Jon Speelman's Best Games

Jon Speelman

To my dear Brother ALEX Best Wishes Phivos x

B. T. Batsford Ltd, *London*

First published 1997
© Jon Speelman 1997

ISBN 0 7134 6477 1

British Library Cataloguing-in-Publication Data.
A catalogue record for this book is
available from the British Library.

Typeset and edited by First Rank Publishing, Brighton
and printed in Great Britain by
Redwood Books, Trowbridge, Wilts
for the publishers,
B. T. Batsford Ltd,
583 Fulham Road,
London SW6 5BY

A BATSFORD CHESS BOOK
Editorial Panel: Mark Dvoretsky, Jon Speelman
Commissioning Editor: Paul Lamford
General Manager: David Cummings

Contents

Part II Four Themes

Bibliography

Chess for Children Raymond Bott and Stanley Morrison (Collins, 1982)
The Chess Apprentice Raymond Bott and Stanley Morrison (Collins, 1982)
London 1980 Stewart Reuben and William Hartston (Pergamon, 1980)
The Pirc for the Tournament Player John Nunn (Batsford, 1980)
The Pirc Defence Raymond Keene and George Botterill (Batsford, 1973)
Developments in the Pirc and Modern Systems 1984-87 Nigel Davies
    (TUI Enterprises, 1987)
The English Defence Raymond Keene, James Plaskett and Jon Tisdall
    (Batsford, 1987)
Informator
The Chess Player
British Chess Magazine (BCM)
New in Chess Magazine
Die Schachwoche

Introduction

When, more than five years ago, a book of my games was first mooted, I realised at once that this would be a serious project. A professional, even then, for a decade and a half – now more than two decades – I wanted to incorporate not only my (more or less) mature output: but also some indication as to how the apparently somewhat 'vegetarian' adult animal developed. Some of this material dated back as far as 1969. There was no way that the traditional chronological approach could do justice to such a body of work.

Unwilling immediately to commit myself to such a large undertaking, I turned to 'masterly inactivity'; failing actually to sign a contract for the work until a few weeks before I finally delivered it and initially taking refuge in a long succession of lists.

Eventually I decided on a mixed approach, including some chronological material but also several chapters devoted to particular themes. As with most such books, the material wasn't written in the order in which it finally appeared. I began with the games against Tony Miles (Game 33) and Zsuzsa Polgar (Game 35), worked my way through the match with Nigel Short, 'Prelate Power' and 'Reginicide' and only towards the very end took in 'Juvenilia' (my thanks to my editors – I'd always assumed the third vowel was an 'a') and 'International Titles' before a final burst of 'Blood on the Board'.

While the initial material was written extremely episodically, the body of the book only took shape over the last year. During this time, despite certain residual Luddite tendencies (as an enthusiastic if very occasional Linux user, I'm certainly not a huge Windows fan) I moved on from using Chessbase 4.0 in DOS and a DOS text editor to the more integrated environment of Chessbase for Windows and eventually even Microsoft Works for Windows, so that I could see the diagrams embedded in the text. I hope both that this has provided for smoother analysis and that the excellent editing has homogenised the text so that the older material isn't too readily apparent.

Nowadays, I try to analyse – if not to play – chess in a fairly episodic way. Quite long tracts of play involve natural moves, which one could perfectly well find in a five-minute game; but then there will be moments which require deep investigation. These can occur when a plan has to be chosen, complex tactics have to be negotiated or on the cusp between results as the game passes from a draw to a win or vice versa. These are always the most tense moments of a game, in which one's body exhibits the most stress; and have tended to call forth a torrent of analysis as I've sought, even away from the cordite, to lay the game to rest. I realise some of these analyses are obsessive; and beg the reader's indulgence for the product of sleepless nights.

There are many people I should like to thank for spurring me on. Firstly, everybody at Batsford and in particular the present incumbents Dave Cummings and Paul Lamford who've guided the book through its final moments. Byron Jacobs and Andrew Kinsman of First Rank Publishing who did the editing and typesetting. John Nunn for his gentle chivvying when he was a Batsford adviser. Bob Wade for endless encouragement and the use of his wonderful library. And last, but far from least, Lindsay and Lawrence who had to endure several months of a rather less domesticated animal than I would usually wish to present at home.

Jon Speelman
London
August 1997

1 Juvenilia

I was taught chess at the age of six on Boxing Day 1962 by my teenage cousin. Naturally I immediately wanted to play a game; and equally naturally I succumbed to scholar's mate – the one where the queen lands on 'bishop two' (presumably he let me start, so it was f2). Despite this outrage, I was fascinated. I saw the game as a very hard puzzle; and to some extent continue to do so to this day. My first chess book was *Chess for Children* by Bott and Morrison, soon followed by their sequel *The Chess Apprentice* – retitled years later, with crashing mundaneness, *More Chess for Children*.

I pestered my mother into buying a fairly decent chess set and on the same day also obtained my first 'real' chess book: Bob Wade's account of the 1963 world championship match in which Petrosian defeated Botvinnik. Although this was many years too advanced for me, it is a lovely book and I still treasure it.

In order for a player to become really strong at chess, there should be some period of his life in which he (or she) is in love with the game. It doesn't have to last; you can't expect somebody who's been a professional player for twenty years to feel the same devotion as a child. But it is only through this obsession that one can suck the essence of the game into one's very being.

For me this lasted right through my childhood, from soon after I learnt the moves right up to my early teens. In common with quite a lot of strong players, I lost my father extremely young – in my case just fifteen months – and my obsession with chess to some extent filled the emotional void left by his absence. (Many years later, I developed a much better understanding of this after reading *The Ego Ideal* and *Creativity and Perversion* both by the splendidly named French

Post-Freudian, Janine Chasse-guet-Smirgel.)

So chess definitely had an emotional significance far beyond its substantive value during my childhood – indeed, I had only learnt to read properly through *Chess for Children*, though in my defence I was already reasonably numerate – and, as with most of my colleagues, it continues to resonate enormously. You only have to observe somebody just after they've lost even a relatively unimportant game to see rivers of emotion way beyond a nought on a tournament table.

My very first chess tournament, at the age of seven or so, was a knockout at the local library. Things went smoothly until the final when I opened 1 e4 (of course it was 1 P-K4 in those days), but the cad to my horror replied 1...e6, defending the bishop two (f7) square, against the obvious continuation. Shocked by what I would later learn is called prophylaxis, I soon fell into difficulties. Nevertheless, I rallied against adversity and eventually succeeded in winning.

In the mid sixties, junior chess was only very loosely organised in the UK. As a southerner, there were the London Junior Championships after Christmas, the British Championships, then as now in August, and junior county matches.

Coaching was practically non-existent, so youngsters developed infinitely slower than later generations. But this was also a great boon since without the constraints of a formal structure you have to develop your own ideas. This has been of great value in the creation of the highly heterodox 'English Chess School' – if such exists.

While my memory of the tournament in the library is pretty clear, things then become something of a blur. There were several London Junior Championships, none of which I won, including an Under-12 from which I had to withdraw with chickenpox. Then there were junior county matches; and I joined Hampstead Chess Club.

Over the years I played many games there with George Stone, an elderly gentleman, now long dead, of about 200 (2200) strength, who specialised in squeezing wins out of almost equal endings. From him I learnt to appreciate small advantages – indeed probably even to overvalue them; and this is a trait I've retained to this day. (Bob Wade tells me that in fact he was originally known as George Stachstein, a German refugee who played in British Championships round about the War.)

My first tournament away from home was the British Under-14 Championship at Rhyl

1969. My mother had arranged for me to be looked after by some slightly older boys; so apart from the rigid timetable of the tournament, I was to some extent on my own.

Compared to the incredibly strong juniors today, I was a beginner. But so was everyone else and this was my first seriously good result: I took first place with 10/11. Although the games are fairly execrable, they at least display the rudiments of the vicious attacking style of my youth. So here, warts and all, is a double rook sacrifice from that tournament.

Game 1
J.Speelman-J.Fletcher
British U-14 Championship, Rhyl 1969
Two Knights Defence, Fried Liver Attack

1	e4	e5
2	♘f3	♘c6
3	♗c4	♘f6
4	♘g5	

Playing for the 'Fried Liver', with which I did well at the time; though John Nunn used to amass a frightful score with the Traxler (Wilkes-Barre) 4...♗c5 and if 5 ♘xf7 ♗xf2+.

4	...	d5
5	exd5	♘xd5?
6	♘xf7	

Initiating the Fried Liver Attack.

6	...	♔xf7
7	♕f3+	♔e6
8	♘c3	♘b4
9	d4?	

9 ♕e4 c6 10 a3 is the correct way to play.

9	...	c6
10	♕e4	♔f7!
11	a3	♕a5?

11...exd4! would have refuted White's play.

12	axb4	♕xa1

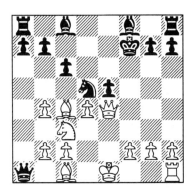

13 ♘xd5?

Too much! 13 0-0 ♗e6 14 ♘xd5 cxd5 15 ♗xd5 ♕a6 16 ♗xb7 ♕c4 17 ♕f3+ ♔g8 18 ♗xa8 wins.

13	...	♕xc1+
14	♔e2	♕xh1

14...♗g4+ 15 f3 ♕xh1 was also plausible; but in those happy days people still generally took any material on offer.

15	♘c7+	♔e7

16 ♕xe5+ ♔d7??

Blocking the bishop's diagonal. After 16...♔d8 17 ♘xa8 ♗g4+ 18 ♔d3! ♕f1+ 19 ♔c3 ♕xf2 20 ♕b8+ ♔e7 21 ♕e5+ it is perpetual check.

17 ♘xa8 ♕xg2
18 ♕c7+ 1-0

Black resigned in view of mate next move.

As with physical growth, chess development is a highly non-linear process: there are periods of sharp improvement interspersed with plateaux and even sometimes small slips backwards.

Competence is achieved in certain areas, but there are extensive badlands in-between in which the intermediate player is only groping. The same applies, for that matter, to grandmasters or the world champion himself but of course the stronger you are, the more territory is already mapped and the greater your confidence in your instinct when faced with the unknown.

I see improvement mainly as a knitting together of the areas of competence so that gradually one learns more and more to sustain good play until there will be whole games without serious error; and even coherent games in which one can discern a single underlying intelligence.

Coherence is the single elusive quality which I most prize, either playing through my colleagues' games; or with a suitable strength adjustment, when examining games by less exalted players. This is the quality which I've also searched for in my own juvenilia. I have no wish to bore either the reader or myself with more than a very few examples from my youth, but the ones which follow were chosen most of all according to that criterion.

Although I played plenty of games during the next year, none of them is particularly memorable. The same could be said of those at the next British Championships, in Coventry 1970. I shared first place in the Under-16s with Jonathan Mestel. But my strongest memories are of a boy only a few years older than us drinking a very considerable quantity of vodka – more than half a bottle I think. (He survived, thank heavens.) And of the gamelet against a fairly strong opponent who had prepared the Marshall Gambit against me (I shan't be so unkind as to name him).

Very quickly we rattled out 1 e4 e5 2 ♘f3 ♘c6 3 ♗b5 a6 4 ♗a4 ♘f6 5 0-0 ♗e7 6 ♖e1 b5 7 ♗b3 0-0 8 c3 d5 9 exd5 ♘xd5 10 ♘xe5. In the heat of the moment, he now played his intended second move first: 10...♘f6?? 11 ♘xc6 1-0.

The Thames Valley Open was held just a few weeks after the British in the last weekend of August 1970. I had a good result, drawing three games and winning three to reach 4½/6; and have included my last round win since it flows rather nicely. But the tournament is most memorable for a remark made by one of my opponents (Brian Hare, I believe) after the final game.

I've always been tall and by this time was quite large enough to get into a pub, at least for a soft drink. I popped in a local hostelry with him but soon had to get some change to phone home. 'Have you got a worrying wife?' he asked.

Game 2
J.Speelman–E.Warren
Thames Valley Open 1970
Queen's Gambit Declined, Chigorin Defence

1	**d4**	**d5**
2	**c4**	**♘c6**

The Chigorin Variation has never been terribly respectable – at least since the end of last century – but some slightly eccentric players have embraced it from time to time; notably Morozevich in the mid nineties. Of course, I must have known next to nothing about it then. I remember first seeing the game Pillsbury-Chigorin many years ago; though surely later than this.

3	**♘f3**	**♗g4**
4	**cxd5**	**♗xf3**
5	**dxc6**	**♗xc6**
6	**♘c3**	**♘f6**

Chigorin's idea was to play 6...e6. After 7 e4 he played 7...♘f6 and got squashed by Pillsbury in their second match-game in St. Petersburg 1895. But two games later, he found a way to attack the centre with

7...♗b4 8 f3 f5. Pillsbury reacted with 9 e5, allowing Black a fine blockade – it is similar to some modern lines of the Queen's Gambit Accepted except that Black has successfully negotiated ...f5 without this being taken en passant. That game continued 9...♘e7 10 a3 ♗a5 11 ♗c4 ♗d5 12 ♕a4+ c6 13 ♗d3 ♕b6 14 ♗c2 ♕a6 15 ♗d1 ♗c4 16 f4 0-0-0 17 ♗e3 ♘d5 18 ♗d2 ♘b6 19 ♕c2 ♖xd4 already winning a pawn – Chigorin won in 38 moves.

Nowadays, however, I believe that the gambit 9 ♗c4 (instead of 9 e5) 9...fxe4 10 0-0 is supposed to be good for White.

7	**f3**	**e5**
8	**dxe5**	**♕xd1+**
9	**♔xd1**	**0-0-0+**
10	**♔c2**	**♘d7**

If Black wants to put the knight on d7 then he should

probably do so without exchanging queens – ...♕h4+ may be annoying sometimes and the black queen can attack the e5-pawn from e7.

After the exchange of queens 10...♘d5 is more dangerous. But although the submissive 11 ♘xd5 ♖xd5 leaves Black extremely active, 11 e4 may be good because 11...♘b4+ 12 ♔b3 ♗c5 13 ♗g5 looks favourable for White and after 11...♘xc3 12 ♔xc3 (not 12 bxc3 ♗a4+) 12...♖d1 13 ♔c2 ♖e1 14 b3 White is only one move away from co-ordinating his pieces. The only way to put a spanner in the works is 14...♗b5 15 ♗b2 ♗xf1!? (or 15...♖xa1 16 ♗xa1 ♗xf1 17 ♖xf1 with a big advantage for White), but 16 ♖xe1 ♗xg2 17 ♖hg1 ♗xf3 18 ♖g5 is very good for White.

11 ♗f4
White could have achieved a clear edge with 11 e6!? fxe6 12 e4.

11 ...   ♖e8
This is somewhat 'cack-handed'. Black would prefer to keep this rook on the d-file, but lines like 11...♗c5 12 e4 ♖he8 13 ♗c4 ♘xe5 14 ♗xe5 ♖xe5 15 ♗xf7 look pretty dubious: Black has the two bishops and active rooks, but White's centre is solid.

12 e4   ♘xe5
13 ♘b5   ♗c5
14 b4!

Gaining space on the queenside.

14 ...   ♗b6
15 a4   a6
16 ♘c3   a5
17 bxa5!?
White could also have gained space with 17 b5 ♗d7 18 ♘d5, but it is better to open the queenside if possible. The question is whether Black can maintain the blockading bishop on a5 after

17 ...   ♗xa5
18 ♗b5!
Creating the 'threat' of ♗xe5 followed by ♗xc6.

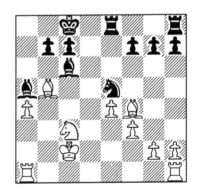

18 ...   ♗xc3?!
A move that I feel could only be played by a strong or a relatively weak player. The strong player would decide that all other options are worse and so simplify, surrendering the two bishops to the opponent but limiting White's attacking options; while a weaker player might not be too concerned about the bishops. Intermediate

players, however, would probably be too concerned about the prelates.

Black would like to wait with for example 18...f6. Now 19 ♗xe5 ♖xe5 20 ♗xc6 ♖c5 21 ♗xb7+ ♔xb7 22 ♖a3 does seem good for White; but Black can simply play 20...bxc6 when he has a bad pawn structure but the knight isn't very happy. I also thought of trying to improve on this with 18...h5 so that the rook can come out via h6 to intensify the 'pressure'.

If he is totally unwilling to play one of the lines above then 18...♗d7 was also perfectly sensible, threatening ...c6. If 19 ♗xd7+ ♘xd7 the crude 20 ♘b5 is met by 20...♘c5!, coming to e6, and something like 20 ♖hd1 c6 21 ♖ac1 can't be too terrible for Black.

19	♔xc3	f6
20	♖hc1	♖e6
21	♔b3	♔d7?

This is walking into trouble. Relocation with 21...♗e8 was better.

| 22 | ♖c5 | ♖c8? |

Black's idea is to give up the e5-pawn for activity, but...

23	♗xe5	fxe5
24	♗xc6+	♖xc6

24...bxc6 keeps material parity, but in a rotten position.

25	♖xe5	♖h6
26	♔c4!	

This kills Black's counterplay since if 26...♖xh2 27 ♖d1+ ♔c6 28 ♖e6 is mate!

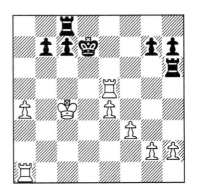

26	...	b6
27	♔b5	♔d6?
28	f4	c5
29	♖d1+	♔c7
30	♖e7+	♔b8
31	♖dd7	1-0

In December 1970, I played in my first Islington Open – the sixth such. This tournament, organised by Islington Chess Club, was the very first to employ the now highly traditional format of six games in a weekend – one on Friday night, three on Saturday and two on Sunday. The first, in December 1965, attracted just twenty-four entrants. But by 1970 there were about 400 players in the various sections; and a year later it had risen to nearly 500.

In the early years, with English chess relatively backward, these weekend tournaments had been easy prey to foreign 'mercenaries'. I still have the bulletin to Islington 1970; and in the introduction Stewart Reuben records how in 1967 they got a £50 grant (think of it in 1997!) from the council to invite Bojan Kurajica over: he romped home. But this rigorous format soon toughened up the 'natives' so that even by the early seventies the invaders often went home empty-handed. And it acted as the springboard from which English chess could quickly develop following the Fischer-Spassky match in 1972.

I had a particularly good tournament in 1970, garnering 5/6 – a year later I could manage only 3½. Perhaps my best game was against Tony Miles – who was much stronger than me at that time – and whom I managed to down with a haymaker. While I have no wish to include too many games against my English colleagues, this one is of particular interest since I wrote notes to it for the bulletin. I've reproduced it as is with various inserts marked '*JS 1997*'.

Game 3
A.Miles–J.Speelman
Islington Open 1970
Sicilian Defence, Löwenthal variation

1	e4	c5
2	♘f3	♘c6
3	d4	cxd4
4	♘xd4	e5
5	♘b5	a6
6	♘d6+	♗xd6
7	♕xd6	♕f6
8	♕d1	♘ge7
9	♘c3	0-0

Too passive. Better is 9...♕g6 and 10...d5. *JS 1997*: Rather simplistic and far from obviously true; but I was very much into the big heave-ho.

10	♗e3	d6
11	♗e2	♕g6

Black has to get some counterplay – how else?

12 ♕d2

If now 12...♕xg2 then 13 0-0-0 must win quickly.

12 ... f5

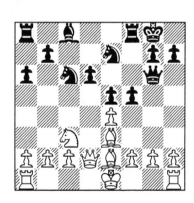

13 ♗f3

13 exf5 looks better to me – Black's pawns are so weak.

13	...	f4
14	♗b6	♗e6
15	♕xd6	

If 15 0-0-0 ♘c8 and now:

a) 16 &c7 &f7 wins. *JS 1997:* Certainly this is true after 17 &xd6? &d7, but 17 ♘d5 ♘d4 18 &a5, while nice for Black, is far from over.

b) 16 ♘a4 and Black seems to have a lot of pressure because of the bad position of the bishop on b6.

15 ...   ♘c8
16 ♕c5   ♘xb6
17 ♕xb6   &ad8
18 ♘e2

If 18 ♕xb7 &c4 and now:

a) 19 ♘d5 &xd5 20 exd5 ♘d4 wins for Black.

b) 19 &c1 ♘d4 20 ♘e2 &xe2 21 &xe2 ♕xg2 is also winning

c) *JS 1997:* But in the supposed rush for White to get castled, I had missed the best reply: 19 b3! Although the black attack is extremely dangerous, White's position is still intact and he has a trump card in many positions of ♘d5. After a couple of hours' analysis, I still can't find anything wonderful. The most natural line is 19...&b8 (19...♘d4 allows the king to slip over to the queenside with 20 0-0-0; and 19...&f7 20 ♕xa6 is a lot of pawns) 20 ♕d7 &fd8 21 ♕g4

(see following diagram)

and now:

c1) If 21...♕d6 22 ♘d5 &xd5 23 exd5 e4 (23...♕b4+ 24 &f1 ♘d4 25 &e4 leaves the bishop very well placed) 24 &xe4

♕b4+ 25 &f1 ♕xe4 26 dxc6 ♕xc2 and although Black has a strong initiative, by the time he has taken the annoying c6-pawn White should be able to get organised.

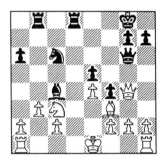

Instead Black can mobilise the knight with tempo to either b4 (variation c2) or d4 (variation c3).

c2) 21...♘b4 22 &c1! (not 22 bxc4 ♘xc2+ 23 &e2 ♕c6 24 c5 ♘xa1 25 &xa1 ♕xc5 hitting both the knight and f2 with a winning attack) 22...♕d6 23 ♘d5! &xd5! 24 exd5 ♘xa2! (if 24...e4 25 &xe4 &e8 26 f3 ♘xd5 27 0-0 ♘e3 28 ♕h4 g6 29 &fe1 the knight is huge on e3, but White does have two extra pawns) 25 &a1 ♕b4+ 26 &f1 ♘c3 27 ♕e6+!? (to remove the dangerous e-pawn; instead 27 &xa6 ♕b5+ 28 &e2 ♘xe2 29 ♕xe2 ♕xd5 30 &a1 e4 gives Black a very powerful attack) 27...&h8 28 ♕xe5. Now if 28...&e8 29 ♕f5 defends but Black can take the vital d-pawn with 28...&xd5! 29 &xd5 ♕b5+ 30 &g1 (not 30 &e1 &e8 and

Black wins) 30...♘e2+ 31 ♔f1 with a perpetual check.

c3) 21...♘d4 allows White to castle, albeit into a very dangerous attack, viz. 22 0-0-0 and now:

c31) The most natural sequence is 22...♕c6 23 bxc4 ♕xc4, but 24 ♖d3! defends since if 24...♘xc2 25 ♖xd8+ ♖xd8 the vicious intermezzo 26 ♕g5!! disrupts Black's coordination. The queen is hitting both the rook and the e5-pawn and 26...♖e8? allows 27 ♔xc2, so Black must try 26...♖c8 27 ♕xe5 ♘d4 (27...♘b4 28 ♔b1 ♕d3+ 29 ♔a1 ♘c2+ 30 ♔b2 ♘d4 31 ♖c1 defends) 28 ♕d5+ ♕xd5 29 exd5 when the powerful d-pawn gives White good chances.

If instead (22...♕c6 23 bxc4) 23...♕b6 24 ♘d5 ♖xd5 25 exd5 ♕b2+ 26 ♔d2 ♕xc2+ 27 ♔e1 ♖b2 forces White to take perpetual starting with 28 ♕c8+ (28 ♗e2 doesn't defend in view of 28...f3!).

c32) 22...♕b6 may be better though, since if 23 ♘d5 ♗xd5 24 exd5 ♕a5 25 ♔b1 (25 ♖xd4 exd4 26 ♔b1 d3 27 cxd3 ♕c3 looks quite good for Black) 25...♘xc2 26 ♕e6+ ♔h8 27 ♕xe5 ♘a3+ 28 ♔a1 ♖xb3 29 ♖c1 Black has the wonderful ♖b1+!! (if 29...♖db8 30 ♗e4 defends) 30 ♖xb1 ♘c2+ 31 ♔b2 ♖c8 when White must jettison the queen with 32 ♕e8+.

18 ...   ♗c4

19 c3?

If 19 ♕c5 ♗xe2 20 ♔xe2 ♘d4+ 21 ♔f1 ♕e6 is probably winning, but this loses at once.

19 ...   ♘d4!

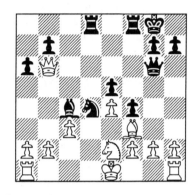

20 ♕c7

If 20 ♕xg6 ♘c2+ 21 ♔f1 ♘xa1! wins nicely.

JS 1997: My aesthetic demands have gone up a bit since then.

20 ... ♘c2+ 21 ♔f1 ♖c8 22 ♕xe5 ♘xa1 23 b3 ♖cd8 24 g4 ♕h6 25 ♔g2 ♗xe2 26 ♗xe2 f3+ 27 ♗xf3 ♖xf3 28 ♔xf3 ♕h3+ 29 ♕g3 ♖d3+ and Black won in a few more moves.

Immediately after the Islington Open there were various closed tournaments, including two for juniors. Junior A was won jointly by Robert Bellin and the Italian IM Sergio Mariotti; while I won Junior B outright with 7½/9, adding a magnificent £5 to the £33 15 shillings I'd won in the Open. (I'm not complaining; it is just that the figures seem so extraordinary today.) Although I made lots of points, my play was still very erratic. As Stewart Reuben put it with typical trenchancy: 'Jonathan Speelman won Junior B extremely convincingly. At 14, though, his play is still extremely immature and crude. He seems to sacrifice incessantly and then win against inferior defence.'

These good results had important long-term consequences, since I believe that it was in Hastings just after this tournament that five of us – Tony Miles, John Nunn, Michael Stean, Jonathan Mestel and myself – were chosen by the BCF for special training. Even more importantly, we were also given preference in tournament selection – an avowedly elitist policy which eventually yielded 5/5 grandmasters; though it presumably had a less beneficial effect on the rest of our generation.

My first international junior tournament was in Nice in April 1971. I travelled with Tony Miles and there were also a couple of Scottish guys: David Bentley who I lost to in the first round; and Ian Sinclair – a problemist with a liking for keys involving queen retreats all the way down the long diagonal – who, some years later, would be (in)famous for his last round game in the C or possibly the D final of the European Junior Championship in Groningen.

Ian, although he was quite a strong player, had somehow contrived to find himself in the bottom section after the qualifying rounds. Two points clear going into the final round, he faced the weakest player in the tournament (whom it would be unkind to name). After a serious night's drinking Ian turned up and the game started something like 1 b3 e5 2 d3 d5 3 ♔d2 ♘f6 4 ♔c3 ♘c6 5 ♔b2, after which White naturally won in fine positional style!

I remember how before the tournament started I had spent a day worrying about what I'd do when the fearsome opponents I was to meet refuted my then favourite Sicilian Najdorf. In fact, this didn't arise: the only opponent who didn't play 1 d4 against me was Bentley in the first round – and that was a 2 c3 Sicilian. But it does contrast wonderfully with the fourteen-year-olds today. (And as it happens I'm writing this the day after fourteen-year-old Etienne Bacrot qualified for his GM title.)

I followed the loss in round one with a further defeat by Frenchman Aldo Haik who, if memory serves, came very close to winning the tournament in the end. [In fact Miles and Werner Hug were first equal on

7/9, while Haik was third equal with Barle (Yugoslavia) on 6½.] But even after a further loss in round four I eventually reached plus one with the game below and finished on 5/9.

Game 4
J.Speelman–Hanau
Nice 1971
Queen's Gambit Declined, Exchange variation

I like this game for my unusually calm approach. My opponent made it very easy for me by allowing the forced exchange of queens, but there is still a real feeling of a plan being formed and executed, which was not so common at a time when my main strength was the haymaker. I'm also interested today in the status of the rook ending which arose; and so have included quite detailed notes which have nothing to do with my thoughts at the time.

1	d4	d5
2	c4	c6
3	♘f3	♘f6
4	♘c3	e6
5	cxd5	exd5
6	♕c2	♗e6

Slightly passive. If Black doesn't want to play the most trenchant move, 6...g6, then 6...♗d6 or 6...♗g4 are normal.

7	♗f4	♗d6
8	♗xd6	♕xd6
9	e3	0-0
10	♗d3	♘bd7
11	♖d1	

Very odd – normal is to castle short and start a minority attack with ♖ab1 and b4.

11	...	♖ac8
12	h3	

It is useful to deny the enemy pieces the g4-square, but this move is also slightly weakening and increases Black's chances of creating a kingside attack.

12	...	c5!?

Encouraged by my time wasting, my opponent opens up the queenside; but this creates an isolated d-pawn for indeterminate compensation.

13	dxc5	♖xc5
14	♕d2	♘e5
15	♘xe5	♕xe5
16	0-0	♕h5
17	♗e2	

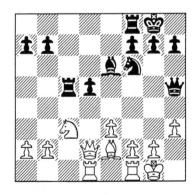

Although Black has a bad pawn structure, the weakening of h3 gives him some counterplay. Now 17...♕g6 looks right, threatening ...♗xh3.

Now 18 ♔h1 may look natural but has the significant disadvantage that ...♗xh3 is left in the air. So Black can play 18...♘e4! 19 ♕d4 ♘xc3! 20 ♕xc5 (20 bxc3 b6 leaves the c3-pawn at least as weak as the one on d5) 20...♘xe2 (20...♘xd1 21 ♖xd1 ♖c8 will surely leave White with an edge), winning material but trapping his own knight. This would be losing with the white king on h2, but here Black will gain a tempo through the threat of ...♗xh3, e.g. 21 ♖fe1 ♕h5 22 ♔h2 (22 f3 ♘g3+ 23 ♔h2 ♘f5) 22...♕e5+ 23 f4 ♕xb2, freeing c3 for the horse's escape.

18 ♔h2 is therefore better, as 18...♘e4 19 ♕d4 ♘xc3 20 ♕xc5 ♘xe2 21 ♕b5 ♗g4 (21...♕h5 22 ♖d2 ♗g4 23 ♖xd5 ♕h6 is also bad) 22 ♖xd5 leaves the horse stranded. Black has no attack while White can easily annex some more queenside pawns; and should always be able to win both minor pieces for a rook when he so desires. But at worst Black can play something like 18...♖fc8 19 ♕d4 a6 instead of 18...♘e4.

17 ...   ♕h4?

A blunder, allowing White to force the exchange of queens, after which White's position almost plays itself.

18 ♕d4!   ♕xd4
19 ♖xd4   ♖fc8
20 ♖fd1   ♔f8
21 ♗f3   a6
22 ♔f1!

White shouldn't hurry but first centralises the king. If 22 ♘xd5? ♘xd5 23 ♗xd5 ♗xd5 24 ♖xd5 ♖xd5 25 ♖xd5 ♖c1+ 26 ♔h2 ♖c2 is at least equal.

22 ...   ♔e7
23 ♔e2   b5

He can't defend the d-pawn since if 23...♔d6 24 e4.

24 ♘xd5+   ♗xd5
25 ♗xd5   ♘xd5
26 ♖xd5   ♖xd5
27 ♖xd5   ♔e6
28 ♖d2   f5?

28...♖c1! 29 ♔d3 a5 creates much better chances. A very similar position arose in the third game of the Ribli-Adorjan match in Budapest 1979 to determine third place in the Riga Interzonal and thus who would qualify to the Candidates.

**Ribli-Adorjan
Budapest (match) 1979**

Ribli eventually won the game, though it was a very hard fight and, while it is nothing to do with the present game, his approach is very interesting.

33 ♖c2 ♖d1+ 34 ♔c3 a5 35 ♖d2 ♖c1+ 36 ♔b2 ♖g1 37 g3 ♔e6 38 ♔c3 ♔e5 39 ♔d3 ♖h1 40 ♖c2 ♔d5 41 e4+ ♔d6 42 h4 ♖e1 43 ♔d4 ♖d1+ 44 ♔e3 ♖a1 45 ♔f4 ♔e6 46 f3 ♔d6 47 ♖g2 ♔e6 48 ♖d2 b4 49 ♖c2 ♔d6 50 ♖g2 ♖d1 51 g4 ♖h1 52 gxh5 ♖xh4+ 53 ♖g4 ♖xh5 54 ♖xg6 ♔e6 55 ♖g2 (After considerable manoeuvring, Ribli has created a haven for his king menacingly near to the enemy forces.) 55...♖h4+ 56 ♔e3 ♖h1 57 ♖c2 ♖e1+ 58 ♔f4 ♖a1 59 ♖h2 (Decisive zugzwang.)

Ribli-Adorjan

59...♔f7 60 ♔f5 ♖c1 61 ♖h7+ ♔g8 62 ♖a7 1-0.

29 ♔d3

This ending presumably ought to be winning, though there is still plenty of work to do. Generally speaking, White seems to have at least two good possible plans:

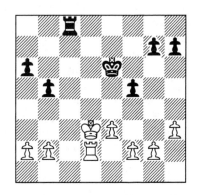

a) He can aim to set up a passed e-pawn on e4 with the king sheltering behind it. Black would like to defend with his king on e6, but White can stretch the enemy defences further by first taking the c-file, after which the defence will be much harder to co-ordinate since only on d6 can the king control the main entry points on the queenside. I could have embarked on this plan immediately by taking control of the c-file with 29 ♔d1 (instead of 29 ♔d3) followed by 30 ♖c2; and later I reverted to it, but only after trying the second plan.

b) To penetrate with his king on the queenside. Black will have some potential counterplay against White's abandoned kingside pawns, but by judicious play White ought to be able to eliminate the entire kingside. Unfortunately, if he is left with an a-pawn then the resultant king, rook and pawn vs. king and rook ending will sometimes be drawn.

29	...	🜶d8+
30	🜶c3	🜶c8+
31	🜶b3	🜶c6
32	🜶c2	🜶d6
33	🜶b4	🜶d7
34	🜶a5	g6

35 🜶b4

A surprisingly sophisticated change of tack which quickly bore fruit. I presume that I would have been very reluctant to take this decision, but there is some justification for it. A normal plan would be to keep the enemy king cut off on the d-file and try to create enough action to exchange one of the kingside pawns in return for setting up a passed pawn on the queenside. In principle, this should be a b rather than an a-pawn; since then almost all rook and pawn against rook endings will be winning. However, if White at some point plays 1 b4 and then 2 a4, 2...bxa4 3 🜶xa4 🜶d1! may be very annoying. Black is

rather near to zugzwang so it may well be possible to achieve this after the rook has moved; otherwise White may have to settle for an a-pawn.

Presumably, Black will try to attack on the kingside himself, and, whilst this will create weaknesses, the result certainly isn't a foregone conclusion. A sample line goes 35 h4 h6 36 b3 g5 37 hxg5 hxg5 38 f3 g4! (38...🜶e6 39 a4 bxa4 40 bxa4 g4 41 fxg4 fxg4 42 🜶f2! transposes to the note below) 39 fxg4 fxg4 40 a4 (not 40 🜶f2 g3! and if 41 🜶f3 🜶d2) 40...bxa4 41 bxa4 g3 (if 41...🜶e6 42 🜶f2! 🜶e5 43 🜶f4 🜶g6 44 g3 🜶d5 45 🜶b4 🜶c5 46 🜶b8! looks over) 42 e4 🜶d4 43 🜶c3 🜶xe4 44 🜶xg3 🜶c7! (not 44...🜶e6 45 🜶a3! or 44...🜶e6 45 🜶g7+) 45 🜶g7+ (45 🜶b3 is met by 45...🜶g4 46 g3 🜶g6) 45...🜶d6 46 g4 🜶e6 47 🜶g6+ (maybe 47 g5) 47...🜶f7 48 🜶xa6 🜶xg4 49 🜶d6 🜶e7.

My first impression was that this would be winning since the black king is so far cut off. But in fact it is quite drawn and Black can even waste some time before undertaking the correct defence. The point is that in order to keep the black king cut off, the rook must retreat down the d-file. Then Black can confine the white king to the a-file – otherwise it has no shelter. The position ♔a8, a7 and ♖d1 (say) vs. ♚e7 and ♜b2 will be reached; and this is dead drawn since by the time the white rook gets to b8 to free the king, the black king will already have reached c7. This theoretical position is extremely well known (and of course I was well aware of it when reaching the diagram above, but imagined that White could somehow arrange to avoid it). However, if the king is cut off one file further on f7 then White does win.

| 35 | ... | h6 |
| 36 | ♔c3 | ♖c6+?! |

Making life easy for White. 36...♚e6 looks slightly more resilient.

37	♔d3	♖d6+
38	♔e2	♚e6
39	♖c7	♚f6
40	b3	g5?!

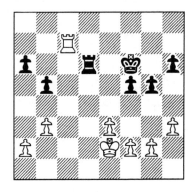

Creating serious weaknesses on both f5 and h6. If he wants to move a kingside pawn then it ought to be 40...h5.

| 41 | g4 | f4? |

41...fxg4 42 hxg4 was very bad, but now he goes down instantly.

| 42 | exf4 | gxf4 |
| 43 | ♖c5 | 1-0 |

In contrast, here is some hackery from a county match just a couple of months later; a game which, although I blundered in the early middlegame, is memorable for the spectacular if somewhat obvious sacrificial attack which I was able to whip up after he let me back into the game just after the first diagram.

The main line, which Rory O'Kelly avoided, involved a queen sacrifice leading to a very pretty mate (see the 'aesthetic diagram'). While I regret not having seen the sacrifice further

in advance I thought it was sufficient to justify inclusion.

Game 5
R.O'Kelly–J.Speelman
Cambridge–Middlesex 1971
King's Indian Defence, Fianchetto variation

1 d4 ♘f6 2 c4 g6 3 g3 ♗g7 4 ♗g2 0-0 5 ♘c3 d6 6 ♘f3 ♘c6 7 0-0 a6 8 h3 e5 9 d5 ♘e7 10 c5 ♘d7

10...♘e8 is very possible, intending to recapture on d6 with the knight.

11 cxd6 cxd6 12 e4 h6 13 ♘e1 f5 14 exf5 gxf5 15 ♔h2 ♘g6?

This blunder loses a pawn and should have led to a decisive disadvantage.

16 ♕h5! ♔h7 17 ♘f3!

It was a very long time ago, but I think I must have seen his previous move but missed this switchback when playing 15...♘g6?

17 ... ♕e8 18 ♘g5+ ♔g8 19 ♘e6 ♘f6

20 ♘xg7?

Letting Black back into the game. Instead 20 ♕xf5! would have led to a large safe advantage, albeit after a slightly complex series of captures: 20...♘xd5 (20...♕f7 21 ♕d3 ♘xd5 22 ♘xf8 is simple) 21 ♘xg7 ♗xf5 (or 21...♔xg7 22 ♕h5 ♘f6 23 ♕xh6+ ♔f7 24 ♘e4 etc.) 22 ♘xe8 ♘xc3 23 ♘xd6 ♗d3 24 bxc3! ♗xf1 25 ♗xf1 ♖xf2+ 26 ♔g1 ♖f3 or ♖c2 27 ♘e4! and Black is squashed flat.

20	**...**	**♔xg7**
21	**♕xh6+**	**♔f7**
22	**♕e3**	**♖h8**
23	**♕b6**	**f4!**
24	**♕xd6**	

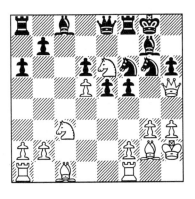

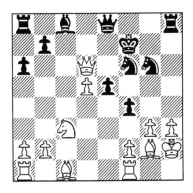

Black is now able to launch a vicious sacrificial attack, but sadly at this point I hadn't yet seen the possible queen sacrifice. So while my instincts were good, I'm somewhat baffled as to what I intended!

24 ...   ♗xh3!
25 ♗xh3   ♖xh3+

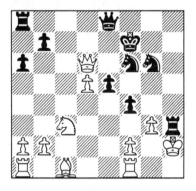

26 ♔xh3?

This leads to forced mate, so he had to try 26 ♔g2! My original instinctive reaction was to dismiss this out of hand as 'grim'; but while this must surely be correct it turns out that White can still put up quite a good fight for at least a few moves since he also has some trumps.

One problem for Black is that he must always watch out for ♕e6+ in the midst of tactical lines; and it is also most important to avoid driving the white king into the centre without good reason, since White's central preponderance may afford His Majesty quite good

shelter.

After 26 ♔g2 Black has three plausible ways to continue the attack:

a) If 26...♘h4+ 27 ♔xh3 ♕h8 gives White enormous latitude so that it would be very surprising if he didn't have at least one reasonable continuation. 28 ♕e6+ is obvious to escape ...♘f5+ and now for some reason my first reaction was 28...♔g6 (rather than to g7) when:

a1) 29 ♘e4!? ♘f5+ 30 ♔g2 f3+ 31 ♔xf3! (not 31 ♔g1 ♘d4 32 ♕xf6+ ♕xf6 33 ♘xf6 ♘e2+ and mates) 31...♘d4+ 32 ♔g2 ♘xe6 33 ♖h1 ♕xh1+ 34 ♔xh1 ♘xe4 35 dxe6 looks about equal.

a2) But 29 ♖h1, and if 29...♖e8 30 gxh4!? ♖xe6 31 ♖g1+ when the good f5-square is taboo in view of ♖g5 mate, looks even better. This line would also be effective with the king on g7.

Since Black is playing for the advantage, these lines are quite enough to put him off 26...♘h4+.

b) 26...♖h2+ 27 ♔xh2 ♕h8+ 28 ♔g1 (not 28 ♔g2? transposing back to the game) 28...♕h5 might just work, though again White has a lot of choice:

b1) If 29 ♘e4 ♘xe4 White gets some checks, but after 30 ♕d7+ ♔g8 31 ♕e6+ ♔h8 32 g4 ♕h3 33 ♗xf4 (33 g5 ♕h4 34

♔g2 f3+ 35 ♔xf3 ♖f8+ is also hopeless) 33...exf4! Black will soon deliver mate.

b2) If 29 ♕c7+ ♘e7? (hoping for 30 d6?? ♖h8 31 ♕xe7+ ♔g6) 30 ♗xf4! ♖h8 31 ♔g2! defends; but conceivably Black can afford to block the back rank with 29...♔g8 with the slow but nasty threat of ...f3 followed by ...♕h3 or ...♘g4.

In any case, in the real world any sane Black would obviously meet 26 ♔g2 with:

c) 26...♕h8! 27 ♖g1! (27 ♕e6+? only helps Black since after 27...♔g7 28 ♕xh3? is impossible in view of ...f3+) when:

c1) My first idea was 27...♕h5 28 ♔f1 fxg3, when White can try 29 ♕b6, defending against immediate disaster since if:

c11) 29...gxf2? 30 ♕e6+ ♔g7 31 ♕e7+ with a perpetual.

c12) 29...g2+ 30 ♔xg2! (not 30 ♖xg2 ♖h1+ 31 ♖g1 ♕h3+ 32 ♔e2 ♖xg1 33 ♕xb7+ ♘e7 and wins) 30...♖xc3 (30...♕f3+ 31 ♔f1 ♕d3+ 32 ♔e1) 31 ♕e6+! ♔g7 32 bxc3 ♖e8 33 ♖h1 ♘h4+ 34 ♖xh4 ♕xh4 35 ♕f5 and White survives.

c13) But 29...♖h1 30 fxg3 ♕h3+ 31 ♔f2 ♘g4+ 32 ♔f3 ♖xg1 33 ♕xg1 ♖f8 is extremely frightening for White.

c14) And so is the restrained 29...♖e8, protecting e6 before striking; for example, if 30 ♗e3 ♘g4 is most unpleasant.

c2) Realising that Black needs to prevent ♕e6+, I then wondered whether it is even better to commit the rook first with 27...♖e8 rather than play ...♕h5, which is often not the best square for the queen. And indeed this looks strong, e.g.

c21) If 28 ♕b6 fxg3 29 fxg3 ♖h2+ 30 ♔f1 ♕h3+ 31 ♔e1 ♘f4 wins.

c22) I was slightly put off by 28 ♕c7+ ♖e7 29 ♕c4, but 29...b5 is very pleasant to annoy the queen and if, for example, 30 ♕b3 fxg3 31 d6+ ♖e6 32 fxg3 ♖h2+ 33 ♔f1 ♕h5 wins.

c23) White can try 28 ♔f1, but after 28...♖h1 29 ♖xh1 ♕xh1+ 30 ♔e2 ♕g2! he does not get far, e.g. 31 ♕c7+ ♖e7 32 ♕c4 fxg3 33 d6+ ♖e6 34 ♗e3 ♘f4+ 35 ♔d2 b5 36 ♕c7+ ♔g6 37 d7 gxf2 and wins.

| 26 | ... | ♕h8+ |
| 27 | ♔g2 | ♘h4+ |

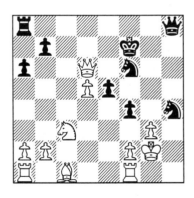

28 ♔g1

For if 28 gxh4 ♖g8+ 29 ♔h3 ♕xh4+! 30 ♔xh4 ♖h8+ 31 ♔g5

♜h5 mate!

The aesthetic diagram

A 'pure mate' (if I understand the definition correctly),
in that all the white king's flight
squares are attacked once and
once only. Indeed, if one removed the pawns on a6, b7 and
f4 then it would be a 'model
mate', since all the other black
pieces are contributing.

28	...	♞f3+
29	♔g2	♛h2+
	0-1	

In view of 30 ♔xf3 ♛h5+ 31
♔g2 f3+ 32 ♔g1 ♜h8 mating.

At the British Champion-
ships in August, I played in the
Under-21s. I started badly with
an abysmal first round loss following my adoption of 1 b3; the
only time I've ever played this
in anger in my life, unless you
count an important five-minute
play-off game against Nick De
Firmian in the GMA rapidplay
tournament in Brussels 1992.
But I rallied with a good series
of wins and draws marred only
by a loss in the sixth round to

Mike O'Hara. This game had,
from my point of view, just two
interesting moments:

M.O'Hara-J.Speelman
British U-21 Championship
(round 6), Blackpool 1971

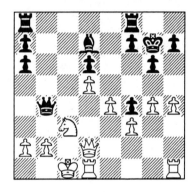

The game had started as a
Sämisch King's Indian. Here I
remember still being so naive as
to be surprised by the transition
to an ending with **18 ♛d4+!**
Surely White was supposed to
play for mate in the Sämisch?

After various adventures we
reached this position:

And here there was general surprise that after **45 ... ♗xd5 46 ♘xd5 ♖xd5+** Black is unable to defend against the a-pawn; but an endgame database confirms that there is indeed no defence in this particular position. **47 ♔b6 ♖d1 48 a6 ♖b1+ 49 ♔c7 ♔d5 50 ♖c6 ♖a1 51 ♔b7 ♖a2 52 ♖b6 ♔c5 53 a7 ♖h2 1-0**

My best game of the tournament was against John Nunn. And while I'm not too keen to include examples against my friends, and quake to offend the mighty doctor, here it is: one of my very first games against a really good player to maintain aesthetic integrity throughout – albeit I didn't have to do so for many moves.

Game 6
J.Speelman–J.Nunn
British U-21 Championship (round 9), Blackpool 1971
English Opening

1 c4	**e5**
2 ♘c3	**♘f6**
3 g3	**c6**

Like 2 c3 against the Sicilian, this can lead to some very sharp lines. Since I haven't been involved in it for years, I was quite interested when annotating this game in May 1997 to find out what the current state of play is; though of course it has no bearing whatsoever on our game in 1971.

4 ♘f3

4 ♗g2 is hardly ever played since 4...d5 5 cxd5 cxd5 6 ♕b3 ♘c6! 7 ♘xd5 ♘d4 8 ♘xf6+ gxf6 9 ♕d1 ♕c7 gives Black a very dangerous initiative though it isn't absolutely clear.

4 ...	**e4**
5 ♘d4	**d5**
6 cxd5	**♕b6!?**

This is Paul Keres's move

which he introduced when the more obvious 6...cxd5 was shown to lead to difficulties. Black's problem is that after 7 d3! he is unable to maintain the centre, and theory still quotes a game Ivkov-Kozomora, Sarajevo 1967, which continued 7...♗c5 8 ♘b3 ♗b4 9 dxe4 ♘xe4 10 ♗d2 ♕b6 11 ♘xe4 dxe4 12 ♗xb4 ♕xb4+ 13 ♕d2 ♘c6 14 ♗g2 f5 15 ♕xb4 ♘xb4 16 0-0 ♗e6 17 ♘d4 ♗d7 18 f3 exf3 19 ♖xf3 0-0 20 ♖b3 a5 21 a3 ♘c6 22 ♖xb7 ♘xd4 23 ♖xd7 and White went on to win in 62 moves.

Black can also play 5...♕b6 a move earlier, introducing a quite different set of complications. Obviously, White would like to play 6 ♘b3, but 6...a5 is a serious nuisance, intending to meet 7 d3 a4 8 ♗e3 ♕b4 9 ♘d2 with 9...a3! – though 7 ♘a4 ♛b4 8 ♘d4 is very unclear.

I was rather surprised to discover that 'theory' gives 6 e3 as best against 5...♛b6, continuing with the rather 'Basmaniac' 6...d5 7 ♛c2 ♝d7 8 a3 ♝e7 9 b4 0-0 10 ♝b2 ♘a6 11 c5 ♛c7 12 f3! exf3 13 ♘xf3 ♜ae8 14 ♝d3 ♘b8 15 0-0 when White was indeed better in Najdorf-Rossetto, Buenos Aires 1968. However, this is hardly sufficient basis to dismiss 5...♛b6.

7 ♘b3   cxd5
8 ♝g2   ♝f5

I found this game difficult to annotate, since a fairly reasonable-looking position for Black disintegrated in just a couple of moves. My feeling is that the whole line is a little shaky.

6...♛b6 gained a tempo since the knight had to retreat, but the queen is somewhat misplaced on b6 in the long term, since she is very likely to get hit by ♝e3. Of course 8...♝f5 shouldn't be too bad; but it seems to make more sense to try to press with ...a5 either now or on the previous move. Neither is supposed to be particularly good, but the evidence of two old Botvinnik games isn't necessarily decisive:

a) 7...a5 8 d4 cxd5 9 ♝g2 ♝e7 10 0-0 0-0 11 ♝g5 ♜d8 12 e3 ♘a6 13 f3 exf3 14 ♛xf3 ♝e6 15 ♛e2 ♘c7 16 ♘c5 ♝xc5 17 ♘a4 ♛b4 18 ♘xc5 ♝g4 19 ♛f2 ♘ce8 20 a3 ♛b5

21 e4 dxe4 22 ♘xe4 ♜a6 23 d5 h6 24 ♘c3 ♛d7 25 ♝f4 ♝h3 26 ♜ad1 ♝xg2 27 ♔xg2 ♘c7 28 ♝xc7 ♛xc7 29 ♜d2 ♘e8 30 ♜e1 ♜f6 31 ♛d4 ♘d6 32 ♜de2 b5 33 ♘xb5 ♘xb5 34 ♜e8+ ♜xe8 35 ♜xe8+ ♔h7 36 ♛d3+ g6 37 ♛xb5 ♛c2+ 38 ♛e2 ♛b3 39 ♜d8 h5 40 h4 a4 41 ♔h3 ♛f3 42 ♛xf3 ♜xf3 43 ♜a8 ♜d3 44 ♜xa4 ♜xd5 45 ♜a7 1-0 Botvinnik-Alexeev, USSR 1968.

b) 7...cxd5 8 ♝g2 a5 9 d3 a4 10 ♝e3 ♛b4 11 ♘d4 a3 12 ♘c2 ♛xb2 13 ♝d4 ♝b4 14 ♘xb4 ♛xb4 15 ♝xf6 gxf6 16 0-0 ♝e6 17 ♜c1 ♘c6 18 dxe4 dxe4 19 ♘xe4 ♝xa2 20 ♘d6+ ♔f8 21 ♘xb7 ♘e5 22 ♘c5 ♜b8 23 ♘a6 ♝b3 24 ♘xb4 ♝xd1 25 ♜fxd1 ♜xb4 26 ♜a1 ♜b2 27 ♔f1 ♝g7 28 ♜xa3 ♜c8 29 ♝e4 ♜e8 30 ♜a4 ♜e7 31 ♝f5 ♜c7 32 ♜h4 h6 33 ♜a4 ♜c5 34 h3 ♘c4 35 ♝d3 ♘e5 36 ♝e4 ♘c4 37 ♝d3 ♘e5 38 ♝e4 ♘c4 39 ♔e1 ♘e5 40 ♜ad4 ♜c3 41 ♜1d2 ♜c1+ 42 ♜d1 ♜c3 43 f4 f5 44 ♝xf5 ♘c4 45 ♜4d3 ♜cc2 46 ♝g4 ♜a2 47 ♜b3 ♔g6 48 ♔f2 ♘d2 49 ♜e3 ♘c4 50 ♜b3 ♘d2 51 ♜e3 ♘c4 52 ♜e8 ♘d2 53 ♜e5 ♔f6 54 ♜f5+ ♔g6 55 ♜e5 ♔f6 56 ♝h5 ♜c3 57 h4 ♜c4 58 ♝f3 ♜cc2 59 ♝d5 ♜a4 60 ♝f3 ♜aa2 61 ♜e1 ♜a4 62 h5 ♜c3 63 ♝g2 ♜c2 64 ♜d1 ♜a3 65 ♝d5 ♜a4 66 ♔e1 ♜d4 67 ♝g2 ♘b3 68 ♜xd4 ♘xd4 69 ♔f2 ♘e6 70 ♝e4 ♜b2 71 ♜f5+ ♔g7 72 ♜d5 ♔f6 73 ♔f3 1-0 was the game Botvinnik-Tal,

World Championship (9th matchgame), Moscow 1961.

9 d3

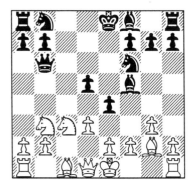

9 ...   exd3?

Somewhat lagging in development and with a centre to defend, Black has very little leeway; and this very bad move renders matters critical. With 9...exd3 Black surrenders his centre, reactivates the enemy bishop on g2, leaves his d-pawn under immediate fire and opens the e-file, which turns out to be a serious problem since White is able to gain a significant lead in development while the d5-pawn is being defended. Black had hoped to gain compensation by kicking White around in the short term. It isn't even clear that this works after the obvious recapture, but White can do even better.

9...♗b4 was the correct way for Black to continue. Then 10 0-0 ♗xc3 11 bxc3 0-0 isn't very cheery for Black but does seem reasonably playable: 12 ♗e3

♕c7 13 ♖c1 ♘c6 14 c4 ♖ad8 15 ♘d4 ♘xd4 16 ♗xd4 and here Keres got into serious trouble against Reshevsky at Los Angeles 1963 after 16...exd3 17 cxd5 ♕d7 18 ♗xf6 dxe2 19 ♕xe2 gxf6 20 ♕b2 ♔g7 21 ♕d4. However, 16...♕e7! is better: 17 cxd5 ♖xd5 18 ♕a4 b6 19 ♗xf6 gxf6 20 ♗xe4 ♖a5 21 ♕c2 ♗xe4 22 dxe4 ♖e8 23 ♖fd1 ♕xe4 ½-½ Jezek-Sapundzhiev, Correspondence 1973.

10 0-0!

Of course it is nice to get the king safe, but in fact the simple recapture 10 exd3 is also good:

a) The main point is that the obvious 10...d4 loses the pawn to 11 ♘xd4! when 11...♕xd4? 12 ♗xb7 ♗b4 13 0-0! gives White a winning material advantage

b) 10...♘c6 11 0-0 transposes back into the game.

c) 10...♗g4! is mildly disruptive since if

c1) 11 ♘xd5? ♕e6+! 12 ♗e3 (12 ♔d2 ♘xd5 13 ♗xd5 ♗b4+) 12...♘xd5! wins.

c2) 11 ♕d2 is a fairly silly square.

c3) But 11 ♕c2 is fine, e.g. 11...♘c6 12 0-0 ♗e7 13 ♗g5 0-0 and now if 14 ♗xf6 ♘b4! 15 ♘xd5 ♘xc2 16 ♘xb6 ♗xf6 17 ♘xa8 ♘xa1 18 ♖xa1 ♖xa8 Black should survive; but 14 ♕d2! d4 15 ♗xf6 ♗xf6 16 ♘d5 ♕d8 gives White a very pleasant edge.

10 ...   ♘c6

If 10...dxe2 11 ♕xe2+ ♕e6 12 ♕b5+ ♕d7 13 ♖e1+ ♗e7 14 ♗g5 is very unpleasant, while 10...♗b4 11 exd3 ♗xc3 12 bxc3 0-0 reaches the same position as after 9...♗b4, but with the difference – very favourable to White – that Black has been induced to exchange on d3. There is now no question of a black space advantage to compensate for the two bishops and the d5-pawn is a little weak.

11 exd3

It is quite possible to defer capture for another move. Polugayevsky-Jongsma, Amsterdam 1970, continued just eight more moves: 11 ♗g5 0-0-0 12 exd3 ♗e6 13 ♖c1 ♔b8 14 d4 ♗e7 15 ♘a4 ♕c7 16 ♘bc5 h6 17 ♗e3 ♖c8? 18 ♗f4 ♗d6 19 ♕b3 1-0.

11 ...   d4

11...♗e7 12 ♖e1 ♖d8 13 ♗g5 is foul.

12 ♖e1+   ♗e7
13 ♘d5   ♘xd5
14 ♗xd5   ♘b4
15 ♕f3!   ♗g6?

Of course the black position can't stand 15...♗e6? 16 ♗xe6 fxe6 17 ♕g4 ♔f7 18 ♘xd4! ♗f6, trying to end up with a knight fork on c2, since 19 ♖xe6 ♕xd4 20 ♖e4 ♕xd3 21 ♖xb4 is simple and 19 ♘xe6 ♘c2 (19...♘xd3 20 ♘g5+ ♔f8 21 ♗e3) 20 ♘g5+ ♗xg5 21 ♕c4+ is even better.

But he should have tried to bail out with 15...♘xd5 16 ♕xf5 ♖d8 when White can easily win a pawn, for example by 17 ♗d2 ♕d6 18 ♘xd4 0-0 and now perhaps 19 ♘b5, when White has a large advantage but Black can certainly fight.

16 ♗g5!

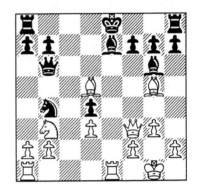

This is already winning by force.

16 ...   f6

If 16...♘xd5 17 ♕xd5 f6 then the variations play themselves. Both 18 ♗d2 ♔f8 (18...♗f7 19 ♕e4; 18...♖d8 19 ♖xe7+ ♔xe7 20 ♖e1+ ♔f8 21 ♗b4+ ♕xb4 22 ♕xd8+ ♔f7 23 ♕d7+ ♔f8 24 ♖e2 ♔g8 25 ♖e7) 19 ♖xe7 ♔xe7 20 ♖e1+ ♔f8 21 ♘c5 ♗f7 22 ♘d7+ ♔g8 23 ♘xb6 ♗xd5 24 ♘xa8 and 18 ♘c5! ♕c7 (18...♖d8 19 ♖xe7+ ♔xe7 20 ♖e1+ or 18...♕d8 19 ♕xb7 fxg5 20 ♖xe7+ ♕xe7 21 ♕xa8+) 19 ♘e6 (or 19 ♗f4 ♖d8 20 ♘e6) are quite decisive.

17 ♖e6   ♕d8

If 17...♕c7 18 ♗f4 ♕d7 19 ♗d6 ♘xd5 20 ♕xd5 ♗f7 (or 20

...♖d8 21 ♖xe7+ ♕xe7 22 ♕b5+ ♕d7 23 ♖e1+ ♔f7 24 ♕d5+) 21 ♖xe7+ ♕xe7 22 ♕b5+ ♕d7 23 ♖e1+ ♔d8 (23...♗e6 24 ♖xe6+ ♔d8 25 ♕d5) 24 ♗e7+ ♕xe7 25 ♖xe7 ♔xe7 26 ♕xb7+.

The queen sacrifice 17...♘xd5 was comparatively best, but 18 ♖xb6 ♘xb6 19 ♖e1 (or 19 ♗f4) 19...fxg5 20 ♕xb7 0-0 21 ♖xe7 ♗f7 22 ♘xd4 is obviously winning.

18	**♗xb7**	**0-0**
19	**♗f4**	**♕d7**
20	**♖xe7!**	**1-0**

I also won in the penultimate round, as White against Roger Webb, which left me just half a point behind Tony Miles going into the last round. But Tony coped with me admirably; I thrashed around against the 2 c3 Sicilian and lost a large pawn. When he confirmed his tournament victory by offering a draw after 23 moves, it was already an act of charity. Still, I was second by myself on 8/11 – a very good result at the time.

As usual, the Islington Open took place just before Christmas. After my 5/6 the previous year I bombed out this time, scoring just 3½/6. The junior internationals followed, and since I had won the B group the previous year, I was promoted to the big boys.

Clearly, I was overawed since I lost to all the top four finishers – Hans-Joachim Hecht, Bojan Kurajica, Robert Bellin and Andrew Law – but I did score three wins against the rest, including this one, which, although it was extremely one-sided, I like for the 'protected passed bishop' which I established in the early middlegame. I found my old notes in the Islington bulletin only after annotating it recently; and have added a few additional comments as '*JS 1971*'.

Game 7
J.Speelman–G.H.Bennett
Islington Junior A 1971
Veresov Opening

1	**d4**	**♘f6**
2	**♘c3**	**d5**
3	**♗g5**	**♗f5**
4	**e3**	

It makes more sense to carry out the 'threat' by doubling the pawns with 4 ♗xf6.

If 4 f3 c5! 5 e4 cxd4 6 ♗xf6 dxc3 7 ♗xc3 dxe4 8 ♕xd8+ ♔xd8 9 0-0-0+ 'and Black has won a pawn' – *JS 1971*.

4	**...**	**♘bd7**
5	**♘f3**	**h6**
6	**♗h4**	**e6**

7 ♗d3   ♗xd3
8 cxd3!?   c6

Playable but not best. In 1971 I criticised it, recommending instead 8...c5 or 8...♗e7.

9 e4   ♛b6

9...♗e7 is sensible, and if 10 ♛b3 only then 10...♛b6.

10 ♛e2   ♗e7
11 0-0

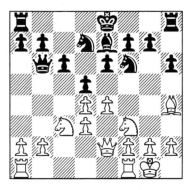

Although White's structure is slightly deformed, he has some very short-term pressure since the obvious 11...0-0?? drops a piece to 12 e5.

11 ...   ♗d8?

But this is a little co-operative. Black could simply have retreated 11...♛d8. Then 12 ♛c2 is mildly irritating, intending to meet 12...0-0 with 13 ♛b3 to try and force a weakening on the queenside. Still, 13...♘b6 14 a4 a5 15 ♘e5 (15 e5 ♘fd7 defends his colleague) 15...♖a7 defends.

And after 11...♛d8 12 ♛c2, 12...a6 is even possible, intending 13 ♛b3 ♖a7, which

reminds me forcibly of this move in a currently fairly trendy line of the Slav.

12 ♗g3   0-0?

If 12...♗c7 13 ♘a4 ♛a5 14 b4 ♛xb4 (14...♛xa4 15 ♗xc7 0-0 16 ♗d6 is rather unpleasant) 15 ♗xc7 ♛xa4 16 ♗d6 and White has dangerous play for the pawn; but 12...♗e7 was quite playable, intending to castle next move.

13 ♗d6!   ♖e8?!

13...dxe4! 14 dxe4 ♖e8 and Black has some chances – *JS 1971*.

14 e5   ♘h7
15 ♘a4   ♛a5

15...♛a6 looks better, preparing to retreat to b7 after ...b6.

16 ♘c5   ♘xc5
17 dxc5

The 'protected passed bishop' radiates power.

Black would like to play 17...b5, so as to close the queenside after which he could try to play round the prelate.

But White can react with 18 a4, when 18...bxa4 19 ♕c2 is tremendous and 18...b4 19 ♕d2 ♘g5 (19...♕a6 20 ♕xb4 ♕xd3 21 ♕b7 wins for White) 20 ♘d4 ♕a6 21 f4! ♘h7 22 ♕xb4 wins at least a pawn.

So the best looks to be 17...♘g5!, trying to disrupt White before he gets organised, as 18 b4 ♘xf3+ 19 ♕xf3 ♕a4! (not 19...♕xb4? 20 ♖ab1) isn't too bad at all. So perhaps 18 ♘d4; but then ...f6 prepares to return the knight to f7.

17	...	♗e7?!
18	b4	♕d8?!

18...♕xb4? 19 ♖ab1 is awful, but 18...♕a4! is a conceivable way to try and annoy White by blockading the queenside.

19	♖fc1	f5?

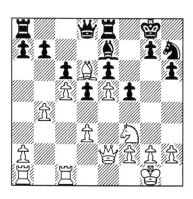

After this Black is quite lost – *JS 1971*; a judgement I concur with today, though the 'quite' seems a little excessive.

20	a4	♘f8
21	b5	

This must already be winning, since if Black waits, penetration down the b-file will surely be decisive, while capturing on d6 is obviously disastrous.

21	...	♗xd6
22	exd6	♖c8
23	d4	♘d7
24	♘e5	♘xe5
25	♕xe5	♕d7
26	♖ab1	♔f7
27	♖b3	♖ed8
28	h4	

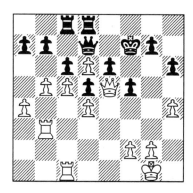

28	...	cxb5?!

Hastening the end. 28...b6 29 h5 is just as horrible as the game, so I suppose Black should try 28...g6. However, there must be lots of ways to win since Black has serious weaknesses all over the board – e6, b7 and h6 to name the three most obvious. Indeed White can almost win (after exchanging on c6) on the b-file alone with the following plan: play a5 and put rooks on b1 and b5 and the queen on b2. Presumably Black will defend with rooks on b8 and d7 and the queen on c6. Then play 1 a6 and if 1...♛xa6 2 ♖a1 ♛c6 3 ♖xa7. 1...b6 may be messier, but 2 axb6 should be sufficient to win in nearly all circumstances..

Black could prevent this by putting the queen on a6 rather than c6, but then White wins at once by moving the queen with tempo to e3 where it hits both h6 and e6. Only the b8-rook can defend both of these two pawns but that would leave b7 en prise.

In practice, White would probably choose to try and win somewhat less thematically. There isn't too much point adducing variations since they will all be more or less the same – attack the various weaknesses until Black loses co-ordination and then strike at a suitable moment. But here is one fairly aesthetic one: (28...g6) 29 bxc6 ♛xc6 ('threatening' ...♖xd6; if 29...♖xc6 30 a5 – to fix the b7-pawn – 30...♖b8 31 ♖cb1 and Black has insufficient time to manoeuvre the c6 rook to the second rank before the white queen reaches the b-file) 30 ♖e1 ♛d7 31 ♖eb1 ♖b8 32 a5 ♛c6 33 ♛e3 ♖h8 and here White can short-circuit the defence at once with 34 a6 when he is winning in each of the following variations:

a) 34...♛xa6 35 ♖a3 ♛c6 36 ♖xa7 ♖h7 37 ♖b6.

b) 34...b6 35 cxb6 ♖xb6 (or

35...axb6 36 a7 ♖b7 37 ♖a3 ♖d7 38 ♖e1 ♖xd6 39 ♖c1 ♛b7 40 ♛e5 ♖hd8 41 a8♛!) 36 ♖xb6 axb6 37 ♖c1! ♛xd6 38 ♛e5! ♛xe5 39 dxe5 ♖a8 (39...g5 40 h5! doesn't help) 40 ♖c7+ ♔e8 41 a7 ♔d8 42 ♖h7 ♔c8 43 ♔f1 b5 44 ♔e2 b4 45 ♔d3.

c) 34...b5 35 cxb6 transposes into the above, though 35 ♛e2 must be an even simpler way to convert White's advantage.

29 axb5   b6

Or 29...g6 30 ♖a1 ♖a8 31 ♛e3 ♖h8 32 ♖a5 b6 33 ♖a6 bxc5 34 dxc5 ♖ab8 35 ♛e5! and White emerges with a winning advantage.

30 h5!   bxc5
31 dxc5   ♖b8
32 ♖g3   ♔f8
33 c6   1-0

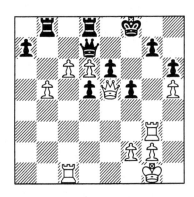

The annual cycle continued with the Hastings Challengers a few weeks later. I started badly but eventually struggled to 5½/10, including these two games.

Game 8
J.Mestel–J.Speelman
Hastings Challengers (round 4) 1971/72
Sicilian Defence, Najdorf variation

This game, played on the first day of 1972, is of interest mainly because of the opening. I played vast numbers of games against my very good friend Jon Mestel around that time. And whilst, after we'd both left university and he became a mathematician while I continued as a professional chess player, my results have been better, from our mid teens until our early twenties he was clearly stronger than me. Although I've never been a serious theoretician, I did play the Najdorf at that time, and here Jonathan hit me with one of the very first outings of a particularly sharp line.

1 e4 c5 2 ♘f3 d6 3 d4 cxd4 4 ♘xd4 ♘f6 5 ♘c3 a6 6 ♗c4 e6 7 ♗b3 ♗e7 8 0-0 0-0 9 f4 b5 10 e5 dxe5 11 fxe5 ♘fd7 12 ♕h5

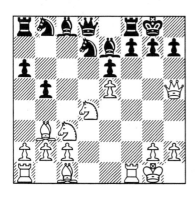

Very new at the time and extremely perturbing to face over the board. Indeed there is only one earlier game in *Informator* – see Walther-Gereben below. While the present somewhat messy game received very little notice, later in the tournament Jonathan used this variation again against the Swiss IM Wirthensohn – and that game did make it to *Informator 13*.

12 ... ♘f6?!

After long thought – though I'm afraid I didn't record clock times in those days. This is inferior since Jonathan's response gives White a clear plus; but it is dismissed by theory for a different reason which, when I looked at the position recently, wasn't at all clear to me.

Mestel-Wirthensohn later in the tournament went 12...♕b6 13 ♗e3 ♗c5 14 ♖f4 ♘c6 15 ♖h4 h6 16 ♖d1 ♘dxe5? 17 ♘e4! ♗xd4 18 ♘f6+!

(see following diagram)

18...♔h8 (18...gxf6 19 ♖dxd4 ♘xd4 20 ♗xd4 leads to mate, e.g. 20...♕a5 21 c3 ♘g6 22 ♕xh6 ♘xh4 23 ♗xf6 etc.) 19 ♖dxd4 ♘xd4 20 ♗xd4 ♕c7 21 ♕g5! ♘g4 22 ♘xg4 f6 23 ♘xf6

♖xf6 24 ♗xf6 ♕a7+ 25 ♔h1
♔h7 26 c3 ♕f7 27 ♖xh6+ 1-0.

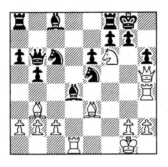

Walther-Gereben, Switzer-
land 1971, also resulted in a
quick win for White: 12...g6 13
♕e2 ♗c5 14 ♗e3 ♗b7

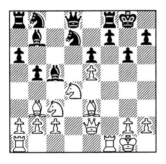

15 ♖xf7! ♗xd4 (worth of attention is 15...♖xf7, as 16 ♘xe6
♗xe3+ 17 ♕xe3 ♕b6 18 ♕xb6
♘xb6 19 ♘d8 ♘c4 20 a4 is not
at all convincing for White) 16
♗xe6 ♗xe3+ 17 ♕xe3 ♖xf7 18
♖f1 ♕b6 19 ♕xb6 ♘xb6 20
♖xf7 ♗c8 21 ♗b3 ♘c4 22 ♖c7
♗e6 23 a4! ♘d7 24 axb5 axb5
25 ♘xb5 ♖a1+ 26 ♔f2 ♘dxe5
27 ♘a3 ♘xa3 28 ♗xe6+ ♔f8
29 bxa3 ♖xa3 30 ♖xh7 ♖c3 31
♗b3 ♘d3+ 32 ♔e3 ♘b4+ 33
♔d4 ♖c6 34 c3 1-0.

Unsurprisingly, a quarter of a
century later, reliable defences
had been found. For example,
the game Anand-Kasparov, Moscow (PCA) Grand Prix 1996,
continued 12...♗c5 13 ♗e3
♗xd4 14 ♗xd4 ♘c6 15 ♗e3
♘cxe5 16 ♖ad1 ♗b7 17 ♖d4
♘g6 18 ♘e2 ♕e7 19 ♘f4 e5 20
♘xg6 hxg6 21 ♕xg6 exd4 22
♗xd4 ♘e5 23 ♕g3 ♖ae8 24
♖f5 ♘f3+ 25 gxf3 ♕e1+ 26
♕xe1 ♖xe1+ 27 ♔f2 ♖d1 28
♗c5 ♗c8 29 ♖f4 g5 30 ♖e4
♖fd8 31 ♖e5 ♖8d2+ 32 ♔g3
♗e6 33 ♖xg5+ ♔h7 34 c4 ♖h1
35 cxb5 axb5 36 ♗e3 ♖xb2 37
♖h5+ ♔g6 38 ♖g5+ ♔h7 39
♖h5+ ½-½.

13 ♕h4

13 exf6 is supposed to refute
12...♘f6 completely on the basis of the game Bednarski-
Zuckerman, Polanica Zdroj
1972: 13...♕xd4+ 14 ♔h1 ♗xf6
15 ♕f3.

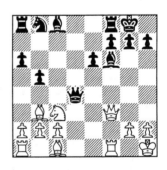

Here Zuckerman continued
15...♕a7 after which Black
certainly seems to be in trouble:
16 ♘e4 ♘d7 17 ♗e3 ♕b8 18
♖ad1 ♔h8? (18...♗e5 19 ♗c5

wins the exchange since 19...♘xc5? allows immediate mate with 20 ♕xf7+ ♖xf7 21 ♖d8+) 19 ♖xd7 ♗xd7 20 ♘xf6 ♕d8 21 ♗g5 h6 22 ♕h5 ♗c6 23 ♗xh6 gxf6 24 ♗g5+ ♔g7 25 ♕h6+ ♔g8 26 ♗xf6 ♗xg2+ 27 ♔xg2 1-0

But I don't really understand why he can't try 15...♕d7 to meet:

a) 16 ♕xa8? with 16...♗b7 17 ♕a7 ♗xg2+.

b) When I happened to mention this (very casually) to Jonathan himself, he suggested instead that White should get to it with 16 ♗h6, but:

b1) 16...♗xc3 17 ♕xc3 gxh6 18 ♕g3+ ♔h8 19 ♕e5+ f6 20 ♖xf6 ♖xf6 21 ♕xf6+ ♕g7 looks like a draw.

b2) And 16...♗b7 17 ♕g3 ♕e7 (not 17...♗xc3? 18 bxc3) isn't clear.

c) Then I wondered about first 16 ♘e4 ♗e7 and then 17 ♗h6, but it looks like Black can get away with taking it: 17...gxh6 18 ♕g3+ ♔h8 19 ♖ad1 ♕a7 20 ♕e5+ f6 21 ♘xf6 ♘c6 22 ♕e4 ♗xf6 23 ♕xc6. So 17 ♕g3 is better, when if 17...♘c6 18 ♗h6 ♕d4 19 ♖ae1 White certainly has a lot of development for the pawn, though he still has to hit home.

Finally, 16 ♘e4 ♗e5 also looks possible and if 17 ♕h5 f6 or 17 ♘g5 h6!

This is probably all only of academic importance since the continuation chosen by Jonathan in the game is rather uncomfortable for Black; and moreover there are other decent defences like the one chosen by Kasparov against Anand above. But it does illustrate how a possibly viable line may be discarded without sufficient testing. And if the other supposedly 'reliable' defences turned out to be 'unreliable' then it could become of real interest.

13	...	♗c5
14	♗e3	♘d5
15	♕xd8	♖xd8
16	♘xd5	

16 ♗xd5 exd5 would remove any residual pressure against f7.

16	...	exd5
17	♖ad1	♗e6
18	♔f2	♘d7

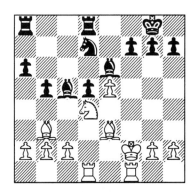

19 ♘c6?

I gave this a question mark at the time. The obvious alternative was 19 ♘f3 ♗xe3+ 20 ♔xe3 ♘b6, when White has a structural advantage but the possibility of ...♘c4 offers some compensation.

19	...	♖dc8
20	♗xc5	♖xc6
21	♗d4	a5!

Black now obtains the necessary time to liquidate the queenside.

22 c3 a4 23 ♗c2 b4 24 ♗d3

bxc3 25 ♗b5 ♖cc8 26 ♗xc3 a3 27 ♗xd7 ♗xd7 28 ♖xd5 ♗e6 ½-½

Here the draw was agreed. After 29 ♖d2 neither 29...axb2 30 ♗xb2 ♖xa2 31 ♖a1 nor 29...♗xa2 30 ♖a1 axb2 31 ♖xb2 is very interesting.

Game 9
Holtzl–J.Speelman
Hastings Challengers (round 9) 1971/72
Alekhine Defence

This game from the penultimate round is awfully one-sided, but I still quite like my purposeful play throughout.

1	e4	♘f6
2	e5	♘d5
3	c4	♘b6
4	c5	♘d5
5	♗c4	e6
6	♘c3	

A somewhat megalithic line in which White's main idea is that if Black takes too soon on c5 White may get a frightful attack with ♕g4. But otherwise the pawns on c5 and e5 can become rather a liability.

6	...	♘xc3
7	dxc3	♘c6
8	♗f4	♕h4!?

To take the g3-square away from the bishop in preparation for ...g5.

9	g3	♕e7
10	♕e2	g5!?
11	♗d2?	

Very submissive. 11 ♗e3

would have given Black much more scope to go wrong, though it is possible to get a rather pleasant position with 11...♘xe5 12 ♗d4 f6 (12...♘xc4 13 ♗xh8 ♕xc5 is a real mess) 13 ♗xe5 fxe5 14 ♕xe5 ♖g8! 15 ♕xc7 ♕xc5 16 ♕xc5 ♗xc5 when the two bishops should give Black a slight edge.

11	...	♕xc5!
12	♗xg5	♕xe5
13	♕xe5	♘xe5
14	♗f6	♘xc4
15	♗xh8	♘xb2

With two pawns for the exchange, the two bishops and some juicy light squares to aim for, Black is obviously doing very well. The only problem would be if White could somehow develop an attack on the kingside. Holtzl's next move pursues this laudable aim, but he leaves his king in the centre too long.

16 h4?!

16 ♔d2 ♗h6+ 17 ♔c2 was recommended (without any enthusiasm) by Barden in *The Chess Player*. And Black might do even better by prefacing the check with 16...b6 17 ♗f6 ♗b7 18 f3 ♗h6+, e.g. 19 ♔c2 ♘c4 20 h4 ♘e3+ 21 ♔b2 ♘d5.

16 ... b6!

17 h5?!

Preparing h6 and ♗g7, but this is easily parried with a good developing move.

17 ... ♗h6!

18 ♖h4? ♗a6!

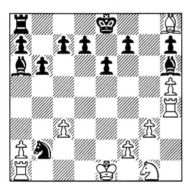

19 ♘h3?!

He had to try to be obstructive with 19 ♗f6 when something like 19...♘d3+ 20 ♔e2 ♘f4+ 21 ♔d1 ♘d5 22 ♗h8 ♔e7 23 c4 ♖xh8 (23...♗xc4 24 ♖xc4 ♖xh8 is also tremendous) 24 cxd5 exd5 25 ♖a4 ♗c4 26 ♖xa7 ♔d6, while dire for White, at least leaves him with some reasonable legal moves.

19 ... ♔e7

20 ♗d4 ♖g8

Stopping ♖g4, after which White is already almost out of sensible moves

21 g4?

But this self-immolation of the rook certainly doesn't help.

21	...	f6
22	f3	c5
23	♗g1	♘d3+
24	♔f1	♗d2
25	♖b1	♗xc3
26	♗e3	d5
27	♔g2	d4
28	♗h6?	♗e1!
	0-1	

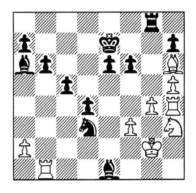

By now I feel that we are near the end of my chess childhood. But I'm including just two more games in this chapter from the next year and a half.

To begin with, my first ever game in the British Championship. Although it went splendidly, I only won once more – in round 9 – and ended up with a miserable 4½/11; a score I repeated the next year until I finally started to get the hang of things with six points in 1974.

Game 10
M.Basman–J.Speelman
British Championship, Brighton 1972
Alekhine Defence

1	e4	♘f6		
2	e5	♘d5		
3	♘c3			

Four rounds later, I lost a miserable – for me that is – game against John Littlewood which I have to confess has rather put me off the Alekhine's to this day, though looking at it now it is clear that I played exceptionally badly: 3 d4 d6 4 ♘f3 g6 5 ♗c4 ♘b6 6 ♗b3 ♗g7 7 exd6 cxd6 8 0-0 0-0 9 ♖e1 h6? 10 a4 a5? 11 ♘a3 ♘c6 12 c3 ♘d7 13 ♕e2 ♖e8 (Inviting the following powerful sacrificial attack.)

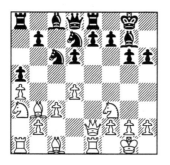

14 ♗xf7+! ♔xf7 15 ♕e6+ ♔f8 16 ♕xg6 e6 17 ♗xh6 ♕f6 18 ♖xe6! ♖xe6 19 ♗xg7+ ♕xg7 20 ♕xe6 ♕f6 21 ♕b3 ♕f7 22 ♕xf7+ ♔xf7 23 ♘b5 d5 24 ♘c7 ♖b8 25 ♖e1 ♘b6 26 b3 ♗f5 27 h4 ♗c2 28 ♘g5+ 1-0.

3 ... e6!?
4 g3!?

To deflect the junior from theory, but the fianchetto is fairly harmless here.

4	...	d6
5	exd6	♗xd6
6	♗g2	0-0
7	♘ge2	♗d7

Offering some bait.

8 ♘xd5?!

Extremely risky, particularly since Michael Basman dislikes being attacked. However, after the sequence 8 0-0 ♘xc3 9 ♘xc3 ♗c6 10 ♘e4 f5!? 11 ♘xd6, both 11...cxd6 12 d4 ♗xg2 13 ♔xg2 ♘d7 and 11...♕xd6 12 d4 ♗xg2 13 ♔xg2 ♘c6 14 c3 ♕d5+ are fine for Black; and 11...♗xg2 is also possible first. In the latter case White has no good zwischenzug and must simply recapture, after which Black can decide how he wishes to take back on d6.

8	...	exd5
9	♗xd5!?	

The logical follow up, though again the discreet 9 0-0 c6 was more sensible.

9	...	♗h3!
10	♗xb7	

Once White has taken one pawn for this awful position then he is quite right to risk taking another, since at least then he has something to play for.

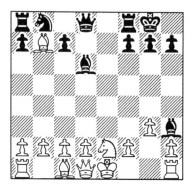

10	...	♘d7
11	d4	

Obviously it would be absurd to take the exchange, e.g. 11 ♗xa8? ♕xa8 12 ♖g1 (or 12 f3 ♕xf3 13 ♖g1 ♖e8 14 d4 ♗g4) 12...♘e5 13 f4 ♘f3+ 14 ♔f2 ♘xh2 15 d3 ♕f3+ 16 ♔e1 ♖e8 and Black wins.

11	...	♖b8
12	♗f3	♕f6
13	♘g1	♖fe8+
14	♗e3	♗f5
15	g4?	

Presumably Michael Basman had some specific reason for this 'pseudo-active' move – perhaps he wanted to make sure that ...♗h3+ is never on the cards later – but as the game goes he never follows it up in any way and it looks merely weak. 15 g4 doesn't in any way assist White's development and creates a potential weakness on f4 which later causes serious problems.

15	...	♗g6
16	b3	c5
17	♔f1	cxd4
18	♗xd4	♗e5
19	c3	♖bd8
20	♔g2	♗xd4
21	cxd4	♘e5
22	♗b7	

If 22 dxe5 ♖xd1 23 exf6 ♖xa1 Black should win.

22	...	♘d3

Hitting not only f2 but also the inviting weakness on the f4-square.

23	♘h3	♖xd4
24	♕f3	♕e6
25	♖hd1	

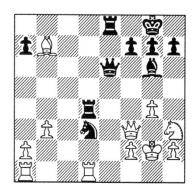

25	...	h6!?

Rather typical of my play then, as now. Given the choice between immediate action and constructive waiting, I will often choose the latter, particularly against an opponent in time trouble. And he may well have been afflicted by this – for while I don't have a time record for the game, I do know that when he lost on time on move 38, having used up the then 2½ hours at his disposal, I was still only on 1hr 51 minutes.

Nevertheless, it would objectively have been at least as strong to hit out at once with 25...♖xg4+ with the following variations:

a) 26 ♔h1 ♖h4 (26...♘e1 was suggested by the irrepressible computer program, Fritz, with the main line of its Silicon analysis continuing 27 ♕e3 ♗e4+ 28 ♗xe4 ♖xe4 when White gets blown away; but it would take an exceptionally calm person to embark on this when 26...♖h4 is so strong) 27 ♘g5 ♕e7! 28 ♖xd3 (if 28 ♗d5 ♕xg5 29 ♖xd3 ♕e5!) 28...♗xd3 winning easily.

b) 26 ♔f1 ♖h4 27 ♘g5 ♕e7 looks immediately winning. Although White can fight on with 28 ♕e3!, 28...♕xe3 29 fxe3 ♖xh2 should certainly be enough.

26 ♖xd3

Cracking. The technical task after this wasn't too onerous, even for a fifteen-year-old. So perhaps he should have tried 26 ♔h1 when 26...♘e5? 27 ♕e3! defends for the moment, but Black does have an immediate win with the vicious 26...♖b8!, threatening ...♖xb7, 27 ♗a8 (if 27 ♕e3 ♖xb7 28 ♕xd4 ♗e4+ or 27 ♗c6 ♘e5) and now:

a) The obvious 27...♘e5 28 ♕g2! (not 28 ♖xd4 ♘xf3 29

♗xf3 ♕f6) 28...♖xg4 29 ♗d5! still leaves Black with a little work, albeit in a dead won position.

b) But 27...♖dd8! is simplest, trapping the bishop and winning instantly.

26	...	♖xd3
27	♘f4	♖xf3
28	♘xe6	♖c3
29	♘f4	♗e4+
30	♗xe4	♖xe4
31	♘d5	♖xg4+
32	♔f1	

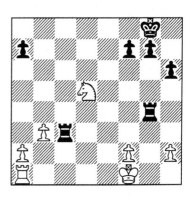

| 32 | ... | ♖c5 |

Nowadays I'd probably play 32...♖d3 33 ♘e3 ♖gd4 here, though it makes little difference.

33	♖d1	♖e4
34	♘e3	♖e7
35	♖d8+	♔h7
36	b4	♖c1+
37	♔e2	♖c2+
38	♖d2	♖xd2+
39	♔xd2	

And in this dead lost position White lost on time: 2:30-1:51.

0-1

Game 11
J.Speelman– Schauwecker
Hastings Challengers 1972/73
Sicilian Defence, Closed variation

I have chosen to publish this traumatic contest partly for its cathartic value. Following my 5½/10 the previous year in the Challengers, this game marked the beginning of the tournament a year later, when I racked up the princely total of 3½/10 – a collapse that was to a great extent due to the present encounter.

Although I didn't play the opening well, I did play it quickly: the one clock time I recorded shows me more than an hour ahead after 17 moves. Then my opponent played a desperate blunder, hurling his queen into a man (or woman) trap whence there was no escape.

Queen for rook ahead and with a considerable time advantage, it looked like I should have been home and dry. But the blunder turned out to be, if not sound, at the very least inspired, for his rooks, bishop and passed pawns were able to create enormous problems for my defenders.

The conclusion, with its initial double blunder in which I played an immediately losing move but he returned the compliment, and then he was still

able to promote a 'space invader', left a scar, in the shape of a slight over-evaluation of such resources, which I am only exorcising today. (Though in the calm light of day it is clear that Black did have serious legitimate chances even before I allowed things to get out of hand.)

1 e4 c5 2 ♘c3 e6 3 g3 ♘c6 4 ♗g2 ♘f6 5 d3 ♗e7 6 f4 d5 7 e5 ♘d7 8 ♘f3 ♖b8 9 a4 a6 10 0-0 0-0 11 ♔h1 b5 12 axb5 axb5 13 d4 Steering into something rather like the 'Classical variation' of the French. **13 ... b4 14 ♘e2 ♕b6 15 ♖e1 cxd4 16 ♘exd4 ♘c5 17 ♗e3 ♕c7** 0:55-2:06! **18 ♘xc6 ♕xc6 19 ♘d4 ♕c7 20 ♕e2 ♘e4 21 ♖f1 ♗c5 22 ♘b3 ♗xe3 23 ♕xe3**

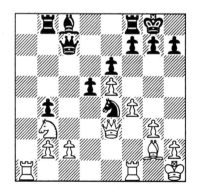

23 ...   ♕xc2??

White may have a pull but this is desperate. The lady is now devoured in just a few moves.

24 ♖ac1! ♛xb2
25 ♗xe4 dxe4
26 ♖f2 ♛a3
27 ♖a1

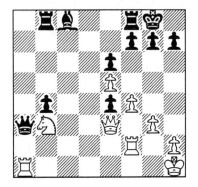

27 ... ♖d8
28 ♖xa3

One should always consider alternatives, even to a move as obvious as this. But delaying capturing the lady doesn't help since after 28 ♖d2 ♖xd2! 29 ♛xd2 ♗b7 (29...g6 is conceivable), threatening ...e3+, White is forced to commit his queen to d6: 30 ♛d6 ♖a8 31 ♖xa3 bxa3, reaching an inferior version of a line he could have in the game.

28 ... bxa3

And certainly not 28...♖d1+? 29 ♔g2 bxa3 30 ♛a7! ♖xb3 31 ♛a4.

Despite – or rather because of – Black's blunder, the position has become extremely interesting. In formal material terms, a rook and two pawns are totally insufficient compensation for the queen, but both pawns are passed and potentially extremely dangerous. The white knight, at present en prise to ...♖d3, lacks an accessible support point; and h1 is the very worst square which one could reasonably choose for the king. On the other hand, Black's back rank is still vulnerable, so he will have to spend an invaluable tempo making *luft* in many lines.

Somewhat to my surprise, I have found no absolutely clear line for White but rather believe that he can choose between several rather unclear endings. Many lines lead to a generic position with Black's bishop on d5 supporting the a-pawn on a2, which is blockaded by the knight on a1 (see 'the generic position', below). Normally, Black will have shed his passed e-pawn to arrange this, so the battle will be between the remaining major pieces. Lacking a passed pawn or any immediate target for the queen, White must try either to penetrate with his king towards e7; or more likely to launch a kingside attack, probably involving f5-f6 followed by something on the dark squares. Obviously only White can be better, but I'm not sure if it is enough to win. Instead of remaining with a knight against the a2-pawn, White could also try to exchange these units off – when life is much simpler but I doubt whether there is a win.

White could also play for an ending with queen, knight and initially three pawns against queen and four (see 'the promotion position', below). In order to evade perpetual, White would have to jettison the g-pawn, but this would still leave a material advantage of queen, knight, f4-pawn and e5-pawn against queen and four pawns – but Black's h-pawn can run.

It is interesting to consider how the evaluation of the position would change if either position were improved. With the white king on g1, I'm sure he'd be winning; while if Black had already played ...h6 then I believe that he would correspondingly be quite comfortable.

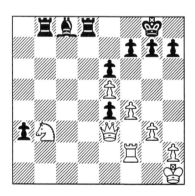

29 ♘c5!
Trying to dominate the bishop; and quite possibly the best move. White has two other plausible possibilities: 29 ♖d2 and 29 ♘c1.

a) 29 ♖d2 and now:

a1) 29...♗b7?! after which Black at best gets an inferior version of the generic position mentioned above: 30 ♖xd8+ ♖xd8 31 ♕a7! (not 31 ♕b6 ♖d7 32 ♘c5 [if 32 ♔g1 h6 followed by ...♗d5] 32...e3+ 33 ♘xb7 e2 34 ♕a5 ♖d1+ 35 ♔g2 h5 and Black will win) and:

a11) Black would like to play 31...e3+?, but the back rank is his undoing: 32 ♕xb7 e2 33 ♕e4! ♖d1+ 34 ♔g2 e1♕ (34...e1♘+ 35 ♔h3) 35 ♕a8+ and mates.

a12) 31...♗d5? 32 ♕xa3 loses for Black.

a13) 31...♗c6? 32 ♕c7 ♖d1+ (32...e3+ transposes to variation a11) 33 ♔g2 ♗e8 34 ♕b8 ♔f8 35 ♕b4+ ♔g8 36 ♕xa3 e3 37 ♕a8 ♔f8 38 ♔f3 is also insufficient for Black.

a14) 31...♗a8! is the only defence, when 32 ♔g1 e3 33 ♔f1 ♗f3 34 ♕xe3 ♗d5 reaches the generic position though in a form where White has more tempi than usual. He might, for instance, play 35 ♘a1 a2 36 g4.

a2) 29...♖xd2 30 ♕xd2 and:

a21) 30...♗b7 was my first thought: 31 ♕b4 e3+ 32 ♔g1 a2 33 ♕b6 g6! (but not 33...h6 when White eventually has a deadly check on the b1-h7 diagonal: 34 ♕c7 ♖a8 35 ♕xb7 a1♕+ 36 ♘xa1 ♖xa1+ 37 ♔g2 e2 38 ♕c8+ ♔h7 39 ♕c2+) 34 ♘a1 ♔g7 35 ♕xe3! (not 35 ♕a7 ♖d8 and Black wins) 35...♗d5

The generic position

Here play might continue 36 ♕c3 (to defend the g3-pawn since if 36 ♕d4 ♖b1+ 37 ♔f2 ♖h1 38 h4 ♖h2+ 39 ♔e3 ♖g2) 36...♖b1+ 37 ♔f2 ♖h1 38 h4 (not 38 ♔e3 ♖xh2 39 ♔d4 h5 40 ♔c5 ♖h3 41 ♔d6 h4 42 ♔e7 hxg3 43 ♕c8 ♖h8 and Black wins) 38...h5 39 ♔e3 ♖d1.

a22) In fact 30...g6 looks even better since after 31 ♔g2 (31 ♕a2 ♖a8 32 ♘c5 ♖a5) 31...♔g7 32 ♕c3 a2 33 ♘a1 Black has even kept the e-pawn.

b) White could also try 29 ♘c1, but Black will surely be able to win the knight for the two passed pawns, after which an ending of queen and four against rook bishop and four must be defensible, e.g. 29...♖b2 30 ♔g2 ♗b7 and now:

b1) 31 ♘a2 ♖d3 (maybe 31...g6) loses a piece after 32 ♖xb2 (not 32 ♕a7 e3+ 33 ♔h3

g6 34 ♖xb2 axb2 35 ♕xb7 e2) 32...♖xe3 33 ♖xb7, but 33...g5 34 ♔f2 ♖f3+ 35 ♔e2 gxf4 36 gxf4 ♖xf4 must draw.

b2) 31 ♔h3 ♖xf2 (not 31...♗d5?? 32 ♖xb2 axb2 33 ♕b6) 32 ♕xf2 ♗d5 to be followed by ...♖a8 and with ...e3 also in the air.

29 ...   ♖b2!
30 ♖xb2??

A blunder, losing immediately to the intermezzo 30...♖d1+! 31 ♔g2 axb2.

30 ♔g2 was correct: 30...a2 (not 30...♖xf2+ 31 ♔xf2 a2 32 ♕a3 ♖d2+ 33 ♔e3 ♖c2 34 ♘xe4) 31 ♕a3 ♖dd2! 32 ♖xd2 ♖xd2+ 33 ♔h3 e3! and now:

a) 34 ♕a8 g6! (again 34...h6 allows a fatal check later: 35 ♕xc8+ ♔h7 36 ♘b3 e2 37 ♕c1 ♖b2 38 ♕xb2 e1♕ 39 ♕xa2) 35 ♕xc8+ ♔g7. Of course White can easily draw by perpetual, but he doesn't seem to have more since the two passed pawns are just too much.

b) 34 ♕xe3! and:

b1) 34...a1♕ 35 ♕xd2 ♕f1+ (not 35...h5 36 ♕d8+ ♔h7 37 ♕xc8 ♕f1+ 38 ♔h4 ♕e2 39 h3 or 35...g6 36 ♘e4 ♕a3 37 ♕d8+ ♕f8 38 ♘f6+ ♔g7 39 ♘e8+) 36 ♔h4 g6 and now 37 ♕d8+? ♔g7 38 ♕xc8 ♕e2 forces a draw, but White can attack with 37 ♘e4! ♔g7 38 ♘f6 h6 39 ♕d8 g5+ 40 fxg5 hxg5+ 41 ♔xg5 ♕f5+ 42 ♔h4 ♕xe5 43 ♘h5+ winning.

b2) So it is better to take the

h-pawn: 34...♖xh2+! 35 ♔xh2
a1♕ 36 ♕d2, reaching the following position.

Black is still going to lose the
bishop, but in return he will get
many checks:

b21) If 36...h5 37 ♕d8+ ♔h7
38 ♕xc8 ♕b2+ 39 ♔h3 ♕c1 40
♕b7! (40 ♕c6 ♔h6) 40...♕xc5
41 ♕xf7 ♕c6 42 ♕xh5+ ♔g8
White has excellent winning
chances.

b22) Black can play 36...h6
so that the pawn isn't en prise at
the end of the above variation,
but I think that it is best to
move the g-pawn instead, since
at the end of the following
variation Black clearly prefers
to have his king on g7 and pawn
on g6 rather than king on h7
and pawn on h6.

b23) 36...g6 37 ♕d8+ (now
that Black has taken the h-pawn
37 ♘e4? ♗b7 38. ♘f6+ ♔g7 is
ridiculous since the crushing
...♕h1 mate is threatened)
37...♔g7 38 ♕xc8 ♕d1 39 ♕c6
♕h5+ 40 ♔g2 ♕e2+ 41 ♔g1
♕d1+ 42 ♔f2 ♕d2+ 43 ♔f3
♕d1+ 44 ♔e3

The promotion position

Here Black can choose be-
tween 44...♕e1+ 45 ♔d4 ♕f2+
(also 45...♕xg3 at once) 46
♔c4 ♕xg3 47 ♘d3 and
44...♕g1+ 45 ♔e2 ♕h2+ 46
♔f1 ♕xg3. Both lines are
highly plausible since the simple plan of advancing the h-
pawn will always cause problems for White. We could continue the latter line: 47 ♕e4 h5
48 ♘d3 h4 49 ♘f2 h3 50 ♔e2
h2 51 ♕f3 ♕g1 with a clear
draw.

30	...	axb2?
31	♕b3	e3
32	♔g2?	

After 32 ♘d3 e2 33 ♕xb2
(not 33 ♔g2? ♖xd3 34 ♕xd3
e1♘+) 33...♖xd3 34 ♕xe2
♗b7+ 35 ♔g1 ♖d8 White is
better since he can try to mount
a kingside attack; but without
any queenside pawns left it
must be drawn.

32	...	e2
33	♔f2	♖d1
34	♔xe2	♖h1!

Obviously, this it what I'd
missed when playing 32 ♔g2.

35 ♕b8   h5!

But not 35...h6? 36 ♕xc8+ ♔h7 37 ♘d7 b1♕ 38 ♘f8+ ♔g8 39 ♘xe6+ ♔h7 40 ♘f8+ with a perpetual check.

36 ♕xc8+   ♔h7

A queen and knight for a rook and pawn ahead, White is totally lost: **37 ♕b8 b1♕ 38 ♕xb1+ ♖xb1 39 ♔f3 ♖b2 40 h3 ♖a2 41 ♘e4 ♖a3+ 42 ♔g2 ♔g8 43 ♘g5 ♔f8 44 ♔f2 ♔e7 45 ♔g2 f6 46 exf6+ gxf6 47 ♘e4 ♖e3 48 ♘f2 ♔f7 0-1**

Never a particularly orderly person, I retain just six scorebooks of games from my youth, running from the end of the British U-14 Championship in Rhyl 1969 up to May 1973, while subsequent output is organised, if that is the word, in envelopes. By coincidence the very last game in the sixth scorebook happens to feature that ghastly memory of the past: an adjudication. This absurd practice is almost dead nowadays, though it still flourishes in some leagues. Soon may it pass! Here with the lightest of notes is, if I may misuse the phrase, a *reductio ad absurdum*.

Goldschmidt–Speelman
Richmond–St Pauls 1973
King's Indian Defence

1 d4 ♘f6 2 c4 g6 3 ♘c3 ♗g7 4 e4 0-0 5 ♘f3 d6 6 ♗e2 e5 7 0-0 ♘c6 8 d5 ♘e7 9 ♗d2 ♘e8
10 ♖c1 h6 11 b4 f5 12 c5 f4 13 ♘a4 ♘f6 14 ♕c2 g5 15 ♘e1 g4 16 f3 g3 17 h3 ♕e8 18 b5 ♕h5 19 ♗b4 ♘e8 20 ♘d3 ♖f7 21 ♖fd1 ♘g6 22 ♘e1 ♘h4 23 ♗f1 ♗f8 24 ♖d2 ♘xg2 25 ♗xg2 ♗xh3 26 ♗xh3 ♕xh3 27 ♕d3 b6 28 cxb6?? White could have refuted the attack by taking control of h3 after 28 cxd6 cxd6 29 ♕f1 ♕d7 30 ♔g2! h5 31 ♖c6 h4 32 ♕h1! **28 ... axb6** But now he has to lose a vital tempo to move the attacked knight. **29 ♘c3 h5 30 ♕f1 ♕d7 31 ♕g2** It is too late to control h3: after 31 ♔g2 h4 32 ♕h1 h3+ 33 ♕xh3 ♕xh3+ 34 ♔xh3 ♖h7+ Black is winning **31 ... h4 32 ♔f1 h3 33 ♕g1 ♘f6**

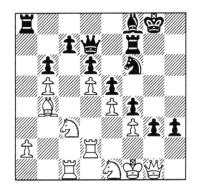

In this splendidly clear position, the game was sent for adjudication. I believe that we both claimed a win, but eventually it was sent to Michael Stean who decided that the possibility of moves like ...♘g4 gave Black the advantage; and he awarded me the game.

2 International Titles

If you aspire to become a professional chessplayer, then you must obtain international titles. Actually, in my case, it was the other way round. I left Oxford in July 1977 with a good second – not good enough, though, to continue doing mathematics – and no great desire to follow the majority of my contemporaries, who were enrolling to become accountants or actuaries.

International Master Title
In contrast to juniors today, the best of whom leave school, let alone university, as IMs or even GMs, I still hadn't obtained even my IM title. Although I was a reasonable player by the end of the previous chapter, my development continued to be marked by long quiescent plateaux, in which there was little visible improvement; and I had consciously decided to put chess on the back burner for the three years while I was, if not always studying, at least enjoying university life.

It is frequently argued nowadays, that in order to get to the very top one needs to specialise at an ever younger age. I suppose this may really be true when applied, say, to female gymnasts; though the damage done to their bodies is nauseating, to say the least. But mind sports like chess, even today when the top players work tremendously hard – much harder than twenty years ago – require relatively less specific preparation and more gathering of inner resources than those which involve physical co-ordination.

The upshot is that I absolutely don't regret according chess such a low priority at this formative stage. And I would argue, in somewhat partisan fashion, that in order to succeed as a chessplayer one requires not only talent but also the maximum quantity of inner strength which one can muster; an elusive virtue which a formal education – apart from being a wonderful thing in itself – is also one of the very best ways of fostering. There is no guarantee that if, following a successful personality transplant, I had spent the years from 1974 to 1977 – or for that matter all my time from puberty onwards – crouched over a hot chessboard, I would have done any better. And it certainly wouldn't have been as much fun.

In any case, I decided to spend some time as a professional chessplayer, initially in search of the International Master title, before getting a 'proper job'; and I remain a professional chessplayer to this very day.

As many readers will know, international titles are obtained by scoring a series of 'norms'. The technical details are rather complex, but in principle these involve obtaining a sufficiently good performance based on rating tables against a field containing a high enough proportion of titled players (IMs or GMs); and against no more than a certain proportion from a single national federation (though nowadays this rule is waived for national championships). Each norm should be in an event of at least nine rounds and the separate norms should add up to at least 24 games.

Grizzled old hacker that I am, I can't resist pointing out that twenty years ago, 'when I was young', these rules were applied fairly strictly, whereas today there are all sorts of exemptions, such as the glorious rule that one can declare a norm before the end of an event of more than nine rounds duration.

The idea is that otherwise players would have to 'fall ill' to preserve their norms. One can understand its application in team tournaments – one certainly doesn't want the best players dropping out before the final rounds – and just about accept it in open tournaments run on the Swiss system – in which by the very virtue of doing well enough to get a norm, one may face exceptionally tough opposition afterwards – but in an all-play-all? Imagine a tournament with two particularly strong players in which a norm contender has the good fortune to be drawn against them in the last two rounds: he makes his norm and then loses to both of them. Bill Hartston lost his last two games one year at Hastings long before this rule applied: bang went his grandmaster title and with it his international career.

I digress. My first norm came just a month or so after leaving university.

Lloyds Bank Masters 1977

This was the very first of the splendid series of annual tournaments in London which ended only in 1994 – one of the main engines for developing British chess over that period. The long-term sponsorship owed much to Sir Jeremy Morse, Chairman of Lloyds Bank and an eminent chess problemist, specialising in 'many movers'. A model for events today, the tournaments, organised by Leonard Barden and Stewart Reuben, were specially designed to create opportunities for title norms, with hopefuls as much as possible given pairings which, at the very least, didn't dash their chances (for instance, they would always ensure that a player with realistic chances of a norm played a sufficient number of titled players and enough foreigners).

Although I'd never previously made a single norm, by this stage I was quite good enough to do so if things went well. The English team only arrived home from the Student Team Championship in Mexico on the morning of the first round. I was therefore allowed to take a half-point bye and slipped through the rest of the event for a final score of 6½/10, drawing with several good players – including Eugenio Torre, John Nunn and Bill Hartston – and winning just three, including the following entertaining encounter:

Game 12
J.Speelman–T.B.Bennett
Lloyds Bank Masters, London 1977
French Defence

With two rounds to go, 1½ points was likely to be enough for the norm. This game is not of a very high standard, but the play on the long diagonal is quite aesthetic. And my opponent's repeated draw offers serve as a platform for a short digression on rudeness at the chessboard.

1	e4	e6
2	♘f3	d5
3	♘c3	

I used to play this against the French quite often at that time,

mainly for the surprise value. It has considerable point against the game continuation; while 3...♗b4 4 e5 avoids a normal Winawer; and 3...c5 4 exd5 exd5 5 d4 is similar to the ...d5 Tarrasch, but with the knight on the better square, c3. However, the main problem is 3...♘f6 4 e5 ♘fd7 5 d4 which transposes back into a standard variation (1 e4 e6 2 d4 d5 3 ♘c3 ♘f6 4 e5 ♘fd7), but with White already committed to 5 ♘f3, whereas the lines with 5 f4 are generally thought to be more dangerous.

3	...	d4
4	♘e2	c5
5	d3	

5 c3, trying to break Black's centre before he can support it, is far from bad. Simon Webb had tried 5...♘f6 against me a few years earlier in the British Championships at Clacton 1974. After 6 cxd4 ♘xe4 7 ♘c3 ♘xc3 8 dxc3 I had a very pleasant game; though I eventually lost in 35 moves. But in this sequence the paradoxical 7...♘g5! is much more challenging.

| 5 | ... | ♘c6 |
| 6 | g3 | e5 |

Reaching a fairly standard King's Indian reversed in which White has two extra tempi in view of the unusually stately progress of the black e-pawn. But since the centre is blocked and White isn't always very pleased to have committed himself to castling kingside in a normal King's Indian, this doesn't have to be too bad for Black, at all.

| 7 | ♗g2 | ♗e7 |
| 8 | 0-0 | ♗g4!? |

To induce the slightly weakening

9	h3!?	♗e6
10	c3	f6
11	cxd4	cxd4
12	♘h4	♕d7
13	♔h2	g5?

A dreadful move, weakening the light squares for no good reason. Of course White is only too delighted to offer a pawn to open the long diagonal.

14	♘f5	0-0-0
15	a3	♗f8
16	b4	♘ce7
17	f4	gxf4?!

17...h6 was sensible, keeping the game closed.

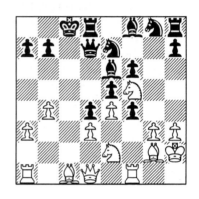

18 ♘xf4!

Offering a piece to take control of the f4-b8 diagonal. If now 18...exf4 19 ♗xf4 ♘c6 20 ♖c1 a6 21 ♕a4 blows Black away. And 18...♗f7 19 ♘xe7+ ♗xe7 (19...♘xe7 20 ♘h5) 20 ♘d5 is most unpleasant; so he feels obliged to give up the light-squared bishop.

18	...	♔b8
19	♘xe6	♕xe6
20	♕h5	

Stopping ...h5 and so provoking a further concession.

20	...	♘xf5
21	exf5	♕e8
22	♕f3	♕d7
23	a4	♘e7
24	a5	♘d5

25	a6	b6
26	♗d2	♛b5
27	♖fc1	♗e7
28	♖c4	♖d7
29	♖ac1	

Setting a fairly obvious trap.

29	...	♖hd8!

Not 29...♛xa6? when White has 30 ♖xd4! when 30...exd4? 31 ♗f4+ ♚a8 32 ♛xd5+ ♖xd5 33 ♗xd5+ ♛b7 34 ♗xb7+ ♚xb7 35 ♖c7+ wins a piece; while if 30...♖hd8 31 ♖dc4 to be followed by d4, blasting open another diagonal.

| 30 | ♖a1 | |

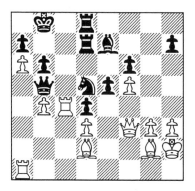

But now Black was threatening to take the a-pawn, so I simply reset. Although White has a beautiful position, it is not so easy to break through. Emboldened by my involuntary repetition, my opponent, who had already, I believe, offered a draw earlier, continued the tactic.

Normally, I would simply say 'I'll think about it' and when rejecting 'No, thank you.' But by offer number three – presumably a few moves later – I blurted out the somewhat tarter 'Not in this position,' though I may have added a 'Thank you.'

Of course, it is rude to continue to offer draws when your opponent has refused – and is arguably in breach of the rules about putting an opponent off. In fact my reply was really pretty restrained. The bluntest reaction to such a kind offer I know of, was in an extremely insignificant club match which a grandmaster – he can only have been an IM at the time – was attending as a favour, at some inconvenience to himself. His opponent, rated all of 130 or 140 (roughly 1700 ELO), produced that most splendidly impertinent of sequences 1 f4 'Would you like a draw?' The instantaneous 1...e5 'F*** off!' led to a very quick victory.

On the subject of rudeness, international players are usually tremendously well behaved, but there are occasional instances, even at a very high level, in which standards lapse somewhat. One situation which can lead to a great deal of fuss, is the sealing of a move before adjournment. I know of at least one case of a very fine player sealing 'Resigns'; while the biscuit for rudest sealed move must surely go to one of our American cousins, who, in the midst of an admittedly extremely trying tournament in Iceland, reached the adjournment a couple of queens down, facing forced mate in just two more moves. It was a tournament in which his opponent would have to get up in the morning to continue this fascinating struggle. The adjournment session duly started, minus the American who had kindly sealed 'Good morning, asshole.'

30	...	♗f8
31	♔h1	♗e7
32	g4	♖g8
33	♕e4	♖d6

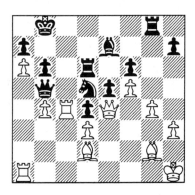

34 g5!
With the black army stretched by the need to defend the long diagonal, it is time to open up a new front.

34	...	♖dd8

If 34...fxg5? 35 ♕xe5 opens the floodgates.

35	♖ac1	♖d7

If 35...♕xa6 36 ♖xd4! again wins.

36	♗f3

Faced with ideas such as ♖g1

or perhaps an improvement of the dark-squared bishop which can go via e1 to g3, taking aim at e5, Black cracked.

36 ... ♕xa6? 37 ♖xd4! exd4? 38 ♗f4+ ♔a8 39 ♕xd5+ ♖xd5 40 ♗xd5+ ♕b7 41 ♗xb7+ ♔xb7 42 ♖c7+ ♔a6 43 ♖xe7 fxg5 44 ♗e5 1-0

A draw in the last round duly secured my first IM norm.

Hastings 1977/78

Although I'd played reasonably well in an all-play-all at Birmingham in 1976, this was my first 'proper' tournament' a category 10 with such luminaries as Tigran Petrosian.

At that time, the players stayed in the Yelton Hotel on the seafront. It was many years ago, and I'm sure that the Yelton has undergone many improvements since, but I have to say that at that time and with hindsight (I'd mind rather more today) it wasn't ideal. The rooms were tiny and extremely cold; and the food far from cordon bleu. Indeed, the dining room in the Yelton is the only eatery where I've ever seen a fly in soup; sadly Jonathan Mestel was either too dumbfounded or too nonplussed to summon up the appropriate response.

The playing hall was next door in the basement of the White Rock Theatre, which, like many such establishments, benefited over the Yuletide period from the annual pantomime. I've always had good concentration and over the years hardly ever noticed the stamping overhead, except perhaps when my position was beyond repair. More sensitive souls were less lucky. Indeed, when Nigel Short decided, a few years later, to amuse himself by going to the pantomime on the free day, he reported later how the children had been exhorted to 'stamp harder to put the Russian grandmasters off'.

For all the problems, it was still thrilling and frightening to be playing in Hastings. Not only was it terribly strong but Hastings is, after all, one of the world's great annual tournaments. (And continues to be. For some years it retained the rather tacky reputation which it arguably deserved at this time. Later they moved to the Queens Hotel, grand in its time but sadly that was a century ago – it is boarded up now. Today's facilities are a great improvement, the players stay, and the Premier is played, in the Cinque Ports Hotel, purpose-built, with help from the Hastings Borough Council, for conferences and with the chess tournament very much in mind.)

In my first Premier I started well with a chaotic draw against Leonid Shamkovich followed by a win against Jonathan Tisdall, but then settled into a steady pattern of draws. Many of the games were very hard fought but my ability to stave off danger was not matched by sufficient power to put opponents away when I held the advantage; and in any case I was rather conservative in my assessments since I wanted, above all, to find my level – to prove that I could survive against this class of opposition.

My run of draws was broken only by a loss to the eventual tournament winner, Roman Dzindzihashvili, who was tremendously strong at that time. Roman's problem has always been that he can't sleep during tournaments; and Tisdall once related to me how, halfway through this particular tournament, an ashen 'Dzindzi' bumped into him on the way to a morning adjournment and asked directions!

Still, one win, one loss and twelve draws was exactly enough for my second IM norm; together with the nine from Lloyds Bank bringing me up to an irritating 23 games – just one short of the overall requirement. My most interesting game was this tremendously chaotic struggle. Played in round 11, nine games after my previous – and eventually only – win of the tournament, it started off quietly but degenerated into chaos just before the first time control. Although I was still winning after the adjournment, the scent of victory overexcited me; and I allowed my opponent to mobilise a fearsome armada of passed pawns which was certainly enough to redress the 'balance of terror'.

Indeed, it appears to have been sufficient for a draw in an analytical sense, as well. (Clock times, where known, are given after the moves. In those days the standard time limit was 40 moves in 2½ hours each, although this has since changed.)

Game 13
J.Speelman–J.Fedorowicz
Hastings 1977/78
English Opening

1	c4	♘f6
2	♘f3	c5
3	d4	cxd4
4	♘xd4	e6
5	♘c3	b6!? 0:13

Offering a hedgehog after 6 e4.

6	♘db5 0:17	♗c5
7	♗f4	0-0
8	♗c7	

Certainly not 8 ♘c7? e5 9 ♗xe5 ♘g4 10 ♗g3, when either piece can capture on f2, but 8 ♗d6 is also possible at once.

8	...	♕e7
9	♗d6	♗xd6
10	♕xd6	♕xd6
11	♘xd6 0:38	

(see following diagram)

White has a slight advantage since the knight is hard to shift, due to the fact that Black has castled.

11	...	♘c6 0:45
12	e3	♖d8

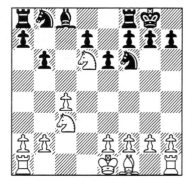

13	♗e2	♔f8
14	0-0-0	♗a6
15	♖d2	♘e7
16	♗f3	♖ab8
17	♖hd1	♘c8
18	♘db5	♗b7
19	♗xb7	♖xb7
20	b3	a6
21	♘d4	

21 ♘d6 was possible, but in view of White's space advantage it makes sense to keep more pieces on.

21	...	♘a7

22	a4		♖c8	
23	♔b2	1:37	♔e7	1:47
24	e4		d6	
25	f3			

Although his space advantage offers a small edge, White is using rather a lot of energy in the shape of both knights to prevent ...b5. John's next move is dubious, since it allows the d4 knight to regroup with tempo.

25 ... ♖c5?!

25...♘e8 looks better, prophylactically defending d6 before considering activating the rook.

26 ♘c2! ♘e8

If 26...b5 27 cxb5 axb5 28 ♖xd6 wins a clear pawn since 28...♘d5? fails to 29 exd5 ♔xd6 30 ♘e4+.

27 ♘b4 1:58 **♖h5!?** 2:08

If Black has to play ...a5 then the rigidity engendered by the weakness on b5 and the lack of a b5 break will certainly give White a serious plus.

27...♖a5 was a reasonable

alternative to the game move. Although this doesn't immediately threaten ...b5, since at present that would lose to capturing twice on b5 followed by ♘c6+, the idea of ...♔f8 followed by ...b5 is certainly in the air. So White might choose to retreat 28 ♘d3, threatening 29 e5 and if 29...dxe5? 30 b4 trapping the rook. Probably Black would now break with 28...b5, but 29 axb5 axb5 30 c5 yields a pleasant plus for White.

28 ♘xa6!?

Deciding to take the opportunity to play with the queenside pawns. These are very powerful, so this is the probably correct decision, but the quiet 28 h3 was perfectly possible, when 28...♖a5!? is more or less identical to the lines with an immediate 27...♖a5. It is possible, though, that John intended 28...b5!? (unplayable a move earlier since then ♘xa6 would have hit the rook). Now White must exchange, but 29 cxb5 axb5 30 a5 obviously gives him some advantage.

28	...	♖xh2
29	♘b4	h5
30	♘b5	♘xb5
31	cxb5	h4
32	♘c6+	♔f8

Not 32...♔d7? 33 ♘e5+ ♔e7 34 ♘g4; but 32...♔f6 is conceivable

33	b4	h3
34	gxh3	♖xh3
35	♖d3	g6

If White could just consolidate then the queenside pawns
should win. But in the next five
moves to the time control, I lost
it a little.

36 ♔c3   ♘f6
37 ♖b1 2:18 **d5!** 2:19

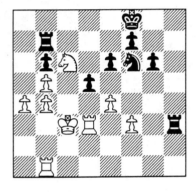

38 a5

I presume that I was worried
about 38 e5 ♘d7 39 a5 bxa5 40
bxa5 ♘c5, but 41 ♘d4! (41 ♖e3
allows 41...♖h4 with serious
play), threatening ♖dd1 followed by a6, looks like it keeps
control, e.g. 41...♘xd3 42 ♔xd3
♖h2 (if 42...♔g7 43 b6 wins) 43
a6 ♖b6 44 ♖a1! ♖b8 45 a7 ♖a8
46 ♔c3! and White is winning.

38 ...   dxe4
39 a6   ♖c7
40 a7 2:20   **♖xa7** 2:21
41 ♖d8+   ♔g7
42 ♘xa7   ♖xf3+

42...exf3 is also very unclear.
Presumably we adjourned round
about here, though my scoresheet unfortunately doesn't say
when. The best time from
Black's point of view would

have been before he had to
make the decision which way to
recapture on f3. In any case, the
first resumption in Hastings was
straight after dinner in those
times and the game reeled on.

43 ♔c2   ♘d5?!

Maybe the best move
'objectively', for if, for example, 43...♖f2+ 44 ♖d2! e3 45
♖xf2 exf2 46 ♔d3 White is well
in control. But from a practical
point of view 43...♘d5 is rather
helpful to White since the
coming liquidation ought to
have been quite sufficient for
victory.

44 ♖xd5!   exd5
45 ♘c8   d4

If 45...♖f2+ 46 ♔c3 ♖f3+ 47
♔d4 ♖d3+ 48 ♔e5 and the b-
pawn should run home

46 ♘xb6   ♖f2+
47 ♔b3   d3

Or 47...e3 48 ♔c4 ♖d2 49
♘d5 e2 50 ♖e1 d3 51 ♘f4! and
wins.

48 ♘c4   ♖h2
49 b6   ♖h8
50 b7 2:49   **♖b8** 2:32
51 ♘d6

Here my scoresheet went to
pieces as I left out 51 ♘d6,
skipping to Black's next move
in my column – the clock times
also disappeared. Nine rounds
after my previous win, I must
have been excessively tense and
it is not so surprising that after
Black's next move I lost the
thread.

51 ...   f5!

51...e3? 52 ♔c3 d2 53 ♔d3 is simple.

52 ♖a1??

After 52 ♔c3! the pawns are stopped and the threat of ♖b1-a1-a8 is decisive: 52...♔f6 53 ♖a1 ♔e5 54 ♖a8.

52	...	e3
53	♔c3	d2
54	♔c2	♖d8!

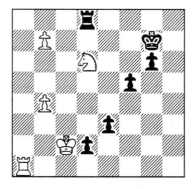

55 ♔d1

Preparing to acquiesce in a repetition. 55 ♖a7 ♔f6 56 ♖a6 is fun to analyse, with or without the help of a computer, but would not have been so enter-taining to play. Here are some lines; though I certainly don't make any pretence of complete-ness. Black continues 56...f4! which, given that it is playable, seems preferable to 56...♔g7 – though that also looks sufficient to draw and indeed can often transpose. White has to choose between the two moves 57 ♘c8+ and 57 ♖b6:

a) 57 ♘c8+ ♔g5 (not 57...♔g7? 58 ♖d6 e2 59 ♔xd2 ♖e8 60 ♖d7+ and wins) 58 ♖d6, which looks very danger-ous in fact leads to 58...e2! 59 ♖xd8! (59 ♔xd2?? ♖e8 60 ♔e1 f3 actually loses!) 59...e1♕ and now:

a1) 60 ♖xd2? ♕e4+ and ... ♕xb7.

a2) If 60 b8♕ at once Black can force an immediate draw by perpetual check as long as he 'forgets' to promote the pawn: 60...♕c1+ 61 ♔b3 ♕b1+ 62 ♔c4 ♕c1+ 63 ♔b5 ♕f1+ 64 ♔b6 ♕g1+ 65 ♔b7 ♕h1+! 66 ♔a7 ♕a1+.

a3) 60 ♖d5+ avoids perpetual but improves the black king so

that after 60...♔g4 61 b8♕
♕c1+ 62 ♔b3 d1♕+ 63 ♖xd1
♕xd1+ 64 ♔c4 ♕e2+ 65 ♔c5
the ending must be fine for
Black. Here he can simply play
65...f3. Perhaps this or some
other line would be playable
even with the black king on g5;
but then ♕g3+ would be in the
air.

b) 57 ♖b6 ♖b8 58 ♖c6 ♖d8!
59 b5! and now:

b1) 59...f3? 60 ♘c4+.

b2) 59...g5?! takes the g5-
square away from the king. After 60 ♘c8+ ♔f5 (60...♔g7?
still loses, as in variation a, to
61 ♖d6 e2 62 ♔xd2 ♖e8 63
♖d7+ ♔f6 64 ♖e7) 61 ♖d6 e2
62 ♖xd8 e1♕ 63 ♖xd2! the b7-
pawn is now protected by a
knight fork due to the place-
ment of the king on f5. Perhaps
it is still drawn, but White must
have chances after, for example,
63...♕e4+ 64 ♔b3 ♕e3+ 65
♔c4 ♕xd2 66 b8♕ since the
knight is threatening to come
back into play with gain of
tempo.

b3) 59...♔g7. By moving the
king out of the potential discovered check, Black appears to
threaten ...f3. This is certainly
the best – indeed the only –
move if the previous variation
is really good for White; but
otherwise there would be
something to be said in practice
for getting the g-pawn moving.
After 60 b6 we reach the following position:

b31) But now if Black does
carry out his 'threat' of 60...f3?
then the weakening of the e3-
pawn would appear to be fatal:
61 ♖c7+ ♔f6 (or 61...♔h6 62
♘f7+ ♔h5 63 ♘xd8 f2 64 b8♕
d1♕+ 65 ♔xd1 f1♕+ 66 ♔c2)
62 ♖d7! ♖b8 (or 62...♖xd7 63
b8♕ f2 64 ♘e4+ ♔f5 65 ♘xf2
exf2 66 ♕f8+ ♔e6 67 ♔d1) 63
♘c4 e2 64 ♔xd2 ♖e8 65 ♖f7+!
♔g5 66 ♔e1 wins for White.

b32) So Black should just
plod on with the 'positional'
60...g5!, maintaining the pawn
chain. Now if 61 ♖c7+?! ♔f6
62 ♖d7 (with the king on c2, 62
♖h7? allows 62...d1♕+ 63
♔xd1 ♖xd6+ 64 ♔e2 ♖d8)
62...♖b8 63 ♘e4+ (not 63 ♔d1
♔e6) 63...♔f5 64 ♘c5 f3 65
♘a6 f2 66 ♘xb8 e2 Black is
winning. So White should reply
61 ♔d1, partly so that with the
rook on e7 he can leave the
knight on d6 under fire without
allowing ...d1♕+ followed by
...♖xd6+. Now Black has further choices:

b321) 61...g4 allows White to
force rook and knight vs. rook

after 62 ♘f5+ ♔f7 63 ♖d6 ♖b8 (63...♖h8 64 ♖xd2 exd2 65 ♘d6+ wins) 64 ♖d4 ♔e6 65 ♖xf4 ♖xb7.

b322) 61...♔h7 should be enough to draw without even having to defend the pawnless ending, since Black is finally threatening ...f3. If 62 ♖c7+ ♔g6 63 ♖e7 (threatening ♖e8; for 63 ♖d7 see variation b3222, where this gets tried on move 71) 63...♖h8 64 ♖e6+ ♔g7 65 ♘f5+ (65 ♖h6 – obviously Fritz – 65...♖d8 66 ♘f5+ ♔f7 comes to the same thing) 65...♔f7 66 ♖h6 ♖d8 67 ♖d6 and now:

b3221) 67...♖h8? allows 68 ♖xd2! (this would also be the answer to 67...♖e8), when 68...exd2 69 ♘d6+ and 70 ♘c8 wins – though it is still far from over after 68...♖b8! 69 ♖d3 ♔e6 70 ♘d6.

b3222) But why give up the beautiful d2-pawn? Simply 67...♖b8 68 ♖c6 ♖d8 makes sense: 69 ♘d6+ (69 ♖d6 is a simple repetition) 69...♔g7! (forced, for if 69...♔e6? 70 ♖c8; 69...♔e7? 70 ♘c8+ ♔f7

71 ♖d6; or 69...♔g6 70 ♘c8+ ♔f5 71 ♖d6) 70 ♖c7+ and while 70...♔f6 may be playable, it is more relevant that 70...♔g6 repeats the position reached after move 62 in variation b322; but in that line the king, which was coming from h7, didn't have the choice of going to the f6-square instead.

There we tried '63' ♖e7. The only other possibility seems to be 71 ♖d7 when 71...♖b8 is sensible. Black is ready to push the g-pawn as well. Apart from 72 ♖e7 ♖h8!, repeating, White can try to manoeuvre the knight towards c6 or a6, but while this knight is in transit awful things can happen. Lines like 72 ♘e4 ♔f5 73 ♘c5 ♖e8 74 ♔e2 f3+ 75 ♔xf3 e2 76 ♖d5+ ♔g6 and 77 b8♕ g4+! or 72 ♘c4 ♔f6 73 ♘a5 g4! (but 73...f3 74 ♘c4! g4 75 ♘xe3 g3 is also enough to draw) 74 ♘c6 g3 75 ♘xb8 g2 (and wins!) are hardly encouraging for White. So my impression is that there is a dynamic balance – both sides should acquiesce in the draw.

Nevertheless, had I been in a better frame of mind there would have been some point in trying these variations starting with 55 ♖a7, as White has quite a lot of latitude before he can get into trouble; while Black has to find some quite difficult moves – the repeated refusal to push ...f3, is not an easy decision in a game.

In reality, the game lasted only two more half-moves.

55 ...   **f4**
56 ♚e2   ½-½

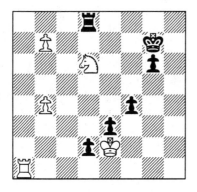

After 58...♜b8 57 ♔d1 f3?! 58 ♘c4 ♜xb7 (or 58...e2+ 59 ♔xd2 ♜xb7 60 ♘e5) 59 ♘xe3 White has chances of reaching rook and knight against rook, so of course Black should repeat with 57...♜d8! 58 ♔e2 ♜b8.

Lone Pine 1978

The tiny town of Lone Pine is in the centre of California near Mt Whitney, the highest point of mainland USA (Mt McKinley in Alaska is higher). The tournament, a very strong open Swiss, was the brainchild of the local magnate, the late Louis Statham, who owned the local water supply.

I remember getting up in the mornings and gazing out of the motel at the most beautiful snow-capped mountains. On the two consecutive rest days we went, however, not to the mountains, but rather across Death Valley to that Paradise of Mammon or – depending on your point of view – hellhole, Las Vegas. I believe that as a man of principle I lost one dollar 25 cents on the slot machines; and was particularly impressed by the marriage parlours (a free bottle of champagne for every third wedding). As you can imagine, I support their particular interpretation of this very fine American institution.

The chess started wonderfully for me when I beat Bent Larsen in the first round: my very first win against a grandmaster – though he went on to win the tournament outright, scoring 7½ from the final eight rounds, drawing only with Polugayevsky. I had good chances to continue the run in the second round against Reshevsky but he got away. The rest of the tournament was less impressive. There were in total five draws, losses to Walter Browne and Peter Biyiasas, and a win against Jay Whitehead. Even so, an overall result of 4½/9 was enough for my final IM norm and the title.

Although the win against Larsen was so important to me, I've already published it – not only in the *BCM* but also in *The Best Chess Games 1970-80* – so instead here is a typically messy draw against Hans Ree.

Game 14
J.Speelman–H.Ree
Lone Pine Open 1978
English Opening

I first analysed this game for the *British Chess Magazine*, August 1978. I've left the annotations practically intact apart from clarifying a couple of variations and chucking in my slightly incomplete record of the clock times.

1 c4 / e5
2 ♘c3 d6
3 ♘f3

3 e3 is a possible alternative, to meet 3...f5!? with 4 d4 when if 4...e4 the white knight isn't attacked. 3 g3 is also perfectly normal. *JS 1997:* But 3 d4!? cxd4 4 ♕xd4 is really the most critical line.

3 ... f5
4 d4 e4
5 ♗g5 ♘f6

5...♗e7 is also sensible, e.g. 6 ♗xe7 ♕xe7 7 ♘d2 (also 7 ♘d5) 7...e3!? 8 fxe3 ♘f6.

6 ♘d2 ♗e7
7 e3 0-0
8 h4!? 0:33

This took me 13 minutes. White is embarking on a rather grandiose plan of undermining the e-pawn by g4; and with this in mind, he wants to protect the bishop on g5. 8 h4 is, in any case, quite a good move positionally since it starts to erect a blockade on the dark squares.

Timman-Ligterink from round five – this game was played in round three – continued more soberly with 8 ♗e2 c6 9 0-0 ♘a6 10 f3 exf3 11 ♗xf3 ♘c7 12 ♕b3 ♔h8 13 ♖ae1 c5. Timman did not seem ever to get anything much, on the contrary Ligterink seemed very comfortable throughout and the game was drawn in 37 moves.

8 ... c6 0:16
9 ♗e2 0:38 **♘a6** 0:20
10 a3!? 0:48

White wants to play g4, and with this in mind he is anxious to prevent ...♘b4 at an unpleasant moment.

10 ... ♘c7 0:22

Black continues with his very sensible plan of strengthening the centre in preparation for ...d5.

11 g4!? 0:52

And here it is!

JS 1997: While I could imagine myself playing this today, it would probably be in a blitz game – which this later rather resembles.

JS 1997: 11 d5 is another wild idea, but White has the problem that if 11...cxd5 he can't really recapture, since after 12 cxd5 (12 ♖c1!? ♗e6) 12...h6! 13 ♗f4 ♘fxd5 14

♘xd5 ♘xd5 15 ♗c4 ♗e6 Black has won a pawn for not a great deal.

11 ... d5 0:38
12 cxd5 0:59 **cxd5** 0:38
13 ♕b3 1:01

White has a certain amount of pressure against the black centre, but his play does rather smack of over-optimism. Black now finds an excellent way to simplify the situation in his favour.

13 ... ♘xg4! 0:45

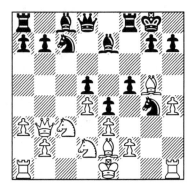

White can now win a pawn by 14 ♗xe7 ♕xe7 15 ♗xg4 fxg4 16 ♘xd5 ♘xd5 17 ♕xd5+ ♗e6 18 ♕xe4, but the state of his light squares at the end of that transaction would be lamentable.

Another try is 14 ♗xe7 ♕xe7 15 ♘xd5 ♘xd5 16 ♕xd5+ ♗e6 17 ♕xe6+, but after 17...♕xe6 18 ♗c4 ♕xc4 19 ♘xc4 ♖ac8 White is in a very bad way since he must allow the black rook to penetrate to c2.

14 ♗f4!? is an interesting idea which I did not consider sufficiently seriously at the time – it looks a bit strange calmly to reposition a piece just after losing a pawn. But after this move Black doesn't seem to have anything wonderful.

The complications after 14...♗xh4 seem to be good for White, since after 15 ♗xg4 fxg4 16 ♗xc7 ♗xf2+ 17 ♔e2 and if 17...♕xc7 18 ♘xd5 ♕f7? 19 ♘e7+ ♔h8 20 ♖xh7+! mates. So Black must try 18...♗e6, which in 1980 I left at that. In fact, although this is very unclear, it seems to be rather good for White. The variation continues 19 ♘xc7 ♗xb3 20 ♘xb3! (20 ♘xa8? ♗c2 is simply bad; while 20 ♖ac1 ♖ac8 21 ♘xb3 transposes to 20 ♘xb3 ♖c8 21 ♖ac1) 20...♖ac8 and now:

a) 21 ♖ac1 offers Black a choice between:

a1) 21...♗g3!? 22 ♘e6 ♖f2+ 23 ♔d1 ♖xc1+ 24 ♘xc1 ♗h2 with a messy position.

a2) 21...g3 is more reliable, though after 22 ♘e6 g2 23 ♘xf8 gxh1♕ 24 ♖xh1 ♖xf8 25 ♘d2 (25 ♘c5 ♖f3!?) 25...♗g3 26 ♘xe4 ♗b8 I imagine that White can't be worse.

b) But in any case 21 ♘e6! seems to be clearly stronger: 21...♖c2+ (21...♖f3 22 ♘d2 ♖c2 comes to the same thing) 22 ♘d2! ♖e8 (22...♖f3 23 ♖ac1 ♖xd2+ 24 ♔xd2 ♗xe3+ 25 ♔e2 ♗xc1 26 ♖xc1 is clearly

better for White) 23 ♘g5! h6
(23...g3 24 ♘h3 ♖f8 25 ♖hf1
wins) when:

b1) My first thought was 24
♖hc1 so that if 24...♖xb2 25
♖ab1 ♖a2 26 ♖xb7! hxg5 27
♖cc7! with at least a draw.
Black can try ...♖xd2+ at some
point in this line, though it may
still be good for White, e.g.
24...♖xd2+ 25 ♔xd2 hxg5 26
♖c5! gets behind the passed
pawn; or 24...♖xb2 25 ♖ab1
♖xd2+ 26 ♔xd2 hxg5 gives
White the additional option of
27 ♖xb7 ♖e6 28 ♖cc7 ♖g6,
though 27 ♖b5 looks safer.

b2) But this is academic since
the calm 24 ♖ad1! (Fritz) is
even better after 24...g3 25 ♘h3
g2 (or 25...♖f8 26 ♖hf1) 26
♖h2 or 24...♗g3 25 ♘gxe4!
♖xe4 26 ♔d3 and White is
winning.

(This analysis of 18...♗e6 is
JS 1997.)

So Black should play something calmer such as 14...♗e6,
when 15 ♗xc7 ♕xc7 16 ♘xd5
is certainly playable for Black
but not marvellous. Maybe
some other 14th move promises
Black more?

Eventually I chose:

14 ♗xg4 1:20 **♗xg5** 0:52

Black could also have played
14...fxg4 immediately.

15 hxg5 1:21 **fxg4** 0:52

16 ♘dxe4 1:24 **♗e6** 1:04

16...♔h8 is a good alternative. Ree was a bit worried by
17 ♘f6 (I can't imagine what

combination of !s and ?s to ap-
pend to this move) 17...gxf6 18
g6. After 18...♔g7 (18...h6 is
also quite sufficient – *JS 1997*),
however, this is shown to be
quite unsound, but in the heat of
battle it is easy to make such
misassessments.

17 ♘g3 1:36

It is important to have the
knight on the kingside to defend
against ideas such as ...g3.

17 ... ♕xg5 1:11

18 ♕xb7 1:40

I felt that this position was
unclear enough for an offer of a
draw not to be impolite and
made one since I feared, however, that in reality my position
was quite a lot worse.

18 ... ♕e7 1:19

18...♖f7 comes into consideration, followed by doubling
on the f-file.

19 ♕b3 1:45

I considered 19 ♘b5, of
course, but rejected it quickly
because ...♕f6(f7) at some
stage would 'surely be good'. I
suspect (without much analysis)
that this must be the case, but
19 ♘b5 certainly merited some
attention since after 19 ♕b3
White is clearly worse.

JS 1997: Of course if 19 ♘b5
♕f7 is simply good for Black:

a) If 20 ♖h2 Black can simply exchange on b5 if he likes –
my note above gives the impression that I'd miscounted
and thought that White had a
pawn for his troubles; but in

fact material is even.

While unsurprisingly taking either way on c7 gets slaughtered. Black only has to take care that the white queen doesn't return home to d3 or c2 with tempo on h7, e.g.

b) 20 ♘xc7 ♕xf2+ 21 ♔d1 ♕f3+ (not 21...♖ab8 22 ♕a6 ♖xb2 23 ♕d3) 22 ♔d2 (22 ♔c2 ♖ab8 23 ♕a6 ♗f5+ 24 ♘xf5 ♕g2+!) 22...♖ab8 23 ♕a6 ♖xb2+ 24 ♔c3 ♕xe3+! 25 ♔xb2 ♖f2+ and mates.

c) 20 ♕xc7 ♕xf2+ 21 ♔d1 ♖ac8 (not 21...♕xb2? 22 ♕c2!) 22 ♕e5 (or 22 ♖f1 ♕xf1+ 23 ♘xf1 ♖xc7) 22...♖c2! 23 ♕xe6+ ♔h8 and mates in a few more moves.

19 ... ♖ab8 1:23
20 ♕c2 1:46 **g6**

White has no very happy long-term home for his king and hence has problems connecting his rooks; while his knights do not have any juicy squares to aim for and his light squares are weak. Black has a safe king, connected rooks and some attractive targets to aim at – some nice light squares his knight might reach one day and a possible pawn push to remove the white knight from g3. We can assert that Black is better, but in order to do anything he will have to find a plan. White should be able to meet any short-term threats against his position but, in view of the general looseness of his game, he

will find it very difficult to get any positive play. In general White would like to provoke Black into 'doing something' quickly, for if Black plays well then his position should improve while White's has got very few ways of getting better and is, on the contrary, likely to deteriorate if he tries anything much.

21 ♖c1 1:50 **♘b5** 1:28

With an exchange of knights, Black would leave White's queenside very weakened. White is unwilling to commit many pieces away from the kingside and will therefore have to contest the queenside with a material deficit there.

22 ♘a4!? 1:59

I decided that 22...♘xd4!? did not win outright and so provoked Black further.

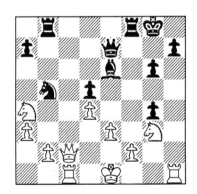

22 ... ♘xd4!? 1:31

Black is tempted but maybe he should just have continued calmly, as White cannot really change the basic characteristics of the position – something along the lines of 'put the bishop on f7 and play ...h5-h4' could be very unpleasant in the long run.

It only took him three minutes! – *JS 1997*.

23 exd4 2:00 **♗d7+** 1:31

If now 24 ♔f1 then 24...♗xa4 25 ♕xa4 ♕e3! wins back the piece. I analysed 26 ♖c2 ♕xg3 27 ♕d7 for a bit (27 ♕xa7 ♕d3+ 28 ♔g1 ♕d1+ 29 ♔g2 ♕f3+ 30 ♔g1 h5 is also horrible – *JS 1997*), so that if 27...♖f7?? 28 ♕xf7+! but then saw 27...♕d3+! and decided to abandon the line.

24 ♘e2 is also very bad: 24...♗xa4 25 ♕xa4 ♖xb2 26 ♕d1 (or 26 ♖c2 ♖b1+) 26...♕e4! (not 26...♖e8 27 ♖c2) is murder.

That only leaves:

24 ♔d1! 2:13

Now Black conceived a 'grand finale'. He could have tried 24...♗xa4 25 ♕xa4 ♖xf2 (also 24...♖xb2) when he would have had some play for the knight, but this isn't entirely clear.

24 ... **♖xf2** 1:52
25 ♕xf2 2:14 **♗xa4+** 1:52
26 b3! 2:16 **♖xb3**

The white king cannot escape the battery so the only chance left is to counterattack.

27 ♖c8+ 2:20 **♔g7**

Ree had (of course) foreseen this position when playing 24...♖xf2 and had analysed the following beautiful variation:

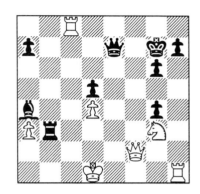

28 ♖xh7+ ♔xh7 29 ♕h2+ ♔g7 30 ♕h8+ ♔f7 31 ♕g8+ ♔f6 32 ♖f8+ ♔g5 33 ♕xd5+ (33 ♖f5+ is nothing) 33...♔h4 34 ♕h1+ ♔xg3 and wins, for after 35 ♕g1+ ♔h4 the black rook will be able to interpose with check.

To this we can add the subvariations:

a) (after 28 ♖xh7+ ♔xh7 29 ♕h2+ ♔g7 30 ♕h8+ ♔f7) 31 ♕h7+ (it is very hard to see checks which give the black king freedom of action when analysing a long way ahead) 31...♔e6 (31...♔f6 32 ♕h4+ ♔e6 33 ♕xg4+ ♔d6 34 ♕xg6+ transposes) 32 ♕xg6+ ♔d7 33 ♕xg4+ ♕e6 and wins, for if 34 ♕xe6+ ♔xe6 35 ♔d2 a piece falls or 34 ♖c7+ (d8+) 34...♔xc7 (xd8) 35 ♕xe6 ♖b6+.

b) (after 28 ♖xh7+ ♔xh7 29 ♕h2+ ♔g7) 30 ♘f5+ ♔f6!! (not 30...gxf5?? 31 ♕h8+).

But he had missed:

28 ♘f5+! 2:25 **gxf5**
29 ♖xh7+!

Now White has a perpetual but no more.

29 ... ♔xh7 1:55
30 ♕xf5+ 2:25 **♔g7** 1:59

Not 30...♔h6?? 31 ♖h8+ ♔g7 32 ♖h7+ ♔g8 33 ♕g6+ ♔f8 34 ♖h8 mate.

31 ♕xg4+ ♔f6
32 ♕f4+ ♔g6
33 ♕g4+ ♔f6
34 ♕f4+ ½-½

This game was adjudged to be the second most interesting (as distinct from 'second best') game of the round.

Grandmaster Title

As with the IM title, I didn't really make a huge attempt to become a grandmaster until I was clearly strong enough. This took a couple more years until 1980, though just as I was starting to consider norms, things got much tougher when FIDE raised the standard from 2550 to 2600 – with inflation I guess 2625 or 2630 at today's ratings. I could easily start banging on again about how things are easier today; though in truth there are far more strong players even than one decade ago, let alone two. Instead I'll move swiftly on.

Phillips & Drew Kings 1980

This superb tournament was the first of three sponsored by the City Stockbrokers at biennial intervals. Held in the sumptuous surroundings of County Hall (the GLC wasn't abolished until 1986), the first in particular attracted huge public interest. There was a glorious hospitality room with drinks and splendid cakes, which, in 1980 was visited by no less than ten per cent of Phillips and Drew's clients!

	1	*2*	*3*	*4*	*5*	*6*	*7*	*8*	*9*	*10*	*11*	*12*	*13*	*14*	
1 Miles	*	1	½	0	1	1	½	½	0	½	1	1	1	½	**8½**
2 Andersson	0	*	½	½	1	0	½	½	½	1	1	1	1	1	**8½**
3 Korchnoi	½	½	*	½	½	½	1	½	1	1	0	½	1	1	**8½**
4 Sosonko	1	½	½	*	0	½	½	½	½	½	1	0	1	1	**7½**
5 Speelman	0	0	½	1	*	1	½	½	½	0	1	1	½	1	**7½**
6 Gheorghiu	0	1	½	½	0	*	½	½	½	1	1	½	0	1	**7**
7 Ljubojevic	½	½	0	½	½	½	*	½	1	½	0	1	½	1	**7**
8 Timman	½	½	½	½	½	½	½	*	0	1	1	0	1	½	**7**
9 Sax	1	½	0	½	½	½	0	1	*	0	½	½	½	1	**6½**
10 Browne	½	0	0	½	1	0	½	0	1	*	0	½	½	1	**5½**
11 Larsen	0	0	1	0	0	0	1	0	½	1	*	½	½	1	**5½**
12 Stean	0	0	½	1	0	½	0	1	½	½	½	*	½	½	**5½**
13 Nunn	0	0	0	0	½	1	½	0	½	½	½	½	*	½	**4½**
14 Short	½	0	0	0	0	0	0	½	0	0	0	½	½	*	**2**

For a player rated only 2495, the tournament represented both a great opportunity and a considerable danger. While it was very exciting to face such excellent opposition, there was also plenty of opportunity to suffer.

Indeed Nigel Short, who was much younger – just 15 – and still considerably weaker (2360) had one of the worst tournaments of his life after he spoilt a won adjournment in the first round against Tony Miles. The adjournment was held in a back room and, presumably partly through nerves, Nigel played Space Invaders when he should have been at the board and only drew. He ended up with just 2/13; and I believe that this defeat set him back several years in his progress towards the summit.

Not very well prepared technically, but extremely keyed up,

I experienced this tournament as a roller coaster in which I reached many bad positions but hacked my way out of the majority, several even to victory, and often by keeping my nerve during critical time trouble situations.

At the drawing of lots the night before the first round, I was lucky to obtain number one and a double white in the first two rounds. Since the tournament was three categories above any that I'd played in before, I was quite happy to start very quietly with a draw in just 20 moves against Gyula Sax. In the next round, against Michael Stean, however, I quickly dissipated, not only the advantage of the first move but any reasonable pretensions to a good position. But instinct took over and I bluffed my way into a violent attack in my own time trouble which led to mate:

Game 15
J.Speelman–M.Stean
London (round 2) 1980
Queen's Indian Defence

1	**d4** 0:03	♘**f6** 0:00
2	**c4** 0:04	**e6** 0:00
3	♘**f3** 0:08	**b6** 0:01
4	♘**c3** 0:11	♗**b7** 0:03
5	♗**g5** 0:14	**h6** 0:11
6	♗**h4** 0:16	**g5** 0:12
7	♗**g3** 0:16	♘**h5** 0:12
8	**e3** 0:18	♘**xg3** 0:12

| 9 | **fxg3** 0:28 |

Dynamic in that it opens the f-file; but spoiling White's pawn structure.

| 9 ... | ♗**g7** 0:32 |
| 10 | ♗**d3** 0:33 |

In the Riga Interzonal the previous year, at which I was

present as Tony Miles's second, Oleg Romanishin had won a nice game against Zoltan Ribli after 10...d6 11 0-0 ♘d7 12 ♗c2 ♕e7 13 ♕d3 a6 14 ♘d2 c5 15 ♘de4 f5 16 dxc5 ♘xc5 17 ♘xd6+ ♔f8 18 ♘xf5 exf5 19 ♕xf5+ ♔g8 20 ♘d5 ♕e8 21 ♖ad1 ♖c8 22 b4 ♘e6 23 ♘xb6 ♖c7 24 c5 h5 25 ♖d6 ♖h6 26 ♖xe6 1-0. Very aesthetic, but Black's play was surely dictated by nerves. For this was in the very last round and had Ribli won or even drawn then he would have got into the Candidates tournament direct; whereas he ended up in a playoff with Andras Adorjan (subsequently drawn 3-3 which meant that Adorjan went through on tie-break).

Romanishin-Ribli was annotated in the booklet on Riga which I co-authored with Tony. And while I've long ago forgotten which of us did what, I presume that he must have taken this one since Michael now adopted a clear improvement that was actually suggested in those notes.

10   ...   ♘c6! 0:36
11   0-0 0:44   **♕e7** 0:39

Much more sensible than Ribli's rush to create light square weaknesses with ...d6. Whatever Michael knew in advance, it is clear that I was floundering; for I now took twenty seven minutes for my next move. Obviously, I was already

regretting my seduction by the Romanishin game – I've never been particularly comfortable with the responsibility engendered by a bad pawn structure at such an early stage.

12   ♖c1 1:11   **0-0-0** 0:48
13   ♕a4 1:17   **♔b8** 0:57

In his notes in *Informator 29*, Michael suggests the obstructive 13...♕b4 14 ♕c2 ♕e7 when 15 a3 would lose a valuable tempo, while 15 c5 ♘b4 exchanges the bishop and 15 ♕a4 ♕b4 only repeats. But presumably Michael was already going for more.

14   c5 1:23   **g4** 1:06
15   ♘h4 1:32   **♗f6** 1:12
16   ♗a6 1:53

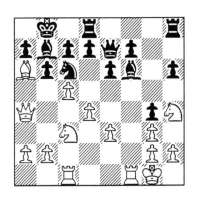

Leaving myself with only 37 minutes for the next 24 moves in an increasingly complex position. If 16 d5, trying to cash in on the momentary 'forkability' of the queen and bishop, Black can utilise the looseness of the bishop on d3. After 16...♗xh4 (16...♗xc3 17 ♖xc3 exd5 18

♘f5 ♕g5 looks less good) 17 dxc6? dxc6! is extremely pleasant; while 17 gxh4 exd5 18 ♘xd5 ♕e5 19 e4 leaves White pretty loose.

16 ...   ♗g5! 1:16
17 ♗xb7?! 2:04

Going into 'swindle mode' rather early. Obviously White doesn't want to defend the pawn with one of his rooks, since 17 ♖ce1 moves the rook away from the attack while 17 ♖fe1 removes the pressure form the f-file. But the latter move is far from clear, e.g. 17 ♖fe1 ♗xh4 18 gxh4 ♕xh4. Now the attack on the e1 rook is annoying, since ♗xb7 followed by ♖xc6 is precluded; and Black is threatening ...g3. But it is White's move and he can certainly create reasonable practical chances with either:

a) 19 cxb6 axb6! (not 19...cxb6 20 d5 exd5 21 ♕f4+ d6 22 ♗xb7 ♔xb7 23 ♕xf7+) 20 ♘b5 runs into 20...g3! (not 20...♗a8 21 d5 exd5 22 ♕f4 ♖c8 23 ♗xc8 ♖xc8 24 ♕xf7) 21 h3 and now:

a1) 21...♕f6? 22 ♖f1 ♕g5 23 ♗xb7 ♕xe3+ 24 ♔h1 ♔xb7 25 ♖xc6 ♔xc6 26 ♕c4+ ♔b7 27 ♕xc7+ ♔a6 is winning for White – one way starts 28 ♘d6 ♖b8 29 b4.

a2) 21...♗a8! is correct when as a result of Black's previous move the d-pawn is pinned. This is certainly still very dangerous for Black but he does

have some counterplay – for instance if 22 ♖c3 ♕e4! is very annoying.

b) 19 g3 ♕g5 20 ♗xb7 ♔xb7 and now:

b1) Immediate violence with 21 ♘b5 invites 21...a6 22 ♘xc7 ♔xc7 23 ♕xa6 ♖b8 24 b4 and if 24...b5 25 a4, but 21...♖a8 looks better and if 22 e4, not my first thought 22...♕d2 in view of 23 cxb6 axb6 24 ♕c4! when if 24...♕xb2 25 ♖e2 ♕b4 26 ♕xb4 ♘xb4 27 ♖xc7+, but now 22...a6 when 23 ♘xc7 ♔xc7 simply doesn't work.

b2) 21 b4 is admirably calm but doesn't seem to do much after, for example, 21 ...h5.

b3) Perhaps 21 ♘e4 ♕d5 22 ♘c3 (not 22 cxb6? ♕xe4 23 ♖xc6 axb6 24 ♖xc7+ ♔xc7 25 ♕a7+ ♔d6 26 ♕a3+ ♔c6! which is dead lost) offering a repetition; though the black queen might choose f5.

17 ...   ♗xe3+ 1:19
18 ♔h1 2:04   **♔xb7!** 1:20

Quite rightly, Michael quickly avoided the appalling mess created by 18...♗xc1 19 ♗xc6 ♗xb2 (19...dxc6 20 ♖xc1 is simply good for White) 20 ♕a6! dxc6 21 ♘b5!

(see following diagram)

which is clearly extremely dangerous.

Obviously if 21...cxb5?? 22 c6 and mate next move. And other defences also appear to fall short.

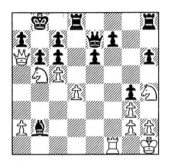

For instance, one nice line goes 21...♗xd4 when 22 ♕xa7?+ ♔c8 23 ♘xd4 ♕xc5 24 ♕a8+ ♔d7 25 ♖xf7+ ♔d6 wins for Black, but 22 ♖d1! is much better at once, e.g. 22...♖d5! 23 ♕xa7+ ♔c8 24 ♘xd4 ♔d7! (not 24...♕xc5 25 ♕a8+ ♔d7 26 ♕xh8) 25 cxb6 ♕d6 26 b7 ♕b4 27 h3! and now:

a) 27...♖d8 28 ♕a8 c5 29 ♕xd8+! ♔xd8 30 ♘c6+ ♔d7 31 ♘xb4 ♖xd1+ 32 ♔h2.

b) 27...c5 28 a3! ♕b6 (28...♕c4 is better; though 29 b8♕ ♖xb8 30 ♕xb8 ♖xd4 31 ♖b1 looks good for White) 29 ♕a4+ c6 and here Black gets hit by 30 ♘xe6!! when all of 30...♔xe6 31 ♕xg4+ ♔e7 32 ♖e1+; 30...fxe6 31 ♖xd5+ exd5 32 ♕xg4+ and 30...♖xd1+ 31 ♕xd1+ ♔xe6 32 ♕xg4+ ♔d6 33 ♕f4+ ♔e6 34 ♕f5+ are winning for White.

There would be no way during a game to be certain that White isn't simply winning in these variations; while after the simple recapture on b7 Black ought to have found a way to simplify to obtain a clear advantage.

19 ♖cd1 2:08 **♗g5!?** 1:31

A brave or foolhardy man might well have tried 19...bxc5. But the common-sense line was 19...♗xd4! 20 ♖xd4 ♘xd4 21 ♕xd4 (if 21 cxb6 ♘c6 the black king is too well protected) 21...♕xc5 22 ♕xg4 when the knights lack good squares and Black's king is pretty safe, while Black's centre pawns should be able to roll up the board, creating unpleasantness: Black must have a safe advantage.

20 d5! 2:14

Stoking the fire

20 ... **exd5** 1:32
21 b4 2:19 **d4** 1:40
22 ♘f5 2:22 **♕e6?!** 1:51

22...♕e5! was better. The queen is quite safe on e5 since if 23 ♖de1 ♗e3 blocks the e-file. After the natural sequence 24 ♘d1 ♖de8 25 ♘dxe3 dxe3 26 ♖xe3 ♕d5 Black is still a pawn ahead and well centralised, with much the better pawn structure – he should win.

23 ♘b5! 2:23

Not 23 ♘xd4? ♕c4, breaking the attack.

23 ... **♗e3** 1:55

23...♖a8! was strong, since if either knight captures on d4, then 24...♕c4 is enormously powerful; while the attempt to whip up an attack with 24 ♘xc7

♔xc7 25 b5 can be met either by the pragmatic 25...bxc5 26 bxc6 ♕xc6 or even the greedier 25...♘a5. It should be impossible to land against such a well co-ordinated position; particularly given that the bishop is covering c1.

24 ♖de1 2:23 **♕d5??** 1:59

After just four minutes' thought Michael blundered, allowing me an immediate haymaker. His alternatives were:

a) If 24...♕c4?? 25 either ♘d6+!

b) 24...♕g6 keeps the b6-pawn protected, but 25 ♘e7! is still winning: 25...♘xe7 26 ♕xa7+ ♔c6 27 ♘xc7 ♘d5 28 b5+ ♔xc5 29 ♕a3+ ♘b4 30 ♖c1+ ♗xc1 31 ♖xc1+ ♔d6 32 ♕xb4+ ♔e5 33 ♕e7+.

c) 24...a6 was natural and – given the time imbalance – should have been very powerful. But, examining this game 17 years after the event in June 1997, I was surprised to discover that by this stage I already had reasonable chances after 25 ♘bxd4 ♘xd4 26 ♘xe3! (not 26 ♘xd4 or 26 ♖xe3, both of which are met by 26...♕c4!), to be followed after most replies by 27 ♕d1! when the knight will be hard to protect and if it moves then White will get an attack, e.g.

c1) 26...h5 27 ♕d1 ♘c6 (the fanciful 27...h4 fails to 28 ♕xd4 hxg3 29 ♘xg4 ♖xh2+ 30 ♘xh2 ♕h6 31 ♕g1) 28 cxb6 cxb6 29 ♘f5 landing on d6.

c2) 26...b5 27 ♕d1 ♘c6 28 a4 attacking.

c3) 26...♕c6! 27 ♕xc6+ dxc6 is quite nice for Black, but White is certainly fighting after 28 cxb6!

d) The attempt to improve on 24...a6 with 24...♖a8 is ill advised in view of 25 ♕d1!

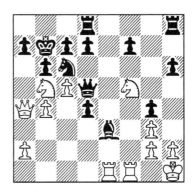

25 ♘e7! 2:25

After this, I became too excited to keep a record of the clock times.

25 ... ♘xe7?

Allowing mate with checks. Given my time shortage, 25...♕e6 would have been more sensible, though it is also quite hopeless after 26 ♘xc6 ♕xc6 27 ♕xa7+ ♔c8 28 cxb6 cxb6 (or 28...♕b7 29 ♘d6+! cxd6 30 ♖c1+ ♗xc1 31 ♖xc1+ ♕c6 32 ♕a8 mate) 29 ♕a6+ ♔b8 when White has to find just one more good move: 30 ♖f6! d6 31 ♕a7+ ♔c8 32 ♖xf7 ♖d7 33 ♖xd7 ♕xd7 34 ♕a8 mate.

26 ♕xa7+ ♔c6

27	♕xc7+	♔xb5
28	♕xb6+	♔c4
29	♕a6+	♔xb4
30	♖b1+	♔xc5
31	♕b6+	♔c4
32	♕b3+	♔c5
33	♕b4+	♔c6
34	♕b6 mate	

The luck continued when Bent Larsen squeezed me in a position with rooks and opposite bishops but allowed counterplay during the time scramble. After the adjournment, he should have acquiesced in a draw immediately; but over-pressed and lost.

I came back down to earth in the next two rounds with losses to Walter Browne and Tony Miles, but I only lost one further game: in round 8 against Ulf Andersson, still the only decisive result in almost a dozen games between us!

In the meantime, I'd drawn with Korchnoi – a relief after the two consecutive losses – and then beaten Gheorghiu after he failed to put me away in a tremendous position and blundered in my time trouble. I remember that he demanded a draw when I had just a minute or so for several moves. I was able to ask him to play a move and by the time he'd done so, was ready to play on.

On fifty per cent with five rounds to go, I now had to face Ljubojevic with Black. 'Ljubo'

built up a very good position with 2 d3 against the Caro-Kann, but I fought back, almost to equalise during the time scramble.

After 36 moves we had reached this position when Ljubo picked up his queen and hurled it towards g8.

L.Ljubojevic-J.Speelman
London (round 9) 1980

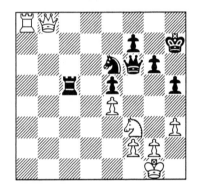

Unfortunately, it landed three-quarters of the way towards h8! By this stage, I was playing blitz; and I instinctively reached out to correct the move and then reply 37...♔h6. At this point Stewart Reuben stepped in and Ljubo started screaming.

There were other time scrambles going on; and in order to control the noise I believe that we went out into the Hospitality Room where, not entirely altruistically – since I thought that I might still be in trouble on the board – I offered a draw which Ljubo quickly accepted.

It is interesting to compare my memory of the incident with Stewart Reuben's perception, as recorded in the tournament book, published by Pergamon, which he wrote with Bill Hartston: 'There was clearly going to be a desperate time scramble and unfortunately Harry Golombek had appointed me in charge of this one, himself concentrating on another. Suddenly Ljubojevic played 37 ♕h8+, one of the most incredible blunders ever played. There is no question but that he intended 37 ♕g8+. He moved his hand away and then went back to put the queen on the other square. Simultaneously I moved to prevent this and Jon's hand came forward, presumably to take the queen, although it was not really the move yet, the clock not having been pressed.

'When I told Ljubojevic the queen had been put on h8, he jumped up shouting, not surprisingly, but even so this was unconscionable with many other games reaching the time control. The clocks were stopped and we tried to settle him down. Then Jon offered a draw and everything was settled amicably. Splendid sportsmanship on Jon's part; personally, I would have won the rook. Incidentally, Jon's hand had not after all been going to take the queen but to adjust it to the intended square – shades of too

much five-minute chess? The rules theoretically would not permit me to allow this, not that I could have known Jon's intentions. If I had known, would it not have been more in the spirit of the game to let the players have their way?

'It is psychologically interesting how difficult it is to ascertain the precise facts about such an incident. B.H.Wood, although standing nearly as close as me, reported that Ljubojevic had made the draw offer.'

This splendid incident had a dramatic effect on my tournament. Not only had I picked up a valuable half-point from a lousy position, but it was very gratifying to be generally perceived to have acted well in difficult circumstances; and I felt that I had in some sense offered a sacrifice to the Goddess Caissa. Down after the loss to Tony Miles, I was galvanised into action for a big push in the last four rounds, particularly after this great piece of luck against the dispirited Nigel Short. Nigel Short, today the happy possessor of a serious theoretical armoury, approached the game in those far off days practically naked – especially against 1 d4. He therefore decided, after 1 d4 ♘f6 2 c4 e6 3 ♘c3 ♗b4 4 e3, to try the provocative 4...a6?! – and proceeded to outplay me until he fell for a sucker punch:

J.Speelman-N.Short
London (round 10) 1980

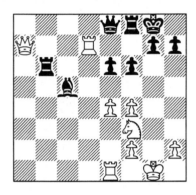

Here 32...♖f7 33 ♖xf7 ♕xf7 would give a small edge. Nigel went for more with:

32 ... ♕g6+
33 ♔f1

And now 33...♖d6 34 ♕c7 ♖xd7 35 ♕xd7 ♕g4 puts White very much on the defensive, but 36 ♘g1 ♕xf4 37 ♕xe6+ ♖f7 38 ♕f5! ♕xf5 39 exf5 should just about hold. But the point of his previous move had been to create immediate threats with:

33 ... ♕g4??
34 ♘g5!

And he had to resign at once.

In the next round, Black against Jan Timman, I decided on a 5...gxf6 Caro-Kann. In a fluctuating battle, he gained the advantage out of the opening, but I tricked him to seize the advantage myself which persisted into a better ending.

I seem to remember a draw offer somewhere, and had imagined that I had made it but he, despite my slight pressure, refused. It may have been the other way round though, since there is the hint of an asterisk – by which I record offers – on his side of the scoresheet; unfortunately it appears right on the fold.

In any case, I blundered a pawn and had to defend a nasty position after the adjournment. But I held with some really rather good play – the ending is analysed in detail in *Analysing the Endgame*. As a result, I now needed 1½/2 for a norm, starting with White against Genna Sosonko, who at this stage was just half a point off the lead on 7½/11.

Game 16
J.Speelman–G.Sosonko
London (round 12) 1980
Sicilian Defence, Dragon variation

At this critical juncture, I decided to shift from my normal flank openings to 1 e4, in the expectation of meeting a Dragon, against which I wanted to try one of my old favourites.

1 e4 c5
2 ♘f3 d6

3 d4 cxd4
4 ♘xd4 ♘f6
5 ♘c3 g6
6 g3 0:03

This quietish system avoids the heavy theory of the main lines or worse still the Yugoslav Attack. Following Jonathan Mestel's example, I had used it quite often a few years earlier when I was still playing 1 e4 regularly. I was surprised how hard it was to track down examples; but eventually unearthed a couple of my games from the late seventies. Both started 1 e4 c5 2 ♘f3 ♘c6 3 d4 cxd4 4 ♘xd4 g6 5 ♘c3 ♗g7 6 ♘de2!?:

a) 6...♘f6 7 g3 0-0 8 ♗g2 d6 9 0-0 ♗d7 10 h3 ♖c8 11 ♘d5 ♘xd5? 12 exd5 ♘e5 (12...♘a5 is better, to keep the diagonal open) 13 a4 ♕b6 14 ♖a2! (one of White's key moves in this variation) 14...♕a6 15 b3 (threatening f4) 15...♗e8 16 ♖a3! (against ...b5) 16...♘d7 17 c4 ♘f6 18 a5 ♗d7 19 ♘d4 b5 20 axb6 ♕xb6 21 ♗e3 ♕c7 22 ♘c6 ♗xc6 23 dxc6 a5 24 ♕d2 e6 25 ♖xa5 d5 26 cxd5 ♘xd5 27 ♖xd5!? (thematic but very slightly extravagant; 27 ♗xd5 exd5 28 ♖xd5 ♕xc6 29 ♖c1 ♕xc1+ 30 ♕xc1 ♖xc1+ 31 ♗xc1 would have given a large simple advantage) 27...exd5 28 ♕xd5 ♖fd8 29 ♕c4 ♖d6 30 b4 ♖e6 31 b5 ♖xe3 32 fxe3 ♗h6? (32...♖f8 was tougher) 33 ♖xf7 ♗xe3+ 34 ♔h2 1-0 Speelman-

Jordan (Australia), World U-26 Team Championship, Mexico 1978.

b) Black can try to exploit this move order with 6...d6 7 g3 (7 h3 looks safer, intending 7...♘f6 8 g3 0-0 9 ♗g2) 7...♗g4 8 ♗g2 ♘d4 9 ♕d3 ♘xe2 10 ♘xe2 ♘f6 11 ♘f4 0-0 12 0-0 ♕c7 13 h3 ♗d7 14 c4 ♖fc8 15 b3 (obviously, this is where Black should strike if possible; presumably because I was worried, I don't have a time record for his previous three moves, though I do know that he'd used 48 minutes after castling and 1 hr 21 after ducking out with...) 15...♗c6 16 ♗d2 b6 17 ♖ac1 ♕b7 18 ♘d5 ♘xd5 19 exd5 ♗e8 20 ♖fe1 (the space should give White the advantage, though Black has obvious potential counterplay with ...b5) 20...♖c7 21 ♖e2 ♗f6 22 ♗h6 ♖ac8 23 a4 a6 24 ♖ce1 b5 25 ♕f3 (threatening 26 ♕xf6)

25...♗h8? (25...♗e5! would have encouraged White to sacrifice the exchange with 26 axb5 axb5 27 ♖xe5 dxe5 28 ♖xe5, but after 28...bxc4 29 ♖xe7 f5! 30 ♖xc7 ♕xc7 31 bxc4 ♕xc4 32 ♕e3 Black is doing quite well) 26 axb5 axb5 27 c5! ♗e5 (if 27...dxc5 28 d6 ♕xf3 29 ♗xf3 ♖d7 30 ♖xe7 ♖xe7 31 ♖xe7 ♖d8 32 ♗g5! is winning, viz. 32...♗d7 [if 32...h6 33 ♖xe8+ ♖xe8 34 d7; or 32...♔f8 33 ♖a7] 33 ♗d5 ♗e8 34 ♖xe8+ ♖xe8 35 d7) 28 c6 ♕a8 (28...♖xc6 29 ♖xe5 dxe5 30 dxc6 ♗xc6 31 ♕e3 ♗xg2?! 32 ♕xe5 f6 33 ♕e6+ ♔h8 34 ♕f7) 29 ♔h2 b4 30 ♖xe5! dxe5 31 ♖xe5 and in bad time trouble Black quickly succumbed: 31...♕a1 32 ♕e2 e6 33 ♕e3 f6 34 ♖xe6 ♗f7 35 d6 1-0 Speelman-D.Wright, Oxford University-Cavendish 1977.

6 ...   ♘c6 0:05
7 ♘de2! 0:03

Received wisdom has it that White should avoid the exchange of a pair of knights; though 7 ♗g2 ♘xd4 8 ♕xd4 ♗g7 is obviously perfectly playable for White.

7 ...   ♗g4!? 0:10

Preparing to exchange off a pair of minor pieces, so preempting any white initiative on the queenside. While this doesn't test White particularly, it is a perfectly reasonable idea. But after:

8 ♗g2 0:05 **♗xe2?!** 0:13

There was no reason to capture at once – I would certainly have played h3 next move if he hadn't.

9 ♕xe2 0:12 **♗g7** 0:14
10 0-0 0:13 **0-0?!** 0:14

10...♖c8 was more accurate, to impede 11 ♘d5?: 11...♘xd5 12 exd5 ♘d4.

11 ♘d5 0:37

Much the most natural move, so I'm slightly surprised to find I took 24 minutes over it.

11 ...   ♖c8 0:19
12 c3 0:39 **♘xd5?!** 0:24

Falling in with White's plan to set up a bind; though the position is still quite playable. 12...e6!? was reasonable, as the very slight weakness of d6 doesn't look remotely important here.

13 exd5 0:40 **♘e5** 0:24

Sometimes in this variation, it is better to move the knight to a5 so as to keep the long diagonal open. But that doesn't look to be the case here, since with the knight on a5, Black would be more or less committed to ...♘c4 at some stage which could often be met by b3 with tempo. 13...♘a5 14 ♗g5 ♖e8

15 ♖ad1 looks pleasant, for example, getting the rook over before retreating the bishop to c1.

White's next task is to try and consolidate on the queenside. I chose to do this with:

14 ♗d2 0:47

But it is far from obvious to me now why I didn't play 14 ♗f4.

14 ... ♘c4 0:31

15 ♗e1 0:47

The disconnection of the white rooks is irritating in the short term.

15 ... a6 0:47

So as to meet 16 a4? with the unpleasant 16...♕b6!

If instead 15...b5 16 a4!? (16 b3 ♘a3 17 ♖c1 is very playable of course) 16...♕a5 17 b3 ♘b6 18 ♖c1 ♗xc3 19 ♖xc3 ♖xc3 20 ♗xc3 ♕xc3 21 ♕xb5 looks very nice.

16 b3 0:52 **♘e5** 0:55

I believe I was more worried at the time by 16...♘a3 to mess up White's queenside; though 17 ♖c1 b5 18 ♗d2 a5, say, isn't too convincing. If instead 17...♘b5, 18 ♕d3 is a good answer since 18...♕a5? can be met by 19 c4 when 19...♕xa2 loses to 20 ♖c2 and 19...♕a3 20 ♗d2 ♘d4 21 ♗c3 ♘f5 22 ♗h3 is very unpleasant.

17 ♗d2 1:02 **♘d7** 0:56

18 ♖ac1 1:05 **♖e8?!** 1:04

18...b5, to prevent c4, must be better; though White has some advantage in any event.

19 c4 1:10

Things have worked out very well for White. I have a space advantage, pressure on the e-file and the two bishops. The ...e6 break would be very weakening, so Black's only reasonable attempt at counterplay is ...b5. But if 19...♖b8 20 b4 looks strong, to meet ...b5 with c5. Instead Genna decided to cement a modest outpost for his knight.

19 ... a5 1:04

20 ♗h3! 1:18

Disrupting the enemy coordination. I would have preferred to preface this with h4; but you can't have everything.

20 ... ♖a8 1:06

21 ♖fe1 1:20 **♘c5** 1:07

22 ♗c3 1:25

Since it would be almost impossible to arrange b4, White offers to exchange bishops, utilising the knight's absence from the kingside to start an attack.

22 ... ♕b6 1:15

22...♗f6 is an idea, when 23

♗xf6?! exf6 gives Black some
dark squares; but 23 ♕f3 and if
23...♔g7 24 ♖c2, preparing
♖c2-e2xe7!, would force Black
to capture in worse circumstances than the game.

23   ♗xg7 1:31   **♔xg7** 1:15
24   ♕b2+ 1:36   **♔g8** 1:15
25   ♖e3 1:36

Of course not 25 ♖c3?? ♘a4.
White is now ready to double
on the e-file, after which Black
would be well on the way to
getting squashed. Sosonko decided to lash out.

25   ...   e5!? 1:18
26   dxe6 1:36   **fxe6** 1:18
27   ♕f6

This is the only significant
clock time I'm missing in the
game. I believe, though, that I
bashed out ♕f6 in some excitement and then was somewhat rocked back on my heels
by his reply.

27   ...   ♕d8! 1:18

This was played instantly,
since the alternative 27...e5? 28
♗g2! e4 29 ♕d4 is completely
hopeless.

28   ♗xe6+ 1:44

After 28 ♖xe6 ♕xf6 29 ♖xf6
♖e2 the knight is extremely annoying.

28   ...   ♘xe6 1:18
29   ♖xe6 1:44   **♕xf6!** 1:19

Not   29...♖xe6?   when   the
continuation 30 ♕xe6+ ♔g7 31
♖d1 is utterly without hope for
Black.

30   ♖xf6 1:44   **♖e2** 1:19
31   ♖d1! 1:45

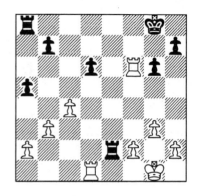

31   ...   ♖xa2?? 1:23

An innocent enough looking
move but absolutely wrong!
Since this game was so important, I spent, if not sleepless
nights, at least hours of soul-
searching about what would
have happened if he'd played
the much better 31...a4! I hope
the reader will excuse the tele-
phone directory which these
long forgotten anxieties gener-
ated when I re-analysed the
game.

The main problem is that if
White plays 32 ♖dxd6? a3! 33
♖d7 ♖xa2 34 ♖ff7 ♖a1+ 35
♔g2 a2 36 ♖g7+ ♔f8 37 ♖df7+
♔e8 then he is a tempo short:
38 ♖xb7 ♖g1+ 39 ♔f3 (or 39
♔xg1 a1♕+ 40 ♔g2 ♔f8)
39...♔f8 with a draw. Instead of
38 ♖xb7, White can try 38
♖g8+, but after 38...♔xf7 39
♖xa8 ♔e6! the a-pawn even
gives Black slightly the more
comfortable side of the draw,
e.g. 40 f4 (40 ♖a5? b6 or 40
♔f3? ♔e5 41 ♔e2 ♔d4 42 ♔d2

♖f1!) 40...♔f5 41 c5 ♔e4 42 b4 ♔d4 43 g4 ♔e4! 44 b5 ♔xf4 45 h3 (avoiding a symbolic disadvantage after 45 c6 bxc6 46 bxc6 ♔xg4 47 c7 ♖c1 48 ♖xa2 ♖xc7) 45...♔e5 46 c6 bxc6 47 bxc6 ♔d6 48 ♖a6 ♔c7 49 ♔h2.

32 bxa4 is therefore sensible, if a bit unfortunate, since now Black's previously passive rook can join in. Black would normally continue 32...♖xa4 when:

a) 33 ♖dxd6 ♖e7! leaves the white rooks looking rather foolish, e.g. 34 ♖d8+ ♔g7 35 ♖b6 and Black can choose between two bad but far from hopeless lines: 35...♖xa2 36 ♖b8 ♖f7 37 ♖8xb7 ♖axf2 38 ♖xf7+ ♖xf7; and 35...♖xc4 36 ♖b8 ♖cc7 37 h4 ♖f7 38 ♖b2 which looks more reliable.

b) 33 ♖fxd6! My initial impression (both then and in 1997) was that Black could then attack with:

b1) 33...♖axa2, but White can win with 34 ♖d8+ ♔f7 35 ♖1d7+ ♔e6 (or 35...♖e7 36 ♖xe7+ ♔xe7 37 ♖h8 h5 38 ♖h7+) 36 ♖d6+ and now:

b11) 36...♔e5 and:

b111) Now if 37 ♖d5+ ♔e6 38 ♖e8+? (but 38 ♖f8! should win) 38...♔f7 39 ♖xe2 ♖xe2 40 ♖d7+ ♖e7 41 ♖xe7+ ♔xe7 the pawn ending is drawn, viz. 42 f4 ♔d6 43 g4 ♔c5 44 f5 gxf5 45 gxf5 ♔d6 46 ♔f2 ♔e5 47 ♔e3 ♔xf5 48 ♔d4 ♔g4 (or 48...♔e6) 49 ♔c5 ♔h3 50 ♔b6 ♔xh2 51 ♔xb7 h5 52 c5 h4 53 c6 h3 54 c7 ♔g1 55 c8♕ h2.

b112) 37 ♖d3! is better, preparing to defend f2 with the rook on f3 while keeping the active rook to maraud. And if 37...♖xf2 38 ♖e8+ ♔f5 39 ♖d5+! ♔g4 40 ♖e4+ ♔f3 (40...♔h3 41 ♖h4 mate) 41 ♖f4+ ♔e3 42 ♖e5+ and White wins.

b12) 36...♔e7 37 ♖8d7+ ♔e8 38 ♖xb7! (38 ♖xh7? ♖xf2 39 ♖xg6 is much worse) 38...♖xf2 39 ♖xh7. An important way of defending against doubled rooks on the seventh that was recently used successfully by grandmaster Matthew Sadler at the European Team Championships in Pula:

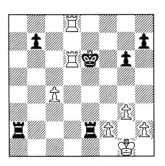

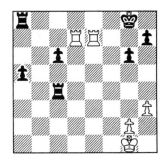

33...♖h4! 34 ♖c7 a4 35 ♖xc6 a3 36 ♖cc7 ♖ha4 37 ♖c1 a2 38 ♖a1 ♖b4 39 ♖cc1 ♖b2 0-1 Rytshagov-Sadler, European Team Championship, Pula 1997.

Returning to my analysis:

In this position Black is dead lost because he has no defence to the plan of ♖d6-d1-b1(or a1)-8th rank. Black can't sit with his rooks on a2 and b2, because pushing the c-pawn would then win without trouble. Here is a sample line of play: 39...♖g2+ 40 ♔h1 ♖gc2 (the rook ending after 40...♖gd2 41 ♖xd2 ♖xd2 42 ♖h4! ♔f7 43 ♖g4 ♔f6 44 h4 is simple; Black can't shift the rook because ...♔f5 is met by ♖g5+ and c5, so White will have plenty of time to bring up his king) 41 ♖d1 ♖xc4 42 ♖b1! ♖ac2 43 ♖b8+ ♖c8 44 ♖h8+ etc.

b2) 33...♖xc4 is therefore, although less obviously worrying for White, worth considering. White should continue 34 ♖d8+ ♔f7 and now White has choice between 35 ♖1d7+ and 35 ♖8d7+:

b21) The obvious line is 35 ♖1d7+ ♖e7 36 ♖xe7+ ♔xe7 37 ♖h8 h5 38 ♖h7+ ♔f6 39 ♖xb7 ♖a4 40 ♖b2 g5, but this leaves White with a great deal of work still to do and might indeed even be drawn. The thing is that in order to win, White will have to bring his king to the queenside; and while this is happening Black can try to attack on the kingside, e.g.

b211) If 41 ♔f1 ♔f5 42 h3 ♖a3 43 ♔e1 h4!; while if 43 ♔g2 Black just sits. Perhaps White can play for g4 but I guess that ...h4 may well be correct then to set up White's h-pawn as a target.

b212) Conceivably, though, White can lash out at once with 41 f4 gxf4 42 ♖f2 when one line goes 42...♔g5 43 gxf4+ ♔f5 44 ♔f1 h4 45 ♔e1 h3 46 ♔d1 ♔e4 47 f5 ♔e3 48 ♔e1 ♖b4 49 ♖e2+ ♔f3 50 f6! ♖b1+ 51 ♔d2 ♖b2+ 52 ♔d1 ♖b6 (or 52...♖xe2 53 f7!) 53 f7 ♖f6 54 ♔e1!

b22) 35 ♖8d7+ ♖e7 36 ♖xe7+ ♔xe7 37 ♖b1 therefore

makes a lot of sense, when White is only one pawn up but with much the better rook. Black must go passive now since if:

b221) 37...h5 38 ♖xb7+ ♔f6 39 ♖a7! is winning by force, albeit after serious technical difficulties. White's plan is to play ♖a8, a2-a4-a5-a6-a7 and then create a passed f-pawn to deflect the black king. After 1 f6+ ♔f7 2 ♖h8! or 1...♔xf6 2 ♖f8+ wins.

The only defence to this is to push the g-pawn right up to g4 to prevent the creation of the passed f-pawn. But then this g-pawn eventually proves too weak, viz. (after 39 ♖a7!) 39...g5 40 ♖a8 g4 41 a4 ♔g6 42 a5 ♖a4 43 a6 ♔h7 44 a7 ♖a1+ 45 ♔g2 ♔g7 46 h3 ♔h7 47 hxg4 hxg4 48 ♔h2 ♖a6 49 ♔g1! ♖a1+ 50 ♔g2 (zugzwang; the king can't go to g7 in view of 50...♔g7 51 ♖b8! ♖xa7 52 ♖b4 winning immediately, so the white king gets out) 50...♖a4 51 ♔f1 ♖a2 52 ♔e1 ♖a5 53 ♔d2 ♖a3 54 ♔e2 ♖a5 55 ♔e3 ♖a4 56 ♖f8! (if 56 ♔d3 ♖a2 57 ♔e4 ♖e2+! defends for the moment – not then 58 ♔f4?? ♖xf2+ with a draw, since White needs an f-pawn to deflect the black king) 56...♖xa7 57 ♖f4! ♖g7 58 ♖f6! and the g-pawn will be surrounded in a few more moves: 58...♖g8 59 ♔f4 ♖g7 (59...♔g7 60 ♔g5 ♔h7+ 61 ♔h5 ♖g7 62

♖f8 is simple)

60 ♖f5! ♔h6 61 ♖f8 ♖g6 (61...♔h7 62 ♔f5 is zugzwang) 62 ♖h8+ ♔g7 63 ♖h5 ♔f6 (against 64 ♖g5) 64 ♖h4!

b222) But passive defence is pretty unpleasant. One sample line goes 37...♖c7 38 ♖b6 ♔d8 (38...♔f8 39 a4 ♔g8 40 ♖b5! ♖c4 41 a5 ♖a4 42 h4 looks easy) 39 ♔g2 ♖d7 40 h4 ♔c7 41 ♖f6 b5 42 h5 gxh5 43 ♖h6 ♖d5 44 a3! h4 45 ♖xh4 ♔b6 46 ♖h6+ ♔a5 47 ♖xh7 ♖d3 48 ♖e7 ♖xa3 49 ♖a7+ ♔b4 50 ♖xa3 ♔xa3 51 f4 b4 52 f5 b3 53 f6 b2 54 f7 b1♕ 55 f8♕+ ♔a2 56 ♕a8+ ♔b2 57 ♕b8+ ♔c1 58 ♕xb1+ and White wins.

b3) Finally, there is the passive 33...♖e7, but White has the happy choice of either 34 ♖d8+ ♔f7 35 ♖8d7 ♖xc4 36 ♖xe7+ ♔xe7 37 ♖b1 ♖c7 38 ♖b6 transposing directly to variation b222 or 34 ♖d7 ♖xd7 35 ♖xd7 ♖xc4 36 ♖xb7 ♖a4 37 ♖b2 g5! with an improved version of variation b21.

Just one final set of variations. When I was wrapping this

analysis up, I suddenly started to wonder about a move I'd completely ignored: 32 ♖fxd6. At first it seemed that this might be a simple win after 32...♖xa2 33 ♖d8+ ♖xd8 34 ♖xd8+ ♔g7 35 ♖d7+, to be followed by 36 ♖xb7. But Black can reply with the important pin 36...♖b2, which should be enough to net a draw, e.g. 35 ♖d7+ ♔g8 (it may be simpler to allow the king to be cut off in this way since 35...♔h6, which would normally be desirable, allows White to play for mate, e.g. 36 ♖xb7 ♖b2 37 h4 ♖xb3 38 ♖a7 ♖b4 39 g4 ♖xc4 40 f3 g5 41 ♖a6+ [maybe 41 ♔g2] 41...♔g7 42 hxg5 ♖c5 43 ♔g2 ♖xg5 44 ♔g3 which is very nasty but theoretically drawn, I presume) 36 ♖xb7 (or 36 bxa4 ♖xa4 37 ♖c7 ♖b4 38 c5 b6 39 c6 ♖c4) 36...♖b2 37 c5 axb3 38 c6 ♖c2. However, even in this line White can obtain reasonable winning chances with 33 bxa4 ♖2xa4 34 ♖b6! (if 34 ♖d7 ♖a1! is the only move but sufficient) 34...♖a1 (if 34...♖xc4 35 ♖xb7 ♖c5 36 ♖dd7 ♔h5 37 h4 must be winning) 35 ♖xa1 ♖xa1+ 36 ♔g2 ♖c1 37 ♖b4.

32 ♖dxd6 1:47 **a4** 1:41

Sosonko had a long think but a move too late. The rest is fairly simple.

33 bxa4 1:48 **♖8xa4** 1:42

34 ♖f4 1:49

There was no reason to hurry to double the rooks, though the thematic 34 ♖d7 ♖xc4 35 ♖ff7 obviously also wins, e.g. 35...♖c1+ 36 ♔g2 ♖cc2 37 ♖g7+ ♔f8 38 ♖df7+ ♔e8 39 ♖xh7 ♖ab2 (39...g5 40 ♖xb7! ♖xf2+ 41 ♔g1! ♖g2+ 42 ♔h1 wins at once) 40 h4! Black can't move the b-pawn since then ♖b7 or a7 would win at once, so he must wait. But there are lots of ways to improve the white position.

34 ... **b5** 1:48

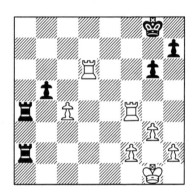

35 ♖d8+! 1:52

After a simple series of checks, White is able to take the pawn with a rook. 35 cxb5?? ♖xf4 36 gxf4 ♖b2 gives Black some chances.

35	**...**	**♔g7** 1:49
36	**♖d7+**	**♔h6**
37	**♖h4+**	**♔g5**
38	**♖d5+**	**♔f6**
39	**♖xb5**	**♖c2**
40	**♖f4+** 1:56	**♔e6** 1:50
41	**♖b6+**	**♔e5**
42	**♖b7**	**♖axc4**

42...h6 and 42...h5 lose to 43 ♖b5+ ♔e6 44 ♖b6+.

43	♖e7+	♔d6
44	♖xc4	♖xc4
45	♖xh7	♔e6
46	♖h4	♖c2
47	♖f4	g5
48	♖f8	♖c5
49	♔g2	♔e7
50	♖a8	

50 ... ♔f6

Making it very slightly easier. White will always be able to exchange off the g5-pawn for the h-pawn, but I suppose Black should have tried 50...♖c4 when one very simple plan is to play h3, g4 and f3 and then arrange for h4, e.g. 51 ♖a6 ♔f7 52 h3 ♔g7 53 g4 ♔h7 54 f3 ♖c1 (54...♔g7 55 ♔g3 ♖c3 56 ♖a5 ♔g6 57 ♖f5 and 58 h4) 55 ♖a5 ♔g6 56 h4! (if White doesn't want to 'sacrifice' a pawn then he can play ♖a2-f2-f1 and ♔g3 first) 56...gxh4 57 ♖h5 ♖c2+ 58 ♔h3 ♖f2 59 ♖f5.

51	♖a4	♖c8
52	h4	**1-0**

That left me needing just half a point as Black against John Nunn, who, very kindly, did not make me suffer; one of the contributing factors being, as he said later, my sportsmanship against Ljubojevic.

J.Nunn–J.Speelman
London (round 13) 1980
Vienna Game

1 e4 e5 2 ♘c3 ♘f6 3 f4 d5 4 fxe5 ♘xe4 5 d3 ♗b4 6 dxe4 ♕h4+ 7 ♔e2 ♗xc3 8 bxc3 ♗g4+ 9 ♘f3 dxe4 10 ♕d4 ♗h5 11 ♔e3 ♗xf3 12 gxf3 ♕e1+ 13 ♔f4 ♕h4+ 14 ♔e3 ½-½

As Reuben and Hartston wrote: 'When a draw has been agreed before the game, the players should not make it so obvious.' To which I would retort that had we been more practised in, and hence competent at, this slightly dubious device which, while not deeply wonderful, I have no great moral objection to – throwing games is another matter entirely – then we would have made a better job of it!

Maribor 1980

This tournament took place in the last week in October and first in November, finishing just three weeks before the Olympiad in Malta – my first. Michael Stean received the original invitation and I believe he had been intending to play before dropping out and passing it on to me. I thus took a plane to

Vienna and then a further flight on to Graz on the Austrian side of the border. The smallest aeroplane I've ever flown in, this tiny machine had more crew than passengers, three and two respectively if I remember correctly. Then I took a train across the border into Yugoslavia, as it then was.

Playing at short notice, I had no particular idea of attempting a norm before the event – particularly since this would involve scoring plus six – 9½/13. But the tournament started off wonderfully well with wins against Vlado Kovacevic, the eventual tournament winner and Tomislav Rakic. After just two rounds, I already had my eyes on the target.

	1	2	3	4	5	6	7	8	9	10	11	12	13	14	
1 V. Kovacevic	*	0	1	1	1	½	½	1	½	½	1	1	1	1	10
2 Speelman	1	*	½	½	½	½	½	½	1	1	1	½	1	1	9½
3 Ree	0	½	*	0	½	½	½	1	½	1	1	1	½	1	8
4 Velimirovic	0	½	1	*	½	0	½	1	1	½	½	1	½	1	8
5 V. Nikolac	0	½	½	½	*	½	0	½	1	½	½	1	1	1	7½
6 Musil	½	½	½	1	½	*	½	½	0	½	½	½	½	½	6½
7 Plachetka	½	½	½	½	1	½	*	½	0	½	½	½	0	1	6½
8 M. Knezevic	0	½	0	0	½	½	½	*	½	½	½	1	½	1	6
9 Kuligowski	½	0	½	0	0	1	1	½	*	1	½	0	1	0	6
10 Polajzer	½	0	0	½	½	½	½	½	0	*	½	½	½	1	5½
11 Rakic	0	0	0	½	½	½	½	½	½	½	*	½	½	1	5½
12 Osterman	0	½	0	0	0	½	½	0	1	½	½	*	½	1	5
13 Supancic	0	0	½	½	0	½	1	½	0	½	½	½	*	½	5
14 Danner	0	0	0	0	0	½	0	0	1	0	0	0	½	*	2

Game 17
J.Speelman–V.Kovacevic
Maribor (round 1) 1980
Catalan Opening

1	d4	♘f6
2	c4	e6
3	g3	d5
4	♘f3	♗b4+
5	♗d2	♗e7
6	♗g2 0:08	0-0 0:08
7	0-0 0:10	♘bd7 0:12
8	♕c2 0:23	c6 0:18

9 ♖d1

Irritatingly, I'm missing the clock time for this, but I imagine it came quite fast and then I spent a quarter of an hour or so on the crucial decision after

9 ... b5!? 0:25
10 c5 0:40

A reasonable reaction. After 10 cxb5 cxb5, unless White can immediately exploit the c-file – which he can't in this instance – then in the generic position he can even easily become worse since the bishop on g2 is biting on granite and so is less effective than its counterpart on e7. But 10 b3 is possible, keeping the tension for the moment.

Five weeks after the present game, I played a very similar one against Ivan Farago at the Malta Olympiad. The only difference was that, because he hadn't inserted 4...♗b4+ 5 ♗d2, my bishop was on c1 rather than d2. That game went 9...♘e4 (of course it is one move earlier as well) 10 ♘bd2 f5 11 ♘e1! e5? (opening the centre prematurely) 12 dxe5! ♘xd2 (12...♘xe5? loses a pawn to 13 ♘xe4 fxe4 14 ♗xe4) 13 ♗xd2 ♘xe5 14 a4 ♗a6 15 ♗c3 ♘d7 16 ♘f3 ♘xc5 17 ♘d4 and Black is blown away by the tactics – there are simply far too many lines converging at c6 and d5:

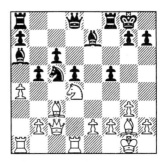

17...♗b7 18 axb5 cxb5 19 ♘xf5 ♘e6 20 ♗xd5! (20 ♖xd5! is also strong) 20...♗xd5 21 ♖xd5 ♕e8 22 ♕e4 ♗c5 23 b4 ♗b6 24 ♖e5 ♖f6 25 ♘xg7! (25 ♘d6 ♕f8 26 ♖xe6 was also quite good enough) 25...♘xg7 26 ♖xe8+ ♖xe8 27 ♕d5+ ♖f7 28 e3 ♘f5 29 ♖d1 h6 30 ♕c6 ♖ee7 31 ♗f6 ♖c7 32 ♕e6 1-0.

But thirteen years later in Brussels 1993, forgetting that game, I had a rather nasty experience against Curt Hansen. After 9...♘e4 10 ♘bd2 f5, this time I tried to follow the Kovacevic game (unbeknownst to me a tempo down) with 11 ♘b3?! a5 12 ♗d2 ♗f6 13 ♗e1 ♖a7 14 ♘c1 e5 15 e3 exd4 16 ♘xd4 (16 exd4 is well met by 16...g5!) 16...♗xd4 17 exd4 f4!

(see following diagram)

18 gxf4 ♖xf4 19 ♘d3 ♖f8 20 ♕c1 ♕f6 21 ♕e3 b4 22 h4? ♕xh4 23 f3 ♕g5! 24 ♕e2 ♕h5 25 ♕e3 ♘g5 26 ♘f4 ♕f7 27

♗d2 h6 28 a3 ♘f6 29 ♕f2 b3
30 a4 ♘h5 31 ♘xh5 ♕xh5 32
♗xg5 hxg5 33 ♖a3 g4 34 ♖xb3
♖af7 35 f4 g3 0-1.

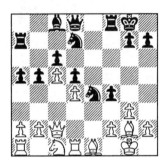

In mitigation, I should point
out that this was a last round
game played in the morning and
starting, if memory serves, at
9:00 AM.

10 ... a5 0:26

To prevent White from deto-
nating the queenside with a4,
though that threat can be met by
...♗a6.

11 ♗e1 0:48

I've always rather liked this
square for the bishop, well away
from marauding knights. Passive for the moment, the prelate
prophylactically defends f2 and
can later emerge after f3 via f2
or sometimes via c3.

11 ... ♘e4 0:36

12 ♘bd2 0:58 **f5** 0:36

Slightly weakening but gaining some space for himself.
After 12...♘xd2 13 ♗xd2 Black
would have had no compensation for White's space advantage.

13 ♘b3 1:01 **♕c7?!** 0:49

On c7 the queen supports a
possible ...e5 or ...f4 later, but
there is also a tactical problem
associated with the square since
if the c-file is opened then she
will be loose, allowing ♗xd5+
utilising the pin. So probably he
should have preferred 13...♗f6
reaching the same position as I
had in the debacle against Curt
Hansen above but with the rook
on a8 instead of a7 (because
Hansen played his bishop to e7
in one move, rather than
4...♗b4+ 5 ♗d2 ♗e7). Cer-
tainly the rook is better on a7
than a8 – off the long diagonal,
ready to swing into play along
the seventh rank. But whether
this makes a huge difference
isn't clear since obviously my
play against Curt could have
been improved.

If now (13...♗f6) 14 ♘c1 e5
(14...g5 is possible) 15 dxe5 (15
e3!? exd4! as in the Curt Hansen game) 15...♘xe5 16 ♘xe5
♗xe5 17 ♘d3, play would
transpose back into the game
after 17...♕c7, but 17...♕e7 is a
better square than c7 – and
17...♗f6 is also possible.

The only disadvantage of this
move order is that without the
inclusion of ...♕c7 and ♘d3
White controls d4, so that after
17 f3 the bishop can't check.
But Black simply retreats
17...♘f6 when if:

a) 18 ♗f2?! f4 19 ♘d3 fxg3
20 hxg3 ♗c7 the white king is
under some fire and the natural

break of 21 e4 is very dubious after 21...dxe4 22 fxe4 ♘g4.

b) 18 ♘d3 allows 18...♗d4+ 19 ♗f2 ♗xf2+ 20 ♘xf2 ♕e7 and now:

b1) 21 e4 is critical but leaves the white king pretty exposed, e.g. 21...fxe4 22 fxe4 and:

b11) If 22...dxe4 23 ♘xe4 ♗f5 24 ♕b3+! ♗e6 (after 24...♔h8 25 ♘d6 the knight is rather threatening, though 25...♗g4 26 ♖e1 ♕d7 is far from over) then perhaps White can get an edge after 25 ♕e3 and if 25...♘d5 26 ♕g5; or less likely after 25 ♘xf6+!? ♕xf6 (better than 25...♖xf6 26 ♕e3!)

b12) In any case, Black can pose more problems with 22...♘g4! when if 23 ♘xg4 ♗xg4 and now:

b121) 24 ♖d2 ♖ae8! when 25 exd5?? (but if 25 h3 ♗f3!) 25...♕e1+! 26 ♖xe1 ♖xe1+ 27 ♗f1 ♗h3 leads to mate!

b122) 24 ♖e1 is better since if 24...♖ae8 25 h3 ♗f3 26 ♗xf3 ♖xf3 27 exd5! ♕xe1+ 28 ♖xe1 ♖xe1+ 29 ♔g2 looks good for White, e.g. if 29...♖ee3, 30 ♕d1! ♖xg3+ 31 ♔f2 is winning. But the modest 24...d4 25 e5 ♗f5! gives Black dangerous attacking chances.

b2) 21 ♖e1 looks like it is getting control, but Black can cause some disruption with 21...f4!? and if 22 gxf4 ♕e3 23 ♖ad1 (23 ♕c1 d4) 23...♘h5.

c) So instead of either of these lines 18 e3 is sensible,

though White is a long way from gaining any serious advantage. Black's light-squared bishop is bad, but White's e-pawn is a slight inconvenience.

14 ♘c1 1:12 **e5** 0:51

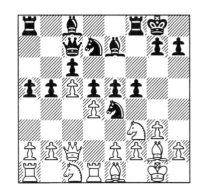

Continuing with his plan, which will give Black a reasonable game if he can maintain his structure. But in the short term, there are various tactical problems which will emerge shortly.

15 ♘d3! 1:19

So that if 15...exd4 16 ♘xd4 White is threatening 17 ♘e6 and the c5-pawn is absolutely taboo since if:

a) 16...♘dxc5? 17 ♘xc5 ♗xc5 (17...♘xc5 18 ♘xc6!) 18 ♗xe4 ♗xd4 19 ♗xd5+.

b) 16...♘df6 leaves White with some positional advantage due to his centralisation and control of the dark squares.

c) 16...♖f6 is the other way to defend e6. Perhaps White can arrange to sacrifice the c5-pawn somehow, but if the worst comes to the worst simply 17 b4 axb4 18 ♗xb4, preparing a4, keeps an edge and if 18...♖a4 19 a3 the rook can be dislodged at some point by ♘b2.

Presumably ♘d3 was an unpleasant surprise for my opponent, who took 25 minutes before replying:

15 ...   ♗f6 1:24
16 dxe5 1:29 **♘xe5** 1:24
17 ♘fxe5 1:37 ♗**xe5** 1:25
18 f3 1:40

Trying to exploit the slight congestion of Black's two centralised minor pieces. If 18 ♘xe5 ♕xe5 19 f3 ♘f6 20 ♕d2 (to stop ...f4, freeing the light-squared bishop and starting an attack) 20...♖e8 21 ♗f1 to be followed by ♗f2-d4 might give White a slight edge but certainly nothing more.

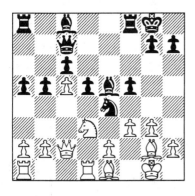

18 ...   ♘f6?! 1:35

Falling in with my plans. Black could have played the obstructive 18...♗d4+! 19 ♔h1 ♘f6, when although the bishop looks slightly uncomfortable, there seems to be no way to ex-

ploit this. If White tees up for e3 with 20 ♗d2 ♖e8 21 ♖e1 then 21...♗e3 is fine.

19 ♕d2! 1:52

Stopping ...f4, though White isn't yet clearly threatening f4 himself since if, for example, 19...♔h8 20 f4? (20 ♗f2! does threaten f4) 20...♗d4+ 21 e3 ♘e4! saves the piece, and while White can win a pawn with 22 ♗xe4 fxe4 23 exd4 exd3, the light squares are disgusting.

19 ...   ♘d7 1:50
20 ♗f2 2:02 **f4??** 1:56

White was doing well, but this is panic. After, for example, 20...♗f6 it is true that Black can't easily get active with ...f4, but there would still have been everything to play for:

a) 21 e4 is obvious – and presumably what Black was afraid of – but very far from clear, e.g. 21...dxe4 22 fxe4 ♘e5! 23 ♘xe5 ♗xe5 24 ♗d4 fxe4 25 ♗xe5 ♕xe5 26 ♕d4 (26 ♕d6 ♕xb2!) 26...♕xd4+ 27 ♖xd4 ♗f5 28 ♗xe4 ♗xe4 29 ♖xe4 and Black is at least equal.

b) So White can try to prepare e4. The obvious way is 21 ♖e1 but the problem is that after 21...♘e5:

b1) 22 ♘xe5 ♕xe5 White doesn't now have the reply ♗d4 which would have given some positional advantage with the rook on d1, so he must defend with 23 ♖ab1 when Black has enough breathing space to get fully mobilised.

b2) While 22 ♖ad1?! ♘xd3!
23 exd3 (23 ♕xd3 ♗xb2 24 e4
♗e6! is unsound) 23...f4! looks
fine for Black.

Instead White can keep the
rook on d1 and prepare with:

c) 21 ♖ac1 or d) 21 ♖ab1.

e) The other move which
might have frightened Black is
21 ♘f4, but 21...♕e5 is very
reasonable when:

e1) 22 ♗d4 is the obvious
positional continuation, but after 22...♕xd4+ 23 ♕xd4
♗xd4+ 24 ♖xd4 ♖e8! threatens
both 25...g5 followed 26...♖xe2
and 26...♘xc5, when if 26 ♖c1
♘e6 27 ♘xe6 he can now recapture 27...♖xe6! So White
should reply 25 ♖d2, defending
the e-pawn and rendering
25...♘xc5? ineffective since
after 26 ♖c1 ♘e6 doesn't now
hit the rook on d4. Instead
Black can play 25...♘e5 with
quite an active position.

e2) The sacrifice 22 e4 dxe4
23 fxe4 is superficially attractive, but the stalwart 23...♘xc5!
is simply good for Black.

e3) So White might prefer 22
♖ab1, but this is hardly terrify-
ing for Black.

21 gxf4 2:05   **♗xf4** 1:56
22 ♘xf4 2:05   **♕xf4** 1:56
23 ♕xf4 2:05   **♖xf4** 1:56
24 e4! 2:08

Smashing up Black's structure before he can get developed. Black can't hold the position since the natural 24...♘f6
loses the exchange to 25 ♗g3.

As a result, the game opens up
and Black must already be lost.

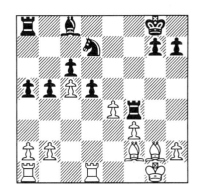

24 ...   ♗b7 2:05

If instead 24...dxe4 25 fxe4
♖f7 26 e5! detonates the position immediately: 26...♘xe5 27
♖d8+ ♖f8 28 ♖xf8+ ♔xf8 29
♗g3 and Black is blown away.

25 ♖ac1 2:14   **♘e5?!** 2:08

I suppose he should have
tried 25...♖a6 but it hardly bears
thinking about. After simply 26
♗g3 ♖f7 27 exd5 cxd5 28 ♗f1
♖c6 (28...♗c6? 29 a4) 29 ♖xd5
the harvest begins.

26 ♗g3! 2:15   **♘xf3+** 2:08
27 ♔h1 2:15   **♖f6** 2:12

While checking my analysis
with Fritz, a question arose
which would hardly occur to a
human: Can Black try to allow a
protected passed pawn on d6
but then blockade it? In order to
do so, it would be necessary to
retreat instead with 27...♖f7 to
control d7, but after 28 exd5: if
28...♖e8 29 ♖d3! ♖ef8 30 ♖f1
wins, while 28...♖af8 29 ♖d3!
and if 29...cxd5 30 ♗d6! is just

as bad.

28 exd5 2:16 **cxd5** 2:12

With the rook on f6 he really has got to recapture since after 28...♖af8 29 d6! there is now no question of a blockade.

29 c6! 2:17 **♗a6** 2:24

If 29...♗xc6 30 ♗xf3 costs a whole piece

30	**♖xd5** 2:18	**♖af8** 2:25
31	**c7** 2:21	**♗b7** 2:25
32	**♖d8** 2:22	**♗c8** 2:27
33	**♖f1** 2:23	**♗b7** 2:28
34	**♗xf3** 2:24	**♖xf3** 2:29
35	**♖xf3** 2:24	**♗xf3+** 2:29
36	**♔g1** 2:24	**♗g4** 2:29
37	**♗d6!**	**1-0**

Daily routines are particularly important in an all-play-all event, and I was able to establish a very good one at this tournament. Apart from the technical preparation each day, I would go for a long walk in the hills around Maribor – peaceful then, though there was a firing range. There was the game in the afternoon and dinner and socialising with the other players in the evening. And while I had only two books to read, both are classics: *One Hundred Years of Solitude* by Gabriel Garcia Marquez and *The Master and Marguerita* by Mikhail Bulgakov.

Under this orderly regimen, I continued with (in order) three draws, two wins, and two more draws, leaving a target of 3/4 for the title.

Obviously, one needs some luck in these circumstances. By now I was very tense and it showed as I quickly fell into a dubious position against Dragoljub Velimirovic.

J.Speelman-D.Velimirovic
Maribor (round 10) 1980

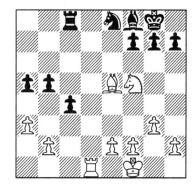

Here it looks as though White might have to defend against a dangerous queenside pawn majority. But I was relieved to make a draw in just three more moves. After twelve minutes I found.

23 ♗c3! **b4**

After just three minute's thought.

24 axb4 **axb4**

25 ♗xg7!!

And Velimirovic offered a draw without replying, which I of course accepted.

After 25...♘xg7 26 ♘h6+ is immediate perpetual while 25...♗xg7 26 ♘e7+ ♔f8 27 ♘xc8 ♗xb2 28 ♘b6! c3 29 ♘c4! is to White's advantage, since Black must try 29...c2 30 ♘xb2 cxd1♕+ 31 ♘xd1.

Of course I had to play 23 ♗c3! first, since if 23 ♗xg7 at once 23...♗xg7 24 ♘e7+ ♔f8 25 ♘xc8 ♗xb2 is very dangerous.

Since Black had simply missed my idea, it doesn't seem so important to look for improvements. But he could have played ...g6 either at once or even after 24 axb4 – though then 24...g6 25 bxa5 gxf5 26 ♖d5 gives White a lot of play for the piece.

So the two main lines are:

a) 23...g6 24 ♘e3 b4 25 axb4 axb4 26 ♗d4 and perhaps now 26...f5, though Black's is somewhat hampered by the looseness of the c4-pawn.

b) 23...♖a8 looks rather frightening until one sees the voluntary retreat 24 ♘e3!, when White must be okay.

The next game was Black against the Austrian Georg Danner, who had a bad time in this tournament. I succeeded in winning, though it was desperately scrappy – a 'Benko Gambit type' sacrifice with the centre already blocked by a Czech Benoni merely lost a pawn; and I only succeeded in rallying in his time trouble.

In the penultimate round I was on the white side of a complex opening variation against the experienced Polish grandmaster Adam Kuligowski.

Game 18
J.Speelman–A.Kuligowski
Maribor (round 12) 1980
Queen's Gambit Declined, Semi-Slav variation

1 d4 0:00 **d5** 0:09

Kuligowski wasn't late but rather deciding what to play.

2 c4 0:01 **c6** 0:12
3 ♘f3 0:02 **♘f6** 0:12
4 ♘c3 0:05 **e6** 0:18
5 e3 0:08 **♘bd7** 0:18
6 ♕c2 0:14

Although hugely analysed today, 6 ♕c2 was much more peripheral then; indeed my normal instinct would be to shy away from a direct theoretical confrontation in such an important encounter.

6 ... **♗d6** 0:20
7 e4!? 0:16

Since I took only two minutes, presumably this decision had been made on the previous move.

7 ... **dxe4** 0:22
8 ♘xe4 0:18 **♘xe4** 0:23
9 ♕xe4 0:18 **e5!** 0:26

Trying to exploit the queen's vulnerable position on the e-file.

10 dxe5 0:23

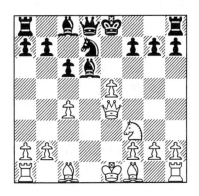

10 ...   ♕e7 0:50

Perfectly playable if some-what accommodating.

10...♘xe5, which did the rounds for a while in the late seventies, had been rendered very dubious a couple of years earlier by Adrian Mikhal-chishin's 11 c5!:

a) His game with Sveshnikov at the 1978 USSR Champion-ship lurched on 11...f5 12 ♕e2 ♕a5+ 13 ♗d2 ♕xc5 14 ♗c3 ♗e6 15 ♘xe5 0-0-0 16 ♕e3 ♕xe3+ 17 fxe3 ♖he8 and of course White is winning, though they drew in 60 moves in the end.

b) 11...♗c7 is a better try, but after 12 ♘xe5 ♕e7 13 ♗f4 (13 f4 f6 14 ♗d3 fxe5 15 0-0 is also possible) 13...f6 14 0-0-0 fxe5 (not 14...g6? 15 ♘g4) 15 ♗e3 White has a pleasant edge.

But the critical line is 10...0-0, when White is more or less obliged to sacrifice his queen with 11 exd6 (11 ♗d3? f5) 11...♖e8 12 ♕xe8+ ♕xe8+

13 ♗e3. I distinctly remember becoming extremely nervous about this variation during my opponent's 24-minute think – though unfortunately I can't remember precisely why. There had been a couple of games with this round about this time. One I certainly knew about was Mikhalchishin-Flear from the World U-26 Team Champion-ship in Mexico 1980, since I had watched it – and it may well have encouraged me to embark on this line. White won that game after 13...♘e5 14 0-0-0 ♘xf3 15 gxf3 ♗d7 16 ♗d3 ♕e5 17 ♖hg1 g6 18 f4 ♕f6 19 f5 b6 20 ♗c2 ♕h4 21 ♔b1 c5 22 ♗g5 ♕xf2 23 fxg6 hxg6 24 ♖df1 ♕d4 25 ♗e7 a5 26 h4 ♗g4 27 ♗f6 ♕xc4 28 h5 gxh5 29 d7 ♕xf1+ 30 ♖xf1 ♗xd7 31 ♗d1 ♗g4 32 ♗xg4 hxg4 33 ♖h1 1-0.

Instead of 13... ♘e5, 13...♘f6 was played in Dorfman-Sveshnikov, USSR Champion-ship 1980. After 14 0-0-0 ♗e6 15 ♗d3 they continued 15...♖d8 16 b3 ♗g4 17 ♗f4 ♗xf3 18 gxf3 ♘h5 19 ♖he1 ♕xe1 20 ♖xe1 and White went on to win.

But in the latter variation 15...b5!?, which I have a very vague memory of fearing at the time, was Sveshnikov's im-provement three years later and is given as best in *ECO* volume D. Naumkin-Sveshnikov, Mos-cow Championship 1983, con-tinued 16 ♘e5 bxc4 17 ♘xc4

⋃d8 18 ⋃he1 c5! which *ECO* deems 'unclear' – though I wouldn't be surprised if it is 'unclearly' somewhat better for Black.

11 ♞f4 0:41 **♞b4+** 0:59
12 ♞d2 0:46

The only sensible move. After 12 ♘d2 (moving the king would be foolhardy in the extreme, of course) 12...♘c5 Black has a tremendously active position. For instance White, though rated more than two hundred points higher than his opponent, was happy to acquiesce in a draw after just four more moves in the game Kindermann-Pokern, Bundesliga 1980/81, i.e. 13 ♕c2 g6! 14 ♞d3 ♕d8 15 ♞e4 ♕d4 16 f3 ♘xe4.

12 ... ♞xd2+ 1:02
13 ♘xd2 0:47 **♕xe5** 1:11
14 0-0-0 0:58

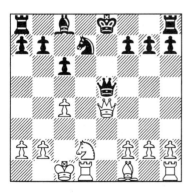

14 ... ♕xe4?! 1:32

If White can induce Black to capture on e4 then he must have a slight advantage, since Black is badly developed and the natural square for the knight (f6) would then become less desirable in view of ♘xf6+, disfiguring the kingside pawns. So Black ought to castle and then hope to threaten to exploit White's slightly unsatisfactory king position with ...♕a5, often to be followed by ...♘c5 when the pieces pour out.

After 14...0-0 15 ♞d3 (15 f4 ♕a5!) 15...g6 Black is threatening ...♘c5!, though any sensible White move should incidentally prevent this. The first outing from this position was 16 ♕h4, but after 16...♕f6! 17 ♕xf6 ♘xf6 18 ♘e4 ♘xe4 19 ♞xe4 ♞g4 White's advantage, if it exists at all, requires a very powerful microscope to be discerned. The riveting game Mikhalchishin-Beliavsky, USSR Championship, Frunze 1981, concluded 20 f3 ♞e6 21 b3 f5 22 ♞c2 c5 23 f4 ♜ad8 24 ♜xd8 ♜xd8 25 ♜d1 ♜xd1+ 26 ♞xd1 ♙f7 27 ♞f3 b6 28 g3 ♙e7 29 ♙d2 ♙d6 30 ♙e3 ½-½.

But a year later Mikhail Gurevich improved White's play significantly with 16 ♞c2!, removing the bishop before the knight can come to c5. He claims in *Informator 34* that his idea was 16...♕a5 17 h4! with an attack. No doubt this was backed up by a considerable amount of home analysis, and, although it may have been a bluff, it does in fact look pretty dangerous – for instance if 17...♕xa2 18 h5 ♘c5 19 ♕h4 ♗f5 and now:

a) Not 20 hxg6?? ♕a1+ 21 ♗b1 (or 21 ♘b1 ♘b3+! 22 ♗xb3 ♕xb1+ 23 ♔d2 ♕xb2+) 21...♕xb1+! 22 ♘xb1 ♘b3 mate.

b) But 20 ♗xf5 ♘a4 21 ♕f6 gxf5 22 h6 and wins.

But in any case after 16...♕a5 17 a3 is simple and good.

In the game M. Gurevich-Novikov, USSR 1982, Novikov decided against any heroics, but after 16...♖e8 17 f4 ♕xe4 18 ♘xe4 White had forced Black to exchange. This is not a position one would want to have as Black against anybody, let alone an excellent technician like Gurevich. White quickly won a pawn and, after a certain amount of resistance, the game: 18...♔g7 19 ♘d6 ♖e7 20 ♖he1 ♔f8 21 g4 ♘f6 22 g5 ♘e8 23 ♖xe7 ♔xe7 24 ♖e1+ ♗e6 25 ♘xb7 ♘g7 26 ♗e4 ♖c8 27 ♘a5 ♔d6 28 b4 c5 29 ♖d1+ ♔c7 30 bxc5 and White won.

15 ♘xe4 0:58 **0-0** 1:37

The only advantage of taking on e4 immediately, would have been to play 15...♔e7 to support ...♘f6. But White keeps a clear edge after either 16 ♗e2 ♘f6 17 ♘c5! or 16 ♗d3 ♘e5 17 ♖he1 ♗e6 (not 17...♖d8?? 18 ♘g3 ♔f6 19 ♘h5+) 18 ♘c5 ♔f6 19 ♘xb7.

16 f4! 1:09

If 16 ♗e2 ♖e8 is annoying.

16 ... **♘b6?!** 1:52

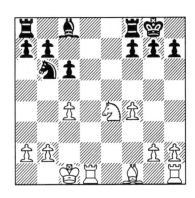

A very bad square for the knight, from which it returns just a couple of moves later. In *Informator 30*, Vlado Kovacevic recommends that Black accept the doubled pawns at once with 16...♘f6 17 ♘xf6+ gxf6 and now:

a) Black has time after 18 ♗d3 to get in 18...f5, securing the e6-square for the bishop, though of course he is still worse even then.

b) 18 g4!? is more challenging, threatening to squash Black after f5. Black can then chose between 18...h5 and 18...f5:

b11) 18...h5!? when:

b111) 19 h3 hxg4 20 hxg4 ♗xg4 21 ♖g1 f5 may equalise – not then 22 ♗d3? ♖fd8!

b112) But 19 f5 hxg4 20 ♗d3 is interesting.

b12) 18...f5 when 19 gxf5 ♗xf5 (19...♔g7? 20 ♗h3 is no good because the king isn't stable on f6: it gets hit by ♖d6+) 20 ♖g1+ ♔h8 21 ♖g5 ♗e6

(21...♗e4 22 ♖d7) 22 ♗d3 (not 22 f5? f6) yields an advantage.

17 ♗e2 1:09 **a5** 1:59

If 17...♖e8?! 18 ♖he1! defends the bishop, preparing to invade on d6. But after 18...♔f8 19 ♘d6 ♖xe2 20 ♖xe2 ♗g4 while White is certainly better, he needs to find the very best lines and Black, having at least freed himself from the bind without immediate catastrophe, does have some decent drawing chances. Indeed, this line could be seen as a reasonable attempt at damage limitation:

a) 21 ♖de1 ♗xe2 22 ♖xe2 gives chances of a big advantage. Black will be in a lot of trouble if he allows White to consolidate with b3, so perhaps he should try 22...♖d8 (22...g6 23 b3 is clearly better for Whitre) 23 ♘xb7 ♖d4. But White can choose between:

a1) 24 c5 ♘c4 25 b3 ♖d7 26 ♘d6 ♘xd6 27 cxd6 (27 ♖d2 ♔e7 28 ♖xd6 ♖xd6 29 cxd6+ ♔xd6 30 ♔d2 looks drawn) 27...♖xd6 28 ♖e5 with a positional advantage.

a2) 24 b3 ♖xf4 25 ♘d6 (25 ♘a5 ♖f6 26 ♔c2 is tempting) 25...g6 26 ♖e8+ ♔g7 27 ♖e7 which should also be pretty good.

b) 21 ♖ed2, which can lead to knight endings after 21...♗xd1 22 ♔xd1 ♖d8, may be even better:

b1) 23 ♘xb7 ♖xd2+ 24 ♔xd2 ♘xc4+ 25 ♔c3 ♘e3 is messy.

b2) But 23 c5 looks very good since if:

b21) 23...♘d5 24 ♘xb7 ♘e3+ 25 ♔e2 ♖xd2+ 26 ♔xe2 ♘xg2 27 ♘d8 ♘xf4 28 ♘xc6 leaves White ahead in the race, while if:

b22) 23...♘a4 24 ♘xb7 ♘xb2+ 25 ♔c2 ♖xd2+ 26 ♔xd2 the black knight is in trouble.

18 b3 1:17 **♘d7** 2:07
19 ♖he1 1:21 **♖b8** 2:09
20 ♗f3 1:23 **h6** 2:11
21 g3 1:25 **♘f6!?** 2:15

In a vile position and getting short of time, Black decided to lash out; but his pieces are on terrible squares so it is not surprising that White can refute the lunge.

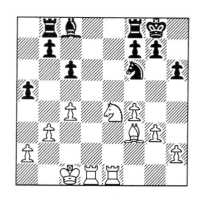

22 ♘xf6+ 1:28 **gxf6** 2:15
23 g4! 1:29

Threatening to strangle the enemy bishop.

23 ... **a4?!** 2:18

After this the prelate is dead. The problem was that after

23...f5 24 gxf5 ♗xf5 25 ♖e5 White wins the a-pawn. But he should have tried this, since after 25...♗h7 26 ♖xa5 (26 ♖g1+ is also possible first) Black can certainly fight by putting the f8- rook on a central file, probably 26...♖fe8.

The other 'wriggly' move was 23...h5, but White can choose between 24 f5 at once and 24 h3, when now if 24...f5 25 gxf5 ♗xf5 26 ♖e5 the inclusion of ...h5 turns out to have been disastrous for Black

24 f5! 1:36

Of course not 24 b4, encouraging 24...♗e6 (also 24...f5) 25 ♗e2 b5.

24 ... **axb3** 2:18
25 axb3 1:36 **♖a8** 2:18

Black can now develop his rook, but with the bishop benched the final result should not be in doubt (easy to write when sitting at a desk 17 years later, not so obvious at the time).

26 ♔b2 1:37 **♖a5** 2:18
27 ♖d6 1:44 **♔g7** 2:18
28 ♔c3 1:45 **♖a2** 2:19

Maybe 28...♖e5!?, while a vile but slightly plausible idea is 28...c5, hoping to get in ...b5. But something like 29 ♖e7 b5 30 cxb5 ♖xb5 31 ♗d5 h5 32 h3 is awful, and White can also go for material at once with 29 ♖b6 ♖d8 (29...♖a6 30 ♖xa6 bxa6 31 ♖e7 is hopeless) 30 ♗xb7 ♗xb7 31 ♖xb7 ♖a2 32 ♖c7 (not 32 ♖ee7? ♖ad2 33

♖xf7+ ♔g8 with a draw) 32...♖xh2 33 ♖xc5 ♖h3+ 34 ♔b4 ♖dd3 35 ♖b1 ♖d4 36 ♖d5 ♖xg4 37 ♔c5 which is presumably winning.

29 h4 1:47

Threatening to bury Black alive after h5, and so more or less forcing Black's response.

29 ... **♖f2** 2:21
30 ♗d1 1:49 **h5!** 2:25

If 30...♖h2 31 h5 there are all sorts of winning plans. Unless Black plays 31...c5, one nice idea is for White to stick in c5 himself. Probably, therefore Black should try 31...c5, for although White will be able to win this pawn, Black has some hope of getting active while that occurs. There are lines such as 32 ♖d5 b6 33 ♖d6 ♖h3+ 34 ♔b2 ♖h2+ 35 ♗c2 ♖g2 36 ♖xb6 ♖d8 37 ♖b5 ♖dd2 38 ♖c1 ♖xg4 39 ♖xc5 which is surely winning for White, but at least Black can move all his pieces.

31 ♖g1! 1:50

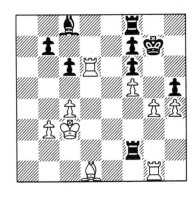

31 ... **hxg4?** 2:25

This makes it easy, but Black is also lost, albeit after creating a few threats of his own, after 31...♖e8 32 gxh5+ and now:

a) 32...♔h8 33 ♖xf6 ♗xf5 when 34 ♔b4 is the simplest, removing the king, before finishing Black off.

b) 32...♔h7 33 ♖xf6 c5!? (33...♗xf5 34 ♖xf5 ♖xf5 35 ♗c2; 33...♖e7 34 ♔b4) hopes to lure White into 34 ♖xf7+ ♔h8 35 ♗c2 ♖e3+ 36 ♗d3 ♖ff3. But after the intermezzo 37 ♖f8+! ♔h7 38 ♖d1 ♗xf5 39 ♖xf5 ♖xf5 40 ♔b2 ♖xd3 41 ♖xd3 White has a straightforward win.

c) 32...♔f8 is much the most challenging, but after 33 h6! the h-pawn seems to win in all variations, viz.

c1) 33...♔e7 34 ♖d2 ♖xd2 35 ♖e1+! ♔d7 36 ♖xe8 ♔xe8 37 h7.

c2) 33...♗xf5 34 ♖xf6 c5 (34...♔e7 35 ♖xf5 ♖xf5 36 ♖e1+ as above) 35 ♖g3 and:

c21) 35...♔e7 still loses to 36 ♖xf5.

c22) 35...♖e4 loses to either 36 h7 ♖xh4 37 ♖xf5 ♖xf5 38 ♖g8+ ♔e7 39 h8♕ or the less impatient but even more decisive 36 h5!

c23) 35...♖d8 36 ♖xf5 ♖xf5 37 h7 ♔e7 38 ♖g8 ♖xd1 39 h8♕.

32 ♖xg4+ 1:50 **1-0**
Black resigned in view of:
a) 32...♔h7 33 ♖xf6, when

Black is still paralysed, e.g. 33...♗xf5 34 ♖xf5 ♖xf5 35 ♗c2.

b) 32...♔h8 33 ♖xf6 ♗xf5 34 ♖g5 ♖d8, when the simplest is 35 ♖gxf5 ♖xf5 36 ♖xf5 ♖xd1 37 ♖xf7.

That left only Black against Ratko Knezevic: a game which did not last long and which, I'm not particularly ashamed to admit, is the only chess game I've ever arrived at armed with a bottle of champagne.

After the tournament, I decided, rather than to fly from Graz to Vienna, to continue on the train to visit John Nunn at the tournament then taking place in Baden-bei-Wien. It seemed polite to inform the airline that I wouldn't be using the return flight; and to my subversive delight I was able to cut through all the bureaucracy by informing the Chairman of JAT directly at the Closing Ceremony, since he was present as a sponsor.

Two years after staggering to the IM title, I had finally made it to Grandmaster. I'm not proud of taking so long compared to the kids today. But I would submit, not entirely unreasonably, that – even if one wasn't forced (together with Monty Python's gentlemen) to domicile oneself in a paper bag on a motorway during the climb – it was tougher back then.

3   Seven Days in London

When I first planned this book, I had been intending to include quite a long section on my various world championship campaigns, running right through from my very first Zonal in Amsterdam 1978 to the Biel Interzonal in 1993; my last event before the convulsions which leave the world championship cycle presently (July 1997) in a state of flux.

But by the time I had included everything else, it had become quite clear that I would have to trim this ambitious project. Eventually I decided to concentrate on just one battle, my first Candidates match with Nigel Short: an event of cardinal importance in my career, eclipsed only by his victory three years later in a murderously close 'return match'.

The Cycle
The relevant cycle started for me with the Bath Zonal in February 1987. With two places at stake among the 10 competitors,

I had a tremendous tournament, eventually racking up 9/10, a point and a half ahead of Glenn Flear.

There were three Interzonals on that occasion. Nigel Short and I were drawn to play in the first of these, which took place in June/July 1987 in Subotica – in the former Yugoslavia just south of the Hungarian border – while the two others were in Zagreb and Szirak, a village near Budapest.

It is not easy to come in the first three of a really strong qualification tournament and I could expatiate on Subotica at some length. The final result, though, was that Sax, Short and myself tied on 10½/15, ahead of Tal and Ribli. I had scored seven wins, losing only to Tal. And I remember how on the last evening Misha gave us, the two English victors, a rousing chorus of 'Oh when the Saints...' Always on the point of physical disaster for the last three decades of his life, but still contriving to play some magnificent fighting chess, it was a great shock when Death did finally catch up with Misha Tal in June 1992.

Saint John

For this cycle and this cycle only, FIDE decided to hold all the first round Candidates matches together. These were played in Saint John, New Brunswick (not to be confused with Saint John, Newfoundland) at the end of January and start of February 1988. Canada is not warm in the winter, but there was a closed tunnel from our hotel right into the huge complex where the event was held. This complex included a shopping centre and various eateries, including one where they had hit upon the notion of naming cocktails after chess players. Various alliterative delights were to be had including, if I recall, the Benko Bomber and Speelman's Surprise. Despite its excellent name, I believe, however, that the latter was inferior to the former – my favourite.

Six-game matches are pretty beastly things – I shall be saying a lot more on the subject when we get into the meat of this chapter with the subsequent match against Nigel. And although my play wasn't terrible good technically, splendidly assisted by Will Watson, I kept my nerve in some hairy situations to run out with a very flattering final score of 4-1 against Yasser Seirawan. Meanwhile Short had cruised through with a smooth 3½-1½ victory against Gyula Sax, while the other results were: Portisch-Vaganian and Timman-Salov both 3½-2½, Yusupov-Ehlvest 3½-1½, Hjartarson-Korchnoi 4½-3½ and Spraggett-Andrei Sokolov 6½-5½.

The latter two matches were decided only after tie-break games and Spraggett-Sokolov, last to finish, turned into quite a circus as they battled through a series of increasingly fast pairs of rapidplay games. The contest was only decided when a shattered Sokolov left his queen en prise to a knight fork in the final fifteen-minute game. It is always difficult to find a totally equitable way of splitting ties, but following this experience FIDE never used a time limit that quick again.

The pairings for the next round were to be made as for St John, 1 vs. 8, 2 vs. 7 etc., but it had not yet been agreed which rating lists to use. Eventually – and here I'm glossing over the no doubt tortuous negotiations since I can't even remember whether I was privy to them, let alone the details – it was decided to carry on with the January and July 1987 lists; though there was an excellent case for replacing January 1987 with January 1988. This led to the following order: Karpov, Yusupov, Short, Timman, Portisch, Speelman, Spraggett, Hjartarson; and the pairings Karpov-Hjartarson, Yusupov-Spraggett, Short-Speelman and Timman-Portisch.

The Match

Sentiment in England was very mixed when the two Englishmen were drawn to meet each other. Certainly this guaranteed that one of us would progress to the semi-finals; but after we had both won so convincingly in St John, it seemed likely that at least one would have won through, anyway.

Personally, I wasn't very happy to be facing the one opponent out of seven who I knew so well and lived almost next door to; but there was nothing to be done. The most important thing was that the match should be played before the Olympiad in mid November.

Excellent sponsorship was forthcoming from Pilkington Glass; and the six-game match was arranged to take place starting on 17 August 1988 in the downstairs cinema at the Barbican. It was scheduled to last until August 25th, but play-offs in the result of a draw could go on right up to the 31st.

Will Watson had acted as my second since the Interzonal in

Taxco (Mexico) in 1985, but his feelings for this match were very mixed since he had also done a certain amount of work with Nigel; and in any case believed that if Nigel did win he would be likely to progress further than I would. All in all, he definitely wanted to stay out of this one, sentiments he very honourably conveyed to me; and we parted extremely amicably.

It was Will himself who suggested that I should employ Jonathan Tisdall in his stead. Tisdall is a Japanese-Irish American who moved to Europe over a decade ago; first considering settling in England but ending up in Norway where his partner, Marianne Hagen, and he, now have a five-year-old son, William. A truly excellent analyst, 'Tis' for many years found it difficult to transfer his full strength to playing but he finally became a grandmaster a couple of years ago.

Meanwhile, Nigel employed John Nunn to beef up still further his considerable theoretical punch, and he also made at least one trip to France, which we only found out about after the match – see the notes to the first game.

Tis, with whom I'm nowadays in very frequent e-mail contact, reminds me that we first met in one of the World Under-26 Team Championships in Mexico in the late seventies; and began working together during one of Ray Keene's Brighton tournaments in the early eighties.

He always used to represent Reuters at big events such as world championship matches; indeed we collaborated on a book on the first Karpov-Kasparov match in 1984-85, *Moscow Marathon* – a book which, like the match itself, expanded to an ungovernable size before foundering; and many years later he was, with Bob Wade and myself, a co-author of *Batsford Chess Endings*. He was an excellent choice for a second since not only is he a strong player and a friend but his presence at all these matches had given him a deep understanding of the psychological aspects of matchplay.

Anyhow, in preparation for the match, I went over to Oslo a couple of times to work with Tis. Preparation has always been the relatively weakest part of my play; a state of affairs which one might expect an intelligent person to be able to remedy, through the very act of identifying it. The problem, though, is getting into the right state of mind.

When people play at tournaments, they tend to get sucked into a 'hypertense' state of being, quite distinct from normal living. Some highly talented players can't sleep properly. Roman Dzindzihashvili, who isn't quite so strong now but was truly formidable in his time – a man with whom Tigran Petrosian would agree a quick draw even when Petrosian was White – is a prime example.

But even if you can cope with the pressure – and the nature of competition is such that it weeds out those who can't – it still demands this shift; the rush of adrenaline that comes with sitting opposite a dangerous opponent. So that it is extremely hard to discern how one would react in combat when one is sitting in a comfortable chair at home. I believe that Kasparov nowadays copes with this problem by analysing, not only with a second but also a couple of computer programs on the latest hardware to check for errors.

Of course we did manage to get some work done, one piece of which, jumping ahead for a moment, was the novelty I employed in the second game. Nigel's first question after the match finished was where this 'piece of rubbish' (I don't remember his exact words but his idiolect would tend to suggest a rather stronger usage) had come from. And the answer is, from when I was in the back of a car on the way to the friendly football match between Norway and Brazil – which I believe the visitors won 2-1.

The prospect of a battle between two Englishmen led to a great deal of brouhaha, some of it, such as being interviewed together with Nigel by Stephen Fry at Simpson's-in-the-Strand, most enjoyable.

The general feeling, not unreasonably, was that Nigel was favourite; and I myself gave him 60:40 in interviews. But both Larsen and Korchnoi said they thought I'd win; and I received tremendous support from my friends at the Kings Head chess club, where I was infinitely more active in those days than I am now.

Since this match was so central to my career, I'm giving the scores of all five games. But while the two crucial wins are analysed properly, the other three games have sketchier notes.

Game 19
J.Speelman–N.Short
London (1st matchgame) 1988
Queen's Gambit Declined, Tartakower variation

The first game of a tournament is always an exceptionally tense affair, let alone a match. Matches create their own space, in that the intensive preparation which they entail, means that there may be theoretical battles fought which will never be continued, at least by the players in question, outside the confined psychological and temporal – it all seems to happen very quickly – conditions of the match itself.

At the drawing of lots the night before, I had been awarded the white pieces for the first game, which must be an advantage in a short match since there is some possibility of winning the match before having to face one's last Black.

This was particularly relevant in our case since both Nigel and I had serious plus scores with White but had never beaten the other in a serious game with Black. Tisdall and I decided that we should use this first game to settle in and test the water. Would Nigel suddenly introduce all sorts of unexpected twists to his repertoire; or was he going to play things straight down the line?

1 d4 ♘f6 2 c4 e6 3 ♘f3 d5 4 ♘c3 ♗e7 5 ♗g5 h6 6 ♗h4 0-0 7 e3 b6 8 ♗e2 ♗b7 9 ♗xf6 ♗xf6 10 cxd5 exd5 11 b4 c6
0:12-0:05

Although Nigel had had problems with this line in the Belfort World Cup earlier that summer, he sticks to his guns.

Later, we discovered that part of his preparation had involved going to see Boris Spassky in France to work on the Queen's Gambit.

Black has to stop his opponent clamping down on his queenside with b5, so the choice is between this and 11...c5 – which had been tested in repeated Kasparov-Karpov games with the two gentlemen prepared to play the position with either colour. The latter leads to a simpler sort of position, in which Black will be doing fine, as long as he survives the opening. Nigel had already played this against Ribli in London 1986, drawing in 37 moves. And he has played it since, though without much success – years later, he even tried it against Karpov in the seventh game of his splendid match victory in Linares 1992, though he did lose that game.

12 0-0 0:14 **♕d6** 0:06

In Belfort, Short had played 12...♖e8 first; and though it all looks very similar, a great deal of work had gone into these nuances, since this is a far from simple position.

White's plan is initially to keep the position under control, clamping down on enemy queenside expansion with ...c5. He can play on the queenside with a4-a5, but Karpov, who does especially well with this line, has generally preferred

rather to prepare for e4. If White does it well, then eventually Black is likely to pre-empt him, often playing ...a5 to start action on the queenside himself, as in the impressive Karpov-Kiril Georgiev game below.

Although his position presently looks somewhat passive, Black has serious long-term chances due to his bishop pair. And if, as in this game, White mistimes his break, then the position can rapidly turn against him.

13 ♕b3 0:16 **♘d7** 0:07
14 ♖fe1 0:19

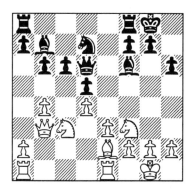

14 ... ♖ad8 0:13
14...♖fe8 would still transpose back directly into Short's two games from the Belfort World Cup 1988: 15 ♗d3 ♗e7 16 ♖ab1 ♗f8 17 e4 a5 18 a3 axb4 19 axb4 g6 20 h3 ♗g7 21 exd5 ½-½ was Speelman-Short; and 15...g6 16 e4 ♗g7 17 e5 ♕e6 18 ♘e2 ♘f8 19 g3 ♕d7 20 ♘f4 ♖ac8 21 ♖ac1 ♖c7 22 ♗f1 ♕d8 23 ♗h3 ♗c8 24 ♗xc8

♕xc8 25 b5 ♘e6 26 ♘xe6 ♕xe6 27 bxc6 ♖ec8 28 ♕a4 a5 29 ♕b5 ♖xc6 30 ♖xc6 ♖xc6 31 ♔g2 ♗f8 32 ♖b1 ♗e7 33 ♕a6 ♔g7 34 h3 h5 35 ♖b3 g5 36 a4 ♕f5 37 ♕e2 g4 38 hxg4 hxg4 39 ♘h2 ♖g6 40 f3 ♖c6 41 fxg4 ♕h7 42 ♖b2 ♗g5 43 ♘f3 ♖c1 44 ♘g1 ♖c3 45 ♘f3 ♖c1 46 ♘g1 ♖c3 47 ♘f3 ½-½ was Karpov-Short.

While six years later 14...♗e7 15 ♖ab1 a5!? 16 bxa5 ♖xa5 17 a4 ♖e8 18 ♗f1 ♗f8 19 ♕c2 g6 20 e4 dxe4 21 ♘xe4 ♕f4 22 ♗c4! ♗g7 23 ♖e2 c5 24 d5 ♖aa8 25 ♖be1 ♖ad8 26 ♕b3 ♗a8 27 g3 ♕b8 28 d6 ♖f8 29 ♗xf7+! ♖xf7 30 ♘eg5 hxg5 31 ♘xg5 ♖df8 32 ♖e8! ♕xd6 33 ♕xf7+ ♔h8 34 ♘e6 1-0 was Karpov-Kiril Georgiev, Tilburg 1994.

15 ♖ab1 0:25 **♖fe8**

16 ♗d3 0:31

Playing for e4, which at the moment would have led to a draw: 16 e4 dxe4 17 ♗c4 exf3 18 ♗xf7+ ♔f8 19 ♗g6 ♖e7 20 ♗h7 ♖f7 21 ♗g6 ♖e7.

16 ... ♗a8

17 ♕a4? 0:41

Black can easily defend a7, after which the queen is misplaced. After this bad move, Black is already doing quite well. If 17 e4 dxe4 18 ♗c4 (18 ♘xe4? ♕f4 19 ♖e3 c5 is already good for Black) leads to a draw again. But in the *BCM*, John Nunn suggests that 17 h3! is best, prophylactically con-

trolling g4 so that the move g3 is stronger in lines where the black queen goes to f4 – she can't run to g4. He gives:

a) 17...g6 18 e4 dxe4 (18...♗g7 19 e5 ♕b8 20 h4 is clearly better for White) 19 ♘xe4 ♕f4 20 ♖e3 (intending g3) 20...♗g7 21 ♖be1 ♕b8?! 22 ♘d6! ♖xe3 23 ♕xf7+ ♔h8 24 ♖xe3 ♕xd6 25 ♖e7 and wins.

b) 17...♖e7 18 e4 dxe4 19 ♘xe4 ♕c7 20 ♖e3 ♖de8 21 ♖be1 ♔f8 22 ♘xf6 ♘xf6 23 ♘e5 ♘d5 (23...c5 24 ♕xf7+!) 24 ♗h7! g6 25 ♗xg6 ♘xe3 26 ♕xe3 fxg6 27 ♕xh6+ ♔g8 28 ♕xg6+ ♔f8 29 ♖e4 with a clear advantage for White.

c) 17...♘f8! 18 e4 dxe4 19 ♗c4 ♘e6 20 ♘xe4 ♕f4 with an unclear position.

17 ... ♕b8 0:32

18 e4?! 0:46

This has been badly prepared and already rebounds unpleasantly.

18 ... c5! 0:52

19 ♘xd5 1:07

Forced, for 19 ♗b5? dxe4! 20 ♗xd7 ♖e7 (20...cxd4 is also good but less so) 21 ♗c6 ♗xc6 22 ♕xc6 ♖e6; 19 e5? cxd4 20 exf6 ♖xe1+ 21 ♖xe1 dxc3 22 fxg7 ♕f4 and 19 bxc5? ♘xc5 20 dxc5 ♗xc3 21 ♖ec1 d4 all lead to a big advantage for Black.

19 ... ♗xd4! 0:59

Better than 19...cxd4 20 ♗b5 with equality.

20 ♘xd4 1:17 **cxd4** 0:59

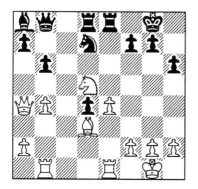

The critical position. Things had gone very badly for me so far, but now I managed to pull myself together and start fighting.

21 h3 1:21

It is a good idea to pre-empt back-rank tricks. If 21 ♗b5?! ♗xd5 22 exd5 ♖xe1+ 23 ♖xe1 ♘f6 24 ♗c4 ♕f4 (threatening ...♘g4) and now:

a) 25 ♕c2? would be nice if it were playable, but after 25...♕d6 26 ♕d2 ♘xd5 27 ♕xd4 ♕xb4 28 ♖d1 ♖c8! Black has won a pawn with wonderful winning chances. In view of the weak back rank, White can't play 29 ♗xd5? ♕xd4 30 ♖xd4 ♖c1+.

b) 25 g3 is better – if rather frightening – when Black has various attacking possibilities, e.g. 25...♕f5 (25...♕f3!?; 25...♕d2!?) 26 ♕xa7 ♘g4 27 ♖f1 ♘e5 as given by John Nunn in the *BCM*. One critical line then is 28 ♕xb6 ♘f3+ 29 ♔g2 ♖e8 (29...♘h4+ is an immedi-

ate perpetual) 30 ♕b5 and:

b1) 30...♕e4 31 ♕xe8+ ♕xe8 32 ♔xf3 when White will be reasonably placed if he doesn't lose at once, e.g. after 32...f5 33 ♗d3 ♕e5 34 ♖b1! ♕xd5+ 35 ♔e2 ♕xa2+ 36 ♔e1 the b-pawn is a powerful unit.

b2) 30...♘e1+ looks like an improvement, but the white d-pawn should not be discounted. Black seems to be winning after 31 ♔g1 ♕e4 32 f3 ♕e3+ 33 ♔h1 d3 (33...♘xf3 34 d6 ♘g5 35 ♕f5) 34 d6 ♕e2 (if 34...♖f8 35 ♕c5!) but this runs into 35 ♖f2! and if 35...♕xf2 36 ♕xe8+ ♔h7 37 ♗xd3+ ♘xd3 38 ♕e4+ g6 39 ♕xd3 and White wins.

21 ... **♘e5** 1:11

If instead 21...♗xd5 22 exd5 ♖xe1+ 23 ♖xe1 ♘f6 I had intended 24 ♗c4! and if 24...♕f4 25 ♕c2 defends since the line above doesn't work once White has made air with h3, i.e. if. 25...♕d6 26 ♕d2 ♘xd5 27 ♕xd4 ♕xb4? 28 ♖d1 is now winning for White.

22 ♗b5 1:21 **♖e6** 1:12
23 ♕b3! 1:22

Nigel had clearly missed this and after seventeen minutes' thought he played:

23 ... **♕d6?!** 1:29

and offered a draw which I quickly accepted (23...♘g6 was a way to play for a win).

Although the opening had gone so badly, I took heart from the fact that I had played some decent moves under pressure; and also had hopes that after achieving such a pleasant game with Black, my opponent would perhaps be tempted to drop his guard slightly.

Game 20
N.Short–J.Speelman
London (2nd matchgame) 1988
French Defence, Burn variation

1 e4   e6

During our pre-match preparation, we had decided that my main weapon, the Caro-Kann, was extremely risky since Nigel would have had ample time to bring some serious ordnance to bear upon it. We were intending to play a Pirc at some point; but in the hothouse atmosphere of the match itself, a problem arose which discomfited me and required a couple of days to solve. So I decided to play the French.

2	d4	d5
3	♘c3	♘f6
4	♗g5	dxe4
5	♘xe4	♘bd7
6	♘xf6+	♘xf6
7	♘f3	h6 0:11
8	♗h4 0:06	g6 0:15

As I mentioned in the general introduction to the match, this novelty was conceived (parthenogenetically, I hasten to add) on the back seat of a car en route to a football match in Oslo. I was wondering what move I would play in this position if I had carte blanche; and realised that 8...g6 was the one which most accords with my style.

Objectively, it may not be a terribly wonderful move; but it suited my purposes admirably. Nigel had blitzed out his first eight moves in just six minutes, a rate of play which presaged serious unpleasantness in the main lines; or at the very least a passage of play in which he felt particularly comfortable. Instead, we now have a completely new position, in which I'd done some work to make sure that disaster wouldn't strike instantly; and he had nothing prepared.

8...g6 is quite logical in that in the normal lines, Black often has to worry about threats on the d3-h7 diagonal – White may play ♗xf6 followed by ♕e4, threatening ♕h7 mate. But it does lose time and renders ...c5 somewhat harder to get in successfully; since after ...♗g7 the bishop won't support that break.

9 ♗c4 0:23

After ...g6, there is less point in putting the bishop on the d3-h7 diagonal, so Nigel simply posts it on a different one – and incidentally prevents ...♕d5 later.

9 ...   ♗g7 0:17
10 0-0 0:29

Of course immediate violence with 10 ♕e2 followed by 0-0-0 was also quite playable. But Nigel decided to be more careful.

10 ...   0-0 0:21
11 c3 0:32

Supporting the d-pawn. After 11 ♕e2 g5 12 ♗g3 g4 it drops off.

11 ...   b6 0:26
12 ♕e2 0:47   **♗b7** 0:33
13 ♖ad1 0:49   **a6?!** 0:42

To prevent the exchange of bishops with ♗a6, but now the black rook is tied to this pawn. 13...♕c8 was a reasonable alternative way of stopping the exchange, to be followed by ...♘d5 and ...c5.

14 ♖fe1 0:53   **♕d6!?** 0:49
15 ♗b3 1:05

Out of the way of the c-pawn to prepare c4.

15 ...   a5 1:07

Played after eighteen minutes thought. Presumably I wanted to play 15...♘h5 but came to the (probably correct) conclusion that 16 d5 in reply is just too strong, e.g. 16...e5 17 ♘d2 ♘f4 18 ♕f3!, threatening ♘c4 or ♘e4 and holding onto the d5-pawn since if 18...♗xd5? 19 ♘e4 ♗xe4 20 ♖xe4 ♕c5 21 ♖c4 ♕b5 22 ♖xc7 with a big advantage.

16 ♗g3 1:10   **♕c6** 1:09

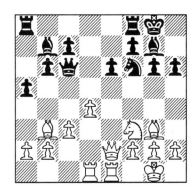

17 ♕f1? 1:12

Up to here, Nigel has played very well, but this allows Black to become active. Instead 17 ♗c4! would have been clearly stronger, returning to annoy the queen. After 17...♖ac8 to defend the c-pawn (if 17...♘e4? 18 d5!; or 17...♕d7 18 ♘e5 ♕e8 19 h3 with good control) 18 ♕f1 is better now that White controls the f1-a6 diagonal. 17 ♗e5 was also reasonable.

17 ...   ♗a6! 1:15

Seizing the opportunity.

18 c4? 1:16

Rather losing the thread. He should have entered the complications with 18 ♘e5!?, when I disliked 18...♕b7?! 19 ♗c4 because c6 is weak, although Black has compensatory activity. In fact I was hoping to be able to play 18...♗xf1 19 ♘xc6 ♗b5 when:

a) 20 ♘e7+ ♔h7 21 a4 and now:

a1) 21...♗a6 22 ♗xc7!? (22

♘c6 ♗b7 is fine for Black, while 22 d5 ♖fe8 23 dxe6 ♖xe7 24 exf7 ♖xe1+ 25 ♖xe1 is very speculative) 22...♖fe8 23 ♘xg6! (both 23 ♘c6 ♖ac8 and 23 ♗d6 ♗f8 are good for Black) 23...fxg6 (23...♔xg6? 24 ♗c2+ ♔h5 25 ♖e5+ and Black will be mated) 24 ♗xe6 is very unclear – my feeling is that unless Black can disrupt White in the next couple of moves then it will be rather more comfortable for White.

a2) 21...♗d7 22 d5 (22 ♗xc7 ♖fe8 is bad for White now that the e6-pawn is defended) 22...♖fe8 23 ♘xg6!? (23 d6 cxd6 24 ♗xd6 ♗f8 25 ♗e5 ♗xe7 26 ♗xf6 ♗xf6 27 ♖xd7 ♔g8 is equal) 23...fxg6 24 dxe6 ♗c6 25 ♗xc7 is another sacrificial variation. Again White has three pawns and this time the e6-pawn is particularly menacing, though there are plenty of Black pieces in the way. But Black can lose quickly if he isn't careful, for instance if 25...♖c8 26. ♗e5 ♘g8? 27 ♖d7! ♗xd7 28 exd7 ♖xe5 29 ♖xe5 ♖d8 30 ♖e8 etc.

b) 20 d5 a4 21 ♘d4 axb3 22 ♘xb5 ♘xd5 is absolutely fine for Black.

So if White doesn't want to risk a piece sacrifice then he should retreat with:

c) 20 ♘e5 a4! and:

c1) 21 ♗c4 is normal, though after 21...♗xc4 22 ♘xc4 any White advantage is absolutely minimal.

c2) 21 ♗c2 is perhaps slightly over-icing the cake. After 21...♘h5 22 ♗e4 ♖a5! 23 ♗h4 ♗xe5 (23...g5 24 ♗f3) 24 dxe5 g5 25 ♗f3 Black can choose between:

c21) 25...♘g7 26 ♗g3 and ...♘f5 possibly preceded by 26...♗c4 27 a3 ♘f5.

c22) The more ambitious 25...♘f4 26 ♗g3 ♘d3.

| 18 | ... | | ♖ad8 | |
| 19 | ♘e5 1:19 | | ♕b7 1:21 | |

Preparing ...c5.

| 20 | ♗a4 1:26 | | c5 1:24 | |
| 21 | dxc5? 1:33 | | | |

After this, Black gains a serious advantage which I quickly proceeded to fritter away. I was rightly much more concerned about 21 ♘c6 ♖c8 22 d5! ♘xd5! 23 ♖xd5 exd5 24 ♖e7, when during the game I thought that

a) 24...♖xc6 was the best way to give up the queen, i.e. 25 ♖xb7 ♗xb7 26 ♗xc6? ♗xc6 27 cxd5 ♗xd5 which is equal. But in the middle of this, 26 cxd5!? is alarming when the d-pawn will be very dangerous.

b) Later we decided that 24...♕xc6! was in fact better, i.e. 25 ♗xc6 ♖xc6 and if 26 b3 (26 ♕d1 looks better) 26...dxc4 27 bxc4 ♖d8, threatening both ...♖d4 and the immediate ...♗xc4.

21	...		bxc5 1:25	
22	♕e2 1:33		♖xd1 1:29	
23	♖xd1 1:33		♘h5 1:29	

24 b3 1:39

24 ... ♘xg3? 1:32

After cursory thought, I gave away most of my advantage. Short had seen that 24...♕c7! is much stronger immediately, since now the defence White uses in the game is impossible: 25 f4 (25 ♘xg6 ♘xg3 26 hxg3 is insufficient – see below) 25...♖d8 26 ♖xd8+ ♕xd8 27 ♗c6 ♕d4+ and wins since the f4-pawn falls.

25 hxg3 ♕c7
26 f4! 1:40

Nigel took just a minute to reject the attempt to complicate matters with 26 ♘xg6? which loses by force, albeit after White has afforded some resistance: 26...fxg6 27 ♕xe6+ ♕f7! 28 ♕xa6 ♕xf2+ 29 ♔h2 ♕e2! (29...♕f5 30 ♖d5 ♗e5 31 ♗d7 is unclear) and now:

a) 30 ♕d6 ♖f5! and both 31 ♗d7 ♖h5+ 32 ♗h3 ♖xh3+ 33 ♔xh3 ♕h5 and 31 ♖d5 ♖h5+ 32 ♖xh5 ♕xh5+ 33 ♔g1 ♗d4+ 34 ♔f1 ♕d1 are mate.

b) 30 ♖d5 (to defend the fifth rank) 30...♖f2 31 ♕a8+ ♔h7 and:

b1) 32 ♖d7 ♖f5 33 ♖xg7+ (forced since if 33 g4 ♕xg4 Black has overwhelming threats) 33...♔xg7 34 ♕a7+ ♔f6 35 ♕b6+ ♕e6 is winning.

b2) 32 ♖xc5 (to keep on the fifth rank) 32...♖f1! (not 32...♕d1? 33 ♗e8) wins since the queen will land decisively on e1 or d1 next move

26 ... ♖d8 1:34
27 ♖xd8+ ♕xd8 1:35
28 ♗c6 1:43 ♗c8 1:41
29 ♔h2 1:44 h5 1:42

29...g5 was possible here, though 30 ♕e3 isn't bad.

30 ♗f3 1:45 h4 1:44
31 ♕e3 1:46 hxg3+ 1:45
32 ♔xg3 1:46 ♕d6?! 1:45

I had to seize the moment with 32...g5 33 ♗h5! (not 33 fxg5? ♕c7 34 ♔f4 f6 winning for Black) 33...gxf4+ 34 ♕xf4 f6 35 ♘c6 ♕d7 36 ♗f3 when the two bishops still give Black some chances.

33 ♔f2 1:47

Now if 33...g5 White can support the f-pawn with 34 g3.

33 ... ♗d7

I don't have the clock time after this, but I think I only took a few minutes over it. Realising that I'd spoilt my chances, I offered a draw here which he readily accepted.

How does one evaluate this game in the match context? Nigel dealt fairly easily with my unusual eighth move but then played some uncharacteristically bad moves after the first diagram. Had 8...g6 caused some sort of delayed reaction? I didn't play too convincingly after springing my surprise but did seize my opportunity on move 17 onwards. Only when I gained a big advantage, did I falter.

I seem to remember not being especially pleased with myself but also far from downcast after this game. Both players were clearly still nervous; I hadn't buckled under the first huge theoretical punch when taking Black; and the real fight lay ahead.

Game 21
J.Speelman-N.Short
London (3rd matchgame) 1988
Queen's Gambit Declined

After my rather pitiful performance with the white pieces in the first game, we had a great stroke of luck. Marianne, Tisdall's girlfriend, had come over to London a day or so previously and happened to buy a Norwegian newspaper on the way. In the chess column, there was the game between Mikhail Gurevich and Andrei Sokolov which had played a couple of weeks earlier in the USSR Championship in Moscow: a game which contained a theoretical bombshell, absolutely ideal for our purposes.

It is hard to credit today, in an age of instant information in which one can download games from big tournaments the day they are played – or even watch them live – that less than a decade ago, the most up-to-date chess information came from the weekly Swiss magazine, *Die Schachwoche*. The next *Die Schachwoche* was due and indeed just two days later it arrived through John Nunn's letter box, with Gurevich-Sokolov as large as life. So we had a window of just this one game, during which the novelty would be effective.

Although initially a little sceptical, I allowed Tisdall to persuade me to give it a try – in a recent e-mail he reminded me that our scepticism was overcome when we realised that Gurevich's idea was not only a gung-ho kingside attack; but also more positional play with ♘f3-d2 to annoy the enemy queen. So I arrived at the game in a state of considerable excitement.

1 d4 0:02

Determinedly played at my

normal rhythm since the most important thing was to avoid arousing Nigel's suspicions. The line with 5 ♗f4 is an obvious one to try; but it is hard not to telegraph a bombshell like 10 0-0-0.

1	...	♘f6 0:01
2	c4 0:02	e6 0:01
3	♘f3 0:04	d5 0:02
4	♘c3 0:04	♗e7 0:02
5	♗f4 0:05	

I remember that between moves one and nine I actually counted to myself to 100 in a couple of languages and possibly also recited poetry so as not to rush and appear too eager.

5	...	0-0 0:02
6	e3 0:05	c5 0:02
7	dxc5 0:06	♘c6 0:02
8	♕c2 0:08	♗xc5 0:02
9	a3 0:09	♕a5 0:04
10	0-0-0!? 0:11	

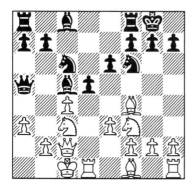

The two minutes were spent, not in decision-making but rather in returning from my area offstage. I played 10 0-0-0 instantly and retreated into the wings, leaving him to it.

Some measure of the spectacular nature of Gurevich's wonderful new idea can be gauged from Tisdall's report in *New in Chess*: 'Michael Stean told me that in his days working with Korchnoi, they periodically tried to revive this variation for White over a span of years – but never considered 10 0-0-0.'

10 ... ♗e7 0:16

Since 1988, there have been literally hundreds of games with 10 0-0-0. I don't want to get too involved in the theory but will adduce a few very relevant examples:

a) When Tis first showed me 10 0-0-0, 10...♘e4!? was what I was most concerned about. Having failed to see 11 ♘b5, we spent some time trying to persuade ourselves that the obvious:

a1) 11 ♘xe4 dxe4 12 ♕xe4 ♗xa3 13 bxa3 ♕xa3+ 14 ♔d2 isn't an immediate draw and, true or not, were sufficiently successful that I was persuaded to play the line.

a2) In fact 11 ♘b5 is very dangerous for Black after 11...a6 12 ♘c7 e5 and now:

a21) 13 ♘xd5 led to considerable excitement in Gelfand-Yusupov, Linares 1992: 13...♘xf2! 14 ♘g5 ♗f5! 15 ♕xf2 exf4 16 ♕xf4 ♘e7! 17 ♘xe7+ ♗xe7 18 ♖d5 ♕e1+ 19 ♖d1 ♕a5 20 ♖d5 ♕e1+ 21 ♖d1 and the draw was agreed. But after that game Short said that he had already analysed the whole thing out with his then second Lubosh Kavalek!

a22) 13 ♖xd5! was Kasparov's improvement in the European Team Championships at Debrecen in November 1992 – Linares had been in February. In the Russia-Armenia match he crushed Vaganian horribly after 13...f5? (in *Informator 56* Kasparov gives 13...exf4? 14 ♕xe4!; 13...♗e6 14 ♖xe5 ♘xe5 15 ♗xe5 ♗f5 16 ♗d3; 13...♘f6!? 14 ♖xe5!; 13...♗f5!? 14 ♘xa8 ♘g3 15 ♕d2 ♘xh1 16 ♕xa5; and 13...♘xf2!? 14 ♘g5 ♗f5!) 14 ♖xe5 ♘xe5 15 ♗xe5 ♖a7? (15...♖b8! was the only move) 16 ♘d5! b6 (or 16...♕d8 17 b4 ♗d6 18 ♗d4 ♖a8 19 c5 ♗e7 20 ♗c4 ♔h8 21 ♘b6 ♖b8 22 ♖d1 ♕e8 23 ♗e5 and wins) 17 ♗d3! ♗d7 18 b4 ♕xa3+ 19 ♗b2 ♕a4 (19...♕a2 20 ♘c3!) 20 bxc5 bxc5 (20...♘xc5 21 ♕xa4 ♗xa4 22 ♗c2) 21 ♘e5 ♕xc2+ 22 ♗xc2 ♗e6 23 ♘f4 1-0.

b) 10...dxc4 was Andrei Sokolov's reaction against Gurevich in the stem game, and after 11 ♗xc4 ♗e7 12 g4 he lashed out with 12...b5? but was downed in just half a dozen more moves 13 ♗xb5 ♗b7 14 ♘d2 ♘b4? 15 axb4 ♗xb4 16 ♘c4 ♕a1+ 17 ♔d2 ♗xc3+ 18 ♔e2 ♕a2 19 ♖a1 1-0.

11 g4 0:21

We hadn't had time to look at much more than 10...♘e4, so I was on my own now too. I presume I was choosing between this and 11 h4 or 11 ♘d2.

11 ... ♖d8 0:30

11...♘e4!? has never been played as far as I know but isn't utterly absurd at first glance.

If instead 11...dxc4 12 ♗xc4:

a) 12...b5 would have transposed back into the Gurevich-Sokolov game.

b) 12...e5 looks dodgy because of 13 g5 exf4 14 gxf6 ♗xf6 15 ♘d5, when Black should acquiesce in doubled pawns with 15...♘e7! 16 ♘xf6+ gxf6, but White, at the moment a pawn down, has expended much of his attacking energy. Indeed Nigel successfully used this in a very recent game against Loek Van Wely at Wijk aan Zee in January 1997. Loek held the advantage for most of the ending but overpressed and eventually lost: 17 ♖hg1+ ♔h8 18 e4 b5 19 ♗d5 ♘xd5 20 exd5 b4 21 axb4 ♕a1+ 22 ♔d2 ♕a6 23 ♕c6 ♖d8 24 ♔c3 ♗b7 25 ♕xa6 ♗xa6 26 ♖d4 ♖ac8+ 27 ♔d2 ♗b7 28 ♖c1 ♖xc1 29 ♔xc1 ♔g7 30 ♘e1 ♖xd5 31 ♖xd5 ♗xd5 32 ♘d3 f3 33 ♔d2 ♗c6 34 ♘f4 f5 35 h4 ♔f6 36 ♔e3 ♔e5 37 ♘d3+ ♔d5 38 ♔f4 ♗a4 39 ♘e5 f6 40 ♘xf3 ♗c2 41 ♘d2 ♗d3 42 ♔e3 ♗c2 43 f3 ♔e5 44 ♘c4+ ♔d5 45 ♘a5 (over-optimistic; 45 ♘d2 would repeat moves) 45...♗a4

46 b3 ♗b5 47 ♔f4 ♔d4 48 ♔xf5 ♔c3 49 f4 ♔xb4 50 ♘b7 ♗c6 51 ♘d8 ♗d5 52 ♔xf6 ♔xb3 53 ♔e5 ♔c4 54 f5 a5 55 f6 a4 56 ♘c6 ♗g8 57 ♘e7 ♗f7 58 ♘f5 a3 59 ♘d6+ ♔c5 60 ♘xf7 a2 61 ♘g5 a1♕+ 62 ♔e6 ♕a6+ 63 ♔e7 ♕b7+ 64 ♔e6 h6 65 f7 ♕c8+ 66 ♔e7 hxg5 67 hxg5 ♕b7+ 68 ♔f8 ♔d6 69 ♔g8 ♕d5 70 g6 ♔e7 71 ♔h7 ♕d8 0-1.

12 h3 0:34

This may appear inconsistent with the previous, very aggressive move. But one of the main effects of 11 g4 is to prepare for g5, attacking the enemy centre at the right moment – which is not now – and the g-pawn is loose.

If instead 12 ♘d2 dxc4 13 ♘xc4 ♖xd1+ 14 ♕xd1 ♕d8 15 ♕xd8+ ♘xd8 16 h3 ♗d7 (also possibly 16...b6) 17 ♘e5 is pretty harmless.

12 ... a6 0:34

Unbeknownst to both players, there had already been a second game played in Moscow. 12...♗d7 13 ♘d2 a6 14 ♗e2 ♖ac8 15 g5 ♘e4 16 ♘dxe4 dxe4 17 ♘xe4 ♘e5 18 ♖d4 ♗c6 19 ♖hd1 ♘g6 20 ♖xd8+ ♖xd8 21 ♖xd8+ ♗xd8 22 ♗g3 ♕e1+ 23 ♗d1 ♕h1 24 ♕d2 ♗e7 25 ♗d6 ♕xe4 26 ♗xe7 ♕xc4+ 27 ♗c2 ♕f1+ ½-½ M.Gurevich-Kharitonov.

As John Nunn explained in the *BCM*, 12...dxc4!? is one of the things they analysed after

the game – and it is certainly playable. After 13 ♖xd8+ ♘xd8 14 ♗xc4 Nunn himself liked 14...♘d5 15 ♘xd5 exd5 16 ♗d3 g6 (16...♗e6!?) – when Black gets developed without undue trouble, but I would slightly prefer to be White – while 14...♗d7 was Short's idea, and if 15 ♘e5 ♗e8, keeping the pawn structure intact and preparing 16...♖c8.

13 ♘d2 0:49

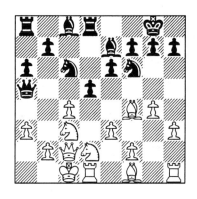

The critical position. After 41 minutes' thought, Nigel wrongly decided to lash out in the centre with:

13 ... e5? 1:15

Here 13...♗d7 would transpose back into M.Gurevich-Kharitonov, but 13...b5 is most combative – and if I remember correctly was what I had decided I was most concerned about during his long think:

a) 14 cxb5? axb5 15 ♗xb5 ♗d7 is horrible. For just one pawn, Black has safeguarded his centre and opened two more lines against the white king. White would be lucky to reach move 25.

b) 14 g5 invites a dangerous looking piece sacrifice with:

b1) 14...bxc4?! 15 gxf6 ♗xf6, but after 16 ♗g2!, threatening ♘xc4, White gains the advantage. John Nunn gives 16...♗b7 (16...♗d7? 17 ♘xc4 dxc4 18 ♖xd7 ♖xd7 19 ♗xc6) 17 h4 intending ♗g5.

b2) 14...♘h5! looks strong since the bishop is embarrassed, but it is far from clear after 15 cxd5 exd5 16 ♘b3 ♕b6 and now:

b21) 17 ♘xd5 ♖xd5! 18 ♖xd5 ♘xf4 19 exf4 ♗e6 is given by Nunn, and if 20 ♗g2 ♖c8 21 ♔b1 ♘b4! 22 ♕xc8+ ♗xc8 23 axb4 ♕xf2 with a big advantage.

b22) 17 ♗g2 was played in a rather obscure correspondence game, which saw 17...♗e6 18 ♗xd5 ♘xf4 19 exf4 b4 20 ♘a4 ♕c7 21 ♗xe6 fxe6 22 ♔b1 bxa3 23 ♘d4 ♖d6 24 ♘xe6! ♕b7 (24...♖xe6? 25 ♕c4) 25 ♕e4 ♖xd1+ 26 ♖xd1 ♖b8 27 ♕d5 ♘b4 28 ♕xb7 ♖xb7 29 bxa3 ♘d3+ 30 ♔c2 ♘xf2 31 ♖f1 ♘xh3 32 ♖f3 ♔f7 33 ♘ac5 ♘g1 34 ♖f1 ♖b5 (34...♗xc5? 35 ♘d8+) 35 ♘xa6 ♖a5 36 ♘ac7 with an edge, Eriksson-Holmberg, Swedish Correspondence Championship 1990.

c) 14 cxd5! would have been most sensible – particularly since at the board it is far from

obvious that the piece sacrifice 14 g5 bxc4 fails – 14...♘xd5 15 ♘xd5 and now:

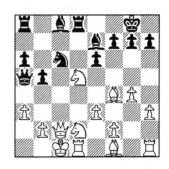

c1) 15...exd5 was given as ?! by earlier analysts. While this may be true, it needs cleaning up. 16 ♕xc6 and now:

c11) 16...♗xg4 turns out to be bad because in the main line White gains a tempo due to the open h-file after 17 ♘b3 ♕a4 18 hxg4 and:

c111) Now 18...♖dc8 is fairly simple, i.e. 19 ♗c7 ♖a7 (19...♕xb3 20 ♗d3 ♖a7 21 ♗xh7+) 20 ♕xd5 ♖axc7+ 21 ♔b1 and wins.

c112) So 18...♖ac8 19 ♗c7 and now:

c1121) 19...♗d6? loses to Fritz's inhuman solution of 20 ♘c5! (Nunn's 20 ♕xd5! is also good) and 20...♖xc7 (or 20...♕xg4 21 ♖xd5 ♖xc7 22 ♖xd6 ♕c8 23 ♖xd8+ ♕xd8 24 ♕b6) 21 ♕xc7 ♕xd1+ 22 ♔xd1 ♗xc7.

c1122) So 19...♕xb3 is best. Now White can gain a simple safe advantage with 20 ♖d3 ♕c4+ 21 ♕xc4 bxc4 22 ♗xd8 cxd3+ 23 ♔d2 ♗xd8 24 ♗xd3, while the more demanding 20 ♗d3, gaining a tempo through the threat of ♗xh7+, looks even better:

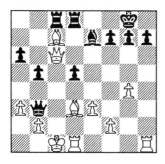

c11221) 20...♗f6? 21 ♗xh7+ ♔f8 22 ♖d2 ♗e5 23 ♕c5+ ♔e8 24 ♗f5 is simple, so Black must first defend h7.

c11222) 20...h6 and:

c112221) 21 ♗c2 ♕a2 22 ♖xh6? fails to 22...gxh6 23 ♕xh6 ♕a1+ 24 ♔d2 ♕xb2 defending.

c112222) 21 ♗f5 ♖d6! 22 ♕c5 ♖d7 23 ♗xd7 ♗xc5 24 ♗xc8 ♗xa3 gives White a lot of material, but the black queen lots of checks and loose men to aim at.

c112223) 21 ♔b1! is simplest, forcing an ending which should be winning after 21...♗xa3 22 ♕c2 ♕b4 23 ♖d2 ♗xb2 (23...♖d7 allows a neat trick: 24 ♗a5! ♖xc2 25 ♗xb4) 24 ♕xb2 ♕xb2+ 25 ♔xb2 ♖xc7.

c11223) 20...g6 21 ♗c2 ♕a2 22 ♕c3! tees up for ♖xh7, e.g. 22...♖d7 23 ♖xh7! ♕a1+ 24

♗b1 f6 (24...d4 25 ♖h8+! ♔xh8 26 ♗e5+) 25 ♔d2 ♖dxc7 26 ♕b3 and White wins.

c11224) 20...h5 was my final thought, trying to gain a tempo after 21 ♖xh5 g6, but White can now attack with, for example, 22 ♗c2 ♕a2 23 ♗xg6 ♖d6 24 ♗h7+ ♔f8 25 ♕c3 d4 26 exd4 ♖d7 27 ♗b1.

c12) 16...♗f5 is better than 16...♗xg4 since the h-file isn't opened:

c121) 17 ♗c7? allows a very nasty accident: 17...♖ac8! 18 ♗xa5 ♖xc6+ 19 ♗c3 ♖xc3+ 20 bxc3 ♗xa3 mate!

c122) 17 gxf5!? ♖ac8 18 ♕xc8 ♖xc8+ 19 ♔b1 gives Black an awful lot of play, though White can play for a win after either:

c1221) 19...♗xa3 20 ♗e5 (20 bxa3 ♕c3! 21 ♗e2 ♕c2+ 22 ♔a1 ♕c3+ is perpetual) 20...♗b4.

c1222) Or 19...♗f6 20 ♘b3 ♕a4 21 ♖d3.

c123) 17 ♘b3 ♕a4 18 gxf5 ♖ac8 19 ♗c7 ♕xb3 when:

c1231) 20 ♗g2 gets hit by 20...♖d6! Fritz (not 20...♗d6? 21 ♗xd5; or 20...♗f6 21 ♖d2 ♗e5 22 ♗xd5 ♖xd5 23 ♕xd5 ♗xb2+ 24 ♔b1! and wins) 21 ♕c2 ♕xc2+ 22 ♔xc2 ♖xc7+ 23 ♔b3, which is conceivably slightly better for White but certainly not more.

c1232) 20 ♖d3! looks best, forcing a better ending after 20...♕c4+! (20...♕a2? is asking for too much: it loses to 21 ♖c3 ♗f6 22 ♗xd8 ♖xc6 23 ♗xf6 ♖xc3+ 24 ♗xc3) 21 ♕xc4 (21 ♖c3 ♕xc6 22 ♖xc6 ♖d7 is equal) 21...bxc4 22 ♗xd8 cxd3+ 23 ♔d2 ♗xd8 24 ♗xd3 with a clear plus.

c2) So instead Black should recapture with the rook, i.e. 15...♖xd5! 16 ♔b1 ♕b6 (16...♖c5?! 17 ♘b3 ♖xc2 18 ♘xa5 ♖xb2+ 19 ♔xb2 ♘xa5 must be better for White, but the exposed position of the white king does give Black some compensation) 17 ♗g2 ♖c5 18 ♕d3.

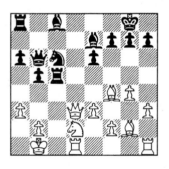

Black has some short-term difficulties, particularly the threat of b4, but if he can circumvent these then he will have a perfectly good game:

c21) If 18...b4 the best may be the illogical-looking 19 axb4 ♘xb4 (19...♕xb4 20 ♘b3 ♗b7 21 ♘xc5 ♗xc5 is clearly better for White) 20 ♘c4!! (this delicious move, found, of course, by Fritz, seals White's advantage) 20...♘xd3 21 ♘xb6 ♘xf4 22 ♗xa8 ♘d5 23 ♘xd5 exd5 24

♗xd5 and wins.

c22) 18...e5 19 ♗g3 (19 b4 exf4 20 bxc5 ♗xc5 21 ♘e4 is unclear) 19...b4 20 ♘c4 ♖xc4 21 ♕xc4 bxa3 22 ♖d2 looks pretty good for White.

c23) 18...a5 looks best when:

c231) 19 ♘b3 ♖c4 20 ♗xc6 achieves nothing after 20...♖xc6 – but not 20...♕xc6? 21 ♘xa5! ♖xa5 22 ♕d8+ ♗f8 and either 23 ♕xa5!?, allowing counterplay after 23...e5 24 ♗g3 b4, or the safer 23 ♗d6 h6 24 ♕xf8+ ♔h7.

c232) 19 ♖c1 can even be met by 19...♖xc1+!? 20 ♖xc1 ♗b7, when 21 ♕d7? ♖d8 22 ♖xc6 ♖xd7! (not 22...♗xc6? 23 ♕xe7 ♖d2 24 ♗c7 ♕b7 25 ♔c1 ♖d3 26 ♗e4! winning for White) 23 ♖xb6 ♗xg2 looks good for Black.

c233) 19 ♗d6 ♗xd6 20 ♕xd6 ♗b7 is also perfectly playable for Black, since if 21 ♖c1 (21 ♘e4 or 21 ♘b3 would both be met by 21...♖c4) 21...♖xc1+ 22 ♖xc1 ♖d8 23 ♕c5 ♕xc5 24 ♖xc5 ♖d2 25 ♗xc6 (not 25 ♖xb5? ♗a6 26 ♖b6 ♗d3+ 27 ♔c1 ♖xf2 28 ♗xc6 ♔f8) 25...♗xc6 26 ♖xc6 ♔f8 or 26...h5 the rook ending is fine for him.

14 g5! 0:53

After this obvious reply, Black has a very hard choice. I presume that Nigel was originally intending 14...♘h5 but lost confidence in it and so retreated.

14 ... ♘e8 1:25

14...♘h5 would be much more desirable if it were possible. However, after 15 ♗h2! Black's centre is collapsing and the knight on h5 is loose. The lines are rather complex, but after very helpful analysis with former Women's World Champion Xie Jun, I now believe that White has at least a couple of ways to get the advantage. Black must try 15...dxc4 (15...d4 16 ♘b3 ♕b6 17 ♘d5; 15...♗xg5 16 ♘b3 ♕b6 17 ♘xd5 ♕a7 18 ♗e2 ♘f6 19 ♖hg1 wins – Nunn) 16 ♘xc4 ♕c7! (not 16...♖xd1+? 17 ♕xd1 when the knight on h5 hangs) and now:

a) Taking the exchange at once with 17 ♘d5?! ♖xd5 18 ♖xd5 ♗e6 looks extremely foolhardy. Black emerges well developed and with dangerous pressure on the c-file, though there is no obvious immediate blow after, for example, 19 ♖d2 ♖c8 20 ♔b1.

b) 17 ♖xd8+ is much more enticing since White keeps many threats. 17...♕xd8! is forced as 17...♗xd8? gets stampeded by 18 ♘d5 and after either 18...♕b8 or 18...♕d7 19 ♘db6 wins. The obvious continuation after 17...♕xd8! is 18 ♗e2 g6! (not 18...♗e6? 19 ♖d1 ♕c7 20 ♘d5 ♗xd5 21 ♖xd5 g6 22 ♘xe5 ♖c8 23 ♘xc6 ♕xc6 24 ♕xc6 ♖xc6+ 25 ♔d2 and wins) 19 ♖d1 ♕f8.

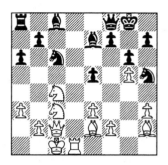

This position would be over at once were it not for the crucial counterblow ...♗f5:

b1) If 20 ♘b6 ♗f5! (not the submissive 20...♖b8? 21 ♗g4! ♗xg4 22 hxg4 ♘g7 23 ♘d7) and:

b11) 21 e4 leads to a great deal of mess:

b111) 21...♗xg5+ 22 ♔b1 ♘d4 23 ♕d3! (23 ♖xd4 leads to only a slight edge after 23...exd4 24 exf5 dxc3 25 ♘xa8 ♕xa8 26 fxg6 hxg6 27 ♗xh5 gxh5 28 ♕xc3) 23...♘xe2 24 ♕xe2 ♗xh3 25 ♘xa8 ♕xa8 26 ♕d3! (26 ♖g1 ♗f4 27 ♕xh5 ♗xh2 28 ♕xh3 ♗xg1 29 ♕g2 ♗xf2 30 ♕xf2 is unclear; while if 26 ♗xe5 ♕e8! is annoying) 26...♗e6 27 ♗xe5 yields a big advantage.

b112) 21...♘d4 is a better move order, e.g. 22 ♖xd4 exd4 and now 23 exf5 ♗xg5+ 24 ♔b1 leads to variation b111, note to White's 23rd move. Instead White can try to improve with 23 ♘cd5! (Xie) but after 23...♗xg5+ 24 f4 ♗xe4! 25 ♕xe4 ♖e8 is unclear since if 26

Wc2 (26 Wxd4? Rxe2 27 fxg5 Rxh2 wins for Black; 26 Wg2 Wc5+ 27 Kb1 Bd8 28 Nd7 Wd6) Black can keep his pawn structure intact with 26...d3 (26...Bd8 27 Bxh5 gxh5 looks vile) and if 27 Wxd3 (27 Bxd3 Re1+ 28 Kd2 Rh1 29 fxg5 Rxh2+ 30 Be2 Wd8 looks worse) 27...Nxf4 28 Bxf4 Bxf4+ 29 Nxf4 Wc5+ 30 Nc4 b5 31 Nd5 Re6.

b12) The self pin 21 Ne4?, hoping to unravel with Nf6+ in a couple of moves, is unsound: 21...Rd8 22 Bxh5 gxh5 23 Nf6+ (23 Rxd8 Wxd8 24 Nf6+ Bxf6 25 Wxf5 Bxg5 and 26 Nd7 fails to the vicious 26...Nd4; while after 23 Nd5 Bg6 the bishop is very powerful) 23...Bxf6 24 Wxf5 Wc5+!

b13) My original feeling was that the simple 21 Bd3!? would lead to a clear edge. But after 21...Bxd3 22 Rxd3 Rd8 23 Ne4 although the horse is superb on e4, Black can challenge it at once with 23...f5! 24 gxf6 Nxf6, which is only a little better at most – the bishop on h2 is out of play.

The conclusion is that if line b112 holds up for Black then 20 Nb6 doesn't work.

b2) In contrast, I originally seriously underestimated 20 Bxh5, which stops ...Bf5 and doubles the h-pawns but at the cost of the two bishops and some potential weakness on the light squares. 20...gxh5 is

forced (20...Bf5? doesn't work now due to 21 e4 Nd4 22 Wd3 Be6 23 Bg4 and wins) and here Xie Jun suggested the overwhelmingly sensible 21 Nxe5!, liberating the dormant bishop, when:

b21) 21...Nxe5 22 Bxe5 Bxh3 23 Nd5 Rc8 24 Bc3! (Xie) intending We4-e5 is tremendous.

b22) 21...Bxh3 22 Nxc6 bxc6 23 We4!, to prevent ...Wc8 followed by ...Bf5 and intending to move the queen and bring up Ne4, is more complex but also extremely good.

b3) 20 Bg4 to defend the h-pawn and prevent ...Bf5, is a more subtle idea.. And this also suffices for a pleasant advantage in lines like 20...Ng7 21 Nxe5 and:

b31) 21...Bxg4 22 hxg4 Nxe5 23 Bxe5 Bxg5 avoids a sickly c6-pawn but leaves White superbly centralised, i.e. 24 f4 Be7 and both 25 Nd5 and the greedy 25 Rd7 Rc8 26 Rxb7 look good.

b32) 21...Bxg5 22 Nxc6 bxc6 23 Ne4 Be7 and White should be able to win the c-pawn.

During the game I also managed to get worked up about 14...Ne4, since I couldn't really see his idea and were the queen sacrifice after 15 Nb3 Wxc3 to work then the game would go round the planet in minutes. But of course White can defend and liquidate to a clear advantage, e.g. 16 bxc3 ♗xa3+ (16...♗f5 17 ♔b2) 17 ♔b1 ♗f5 18 ♔a2! (not 18 ♗d3?? dxc4 19 ♗xe4 cxb3) 18...♗b4 19 ♗xe5. This is the sort of line I tend to see in a game, without of course really knowing what's going on. In fact Black can win back the queen, but at too great a cost, with 19...d4 (19...dxc4 20 ♗xc4 ♘xc3+ 21 ♕xc3 ♗xc3 22 ♗xc3 leaves White a piece up) 20 ♖xd4 ♘xd4 21 ♗xd4 ♘xc3+ (if 21...♖xd4 22 cxb4!) 22 ♕xc3 (22 ♗xc3 ♗xc2 23 ♗xb4 is also good) 22...♗xc3 23 ♗xc3.

15 ♘b3!? 1:04

15 ♘xd5!? was another way to win the exchange, but after 15...exf4 16 ♘b3 ♖xd5! 17 cxd5 ♕a4!? Black has play.

15 ... ♕b6 1:26
16 ♘xd5 1:09 **♖xd5!** 1:26
17 cxd5 1:10 **exf4** 1:26
18 dxc6 1:11 **fxe3** 1:27

At the moment, White is a whole exchange up. In compensation, Black has some potential play against the white king and the two bishops; and White's pawn structure is very ragged. So I played:

19 fxe3! 1:17

Not to take a pawn but rather to open the f-file for an attack against f7. White certainly mustn't sit back and relax but rather must continue as violently as possible.

19 ... ♗xg5 1:28

20 ♔b1! 1:19 **bxc6!?** 1:34

I remember being very pleased with this since now I gain more time and the c-file is closed. 20...♗f6 looks better; and if 21 ♗c4 ♕xc6 White is much better but still has to deal out the decisive blow.

21 ♗c4! 1:24

Taking aim at f7.

21 ... ♖a7 1:38
22 ♖hf1 1:27

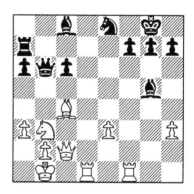

22 ... ♗f6? 1:39

The losing move. After 22...♖e7 23 ♘d4, threatening ♘xc6, is very strong, though there is still lots of fight left. The most combative reply is 23...♗xh3, but as long as White sticks to his guns and plays ♖xf7 at some time then the tactics will always favour him. For example:

a) 24 ♖h1 ♖xe3 25 ♖xh3 ♖xh3 26 ♕f5 (or 26 ♗xf7+ ♔xf7 27 ♕f5+ ♗f6 28 ♕xh3 with a clear plus) 26...♘d6! 27 ♗xf7+ (27 ♖e1? ♖h1; 27 ♕xh3 ♘xc4 28 ♕c8+ ♕d8 29 ♕xc6 is a mess) 27...♘xf7 28 ♕xh3 and White is on top.

b) 24 ♖xf7!? ♖xf7 25 ♖h1! (25 ♗xf7+? ♔xf7 26 ♕xh7 ♗g4! defends) 25...♗xe3 and either 26 ♕e4 ♗d7 27 ♕xe3 or even better 26 ♘xc6 ♘d6 27 ♖xh3 ♗h6 28 ♘e5 ♘xc4 29 ♕xc4 ♕g1+ 30 ♔a2 ♕f1 31 ♕d5 ♕f5 32 ♖f3 ♗f4 33 ♕xf7+.

c) 24 ♘xc6 ♖c7 25 ♖xf7! is not only thematic but also good. One particularly rattractive line goes 25...♖xf7 26 ♘e5 ♗e6 (26...♘d6 27 ♖xd6! ♕xd6 28 ♘xf7 and wins) 27 ♘xf7 when both recaptures favour White:

c1) 27...♔xf7 is prosaic, e.g. 28 ♕f5+ ♘f6 (28...♗f6? 29 ♗xe6+ ♕xe6 30 ♖d7+ wins the queen) 29 ♗xe6+ (29 ♖d7+ ♔e8 30 ♗xe6 g6!) 29...♕xe6 30 ♕xg5 with a big advantage to White.

c2) 27...♗xf7 leads to the spectacular 28 ♖d7 ♗xc4 29 ♕xc4+ ♔h8 30 ♖f7! (30 ♕f7? ♕g6+) 30...♕d6 (30...♕g6+ 31 e4 doesn't help) 31 ♕c6!

23 ♕e4! 1:28

This is decisive since the natural reply 23...♖e7 (23...♗e6 24 ♗xe6 ♖e7 25 ♗xf7+ ♔xf7 26 ♕c4+ ♔f8 would be absolutely hopeless) is poleaxed by 24 ♕xe7! ♗xe7 25 ♖xf7. I remembered this as being absolutely over, but when I started to re-examine the game eight years later, I was surprised to find that Black can still fight a

bit:

a) 25...♘f6 26 ♖xf6+ (26 ♖xe7+ ♔f8 27 ♖f7+ ♔e8 28 ♖xg7 complicates the issue) 26...♔h8 27 ♖f7 ♕c7 28 ♘c5 h5 29 ♘e6 ♗xe6 (29...♕b7 30 ♖d8+ ♗xd8 31 ♖xb7 ♗xb7 32 ♘xd8 wins) 30 ♗xe6 and wins the bishop as well.

b) 25...♔h8 26 ♖xe7 ♘f6 and now:

b1) 27 ♖d6 ♗f5+ (27...h5 28 ♖xf6 gxf6 29 ♖e8+ ♔g7 30 ♖xc8 ♕xe3 is clearly better for White) 28 ♔a2 h5 is still very messy.

b2) But 27 ♔a2! is the very cleanest, i.e. 27...h5 (27...♗xh3 loses to a back-rank trick 28 ♖b7! ♕xe3 29 ♖d8+ ♘e8 30 ♗f7) 28 ♖g1! ♗xh3 29 ♖gxg7 ♕d8 30 e4 etc.

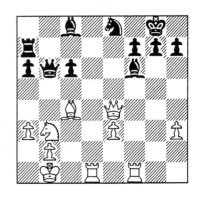

23	...	♔f8 1:51
24	♕xh7 1:29	g6 1:51
25	e4 1:34	c5 1:52
26	e5 1:36	♗g7 1:52
27	e6! 1:37	**1-0**

Short resigned in view of 27...♗xe6 28 ♕xg6.

Game 22
N.Short–J.Speelman
London (4th matchgame) 1988
Pirc Defence, Austrian Attack

Before the match, I had also done some work with Nigel Davies. Nigel is a somewhat idiosyncratic player, who at that time was doing very well as Black with various dark square systems involving an early ...g6 and ... ♗g7; systems that I had had the opportunity to observe in action a couple of years earlier when we played together in a small open tournament in Cala d'Or in Majorca.

At that time Spain, today a chess superpower, was still relatively undeveloped. So, like England in the early seventies, it was fair game for foreign pillage. While I did perfectly well in the tournament, I had envied Nigel the tremendous positions he regularly obtained as Black right out of the opening, indeed some of his white opponents didn't even survive to the early middlegame; and resolved to include the Pirc/Modern complex in my own opening repertoire.

Generally, I had had very good results with it, though my previous Pirc/Modern outing against Nigel Short had lasted just 16 moves: 1 e4 g6 2 d4 d6 3 ♘c3 ♗g7 4 ♗e3 a6 5 a4 ♘f6 6 h3 b6 7 ♘f3 0-0 8 ♗c4 ♘c6 9 e5 ♘e8 10 ♗f4 ♘a5 11 ♗a2 c5 12 dxc5 bxc5 13 0-0 ♖b8 14 exd6 ♘xd6 15 ♘d5 e6?? 16 ♗xd6 1-0 was the offending game (Short-Speelman British Championship, Swansea 1987) – one of my fastest ever losses.

The element of risk was compounded by the fact, known to all parties, that Nigel's second John Nunn had just completed his revision of *The Pirc for the Tournament Player*. But as I said in my notes in *New in Chess*, (which I shall to a great extent be following here) '...with things clearly going my way, Jonathan Tisdall and I felt that some mild provocation was in order.'

1	**e4** 0:00	**d6** 0:02
2	**d4** 0:00	**g6** 0:02
3	**♘c3** 0:01	**♗g7** 0:02
4	**f4** 0:01	

Quite a surprise. 4 f4 seems slightly alien to Nigel's style and so we were more expecting something slightly toxic in the 'Spassky System' as in our game above or perhaps in the Classical.

4	**...**	**♘f6** 0:04
5	**♘f3** 0:01	**0-0** 0:06

At the time 5...c5 was doing well following the sensational game Sax-Seirawan at the Brussels (SWIFT) World Cup in April. After 6 ♗b5+ ♗d7 7 e5 ♘g4 8 e6 Seirawan had unveiled the massive novelty 8...fxc6!! with the point that after 9 ♘g5 ♗xb5 10 ♘xe6 ♗xd4 taking the queen leads only to a draw by perpetual check. After considerable thought Sax acceded with 11 ♘xd8 and they concluded 11...♗f2+ 12 ♔d2 ♗e3+ ½-½ – a game which has since been repeated many times.

There had also been further satisfactory experiences for Black, but it would have taken extraordinary theoretical self-confidence to venture upon this in such an important game against an opponent so heavily armed and with such a second.

6   ♗e2 0:01

A very old move, about which I knew next to nothing. So unusual is it that there is very little coverage in modern opening literature, even in tomes as comprehensive as John Nunn's. But I subsequently discovered that there is an excellent chapter on it in Keene and Botterill's *The Pirc Defence* (1973) – now, of course, out of print for many years.

6   ...   c5 0:13
7   dxc5 0:02   **♕a5** 0:15
8   0-0 0:03   **♕xc5+** 0:18
9   ♔h1 0:03

Of course I wanted to play 9...b5 now but simply didn't believe that it could work. In fact Keene and Botterill give 9...b5 10 e5 dxe5 11 fxe5 ♘g4 12 ♕d5!, after which if 12...♘f2+ 13 ♖xf2 ♕xf2 14 ♕xa8 b4 15 ♘d5 ♕xe2 16 ♗g5! is supposed to be winning. Instead Fritz Nijboer played 18 ♗f4 (it really was move 18 since they'd repeated once with 13 ♔g1 ♘h3+ 14 ♔h2 ♘f2+ 15 ♖xf2) against Zurab Azmaiparashvili in the Reykjavik Open 1990. After a few more moves he had a very dubious position: 18...♔h8 19 ♘xb4 ♕b5 20 c3 a5 21 ♘d4 ♕b6 22 ♘d5 ♕xb2 23 ♖d1 e6 24 ♘e3 ♗b7 25 ♕a7 ♗e4 26 ♕e7 and 'Azmai' won in 53 moves. But the most interesting thing about this is not the exact moves, but rather that Azmai would play 9...b5 at all. If somebody as erudite as Azmai believes in 9...b5 then maybe it isn't so bad after all?

9   ...   ♘c6 0:26

So the choice was between this and 9...♘bd7. But ...♘bd7 looked a much more modern move and, moreover, had alarming similarities with variations of the 6 f4 Najdorf about which Nigel knew a great deal and I next to nothing; so the decision wasn't too difficult.

10   ♗d3 0:10

10 ♕e1 ♗g4 11 ♗d3 transposes back to the game, while in the *BCM* John Nunn noted that it also allows 10...d5 11 e5 ♘e4.

10 ♘d2 a5 11 a4 ♘b4 12 ♘b3 ♛b6 13 g4? ♗xg4! was the famous game Fischer-Korchnoi, Curaçao 1962, which Korchnoi subsequently won.

10 ...   ♗g4 0:35

11 ♛e1 0:10   **♗xf3** 0:40

Getting rid of the knight to prevent the obvious attack with ♘g5 and ♛h4 .

12 ♖xf3 0:14   **♘b4** 0:45

Strangely, this enormously natural move may have been a novelty. Keene and Botterill gave 12...♘d4 13 ♖f1 and now 13...♛h5! is supposedly best and enough to equalise; though it all looks a bit tenuous.

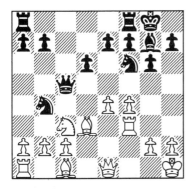

13 ♗e3 0:14   **♘xd3** 0:51

14 cxd3 0:14   **♛b4!?** 0:51

As I wrote in *New in Chess*: 'Trying to irritate White by tilting at the queenside pawns.' From the clock times it is clear that I'd decided on this before taking on d3. 14...♛a5 looks more 'normal'; but provocation was the order of the day.

15 ♖b1 0:21   **a5** 1:01

Not the ideal move, but if 15...♖ac8 I was frightened of 16 ♗xa7 and if 16...b6 17 ♛g1!; while 15...♖fc8 leaves the rooks looking cack-handed and specifically weakens f7.

16 f5 0:30

Seirawan suggested immediate evacuation of the bishop with 16 ♗g1!? and if 16...a4 17 a3 ♛b3 18 d4.

16 ...   ♖ac8?! 1:10

16...a4 first was more logical. I wanted to prevent ♛h4, but this not only doesn't seem too important but wasn't even achieved. Much more relevant, by moving off the a-file I've left the a-pawn badly defended in subsequent lines in which White forces the black queen to flee for her life.

17 ♗g1 0:43

I hadn't prevented 17 ♛h4 anyway since if 17...♖xc3? 18 ♗d2! wins material after, for example, 18...♖fc8 19 ♛e1. 17 ...a4 18 ♖h3 (threatening ♘d5) 18...h5 is therefore necessary. This seriously weakens g6 so that a race will follow between White's attack and Black's queenside counterplay. But the white queen and rook are temporarily, at least, very clumsy; so I imagine it is perfectly good for Black.

But the critical line, on which Nigel spent his 13 minutes, was 17 ♛d1!, a move of which I remained blissfully unaware throughout proceedings. (Don't believe ex- or even present World Champions if they tell you they see everything. It just doesn't happen that way.)

The threat is to trap my queen at once with 18 a3! Now 17...d5 is forced (since if 17...a4 White can simply take it): 18 e5 ♘g4 19 ♘xd5 ♘xe3 20 ♖xe3 ♕c5 21 ♕f3. Nigel rejected this line in view of:

a) 21...♖fd8 but he'd missed 22 ♘xe7+! ♕xe7 23 f6 and:

a1) 23...♕b4? 24 fxg7 ♕xb2 25 ♖f1 ♕xa2 unsurprisingly loses at once to 26 e6, when Black can hang on for only a few more moves: 26...♖c7 (26...f5 27 ♕xb7) 27 ♕f4 ♖e7 (27...♖dc8 28 e7) 28 ♕f6 ♖de8 29 exf7+ ♕xf7 30 ♕xf7+ ♖xf7 31 ♖xe8+.

a2) So 23...♕e6 24 fxg7 is the critical variation and perhaps then 24...♕xa2 since otherwise White remains a pawn up, albeit not an especially good one. I stopped here in *New in Chess*, assessing it as somewhat better for White, but Nunn in the *BCM* went further: 25 ♖f1 (threatening e6) 25...♕e6 26 ♕f6 ♖e8 when White can choose between:

a21) 27 ♖ef3 so that if 27...♕xf6 28 exf6 ♖c2 29 h3 the g7-pawn is very dangerous. If Black tries to attack with 29...♖ee2 then 30 ♖f4 ♖xg2 31 ♖e1 wins immediately.

a22) And 27 ♕g5 is also possible, i.e. 27...♖c2 (27...♔xg7

28 ♖h3!) 28 h3 preparing to attack with ♖f6.

b) 21...♕c1+ 22 ♖e1 is hopeless.

c) As is 21...gxf5 22 d4 ♕c1+ 23 ♖e1 ♕g5 24 ♕xf5.

d) But Tisdall and I did investigate 21...e6 on the rest day. However, we decided that 22 fxe6 fxe6 23 ♘f6+ ♗xf6 (maybe 23...♔h8) 24 exf6 ♖xf6 25 ♕xf6 ♕xe3 26 ♖f1 was extremely unpleasant.

17 ...   a4 1:18

By removing his bishop from the black knight's ambit, Nigel's last move threatened ♕d1 in earnest. Still oblivious to this blow, I rejected 17...e6, the only other move I considered, because of 18 a3 ♕b3 19 d4, when White gets in e5 and f6. But of course 18 ♕d1 is even stronger: 18...d5 19 e5 ♘d7 20 f6 looks horrible for Black.

18 a3 0:47   **♕b3** 1:24

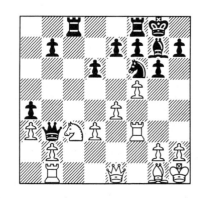

18...♕a5 is also possible since if 19 ♘d5? ♕xe1 20 ♘xe7+ ♔h8 21 ♖xe1 ♖ce8

White loses material. But the queen is more active on b3.

19 &d4 0:56

By defending his knight Short frees the queen, which couldn't leave the first rank in view of ...&xc3. The alternative was 19 d4, which threatens &d5 but loosens the white position. I hadn't yet chosen between 19...&c2 and 19...&c4, but in his notes in the *BCM*, Nunn demonstrates that the former is dubious:

a) 19...&c2?! gets hit by 20 e5 dxe5 21 dxe5 &g4 22 &d5 &fe8 23 e6 gxf5!? 24 exf7+ &xf7 25 &b4! &c4 26 &xf5+ &g8 27 &g3 when Black is very loose, though he can fight off the immediate threats with 27...&e4 28 &bf1 &e5.

b) 19...&c4 20 &d1 &fd8 21 &h4 b5 is still very unclear but looks fairly pleasant for Black to me now. I don't believe that White can either develop a really strong attack or bash through in the centre; but Black has good play on the queenside. John continues with the sample line 22 &h3 h6 23 &e3 and:

b1) 23...g5 24 &xg5 hxg5 25 &xg5 which looks pretty dangerous for Black to me: in return for the piece White has annoying threats on the g-file and has brought Black's counterplay to a halt for the moment.

b2) 23...&b3 looks better, to harass the enemy pieces before allowing the sacrifice. If then

24 &e1 g5 25 &xg5 now fails to 25...hxg5 26 &xg5 when:

b21) 26...&xc3? was my first idea, but 27 &xc3 &xe4 28 &xe7! poleaxes Black.

b22) 26...&xb2! wins, however, after 27 &g3 &h5! 28 &xh5 (28 &d5 &xg3+ 29 hxg3 &xd4 30 &xe7+ &f8 31 &d5 can't possibly work) 28...&xc3 and Black is a tempo ahead: 29 &xg7+ (29 &g4 &d2! wins) 29...&xg7 30 &g5+ &f8 31 f6 exf6 32 &xf6 &e8 escapes the perpetual.

19 ... e6 1:29

Running fairly short of time, I played this committal move quite quickly. It stops any ideas of &xf6 and &d5 stone dead but does weaken the f6-square. I seemed to play this whole game in something of a fugue, choosing moves more through judgement than analysis – usually with me it is the other way round. So in *New in Chess* I wrote that 'I considered 19...e5 as an alternative but wasn't terribly struck on it and felt that if necessary e5 could always be played a move later.'

John Nunn in the *BCM* gives much more cogent analysis. As he points out, Black can play ...e5 followed by ...d5 at various moments in the next move or so. He analyses 19...e5 20 &f2 (20 &e3 d5 21 exd5 &xd5 22 &xd5 &xd5 23 f6 &h8 is unclear) 20...d5 and now:

a) 21 exd5 &xd5 22 &e4

gives White a pleasant edge.

b) 21 ♗h4 d4 22 ♗xf6 dxc3 23 ♗xg7 leads to more forcing play:

b1) 23...c2? loses to 24 ♖c1 ♔xg7 25 f6+ ♔h8 26 ♕h4 (for what it matters, John gave 26 ♕e3 after which 26...g5 27 ♕xg5 ♖g8 at least stops immediate mate; though White can take another pawn with 28 ♕xe5, winning easily since if 28...♖ge8 29 ♕h5 ♕xb2 30 ♕h6 ♖g8 31 ♖h3) 26...♕xb2 27 ♕h6 and Black must play the hopeless 27...♕xc1+ since 27...♖g8 allows mate in two: 28 ♕xh7+ ♔xh7 29 ♖h3.

b2) 23...♔xg7 24 f6+ ♔h8 25 bxc3 ♕xc3 26 ♕e3 is more interesting. Nunn continues with the very plausible:

b21) 26...♖g8? with the idea that if 27 ♕h6? g5 defends through the threat of ...♕c1+; or 27 ♖h3 g5! But White has 27 ♕g5!! when there is absolutely no defence to the threat of ♖h3 followed by ♕h6, e.g. 27...♕xa3 28 ♖h3 ♕f8 29 ♕h4 h5 30 ♕xh5+!

b22) 26...g5! is therefore forced at once with very unclear play which can swing enormously on a single tactic. For instance, if 27 ♕xg5 ♖g8 28 ♕h6 (28 ♕h4?? allows 28...♕c2 29 ♖g1 ♕xg2+! and mates) Black has a nasty hit not with the obvious 28...♖g6? 29 ♕h3 ♖cg8?! 30 g3!, re-establishing co-ordination, but

rather 28...♕c2 29 ♖g1 ♖xg2! 30 ♖g3 (30 ♕xh7+ ♔xh7 31 ♖h3+ ♔g6 32 ♖xg2+ ♕xg2+ 33 ♔xg2 looks very unpleasant for White) 30...♖xg3 31 hxg3 ♖g8 with a big advantage.

Finally, instead of moving the e-pawn at all, 19...b5 was also well worth considering, to avoid weakening the f6 point.

20 ♕g1?! 1:08

20 ♕h4? loses a piece to 20...e5 21 ♖h3 h5 or 21...h6! (21...exd4? is much less clear after 22 ♘d5 ♘h5 23 g4) 22 ♗e3 ♖xc3.

And, as Nunn points out, 20 ♕d2?, is a bad square since 20...e5 21 ♗f2 d5 22 ♗h4 d4 23 ♗xf6 now loses in view of 23...dxc3, while if 21 ♗g1 d5 22 exd5 ♘xd5 23 ♘e4 Black has a tempo with 23...♖c2.

But Nigel spent what seemed ages but was actually just twelve minutes on 20 ♕f1! which he rejected because of

a) 20...♘xe4? which I had vaguely seen was possible but strongly mistrusted. In subsequent analysis, Tisdall and I established that it does indeed lose to 21 ♗xg7! (21 dxe4 ♗xd4 22 ♘d5 exd5 23 ♖xb3 axb3 is much less convincing) 21...♘d2 22 ♕c1! ♘xb1 23 ♕h6 ♘xc3 (23...♖xc3 24 ♖f1 is simple) 24 ♖f1 ♘d5

(see following diagram)

25 ♗h8!! (the move Nigel

had missed) 25...♔xh8 26 fxg6 ♘f6 27 g7+ ♔g8 28 gxf8♕+ ♖xf8 29 ♕g5+ ♔h8 30 ♕xf6+ ♔g8 31 h3 and the horribly exposed king will most likely quickly be beheaded. Certainly after 31...♕xd3 (perhaps 31...♕d5 but it is pretty grim) 32 ♖f3 ♕g6 33 ♕c3 ♕b1+ 34 ♔h2 e5 (34...f6 35 ♕c7 ♔h8 36 ♕e7 finishes things off) 35 ♕c7!, and the threat of ♖g3+ followed by ♕e7 is immediately decisive.

b) 20...e5 was my bail out *in extremis*, but after 21 ♗f2 d5 White should choose the simple

b1) 22 exd5! ♘xd5 23 ♘e4 with a nice safe advantage.

b2) Instead 22 ♗h4 d4 23 ♗xf6 dxc3 24 bxc3 ♕xc3 25 ♗xg7 ♔xg7 is less good. With the queen on f1, White can't attack on the dark squares. There is some pressure against f7 but after 26 fxg6 (not 26 ♖xb7 ♕xa3 27 fxg6? ♖c1 and Black wins) 26...hxg6 27 ♖xb7 ♖c7 28 ♖xc7 (28 d4 ♕xf3 29 gxf3 ♖xb7 doesn't look dangerous for Black) 28...♕xc7

White's ragged pawn structure and temporary lack of co-ordination, allied to the strong black pawn on a4, give Black very reasonable compensation.

20 ... b5 1:31

The natural move, preparing to undermine Black's queenside structure. Nigel now took ten minutes to play:

21 g4 1:19

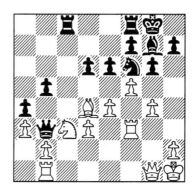

Here I was really rather lucky. After just four minutes I lashed out with:

21 ... ♘xg4!? 1:35

Not a bad move, particularly in time trouble, but the four minutes were spent on calculating the consequences of White attempting to mate Black and nothing else.

After 22 ♗xg7 ♔xg7 23 ♕xg4 ♖xc3, 24 fxe6 ♖c7 looked absolutely fine and 24 ♕h3 exf5 25 exf5 ♖c5 defends, so I concentrated on 24 f6+ ♔h8 when if:

a) 25 ♕g5? ♖xd3 26 ♕h6 ♖g8 and wins.

b) 25 ♖h3 ♖xd3 26 ♖xh7+ ♔xh7 27 ♕h4+ ♔g8 28 ♕h6 ♖d1+ 29 ♖xd1 ♕f3+ 30 ♔g1 ♕xd1+ (30...♕xf6 is enough to assess the variation as decisive for Black) 31 ♔g2 ♕e2+ and after a couple more checks Black will be able to capture the f6-pawn.

c) 25 ♕h3! is critical when:

c1) 25...h5? is obviously very dangerous, and indeed after 26 ♕g3 White seems to be winning:

c11) 26...♕c2 27 ♖e1 ♕xb2 (27...♖c5 28 d4 h4 – if the rook moves ♕g5 wins – 29 ♕xd6! wins) 28 ♕g5 ♔h7 29 ♖h3.

c12) 26...♖c5 27 d4 ♕c2 28 ♖e1 transposes.

c13) 26...♖fc8 27 ♕g5 ♔h7 28 ♖h3.

c2) 25...♖c5! is of course the move you look at from afar. I decided that 26 ♕h6 (26 d4? ♕c2!) 26...♖g8 is obviously not losing for Black; though, as Short later pointed out, White can draw with 27 ♖h3 ♖h5 28 ♖xh5 gxh5 29 ♖g1! ♖xg1+ 30 ♔xg1 ♕d1+.

I felt that with twenty moves to make in less than half an hour that was enough calculation and so hardly considered any alternatives for Black. At first glance these look dire, but when I re-examined the game recently I wasn't nearly so sure. Black can try:

a) 21...h6? weakens the g6-square. White should reply 22 h4! when:

a1) 22...♘xg4? 23 f6 ♘xf6 24 ♗xf6 ♗xf6 25 ♖xf6 is much worse than in the game since Black must lose a tempo to prevent ♖xg6+, e.g. 25...♔g7 26 ♕d4 e5? 27 ♕xd6 ♖xc3 28 ♕xe5 ♖c5 29 ♖xg6+ ♔xg6 30 ♖g1+ ♔h7 31 ♕g7 mate.

a2) 22...e5 is considerably worse than in the variations below. I'll return to it after examining them.

b) 21...e5 looks ridiculous but seems to be playable because of various tactical finesses made possible by the temporary looseness of the white position:

b1) 22 g5 exd4 23 gxf6 dxc3 24 fxg7 ♔xg7 25 f6+ ♔h8 26 bxc3 ♕xc3 27 ♕g5 ♖c5 defends. After 28 ♕h6 ♖g8 and if 29 ♖h3 ♖h5 Black is doing well.

So the bishop must move:

b2) 22 ♗a7 and:

b21) Now the obvious 22...♘xg4? is bad after 23 ♘d5 when if:

b211) 23...♘f6 24 ♘e7+ ♔h8 25 ♘xc8 ♖xc8 Black doesn't have enough for the exchange.

b212) Black can try to complicate with something like 23...gxf5 24 ♖bf1 ♖c2, but after 25 ♖h3 he is soon dispatched after, for example, 25...♖a8 26 ♘e7+ and 27 ♘xf5; or 25...♔h8 26 ♖xf5 ♖g8 27 ♘e7 ♖e8 28 ♕xg4 ♖xe7 29 ♖fh5.

b22) But Black has a trick 22...d5! based on the fact that

after 23 g5 (23 exd5 ♘xd5 24 ♘e4 is better but a pretty good version for Black) 23...dxe4 24 dxe4 ♘xe4 is possible due to the pin on the third rank. If then 25 f6 ♘d2 26 fxg7 ♖fd8 White is very loose – unless the knight can get into play he is in trouble) Instead of 24 dxe4, 24 ♖e3 ♘d5 25 ♘xd5 ♕xd5 26 dxe4 ♕b7 is good for Black and 24 gxf6 exf3 25 fxg7 ♔xg7 is unclear.

b3) 22 ♗f2 d5 is very similar to b2.

b4) But if White instead plays 22 ♗e3 then now there is no pin on the third rank, so:

b41) 22...d5? 23 g5 dxe4 24 dxe4 is bad. Black can try 24...♘xe4 but it fails to 25 ♘xe4 ♕d5 26 ♕g4! (26 ♘d2? gxf5 is unclear) 26...♖c4 27 ♘c3!! ♕d3 28 ♕g1! defending the rook on b1 and threatening to co-ordinate with ♖d1.

b42) But now 22...♘xg4! is playable because the natural 23 ♘d5? is a blunder, allowing ♕xd3, and 23 ♕xg4 ♖xc3 24 f6 ♗h8 seems good for Black, because in the obvious attacking line 25 ♕h4 ♖xd3 26 ♖h3 Black wins with 26...♖d1+! (but not, of course, 26...h5?? 27 ♕xh5! gxh5 28 ♖g1+ and mate in two).

Returning now to line a2. After the weakening 21...h6 22 h4 e5 23 ♗e3! ♘xg4 24 ♕xg4! ♖xc3 25 f6 is now strong, in contrast to line b42 above. After

either variation a21 or a22 below White wins a piece for what must be inadequate compensation:

a21) 25...♖xd3 26 fxg7 ♔xg7 27 ♖e1.

a22) 25...h5 26 ♕g1! (not 26 ♕g5? ♗h8 27 ♖g1 ♖xd3 28 ♕xh5 ♖d1! repelling the attack) 26...♖xd3 27 fxg7 ♔xg7 28 ♖bf1.

a23) Retreating the bishop is now disastrous: 25...♗h8 26 h5 g5 27 ♗xg5! crashes through, e.g. 27...hxg5 28 ♕xg5+ ♔h7 29 ♖g1 ♖xd3 30 ♕f5+ ♔h6 31 ♖g6+! ♔h7 32 ♖g7+ ♔h6 33 ♖h7 mate.

Nigel now thought for more than half of his remaining time before replying:

22 f6 1:40

I remember that I was off-stage when the realisation hit me that he could win a piece. At first I was shocked and wondered why he was taking so long to see it, but by the time he made his move I'd realised that it would be quite playable for me. Had I had the misfortune to foresee 22 f6 – and the reason it is (slightly) hard to see is that the knight has just vacated the square – then I would have wasted quite a while in the diagram position looking at the alternatives; and probably ended up playing 21...♘g4 anyway; but with much less time left than in the game.

22 ... ♘xf6 1:37

Of course not 22...♗xf6? 23 ♖xf6.

23	♗xf6 1:40	♗xf6 1:37
24	♖xf6 1:40	b4! 1:38
25	axb4 1:46	a3 1:38

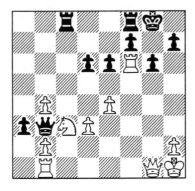

Despite White's extra piece, Black has excellent chances of holding the game. He will not only be able to eliminate all the queenside pawns but also one of White's centre pawns. A likely result will be an ending of rook knight and h-pawn against rook and f-, g- and h-pawn which would be an easy draw.

Today, I would be worried about playing this position against a computer, which, unafraid of checks and hurricane fast at calculation, might well find a way to co-ordinate the white forces effectively. But of course, Nigel was under great pressure due to the match situation and, moreover, was drifting into time trouble. Under those circumstances Black's position is fully playable.

| 26 | ♕d1 1:46 | ♕xb4 1:39 |

| 27 | ♖f2 1:47 |

27 ♕a4 would get hit by 27...♕b6! and if 28 ♕xa3 28...♖a8 29 ♘a4 ♕d4 and wins; or 28 bxa3 ♕d8 29 ♕d4 e5.

| 27 | ... | axb2 1:43 |

In principle one would prefer to keep the tension with 27...♕d4, but after 28 ♖c2 axb2 29 ♘e2 ♕e3 30 ♖cxb2 White has regained his co-ordination.

| 28 | ♘a2 | ♕d4 |
| 29 | ♖fxb2 1:47 |

It was also possible to take with the other rook, but 29...d5 would still be playable for Black. In any case, White's mistakes come later.

| 29 | ... | d5 1:44 |
| 30 | ♖b4?! 1:48 |

Much too ambitious. Nigel's problem was that in view of the match situation he felt he had to win; so he avoided solid moves in the hope of gaining more. I'd expected either 30 ♕f3 or 30 ♕e2!?, when if, for example, 30...dxe4 31 ♕xe4 (31 dxe4!?) 31...♖fd8 32 ♕xd4 ♖xd4 33 ♖b8 ♖xb8 34 ♖xb8+ ♔g7, I felt that Black should be able to draw without undue difficulty.

| 30 | ... | ♕a7 1:47 |
| 31 | ♘c1?! 1:49 |

Nunn prefers 31 ♖a4.

| 31 | ... | dxe4 1:48 |
| 32 | dxe4?! 1:48 |

It was imperative to recapture with the rook, but, as Nunn explains, Short was still pursuing the elusive win and reasoned that by keeping the e-pawn he could later aim to set up the pawn on e5 and transfer the knight to f6. 32 dxe4 might be reasonable in a postal game or played by a computer, but it was madness for a human being in time trouble. Instead 32 ♖xe4 ♕a8 should be fine for Black.

32 ...   ♕e3! 1:50

White is on the brink. In fact he can still defend and indeed play for the advantage with either 33 ♘b3, and if 33...♖fd8 34 ♕f1 ♖c2 35 ♖e1! ♕h6 36 ♖e2; or even 33 ♘d3, and if 33...♖fd8 34 ♖1b3 but neither of us saw anything clearly at the time. Instead Nigel panicked with:

33 ♕g1? 1:56

The losing move.

33 ...   ♕f3+ 1:53
34 ♕g2 1:56   **♕d1+** 1:55
35 ♕g1 1:55   **♖fd8** 1:57

Luckily I had a way to improve while definitely keeping the perpetual. There is now no good defence to the threat of ...♕f3+ and ...♖d1. At this point

the excitement got too much and I finally stopped recording all the clock times.

36 ♘b3

If 36 ♘a2 ♕f3+ 37 ♕g2 ♖d1+ 38 ♖xd1 ♕xd1+ 39 ♕g1 ♕f3+ 40 ♕g2 ♕xg2+ 41 ♔xg2 ♖c2+; or 36 ♖4b3 ♖xc1!; while 36 ♖4b2 doesn't prevent the threat of 36...♕f3+ 37 ♖g2 ♖d1.

36 ...   ♕f3+
37 ♕g2   ♖d1+ 1:58
38 ♖xd1   ♕xd1+
39 ♕g1   ♕e2 1:58
40 h3

Or 40 ♕a1 e5 41 ♔g1 ♕g4+ 42 ♔h1 ♕f3+ 43 ♔g1 ♖c2 44 ♖b8+ ♔g7 45 ♕xe5+ ♔h6 and wins.

40 ...   ♖c2 1:59

And after a few minutes' thought, Nigel resigned. This was the first time that either of us had beaten the other with Black in a proper tournament game. Of course, I was lucky in that I missed some very dangerous moves and it turned out not to matter. Had I seen everything in advance then I would have been immensely proud of this game, but even so I have a serious soft spot for it.

There is a slightly dreamlike quality to some of my play – the way reasonable positional moves held up if not completely, at least to a sufficient degree, against all sorts of direct threats – which would not normally appear if I were more on the planet and calculating rationally. This is not the way I usually aspire to play chess, but steering by instinct does lead to a good flowing course, even if the barnacles underneath the craft are constantly alarmed by hidden reefs, barely avoided.

Game 23
J.Speelman–N.Short
London (5th matchgame) 1988
Catalan Opening

1 ♘f3 0:02

Of course we had no idea how Nigel would try to play this game. He had seemed pretty shattered after the end of the previous game, but chessplayers are tough people, none more so than Nigel; so we were certainly expecting some serious trouble. One of the advantages of 1 ♘f3 is that, as Tisdall put it in *New in Chess*: 'A wise and wily Swede once told me that this was a good choice against Stonewall Dutch players. That is how Seirawan chose to exit the cycle against Speelman, and Short, of course, has tried it before.'

1 ... ♘f6 0:04
2 c4 0:03 **e6!?** 0:08

Offering another battle in the Queen's Gambit, but they can't have been too surprised when I opted instead for a Catalan.

3 g3 0:06 **d5** 0:09
4 ♗g2 0:08 **dxc4** 0:09

Nigel decides to play it simple and hope that the tension will get to me later.

5 ♕c2!? 0:10

Polugayevsky had recently been doing rather well with this move. For instance, 5...c5 6 ♘a3 ♘c6 7 ♘xc4 ♕c7 8 d3 ♘d5 9 0-0 ♗e7 10 a3 ♘d4 11 ♘xd4 cxd4 12 ♗d2 0-0 13 ♖ac1 ♗f6 14 ♕b3 ♕d7 15 ♖c2 b6 16 ♗f4 ♗b7 17 ♗e5 ♗xe5 18 ♘xe5 ♕d6 19 ♘f3 e5 20 ♖fc1 ♖ad8 21 ♘d2 ♗a8 22 a4 h6 23 a5 ♖b8 24 axb6 axb6 25 ♕b5 ♖fd8 26 ♖a1 ♘c7 27 ♕c4 ♗xg2 28 ♔xg2 ♘e6 29 ♕c6 ♕e7 30 ♖a6 ♖d6 31 ♖a8 ♖xc6 32 ♖xb8+ ♔h7 33 ♖xc6 ♕b4 34 ♖c2 ♕d6 35 ♖cc8 ♕d5+ 36 f3 b5 37 ♔f2 ♘c5 38 ♖d8 ♕c6 39 ♖dc8 ♕d5 40 h4 b4 41 ♖d8 ♘d7 42 ♖bc8 ♕e6 43 ♘e4 f6 44 ♖c7 1-0 Polugayevsky-H.Olafsson, Akureyri 1988.

5 ... a6 0:13
6 ♘e5 0:14 **♘d5!** 0:20

This excellent move neutralises White's slightly pretentious scheme.

7 ♘xc4 0:22 **b5** 0:24
8 ♘e3 0:27

The critical point of the game. Under the extreme stress of the occasion, I was pretty nervous about 8...♗b7 when Black has a free game. There is nothing obviously better than 9 ♘xd5 ♗xd5 10 ♗xd5 ♕xd5 11 0-0 and here I believe I started to wind myself up about 11...♘c6. Instead in a game five years later, Epishin played 11...♕c6 against Polugayevsky – a move I also have a vague memory of having noticed – and they quite quickly drew: 12 ♕c3 b4 13 ♕xc6+ ♘xc6 14 e3 0-0-0 15 a3 ♔b7 16 ♖d1 a5 17 ♔f1 ♗e7 18 ♔e2 ♖d5 19 axb4 axb4 20 d3 ♖hd8 ½-½ Polugayevsky-Epishin, Tilburg 1993. This is a draw based on serious mutual respect. White has the better pawn structure but Black much the better development. With an effort, one could convince oneself one was worse with either colour!

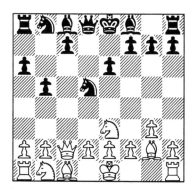

8 ...   ♘xe3?? 0:27
Quite the reverse of the strategy implied by 2...e6 and 4...dxc4. This unbalances the position but greatly in White's

favour. All my nerves disappeared and the rest was relatively painless.

9	**dxe3**	**♖a7**
10	**a4**	**♗b7**
11	**e4**	**♖a8**

11...♘c6 12 0-0 followed by ♗e3 and ♖d1 would be similar.

12	**0-0**	**♗e7**
13	**♖d1**	**♕c8**
14	**♗f4**	**♘c6**
15	**♘a3!**	

Forcing Black to cede the c4-square.

15	**...**	**e5**
16	**♗e3**	**b4**
17	**♘c4**	**0-0**
18	**♖ac1!**	

18 a5 was no doubt also strong, but I didn't want any stray pawns, even one as well guarded as this. Why not keep it simple?

18	**...**	**♖e8**
19	**♘d2**	**♖d8**
20	**♘b3**	**♖xd1+**
21	**♖xd1** 1:12	**♗d6** 1:21
22	**♗c5** 1:17	

The holes on the queenside render Black's position extremely unpleasant. And Nigel's coming attempts to stir up trouble merely exacerbated matters.

22	**...**	**♕e6**
23	**e3**	**♖c8**
24	**♗f1**	**♘e7**
25	**♖c1**	**♕g4**
26	**♗g2**	**h5!?**
27	**♘a5**	**♗a8**
28	**♕c4**	**♗xc5**
29	**♕xc5**	**♘g6**
30	**h3**	**♕e2** 1:42

31 ♕xb4 1:33

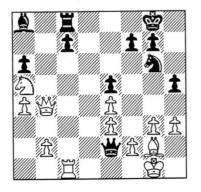

Since this position is not only more or less winning but I was also ahead on time, I decided that it wouldn't be impolite to offer a draw. But after eight more minutes, Nigel resolutely continued.

31	...	**♖d8** 1:50
32	**♗f1**	**♕f3**
33	**♗g2** 1:40	**♕f6** 1:50

Otherwise, I was quite happy shamelessly to repeat.

34	**♘c4**	**♗c6**
35	**♕a5**	**♗e8**
36	**♕xc7**	**♗xa4**
37	**♕b6** 1:46	**♗b5** 1:56

Here Nigel offered a draw himself; an offer I was more than happy to accept, despite White's overwhelming position.

4 Skirting the Precipice

This chapter consists of three examples of the power of the irrational – games in which I succeeded in changing the course of events by a totally unexpected move. It is perhaps no coincidence that I was Black in all three: it is normally only when one is under pressure that one feels the need for such shock tactics.

Actually this generalisation only applies to the latter two games, since in the first against Murray Chandler it was I who was dictating events and deliberately aimed for the combination. For all their charm neither of the other two is very sound. But I don't greatly regret this since in battle one must use all the weapons at one's disposal. And I certainly fared better by skirting the precipice than I would have by meekly awaiting my fate in the valleys below.

Game 24
M.Chandler–J.Speelman
British Championship, Edinburgh 1985
Caro-Kann Defence, Advance variation

1 e4 0:01   c6 0:02
2 d4 0:01   d5 0:03
3 e5 0:02

Not an unwelcome choice since the Advance variation, while quite dangerous, gives Black good long-term prospects.

3 ...   ♝f5 0:06
4 h4 0:03

This has often been played by Boris Spassky. White induces the slightly weakening ...h5, at the cost of his own slight weakness on h4.

Nowadays white players usually follow Nigel Short's deceptively quiet 4 ♘f3 intending ♗e2 and 0-0. Black 'has a good game', but the break ...c5 will lose another tempo and White often manages to whip up a serious attack. The aggressive 4 ♘c3 e6 5 g4 was all the rage for some years but is much less well regarded now.

4 ...   **h5** 0:07
Essential to fight for some space on the kingside, though the g5-square is slightly weakened.

5 c4 0:03   **dxc4** 0:10
Sometimes they play 5...e6 first and only capture on c4 later. But this doesn't seem to have any great advantages; and it is nice to fix the pawn structure with the slightly weak d-pawn, rather than leave White the option of cxd5!?

At one time, it was thought Black could equalise with 5...♗xb1 6 ♖xb1 e6. But this is a very simplistic approach, as Boris Spassky amply demonstrated in a fine win against Yasser Seirawan in the second Phillips and Drew Kings, London 1982: 7 a3 ♘d7 8 ♘f3 g6 9 ♗g5 ♗e7 10 cxd5 cxd5 11 ♗d3 ♖c8 12 0-0 ♔f8 13 ♖c1 ♖xc1 14 ♕xc1 ♔g7 15 ♕f4 ♗xg5 16 ♘xg5 ♘h6 17 ♖c1 ♕b6 18 b4 ♖e8 19 ♖c3 ♖e7 20 ♖c8 ♘g8 21 g4 hxg4 22 h5 f5 23 exf6+ ♘dxf6 24 ♕e5 g3 25 ♖xg8+ ♔xg8 26 ♕xf6 gxf2+ 27 ♔g2 ♕c7 28 ♕xg6+ ♔f8 29 ♕f6+ 1-0.

6 ♗xc4 0:04   **e6** 0:11
7 ♘c3 0:08   **♘d7** 0:17
8 ♘ge2!? 0:13

The idea is to play ♘g3-e4 and then ♗g5, attacking on the dark squares and hoping to get in ♘d6(+).

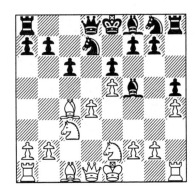

8 ...   **♗e7** 0:38
Eight years later, forgetting exactly what I'd played against Murray, I tried instead 8...♘b6!? against Ekström in a European Club Cup match. This does have the advantage that the bishop has to retreat before it can go to e2. After 9 ♗d3!? (maybe 9 ♗b3) 9...♗xd3 10 ♕xd3 ♕d7 11 ♗g5 f6, he meekly retreated with 12 ♗f4 (the forcing 12 ♘f4 fxg5 13 ♘g6 ♖h6 14 hxg5 ♖xg6 15 ♕xg6+ ♕f7 16 ♕xf7+ ♔xf7 17 ♖xh5 was well worth considering) and the game continued 12...♘e7 13 0-0 ♘ed5 14 ♘e4 ♕f7!? 15 exf6 gxf6 16 ♘d6+? (16 ♗d6 is better, as after 16...0-0-0 17 ♗xf8 ♕xf8 18 ♘c5 White has play against the e6-pawn; while Black must also keep his eye on the h5-pawn if the position begins to simplify)

16...♗xd6 17 ♗xd6 ♖g8 (the g-file and Black's central control give him an edge) 18 ♖fe1 ♕g6 19 ♕h3 ♔d7 20 ♗c5 ♖ae8 21 ♗xb6!? axb6 22 a4 ♖e7 23 ♕f3 ♖eg7 24 g3 ♕f5! 25 ♔g2 ♖g4 26 ♕xf5 exf5 27 ♔f3 ♖e8 28 ♖ed1! (forced)

28...f4! 29 gxf4 (if 29 ♘xf4 ♘xf4 30 gxf4 ♖xh4) 29...f5 30 a5 bxa5 31 ♖xa5 ♖xh4 32 ♖g1 ♖g4 33 ♖ga1 h4 34 ♖a7 ♔c7 35 ♖a8 ♖gg8 36 ♖xe8 ♖xe8 37 ♖g1 ♘b4 38 ♖g7+ ♔b6 39 ♘c3 ♘d3! (threatening 40...♘e1 mate) 40 ♔g2 ♘xf4+ 41 ♔h2 ♘e2 42 ♔h3 ♘xc3 43 bxc3 ♖e2 44 ♖g1 ♖xf2 45 ♔xh4 ♖f3 46 ♖b1+ ♔c7 47 ♖b3 b5 48 d5 c5! 49 ♖xb5 ♖xc3 50 ♔g5 ♔d6 51 ♔xf5 ♔xd5 and I won in a further 14 moves.

9 ♘g3 0:17 **♗g6** 0:40
10 ♘ce4 0:22
Aiming at d6; but after my reply, Black holds the dark squares. 10 ♗e2 seems better because 10...♗xh4 11 ♘xh5 ♗xh5 12 ♗xh5 looks better for White. The attempted combination 12...♘xe5 fails to 13 dxe5

♕xd1+ 14 ♔xd1 ♖xh5 15 g3. So perhaps Black must destabilise the centre with 10...c5, when my initial reaction today, a dozen years later, was that 11 d5 would be dangerous, and indeed after 11...♘xe5 12 ♗f4 (12 dxe6 ♘f6 looks much less convincing) gives White a very dangerous initiative.

10 ... ♘h6! 0:42
Now the knight will always be able to come to f5, covering d6.

11 ♘g5?! 0:49
Very odd. Although there are some vague threats against e6, these are easily dealt with. 11 ♗g5 was natural, but after 11...♗xe4 (11...♕a5+ 12 ♔f1 ♘f5 13 ♘xf5 ♗xf5 14 ♗xe7 ♗xe4 15 ♗d6 is playable for Black but unnecessary) 12 ♘xe4 ♘f5 Black is comfortable.

11 ... ♕a5+ 0:50
With White's pieces somewhat lacking in co-ordination, this is surprisingly strong.

12 ♗d2 1:08
Or 12 ♔f1 0-0-0 with pressure against d4 and e5.

12 ... ♗b4 0:56
13 ♘5e4 1:14
If 13 a3 ♗xd2+ 14 ♕xd2 ♕xd2+ 15 ♔xd2 0-0-0 – or maybe 15...♖d8 when the king will be very happy on e7 – 16 ♔c3 c5!

13 ... ♗xe4 0:59
14 ♘xe4 1:16 **♘f5** 0:59
As a result of the tempo loss

♘e4-g5-e4, White's centre is now under serious pressure.

15 ♗c3!? 1:17 **♗xc3+!** 1:09

Of course, I would have preferred not to strengthen White's centre; but the various pins prove extremely unpleasant in the short term, so I can smash it up before White gets organised. If instead 15...♖d8 16 ♕d2, intending 16...♗xc3 17 ♕xc3!; or if 15...0-0-0 either 16 ♕d2 or16 ♕b3.

16 bxc3 1:18 **♖d8!** 1:10

Clearly I had taken this decision when playing 15...♗xc3+. It would be nice to castle, but after 16...0-0-0? 17 ♕b3 ♘xe5 not (17...♘xd4?? 18 ♘d6+) 18 ♗xe6+! (18 ♖b1!? also worried me at the time) 18...fxe6 19 ♕xe6+, the natural 19...♘d7 allows a hit 20 ♕xf5!, repulsing the black attack and keeping an extra pawn; while if 19...♔b8 20 ♕xe5+ ♕xe5 21 dxe5 ♖he8 22 f4 White keeps control.

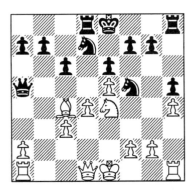

17 ♗d3 1:40

If 17 0-0? ♘xe5 is simple.

But 17 ♕c1 was conceivable, though it leaves Black with a very wide choice of attacking continuations:

a) If 17...♘xe5!? 18 dxe5 ♕xe5 19 f3 I could choose between:

a1) 19...♘d6 20 ♗e2 (20 ♕g5? ♘xc4) 20...♘xe4 21 fxe4 when there probably isn't anything better than 21...♕xe4 which is pretty unclear.

a2) 19...♘g3 20 ♕g5! ♕xg5 21 hxg5 ♘xh1 22 ♔e2 when the ending looks reasonable for White.

b) 17...♘xd4 isn't a move which I examined at the time, since the alternatives seemed so appealing and it is always nice to avoid a knight on d6 if possible. 18 ♘d6+ ♔f8 (not however 18...♔e7? 19 ♕g5+ ♔f8 20 ♔f1 ♘xe5 21 ♘xb7 f6 22 ♘xa5 fxg5 23 cxd4 ♘xc4 24 ♘xc4 and wins) looks somewhat like the game:

b1) Now 19 0-0 ♘f3+! 20 gxf3 ♘xe5 21 ♖d1! (not 21 ♘xb7 ♘xf3+ 22 ♔g2 ♕f5 23 ♖d1 ♕g4+ 24 ♔f1 ♕xc4+ and Black wins) 21...♖xd6! 22 ♖xd6 ♘xc4 23 ♖d4 ♘e5 is unclear.

b2) And 19 ♔f1 can be met by either:

b21) 19...♘f5 20 ♘xb7 ♕a4 21 ♘xd8 ♕xc4+ 22 ♔g1.

b22) Or even 19...♘b5, when the continuation 20 ♘xb7 ♕a4 21 ♗b3? (21 ♘xd8 ♕xc4+ 22 ♔g1) 21...♕a6! is bad for

White; though 20 ♗xb5 ♘xe5 21 ♘xf7 ♘xf7 is less clear.

b3) But White's best reply is the surprisingly strong 19 ♘xb7!, trying to commit the black queen to e5 too early so that if

b31) 19...♕xe5+ 20 ♔f1 ♖b8 21 cxd4 with a big advantage.

b32) 19...♕a4 is a better try, but simply 20 cxd4 ♕b4+ 21 ♔e2 ♕xb7 22 ♖d1 is nice for White; while 20 0-0! looks even better.

c) 17...♘b6! is most sensible. 18 ♘d2 and now:

c1) 18...♘xd4 is very appealing, as after 19 cxd4 ♖xd4 Black has a very dangerous attack for the piece, e.g. 20 ♗e2 0-0 21 ♕c2 ♖fd8 22 0-0-0 ♕xe5!? (threatening 23...♖xd2) when:

c11) 23 ♘f3 ♕f4+ 24 ♖d2 (24 ♔b1? ♖b4+ 25 ♔a1 ♕f6+) 24...♖xd2 25 ♘xd2 is foul for White.

c12) 23 ♘b3 ♕f4+ 24 ♔b1 ♖xd1+ 25 ♖xd1 ♘d5! also looks very nice for Black.

But if Black doesn't want to risk sacrificing a piece then the safest is to take a pawn which, if heated at all, is lukewarm at most with:

c2) 18...♘xc4 19 ♘xc4 ♕d5 20 ♘e3 ♘xe3 21 ♕xe3 ♕xg2 22 0-0-0 ♕d5. This simple line effectively refutes 17 ♕c1.

17 ...   ♘xd4 1:15
18 ♘d6+ 1:45 **♔e7** 1:18
19 0-0 1:45

Andrew Martin reported in the *BCM* that 'White made this move with a confident air.' Certainly, it looks as though he is getting out, since if 19...♕xc3 20 ♖c1 ♕a3 21 f4 with an attack. It is perfectly possible that Black, who is two pawns up at the moment, could survive, but I had no wish to defend.

While if 19...♘xe5 20 cxd4 ♘xd3 21 ♘xb7 ♕f5 22 ♘xd8 ♖xd8 23 ♕a4! Black has play for the exchange – the knight will be very dangerous when it goes to f4 – but White is active too. However, this variation only works for White because the knight on d4 is en prise, which makes it a desperado: a doomed piece trying to sell its life as dearly as possible. When selecting this continuation I'd already decided on:

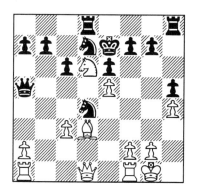

19 ...   ♘f3+!! 1:20

A shocking sacrifice which leaves White with serious problems. I can't remember now, when I first noticed it, but the ten-minute think before playing 15...♗xc3+ suggests that it was then – or perhaps during Murray's time, while he was deciding on 17 ♗d3.

20 gxf3 1:51

Winning the exchange, but at the cost of a filthy kingside pawn structure.

The alternative 20 ♕xf3 ♘xe5 is extremely complex:

a) If 21 ♕g3? ♖xd6 22 ♕xg7 ♕xc3! and if 23 ♕xh8 (23 ♔h1 ♖xd3 24 ♕xh8 ♖h3+ 25 gxh3 ♕xh3+ 26 ♔g1 ♘f3 mate) 23...♘f3+!

b) So White must play 21 ♘f5+! to open the e-file. He will get some dangerous threats in the very short term, but if Black defends properly then it should be very good for him. While I was waiting for Murray's reply, I first glanced briefly at 21...exf5 22 ♖ae1 and then noticed 21...♔f8, which looked like an improvement until I realised that 22 ♕g3! exf5 23 ♗xf5 would be annoying. Of course, one couldn't possibly hope to analyse such a position out during a game. But I think I had come to the conclusion that 21...exf5 22 ♖ae1 ♖he8! ought to be alright; and my instinct seems to have been correct. The lines go:

b1) 21...exf5 22 ♖ae1 or perhaps the other rook, but it is nice to keep a rook on the f-file in attacking lines. And if the rook stays on a1 then ...♕xc3

may be stronger.

b11) 22...♕xc3 is extremely foolhardy, since 23 ♕xf5 f6 24 ♗b1! (24 ♗c2 loses a crucial tempo after 24...♖d2 25 ♗b3 ♔d8! 26 ♖d1 ♔c7 27 ♖xd2 ♕xd2 28 ♖d1 ♕b4) 24...♔f7 25 f4! is surprisingly annoying, e.g. 25...g6 26 ♕e4 ♕c5+ 27 ♔h1 ♖d4 28 ♕e3 ♘g4 29 ♕b3+! ♔g7? (29...♕d5 30 ♕xb7+ ♕d7 keeps the advantage) 30 ♕xb7+ ♔h6 31 ♕f7 and White wins!

b12) 22...♖he8! is much more solid:

b121) 23 ♕xf5 is most worrying, as after 23...♔f8 White can cause some confusion with 24 ♕xh5 (24 ♕h7 ♖xd3 is worse – 25 f4 ♘g6 doesn't work so White has to play 25 ♕h8+ anyway, but without taking the h-pawn – and 24 f4? loses at once to 24...♕c5+ 25 ♔h2 ♘xd3) 24...♖xd3 25 ♕h8+ ♔e7 26 ♕xg7, but Black must be winning even if some care is needed. 26...♔d8! is best, to reserve d7 for the knight (26...♔d7? 27 f4! ♕c5+ 28 ♔h2 ♘g6 29 ♕xf7+ ♘e7 is very messy) 27 h5! (now 27 f4 ♕c5+ 28 ♔h1 ♘d7 is hopeless) 27...♕xc3 (27...♖d6) 28 h6 and here I was temporarily convinced that Black couldn't play 28...♘f3+! 29 gxf3 ♕xg7+ in view of 30 ♖xe8+. But of course White is in check, so 30 hxg7 ♖g8 is a trivial win.

b122) 23 ♗xf5 g6! defends

the h5-pawn and so threatens ...♔f8. After 24 ♗c2 ♔f8 White has to try 25 ♕f6, since otherwise ...♔g7 will leave Black totally safe. Black plays 25...♖e6, and now perhaps 26 ♖xe5!? (26 ♕h8+ ♔e7 will soon be over) 26...♖xe5 27 ♗xg6, but after 27...♖d7 White's attack comes to an end. Black is much too well centralised.

b2) 21...♔f8!? hardly even needs analysing, given that 21...exf5 is strong. After 22 ♕g3! exf5 23 ♗xf5! Black is happy to be a pawn up but still needs one more tempo to get completely organised. 23...g6 24 ♖ae1! looks best, keeping the other rook on f1 to support f4:

b21) 24...♘c4? allows 25 ♗xg6!, when 25...♖g8 26 ♕f4! ♖xg6 27 ♕xc4 ♕d5 28 ♕xd5 ♖xd5 leaves Black with a slight edge but probably no more.

b22) But 24...♖e8, although it looks slightly awkward, does seem to keep the advantage, e.g. 25 ♗h3 (to keep control of g4; 25 f4 ♘f3+! 26 ♕xf3 ♖e1 27 ♖xe1 ♕xf5 is easy for Black) 25...♔g7, when White can thrash around, but it doesn't seem to work since if 26 f4 ♘g4 Black will emerge at least a pawn up; while 26 ♖e4 ♕d5 27 ♖fe1 fails to 27...♘g4! with a vicious back-rank trick.

| 20 | ... | ♘xe5 1:22 |
| 21 | ♘xb7 1:52 | ♕c7 1:27 |

Instead 21...♕xc3 22 ♘xd8 ♖xd8 23 ♖c1 ♕xd3 24 ♕xd3 ♖xd3 was also very pleasant, but I preferred to keep the queens on. My decision depended on the evaluation of the ending in the note to 24 ♕xh5.

22 ♘xd8 2:03

After 22 ♘c5 my only real problem would have been in choosing between the myriad strong continuations, e.g.

a) 22...♖d5 and now:

a1) 23 ♘a6 ♕d7 24 ♘b4 ♖d6 25 ♕a4 ♘xd3 26 ♘xd3 ♖xd3 27 ♖d1 c5!

a2) 23 f4 ♘xd3 (23...♘g4 is also strong) 24 ♘xd3 and now 24...♕d6 25 ♘e5 ♖xd1 26 ♖fxd1 ♕c7 27 ♖d7+ ♕xd7 28 ♘xd7 ♔xd7 is cleanest; though 24...♖hd8 25 f5 ♖xd3 26 ♕xh5 ♖h3 27 ♕g5+ ♔f8 28 ♕g2 ♖xh4 29 fxe6 ♖h6 must also win.

b) 22...♕d6 23 ♘b7 (23 f4 ♘g4! is horrible, e.g. 24 ♘e4 ♕xf4 25 ♘g3 ♘e5) 23...♕xd3 24 ♘xd8 ♘xf3+ 25 ♔h1 (25 ♔g2 ♘xh4+ 26 ♔h2 ♕e4) 25...♕f5 26 ♘xc6+ ♔f6 and wins.

22	...	♖xd8 1:27
23	f4 2:08	♖xd3 1:27
24	♕xh5? 2:13	

Allowing a crushing attack. He had to try 24 fxe5 ♖xd1 25 ♖fxd1 ♕xe5, when Black is clearly better but White can still fight.

| 24 | ... | ♘f3+ 1:29 |
| 25 | ♔g2 2:13 | ♕xf4 1:29 |

26 ♖fd1 2:13

Unsurprisingly, there is simply too much fire power aimed at the white king. If 26 ♕c5+ ♔f6! 27 ♖h1 ♕g4+ 28 ♔f1 ♘d2+ 29 ♔e1 ♕e4+ finshes

off; while 26 ♖h1 ♕e4 is speedily decisive

26 ... **♖xc3!** 1:39

Since there is no win with checks, the rook simply moves away, preparing to land on c2; and controlling c5 so that ...g6 is now an additional threat, moving the queen off before the final blood bath initiated by ...♕g4+.

27	♖ab1 2:16	♕h2+ 1:40
28	♔f1 2:16	♕h3+ 1:40
29	♔e2 2:16	♖c2+ 1:41
30	♔e3 2:18	

Or 30 ♔d3 ♘e1+ and mate in a few moves

30 ... **♘xh4+** 1:41

0-1

Game 25
L.Psakhis–J.Speelman
Hastings 1987/88
Queen's Gambit Accepted

1	d4	d5
2	c4	dxc4
3	♘f3	c5
4	d5	e6
5	♘c3	exd5
6	♕xd5	♕xd5
7	♘xd5	♗d6

In this line of the Queen's Gambit Accepted, Black sets up a position which will be very pleasant for him unless White reacts immediately. But this costs time; and one way White can exploit his slight lead in development is by moving his knight round to c4.

8	♘d2	♘e7!?

Surrendering both bishops for knights. A few months later 8...♘c6 was introduced, which keeps the bishops but at the cost of some time.

9	♘xc4	♘xd5
10	♘xd6+	♔e7
11	♘xc8+	♖xc8
12	g3 0:01	♘c6 0:12

Fairly simplistic. Seirawan has often played 12...♘b4 13 ♗h3 ♖d8, though without particularly good results.

| 13 | ♗g2 0:06 | |

When he knows what he is

going to play, Lev Psakhis tends to get on with it. So before this move he'd spent just one minute. But my perfectly natural 12th move was less common than ...♘b4, and so he started to think.

13 ...   ♖d8 0:17
14 ♗g5+!? 0:19

Inducing a slight weakness, though it is not immediately clear whether this will be useful to White or not. 14 ♗d2 is also perfectly playable at once.

14 ...   f6 0:17
15 ♗d2 0:19   **♖d6** 0:26
16 0-0 0:27   **♖ad8** 0:34
17 ♖fc1 0:43

The other rook was also possible and indeed had been played in Bellon-Seirawan, Zurich 1984.

17 ...   b6 0:35

Here I offered a draw. Black has a well centralised position with at the moment even a slight space advantage; but if he drifts then he is likely gradually to be driven back. White will hope to exchange one or both pairs of rooks; and then slowly exploit the advantage of the two bishops. I felt, therefore, that some serious measures might be necessary. But I didn't want to burn my bridges without first testing the water – if he accepted the draw then well and good; otherwise it was total war. Lev took just three minutes to refuse my offer.

18 ♔f1 0:46   **a5** 0:39

19 ♗e1 0:54   **g6** 0:50

It was also possible to try to use the 'weakening' ...f6 with 19...♔f7 or even to initiate some kingside play with 19...h5!?

20 ♖ab1 1:02

The position is threatening to stabilise with White holding a pleasant edge.

20 ...   ♘db4!? 0:59

I'd already more or less decided on the following rather desperate expedient.

21 a3 1:04

21 ...   ♘a2?! 1:00

How should one annotate a move like this? The rationale is that Black is beautifully centralised and in particular controls the d-file. White will be temporarily inconvenienced by the knight on a2 and for the next few moves at least must watch out for all sorts of tactical tricks from it and its colleague on c6. Moreover, in the very short term White must be careful to avoid back-rank tricks since the e- and f-pawns combined with the bishop on g2 give the king no flight square. Of course, such a move is extremely aesthetically pleasing, if one can get away with it. But it is equally unsurprising that analysis proves 21...♘a2 to be unsound.

There is also an important psychological component. A move like this would be suicidal against a computer, which not only would be able to calculate its way through the coming thicket of variations; but also would feel no surprise at it. However, a person has to deal with serious shock value which may influence him for the rest of the game.

22 ♖c4 1:19

If I remember correctly, I was much more expecting 22 ♖c2, so I now sank into thought myself. 22 ♗xc6 didn't occur to either of us at the time, as far as I recall, but looking at the game nearly a decade later it seems at least worth consideration. The main line goes 22...♘xc1 23 ♗a4 ♖d4 24 ♗c2 ♖d1, which looks rather dangerous for Black in the long term. White can just leave the rook on d1 and improve his position – though there is no obvious way to do so beyond playing f3 and ♔f2.

22 ...   ♘d4 1:14

I think I'd intended 22...♘e5, but after 23 ♖e4! (23 ♖h4 h5 24

♖a1 ♖d1 25 ♖xa2 ♖b1 26 f4 ♘g4 27 ♖xg4 hxg4 28 ♔f2 is much less convincing) 23...♔f7 24 ♗h3! (24 f4? ♘g4 25 ♗h3 [25 h3 f5!] 25...f5! is unclear) 24...♖d1 25 ♖xd1 ♖xd1 26 f4 White wins a piece.

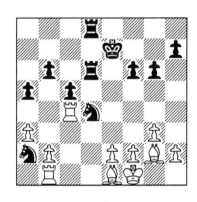

23 b3 1:31

Joel Benjamin later pointed out the refutation. 23 ♗e4 ♘b3, intending 24 ♗c2 ♘ac1, is a mess; but White should play 23 ♖a1! ♘b3 24 ♖xa2 ♖d1 25 ♖e4+ ♔f7 26 f4! and now:

a) 26...♘d2+ 27 ♔f2 ♘xe4+ 28 ♗xe4 leaves White with too much material. If 28...c4 29 a4 is good; or if 28...a4 29 ♗c2 b5 White can ignore the invitation to immure his rook with 30 b3!?, e.g. 30...♖1d4 31 ♗c3 axb3 32 ♗xb3+ c4 33 ♗c2 with a big advantage.

b) 26...f5 27 ♖e3 c4 28 ♖e5.

c) 26...♖b1 was my intention but, as Benjamin pointed out, White can reply 27 ♖e3! (not 27 ♔f2 ♘c1!) when 27...♘c1 is now met by 28 ♗e4! winning.

23 ... ♘b5 1:16
24 ♖b2 1:38

If instead 24 ♖a1:

a) The forcing 24...♘bc3!? 25 ♖xc3 ♘xc3 26 ♗xc3 ♖d1+ 27 ♖xd1 ♖xd1+ 28 ♗e1 leaves Black just one move's grace to get some play on the queenside, so 28...a4 29 bxa4 c4 30 e3 c3 (not 30...♖a1 31 ♔e2 ♖a2+ 32 ♔f3!) 31 ♗e4 f5 32 ♔e2! ♖a1 (32...♖xe1+? 33 ♔xe1 fxe4 34 ♔d1 wins for White) 33 ♗c2! ♖c1 34 ♗d3. It is hard for White to untangle, but Black's kingside pawns are weak and his king can't enter unless White plays e4. I guess that White will always be able to reach a position with a lot of pawns for the exchange – and may well even avoid giving up a bishop for the c-pawn.

b) Psakhis was much more concerned about the murky 24...♖d2!

24 ... ♘ac3 1:19

24...♘bc3 25 ♗e4 (not 25 f4? ♖d1 26 ♔f2 ♖c1!) 25...b5 26. ♖xc3 ♘xc3 27 ♗xc3 ♖d1+ 28 ♗e1! looks very bad for Black.

25 a4! 1:40

With the bishop on g2 rather than e4 as in the above note, 25 ♖xc3!? ♘xc3 26 ♗xc3 ♖d1+ 27 ♗e1 ♖a1 is very unclear. After 28 e3! ♖dd1 29 ♖e2 ♖xa3 White does have the defence 30 ♗e4!, but there is a lot to be said then for 30...♖xb3 31 ♗c2 and perhaps 31...♖db1 to keep a rook on the b-file. The three connected passed pawns will be very dangerous.

25 ... ♘d1 1:25

If 25...♖d1 then 26 f4 is forced but strong (not 26 axb5?? ♖xe1+) 26...♖xe1+ 27 ♔xe1 ♖d1+ 28 ♔f2 ♖d6 (if 28...♖a1 29 ♖d2! wins) 29 ♖c2 ♘d1+ 30 ♔e1 ♘a3 31 ♖e4+ with a big advantage.

26 ♖b1 1:45

Psakhis suggested 26 ♖a2!? ♘d4 27 ♖a3, hoping to play against the stray horse on d1.

26 ... ♘a3 1:26
27 ♖cc1! 1:52

Not 27 ♖e4+ ♔f7 28 ♖c1 ♘b2! with ...♖d1 coming.

27 ... ♘xb1 1:28
28 ♖xb1 1:52

By sacrificing the exchange, Psakhis has trapped the knight on d1 and can now at last start to play 'natural moves' – a very important consideration in time trouble.

28 ... f5 1:34

28...♘c3!? is extremely committal, so one would have to be remarkably confident to play it. But it may be playable for Black, e.g. 29 ♗xc3 ♖d1+ 30 ♖xd1 ♖xd1+ 31 ♗e1 b5 when:

a) The race starting 32 axb5? c4 is lost for White unless he can improve on 33 b6 ♔d8 34 bxc4 a4 35 c5 a3 36 c6 a2 37 c7+ ♔c8 and wins.

b) So 32 e3! looks best, but with 32...c4 33 ♔e2! (not 33 bxc4? bxa4 34 ♔e2 ♖xe1+ 35 ♔xe1 a3) 33...♖a1, and if 34 bxc4 b4, Black looks to be winning a bishop for the b-pawn.

Instead 28...b5? 29 axb5 ♘c3 attempts to transpose into the race in variation a above, but White can simply reply 30 ♖c1! with a material advantage.

29 ♗b7! 1:52 **g5!** 1:42

If 29...♖d2 30 ♗xd2 ♖xd2 and now:

a) 31 ♔e1!? leads to some interesting complications after 31...♖d7 32 ♗c8 (32 ♖xd1 is sensible, with about equality) 32...♘c3 33 ♖c1 and now:

a1) 33...♖d8 34 ♗xf5 when Black must choose between the reasonably safe ♘xe2 35 ♔xe2 gxf5 36 ♖d1 and 34...♘a2?! 35 ♖a1 ♘b4 36 ♗b1! when, despite the temporary inconvenience, White has good chances of emerging with the advantage.

a2) 33...♘a2!? 34 ♖a1 ♘b4 35 ♗xd7 ♘c2+ 36 ♔d2! (36 ♔d1 ♘xa1 37 ♗b5 ♘xb3 38 e3 c4 39 ♗xc4 ♘c5 40 ♗b5 ♘e4! is unpleasant) 36...♘xa1 37 ♗xf5 gxf5! (not 37...♘xb3+? 38 ♔c3 gxf5 39 ♔xb3 with a clear plus for White) 38 ♔c3 ♔e6 39 ♔b2 ♘xb3 40 ♔xb3 ♔d5 and the pawn ending looks rather good for Black.

b) But unfortunately all these lines are irrelevant since White can simply trap the knight with 31 ♖c1!, when he must be winning.

30 ♗a6 1:52 **f4!** 1:42

Forced, to prepare ...f3+ in the coming melee.

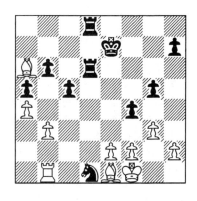

31 ♗d3? 1:53

This simplistic move makes Black's life easy. After a waiting move like 31 ♗b5 Black has no way to free his knight, but equally it is hard to see how White will improve his position.

31 ... **♖xd3** 1:43
32 exd3 1:53 **♖xd3** 1:44
33 ♔e2 1:53 **♖d5!** 1:45

I think Lev may have been expecting 33...♖d4?, which loses after 34 gxf4 gxf4 35 ♗d2 ♘xf2 36 ♗c3! ♖d3 37 ♗e1!

34 gxf4 1:57

Not 34 ♖xd1? f3+!; but 34 ♔f3 is playable, e.g. 34...♖d4 (if 34...♘c3 35 ♗xc3 ♖d3+ 36 ♔g4 ♖xc3 37 ♔xg5 the ending isn't clear; but later in the game after the exchange 34 gxf4 gxf4, the corresponding endgame would be clearly in Black's favour) 35 ♔e2 and Black must either repeat with 35...♖d5 or engage in the speculative 35...♔e6?! 36 gxf4 gxf4 37 ♗d2 ♘xf2 38 ♗c3 ♘e4 39 ♗xd4 cxd4 when the two pawns are annoying for White, but if the rook gets going Black will be in dire trouble.

34 ...   gxf4 1:46

35 ♖c1 1:59

Now 35 ♔f3 ♘c3 (35...♖d4 repeats after 36 ♔e2 ♖d5) is much more playable for Black due to the exchange of g-pawns: 36 ♗xc3 ♖d3+ 37 ♔xf4 ♖xc3 and Black looks better.

35 ♗xa5 is an attempt to bail out. Since it is a quintessentially analysable rook ending, I got rather involved in doing so. But it takes little analysis to determine that White is extremely close to the abyss, so this would be a rather unlikely course in time trouble: 35...bxa5 36 ♖xd1 f3+ 37 ♔e1 ♔d6 38 ♖c1 (38 ♖d2 ♖d4 39 ♖c2 ♖d3 40 ♖c4 ♖xb3 41 ♔d2! transposes; and 38 ♖xd5+ ♔xd5 39 ♔d2 ♔d4 is a simple lost pawn ending, viz. 40 h3 h6 41 h4 h5 42 ♔c2 c4 43 bxc4 ♔xc4 44 ♔d2 ♔b3 45 ♔e3 ♔xa4 46 ♔xf3 ♔b3) 38...♖d3 39 ♖c4 (or 39 ♖d1 ♖xd1+ 40 ♔xd1 ♔d5 and Black wins) 39...♖xb3 and now:

a) 40 ♖h4 ♖d3 is over since the c-pawn is too strong. White's best defence is 41 ♖h6+! (Luke McShane) but after 41...♔d5 42 ♖xh7 ♔c4! (not 42...c4 43 ♖d7+ ♔e4 44 ♖xd3 ♔xd3 45 ♔d1 c3 46 h4 c2+ 47 ♔c1 ♔e2 48 h5 ♔xf2 49 h6 ♔e2 50 h7 f2 51 h8♕ f1♕+ with a draw) 43 ♖c7! ♔b4 44 h4 c4 45 h5 c3 46 h6 ♔b3 47 h7 c2! (not 47...♔c2?? 48 ♖xc3+) Black is a tempo too fast: 48 ♖b7+ (48 h8♕ ♖d1 mate) 48...♔xa4 and wins (though even 48...♔a2?! 49 ♖b2+ ♔xb2 50 h8♕+ ♖c3 51 ♕b8+ ♔a1 wins).

b) 40 ♔d2! puts up a much better fight, but I now believe that Black is winning after the continuation 40...♔d5! 41 ♖h4 ♖b2+, as the following variations demonstrate:

b1) 42 ♔d3 c4+ 43 ♔c3 (43 ♖xc4 ♖b3+ 44 ♖c3 ♖xc3+ 45 ♔xc3 ♔c5 46 h3 h6 47 h4 h5 48 ♔d3 ♔b4 is over) 43...♖xf2 44 ♖xh7 ♖a2 45 ♖f7 f2 46 h4 ♔e4 47 ♔xc4 (47 h5 ♖a3+ 48 ♔xc4 ♖f3) 47...♔e3! (the alternative 47...♖xa4+ 48 ♔b5 ♖a2 49 h5 ♔e3 50 h6 ♖a1 51 h7 ♖h1 looks like a draw) 48 ♔b5 ♖a1 49 ♔xa5 f1♕ 50 ♖xf1 ♖xf1 51 ♔b6 ♔d4 52 a5 ♔d5 53 a6 ♔d6 54 ♔b7 (or 54 a7 ♖b1+ 55 ♔a6 ♔c7 56 a8♘+ ♔c6 57 ♔a7 ♖h1 and wins) and although this would be a draw without the h-pawn, here there is no stalemate, i.e. 54...♔d7 55

a7 ♖b1+ 56 ♔a8 ♔c7 57 h5
♖d1 58 h6 ♖d8 mate.

b2) 42 ♔e3 ♖e2+ 43 ♔d3! (if
43 ♔xf3 ♖e7 the c-pawn should
decide) 43...♖xf2 (if 43...c4+ 44
♖xc4 ♖d2+ 45 ♔xd2 ♔xc4 the
pawn ending now appears to be
drawn, e.g. 46 ♔e3 ♔b3 47
♔xf3 ♔xa4 48 ♔e4 ♔b5 49
♔d4 h5 50 ♔c3 h4 51 ♔b3 h3
52 ♔a3 ♔c4 53 ♔a4 ♔d4 54
♔xa5 ♔e4 55 ♔b4 ♔f3 56 ♔c3
♔xf2 57 ♔d2 ♔g2 58 ♔e2
♔xh2 59 ♔f2) 44 ♖h5+ ♔d6 45
♖h6+ ♔e5 46 ♖h5+ ♔f4 47
♖h4+ ♔g5 48 ♖xh7 ♖a2 49 ♖f7
♖xa4 50 ♔e3 ♖a3+ 51 ♔f2 a4
and wins.

35 ...   ♘b2 1:48
36 ♗c3 1:59

From an asterisk on my
scoresheet, it appears that White
offered a draw here; but it is
already too late.

36 ...   ♘d3 1:48

Not only was White in serious time trouble, but the knight
escapes and White finds himself
a pawn down with the worse
position.

37 ♖g1 1:59

If 37 ♖d1 ♘b4 38 ♗xb4 f3+!
39 ♔e1 ♖xd1+ 40 ♔xd1 axb4
wins easily.

37 ...   ♘b4 1:50
38 ♖g7+? 1:59

Losing immediately, but the
rook ending after 38 ♗xb4 axb4
39 ♖g7+ ♔d6 40 ♖xh7 f3+! 41
♔e3 ♖d1 seems lost. Black's
connected pawns will be very
quick.

38 ...   ♔f8! 1:51
39 ♗b2 1:59

If 39 ♖xh7 f3+!; or 39 f3 ♖d3
40 ♗xb4 ♖e3+.

39 ...   ♖d3 1:51

And Psakhis resigned.
0-1

Game 26
G.Kasparov– J.Speelman
Linares 1992
Caro-Kann Defence

My second appearance at Linares was one of the worst tournaments of my life. I started
fine, with a draw as Black

against Beliavsky, but then lost
a rather limp game as White
against Yusupov's splendidly
iron logic. This was followed by

a loss as Black against Ljubojevic in a 4 ♕c2 Nimzo-Indian where I appeared to take the initiative but at the cost of a bad pawn structure, was repelled and then outplayed in time trouble.

Things looked up after a fighting draw White against Karpov and a squeeze in which I almost succeeded in beating Anand on the black side of the Caro-Kann. But now I was Black against Kasparov, never an easy pairing even at the best of times.

Although I eventually succeeded in drawing this game, things went from bad to worse and I lost three more games without winning to end up on a magnificent 4/13 – tied for last with Nigel Short!

Nevertheless, there are some good memories, notably my 21st move in the following game.

The course of play must surely have been influenced by our battle at Linares a year earlier. After a short skirmish in the opening, I had obtained a position so dire that a true aesthete might have been tempted to resign.

The following diagram was the position after his 22nd move: ♘f3-e5. I shall spare the readers' sensibilities by drawing a veil over how I reached this delightful position and the many fine moves which fol-

lowed it. But somehow I managed to survive and on move 50, to my opponent's great disgust, we shook hands, agreeing to a draw.

G.Kasparov–J.Speelman
Linares 1991 (after move 22)

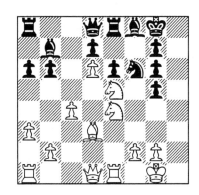

In 1991, Kasparov had started with 1 c4, but this time he decided to try:

1 e4 0:01   **c6** 0:01

Although I play many other openings, the Caro is my most solid – or rather least leaky – defence against 1 e4. So, quite quickly it seems, I decided to see what he had in mind.

2 d4 0:02   **d5** 0:01
3 ♘d2 0:02   **dxe4** 0:06
4 ♘xe4 0:02   **♘d7** 0:06
5 ♗c4 0:03   **♘gf6** 0:07
6 ♘g5 0:04   **e6** 0:09
7 ♕e2 0:04   **♘b6** 0:12
8 ♗b3 0:04   **a5** 0:20

Normally, 8...h6 is played first and after 9 ♘5f3, both 9...a5 and 9...c5 are possible. By playing 8...a5 first I give White the opportunity to support the d-pawn so that in the event of ...h6 the knight can retreat to e4. Kasparov clearly felt that my move was inaccurate; and produced a magnificent look of mildly contemptuous puzzlement before replying:

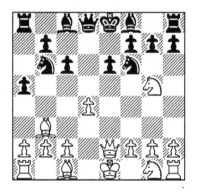

9   c3 0:10   **a4** 0:25
10   ♗c2 0:10   **a3** 0:28

To undermine the dark squares, though of course this pawn can be very weak in an ending. If memory serves, Garry wasn't too impressed with this, either.

11   b3 0:11   **♘bd5** 0:33
12   ♗d2 0:14   **♗d6** 0:46

Of course, I wanted 12...♘xc3 13 ♗xc3 ♘d5 to work. But equally obviously it doesn't: 14 ♗d2 ♘b4 15 ♗e3! ♕a5 16 ♔f1 b6 17 ♕d2 and Black has nothing like enough for a piece.

13   ♘1f3 0:29

13 g3 was also possible, to prevent ...♘f4

13   ...   **♘f4** 0:50

14   ♕f1 0:30   **h6** 0:56

Here, perhaps because of the passive enemy queen on f1, I remained oblivious to the dangerous 15 ♘xf7?, which Kasparov investigated but rejected in view of 15...♔xf7 16 ♘e5+ ♗xe5 17 dxe5, which would not be pleasant at all if Black had to move the knight, but fails to 17...♕a5! 18 exf6 ♕e5+ 19 ♔d1 ♖d8.

15   ♘e4 0:31   **♘xe4** 0:56
16   ♗xe4 0:31   **0-0** 1:02
17   g3 0:40   **♘d5** 1:04
18   ♕e2 0:40   **c5** 1:16

A 'natural break', but after just two more moves I felt a little uncomfortable.

19   dxc5 0:44   **♗xc5!** 1:16
20   ♘e5! 0:55

It is vital to maintain the bishop on the long diagonal. The thoughtless 20 0-0? would allow 20...♘f6 21 ♗c2 b6, when the weak long diagonal is very likely to be a worry for White at some stage.

20   ...   **♕c7** 1:21
21   0-0! 0:56

Behind on the clock and with White starting to get organised, I started to feel very nervous, particularly given my atrocious tournament position as outlined in the introduction. Then I suddenly spotted a move to change the course of the game. I make no claim for its soundness, but after just eight minutes, before I could talk myself out of it, I bashed out:

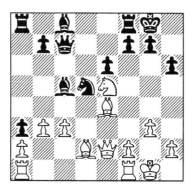

21 ...　　　　　　&e3!?! 1:29

Kasparov returned to the board. If 8...a5 and 10...a3 had caused something of a reaction, this was altogether in a different league. His eyebrows arched and he sank into deep thought.

22 fxe3! 1:34

I had definitely underestimated this when playing 21...&e3. Though by the time it came, 40 minutes later, I was fairly clear how I was going to respond.

The more obvious 22 &xe3 gives White some dangerous threats in the short term. Black must play 22...&xc3! (not 22...&xe5? 23 &d4 and if 23...&xc3? 24 &h7+!) 23 &h5 (23 &h7+!? &xh7 24 &d3+ &g8 25 &d4 &d5 defends) 23...&xe4 (maybe 23...&a5) 24 &ac1 &a5 25 b4 and now:

a) In my notes at the time, I now recommended 25...&b5 26 &c5 &f6 and stopped here. In fact after 27 &h4 it looks sensible to sacrifice the exchange

with 27...b6 (27...&e8 28 &c4! does very bad things to Black's co-ordination) 28 &xf8 &xe5 29 &e7 (29 &fd1 &b7) 29...&d5, which looks very pleasant for Black.

b) The more daring 25...&d5 also looks playable if foolish since:

b1) 26 &fd1 weakens f2 so that Black can play 26...&xa2 (26...&f6 27 &xd5 &xh5 looks ropey with the white rooks so active) 27 &d8 &xd8 28 &xf7+ &h8, and here 29 &xh6? fails to 29...&xf2+!; while 29 &c7? &a1+ 30 &g2 &xe5 31 &xh6 &d7 loses; though 29 &d4! forces a draw.

b2) 26 &cd1 keeps f2 defended so that:

b21) 26...&xa2? now gets hit by 27 &d8! There is no real need to calculate further – White has at least a draw – but I rather obsessively did in fact work my way through. The main line runs 27...&xd8 28 &xf7+ &h7 (or 28...&h8 29 &xh6! &g8 30 &h5 g6 31 &g7+ &xg7 32 &xg6+) 29 &xh6 &d7 30 &xd7 &b2 31 &f8+ &h8 32 &g6+ &h7 33 &e7 &d7 (33...&f6 34 &g8+ &xh6 35 &h8+ &g5 36 &h4 mate) 34 &g6+ &h8 35 &xe4 &f6 (35...gxh6 36 &xb7 &d8 37 &c7 and wins) 36 &xg7+ &xg7 37 &xb7 &f8 (37...&d8 38 &c6; or 37...&e8 38 &c6) 38 &xd7 &f7 39 &d3 a2 40 &a3 wins.

b22) So here Black must play 26...♘f6! 27 ♖xd5 ♘xh5, but with the rook on f1 rather than c1 this looks playable for Black.

| 22 | ... | ♕xe5 1:29 |
| 23 | ♕d3 1:34 | |

Played instantly. If 23 ♗c2 Black ought to try 23...f5 24 ♕d3 ♘f6, since 23...b5 24 ♕d3 f5 25 e4 fxe4 26 ♕xe4 ♕xe4 27 ♗xe4 ♗a6 is very ragged; the a3-pawn, in particular, is in serious trouble.

| 23 | ... | ♖a6! 1:35 |

Much the best way to get active.

| 24 | c4 1:43 | ♘f6 1:35 |
| 25 | ♗g2 1:45 | ♖d6 1:39 |

Black seems to have achieved some activity, but a couple of excellent moves by the World Champion promptly dispelled this illusion:

| 26 | ♕c3! 1:45 | ♕g5 1:40 |
| 27 | ♕a5! 1:48 | |

Black can't afford to exchange queens, but now the weaknesses on a3 and b7 are very pronounced.

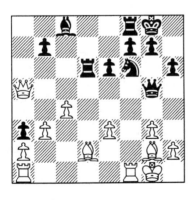

27	...	e5 1:43
28	♗b4 1:49	♖a6 1:46
29	♕b5 1:50	♗d7!? 1:50

In time trouble, I didn't want to be attacked after 29...♖d8 30 ♗e7.

| 30 | ♕xb7 1:51 | ♕xe3+ 1:51 |
| 31 | ♔h1 1:51 | ♖a7 1:51 |

Not 31...♖b6 32 ♕a7.

| 32 | ♗d2? | |

32 ♕f3 would have kept a large safe advantage. Here my record of the times disappeared as we bashed our way through the time scramble.

32	...	♕d4
33	♗c3	♕c5
34	♕b4?	♕c7
35	c5?	

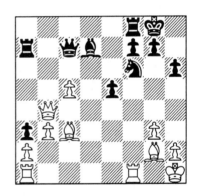

| 35 | ... | ♗c6? |

Missing an excellent chance. 35...♖b8! would have won the c-pawn.

36	♕b6	♗xg2+
37	♔xg2	♘d5
38	♕xc7	♖xc7
39	♗xe5	♖xc5
40	♗d6	♖c2+
41	♖f2	

41 ...   ♖fc8! 2:17

After 41...♖d8 42 ♖xc2 ♘e3+ 43 ♔f2 ♘xc2 44 ♖d1 ♘b4 45 ♖d2 ♘xa2 46 ♗f4! ♖xd2+ 47 ♗xd2 White traps the knight, which I judged to be decisive. And certainly only White can win, though it will take a lot of time to win the knight, requiring the white king to travel a long way. Black can often create a passed f-pawn, so White must play accurately:

a) 47...f5 48 ♔e3 g5 49 ♔d4 ♔f7 50 ♔e5 ♔g6 51 b4 ♘xb4 52 ♗xb4 a2 53 ♗c3 looks hopeless as long as White negotiates the stalemate trap 53...g4 54 ♔e6 ♔g5 55 ♗e5 ♔h5 56 ♔xf5?? (56 ♔f6!) 56...a1♕ 57 ♗xa1.

b) 47...♔f8 48 ♔e3 ♔e7 and now:

b1) After 49 ♔d3 ♔d6 50 b4 (50 ♔c2? ♔c5 rescues the horse) 50...♔d5 51 b5! ♔c5 52 ♔c2 ♔xb5 53 ♔b3 ♔c5 54 ♔xa2 ♔d4 the white king is a long way away.

b2) 49 ♔d4! is much more controlled, as after 49...♔d6 50 b4 f5 either 51 b5 g5 52 ♔c4 ♔c7 53 ♗e3! or 51 ♔c4 ♘xb4 52 ♗xb4+ ♔e5 53 ♔d3 must win.

42   ♗xa3 2:03   **♘e3+** 2:19
43   ♔g1 2:05   **♖a8!?** 2:31

After quite a long think I rejected 43...♘g4 44 ♖xc2 ♖xc2, since I felt that despite my considerable activity the queenside pawns would be too strong:

a) My notes in *Informator* continue 45 ♗c1 ♘xh2 and:

a1) Here I produced 46 a4?? ♘f3+ 47 ♔f1 which, in my terror at the a-pawn, I assessed as winning for White; but after 47...♘d4! Black is absolutely fine since if 48 ♖b1 ♘xb3.

a2) If 46 ♗e3? ♘f3+ 47 ♔f1 ♖h2! and White has nothing better than 48 ♗c1.

a3) So 46 b4! is correct, when the pawns really are dangerous

b) 45 ♗b4 ♘xh2 46 a4 ♘f3+ 47 ♔f1 ♘d4 (better than 47...♖h2 48 ♖a3!) 48 ♖b1! is also very threatening.

c) The calm 45 h3 is also possible, when if 45...♘e5 46 ♗c1 ♘f3+ 47 ♔f1 White has an extra h-pawn compared to variation a but Black has an extra tempo; though 45...♘e3 is also interesting.

In conclusion lines a3 and b are pretty worrying, so I can well see why I preferred 43...♖a8, particularly since it sets some rather vicious little traps which must have appealed to me, even against Garry, just after a time scramble.

44 ♗b2! 2:26

But of course Kasparov played the best move. Certainly not 44 ♗b4?? ♖axa2 45 ♖xa2 ♖c1+ winning; while 44 ♗c1? ♖axa2 45 ♖xc2 ♖xa1 46 ♖c8+ ♔h7 47 ♔f2 looks reasonably playable for Black, who can try either the centralising 47...♘d5 or the more ambitious 47...♘g4+!?

44	...	♖xf2 2:31
45	♔xf2 2:25	♘c2 2:31
46	♖c1 2:25	♘b4 2:31
47	♖b1 2:16	♖xa2 2:32
48	♔e3 2:26	

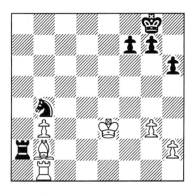

The powerful b-pawn together with the centralised king and advantage of bishop for knight give White a large advantage.

48	...	f6 2:36
49	♔d4 2:27	

Allowing me to force the exchange of minor pieces, albeit not in a wholly satisfactory

way. I was also worried about 49 ♔e4 followed by ♗c3, preparing the pawn's advance.

49	...	♘c2+ 2:40
50	♔c3	

50 ♔c5 would be good for the rook ending, though I might try 50...♖a8; and 50 ♔c4 was also possible.

50	...	♘a3! 2:41
51	♗xa3 2:39	♖xa3 2:41

Although I was very pleased to get rid of the bishop, the b-pawn is very dangerous. It is touch and go whether Black can draw.

52 ♔b2!? 2:29 **♖a7** 2:41

It looks slightly odd to retreat here rather than a8, but I wanted to keep the rook on the second rank to defend the g7-pawn.

53	b4	♔f7
54	b5 2:46	♔e6 2:45
55	♔b3 2:46	

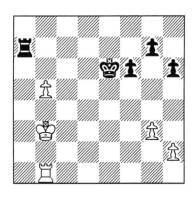

55	...	♔d7 2:50

It is vital to get the king in front of the pawn. I had thought that 55...♔d6 is a mistake. 56 ♖c1 ♖a5 is similar to the lines below; but in a race where White wins the rook for the b-pawn and Black mobilises his kingside, it is better to have the king on d6 rather than d7. The only disadvantage of d6 as compared to d7 is that the white king might be able to go to c8 at some point.

However, I was worried about 56 b6:

a) 56...♖b7? 57 ♔a4 is hopeless because Black can't prevent the white king from entering:

a1) 57...♔d7 58 ♔b5 ♔c8 (58...♖b8 59 ♖d1+!) 59 ♖e1!

a2) 57...♖b8 58 ♔b5 ♔d7 59 ♖d1+.

b) 56...♖a8 is much stronger, however: 57 ♔c4 ♔c6! (not 57...♖b8? 58 ♔b5) and now:

b1) 58 ♔d4 ♔b7! looks alright (but not 58...♔d6 which I originally gave and looks to be losing after 59 ♔e4 ♔e6 60 b7 ♖b8 61 g4).

b2) 58 b7 ♖b8 59 ♔d4 forces Black to go into the pawn ending, since 59...♔d6 60 ♔e4 ♔e6 61 g4 transposes back to the line above; but Black seems to be able to draw by a tempo 59...♖xb7 60 ♖xb7 ♔xb7.

(see following diagram)

Now if White runs straight towards the g-pawn then Black draws by advancing his f-pawn:

b21) 61 ♔e4 and:

b211) Not 61...g6 62 ♔d5 f5

63 ♔e5 ♔c6 64 h4! h5 65 ♔f6 ♔d5 66 ♔xg6 ♔e4 67 ♔g5! (zugzwang) 67...♔f3 68 ♔xf5 ♔xg3 69 ♔g5 ♔f3 70 ♔xh5 ♔f4 71 ♔g6.

b212) But 61...♔c6! 62 ♔f5 ♔d5 63 ♔g6 (or 63 h4 h5 64 ♔g6 ♔e4 65 ♔xg7 f5! 66 ♔g6 f4 67 gxf4 ♔xf4 68 ♔xh5 ♔f5) ♔e4 64 ♔xg7 f5 65 ♔xh6 f4 66 gxf4 ♔xf4 draws.

b22) 61 ♔d5 is more subtle, but after 61...h5! White can never fix the h-pawns with h4, so as to aim for the zugzwang in variation b211 above, in view of ...g5! So the line continues 62 ♔e6 ♔c6 63 h3 (if 63 ♔f7 ♔d5 64 ♔xg7 f5 65 ♔g6 ♔e4 66. ♔g5 h4! with a draw; and of course 63 h4 g5! is simple) 63...♔c5 64 ♔f7 ♔d4 65 ♔xg7 f5 66 ♔g6 ♔e4 67 ♔xh5 f4 68 gxf4 ♔xf4 with a draw.

56 h4? 2:47

A bad mistake since after my reply, I'm able to oppose rooks on the c-file and the draw is easy.

Instead 56 ♖c1!, cutting off the king, gives good winning

chances. It would be very difficult to analyse this out; but I was interested in getting a reasonable idea of the position, so here are some lines: 56...♖a5 (56...h5!?) 57 ♔b4 ♖a2 and:

a) 58 b6 is most obvious, e.g. 58...♖xh2 59 ♔b3 (not 59 ♖c7+ ♔d6 60 ♖xg7 ♔c6) 59...♖h5 60 ♔a4 ♖h2 61 ♔b5 ♖b2+ 62 ♔a6 ♖a2+ 63 ♔b7 g5 64 ♖c6 looks most dangerous, cutting the king off.

a1) Now 64...h5 creates a passed pawn, but a long way from the support of the black king. This looks fatal, e.g. 65 ♖xf6 h4 66 gxh4 gxh4 67 ♖h6 ♖h2 (67...♖a4 68 ♔b8 also looks lost) 68 ♔b8 h3 69 b7 ♖h1 70 ♖h4! h2 71 ♖d4+ ♔e6 72 ♖d2! ♔f5 73 ♖c2 ♔g4 74 ♔c7 wins.

a2) 64...f5! is much better, e.g. 65 ♖xh6 (if 65 ♖f6 ♖a3!) 65...f4 66 gxf4 gxf4 67 ♖f6 ♖a4 68 ♔b8 ♔e7! Now if the rook allows the king to cross the third rank then Black will always be able to draw with pawn against rook. (It is vital to get across this rank to support the pawn. Otherwise Black would be in danger of reaching a totally lost ending like the diagram below – cutting off the king.) Therefore White must keep the king cut off with, for example, 69 ♖c6, but then the f-pawn can advance: 69...f3 70 b7 f2 71 ♖c1 ♔d7 with a draw.

a3) Even 64...♖f3 might also

be possible.

Cutting off the king

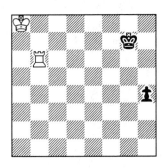

Although the white king is streets away, Black is helpless since he can't advance the pawn: 1...h3 2 ♖b3 h2 3 ♖h3 captures it.

b) 58 h3 leaves the pawns vulnerable on the same rank: 58...♖b2+ 59 ♔a5?! (maybe 59 ♔a4!) 59...♖b3 60 b6 (60 ♔a4 ♖xg3 61 b6 ♖g2 62 ♔a3 ♖g5) 60...♖xg3 61 b7 ♖b3 62 ♔a6 ♖a3+ 63 ♔b6 ♖b3+ 64 ♔a7 ♖a3+ and 65 ♔b8? ♖xh3 would only give Black chances to win.

c) 58 h4 is more dangerous: 58...♖b2+ 59 ♔a5 h5 60 b6 g5 and now:

c1) The manic 61 g4 hxg4 62 h5 doesn't work after 62...♔e6 63 h6 ♔f7 64 ♖c7+ ♔g8 65 b7 g3 66 ♖c8+ ♔h7 67 b8♕ ♖xb8 68 ♖xb8 g2 69 ♖b1 ♔xh6.

c2) 61 ♖c5 ♖b3 62 hxg5 (not now 62 g4 hxg4 63 h5 g3 64 h6 g2 65 ♖c1 ♖a3+ 66 ♔b4 ♖h3 67 b7 g1♕ 68 ♖xg1 ♔c7 and Black is probably winning!) 62...fxg5 and:

c21) 63 ♖xg5 ♔c6 is an easy draw, e.g. 64 ♖g6+ ♔b7 65 ♖g7+ ♔b8 66 ♔a6 ♖a3+ 67 ♔b5 ♖c3!

But the more I look at this the more complex it becomes:

c22) White can try 63 ♔a6 ♖a3+ 64 ♔b7 ♖xg3 and:

c221) 65 ♖d5+ ♔e6 66 ♖a5 ♔f6 67 ♔a7 ♖b3 68 b7 h4! 69 ♖a6+ ♔f5 70 ♖b6 ♖a3+ 71 ♔b8 ♖e3! ensures that the rook can sacrifice itself for the pawn.

c222) 65 ♖a5 h4 66 ♔a7 h3 67 b7 ♖b3 and both 68 ♖xg5 ♖a3+ 69 ♔b8 h2 and 68 b8♕ ♖xb8 69 ♔xb8 h2 70 ♖a7+ ♔e6 71 ♖h7 g4 72 ♖xh2 ♔f5 are drawn.

56 ... **h5!** 2:52
57 ♖**c1** 2:54 ♖**c7!** 2:53
58 ♖**d1+** 2:54

The pawn ending is now drawn by a tempo after 58 ♖xc7+ ♔xc7 59 ♔c4 ♔b6 60 ♔d5 g5 61 ♔e6 gxh4 62 gxh4 ♔xb5 63 ♔xf6 ♔c6 64 ♔g6 ♔d7 65 ♔xh5 ♔e8 66 ♔g6 ♔f8.

The relief of having finally equalised again disrupted my time record.

58 ... ♔**c8**
59 ♖**d5** ♖**e7**
60 ♔**c4** ♖**e3** 2:55

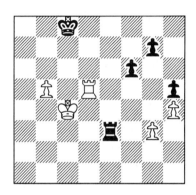

Here Kasparov offered a draw and, upon my acceptance, left the stage, none too pleased. The next day, however, he came to chat about the game and mentioned 35...♖b8!

5 'Reginicide'

The queen sacrifice – the triumph of energy over matter – has always appealed to me in the abstract; and over the years I probably have had recourse to this weapon rather more often than I should. Nevertheless, it was quite a coincidence when in the British Championship in Torquay 1982, I sent no less than three Ladies to the Guillotine in just eleven games.

From their blood I reaped three points, which – combined with other acts of barbarism – sufficed for eight points from 11 games, clear second a point behind Tony Miles.

Here are those three 'reginicides'.

Game 27
J.Levitt–J.Speelman
British Championship (round 1), Torquay 1982
Albin Counter-Gambit

1 d4 0:0   **d5** 0:04
2 c4 0:00   **e5!?** 0:04

The first round is always that little bit tenser, even if you're one of the stronger players. Jonathan Levitt is an excellent strategist but tends to react less well to randomness either on the board or the clock. So this was the occasion for my first and thus far only Albin Counter-Gambit, which I risked, if I recall, partly under the influence of the Welsh player Paul Lamford, who had recently had surprisingly good results with it.

Objectively good or not, the Albin certainly had the effect of winding both of us up extremely early. And the mounting chaos on the board, was, as you can see from the time record, matched by huge expenditures of time in the opening and early middlegame. These were still the days of 40 moves in two-and-a-half hours, but by move 20 I was already in a slight rush and he in a serious hurry.

3	dxe5 0:02	d4 0:05	
4	♘f3 0:03	♘c6 0:05	
5	g3 0:05	♗e6 0:07	
6	♘bd2 0:05	♕d7 0:07	
7	a3 0:14	♘ge7 0:14	
8	♘b3 0:37	♘g6 0:25	
9	♘bxd4 0:42	0-0-0 0:58	

After 33 minutes' thought. The more modest 9...♗xc4 was also quite playable.

10	♗e3 0:43	♘gxe5 1:06	
11	♘xe5 1:07	♘xe5 1:07	
12	♗g2 1:25		

Not 12 b3 ♘g4!

12	...	♗xc4 1:16	
13	♕c2 1:38	♗c5 1:25	
14	♘f5 1:45		

14 0-0-0!? occurred to me as a very sensible alternative on re-examining this game fourteen years later.

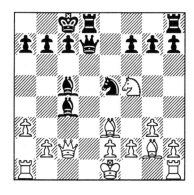

14	...	♗xe2!? 1:45	

Creating a serious mess.

15	♗xc5! 2:02		

15 ♔xe2 loses the queen after a few checks: 15...♕b5+ 16 ♔e1 ♘d3+ 17 ♔f1 ♘f4+ 18 ♔g1 ♘e2+ 19 ♕xe2 ♕xe2 20 ♗xc5. Not only does Black have a nominal material advantage, but White's forces are much too loose.

15	...	♗a6 1:50	

15...♘d3+ 16 ♔xe2 ♕xf5 17 ♖hc1 is good for White. Black has no better than 17...♘xc1+ (if 17...♖he8+ 18 ♔f1 defends – but not 18 ♗e3?? ♕xf2+) 18 ♖xc1 ♖he8+ 19 ♗e3 (even 19 ♔f1 is legal since White can interpose 19...♕xc2 20 ♗h3+!) 19...♕xc2+ 20 ♖xc2 and the two bishops yield a big endgame advantage.

15...♗c4 was possible, to block the c-file and so prevent the game continuation. But at the time I was positively hoping to be able to sacrifice my queen.

16	♘d6+! 2:07		

If 16 ♗e4 (16 ♘e7+ ♔b8 17 ♗e4 ♘d3+ transposes after 18 ♗xd3 ♗xd3) 16...♘d3+ 17 ♗xd3 ♗xd3 18 ♘e7+ ♔b8 Black has sufficient play to regain the piece:

a) 19 ♕b3?? loses at once to ♕g4!

b) 19 ♕c3? ♕e6+ 20 ♗e3 ♕xe7.

c) 19 ♕d2 b6 20 ♗b4 a5 21 0-0-0 axb4 22 ♕xb4 and Black has a nice position after the simple 22...♔b7 23 ♖he1 ♕d4.

d) 19 0-0-0 is most forcing: 19...♗xc2 20 ♖xd7 ♖xd7 21

♔xc2 b6 22 ♗b4 (not 22
♘c6+? ♚b7 23 ♘e5 ♖d5 24
♘xf7 when 24...♖xc5 is check)
22...c5! (22...a5? 23 ♘c6+ ♚b7
24 ♘e5 ♖d5 25 ♗c3) 23 ♘c6+
♚c7 24 ♘e5 cxb4 25 ♘xd7
♚xd7 looks equal.

16 ... ♚b8 1:52
17 0-0-0 2:07 **cxd6!** 1:53
18 ♗xd6+ 2:10 **♕xd6!** 1:53
19 ♖xd6 2:10 **♖xd6** 1:53

Although Black has just a
rook and knight and no pawns
for the queen, the white king is
looking pretty shaky and I was
feeling fairly confident.

20 ♕a4 2:22 **♖hd8** 2:03
21 ♚b1 2:23 **♘c4** 2:05
22 ♖c1 2:25 **♖d4** 2:06
23 ♚a1 2:25

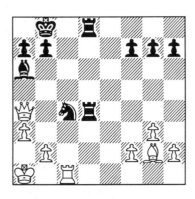

Here I perhaps should have
taken longer. Black obviously
has reasonable compensation
for the queen, but I persuaded
myself that immediate action
didn't seem to work very well.
This was a conclusion I was
predisposed to come to since,
with the opponent in time trou-

ble, it is best to avoid forcing
moves unless they really are
strong: he will usually have
prepared a reply to direct
threats, but will have to reorient
himself against more subtle ap-
proaches. So after just six minutes I kept the tension with a
positional move to support the
knight on e5.

23 ... f6?! 2:12

But objectively Black should
have got on with it:

a) 23...♘xb2 looks good but
after 24 ♕c2 (24 ♕a5 ♘c4 25
♕f5 transposes to variation a2
below) 24...♘c4 White has two
good lines:

a1) 25 ♕xh7? invites
25...♖d3! with a dangerous attack.

a2) But 25 ♕f5 ♖d3 26 ♖xc4
♗xc4 27 ♕f4+ ♚a8 28 ♕xc4
♖d1+ 29 ♚b2 ♖8d2+ 30 ♚b3
♖d3+ is an immediate draw (not
30...♖b1+? 31 ♚a4 when the b-
pawn is pinned).

a3) And 25 ♗f1! covers the
d3-square, giving White a relatively easy game and leaving
Black pretty uncomfortable;
though after a sensible move
like 25...g6 it is far from clear
how White can improve his position.

b) But 23...♘d2 looks best:

b1) 24 b4 would be unrea-
sonably brave when short of
time: 24...♖d3 25 ♚a2 (after 25
b5 ♘b3+ 26 ♚b2 ♘xc1 27
bxa6 ♘e2 Black has at least a
draw) and now:

b11) The ending after 25...♘c4!? 26 b5 ♖xa3+ 27 ♕xa3 ♘xa3 28 bxa6 ♘b5 29 axb7 (29 ♗xb7 ♖d2+ 30 ♔b3 ♘d6) 29...♖d2+ 30 ♔b3 ♘d6 looks pretty good for Black.

b12) 25...♘b3! 26 ♖c2 ♘d4 gives Black an extremely dangerous attack.

b2) Of course, in practice White would always reply 24 ♕d1 when 24...♗c4!? wins the exchange, but after 25 ♖xc4 ♘xc4 White has reasonably obvious moves to make. Against an opponent in time trouble, 24...g6! looks even better as long as White doesn't have a way to avoid shedding material later.

24 ♕c2! 2:25

24 ♗h3? fails to 24...♘d2! 25 b4 (25 ♕xd4 ♘b3+; 25 ♕c2? ♖c4; 25 ♕d1 ♗c4) 25...♗c4 26 ♔b2 b5 27 ♕c2 (27 ♕a6 ♖4d6 28 ♕a5 ♘b3) 27...♘b3.

24 ... ♖d2 2:11

25 ♕f5

It is best to centralise. The greedier 25 ♕xh7 leads to the following variations:

a) 25...♖xb2? loses to 26 ♖xc4 ♖xf2 27 ♖c2.

b) If 25...♖xf2 26 ♗h1 ♘a5 or 26...♘d2 (not 26...♘xb2 27 ♕xg7 ♘c4 28 ♗d5) 27 ♗d5!

c) 25...♘a5 (best) 26 ♖c3 ♗c4! 27 ♖xc4 (27 ♗e4? ♖d1+ 28 ♗b1 ♘b3+ 29 ♖xb3 ♗xb3 and wins) 27...♘xc4 and now:

c1) 28 ♕xg7!? leads to a draw after 28...♖xb2! 29 ♗d5!

♖b6 (or 29...♖b5 30 ♗xc4) 30 ♗xc4 ♖d1+ 31 ♔a2.

c2) 28 ♕e4 ♘a5 29 ♕f4+ looks fairly balanced – though of course White is doing much better than in line b2 in the note to 23...f6.

25 ... ♘e5 2:12
26 ♗h3 2:27 **b6** 2:13
27 ♕xh7 2:28

27 ♖c2 is legal, since 27...♖d1+ 28 ♔a2 ♗d3 (or first 28...♗c4+ 29 b3 ♗d3) loses to 29 ♖c8+ ♔b7 30 ♖xd8 ♗xf5 31 ♗g2+!

But Black can reply 27...♖2d7 when if 28 f4? ♗d3 29 ♕h5 ♗xc2 30 ♗xd7 ♘xd7 wins material.

27 ... ♗c4 2:16

27...♘d3 is better but both of us totally missed White's refutation of the attack.

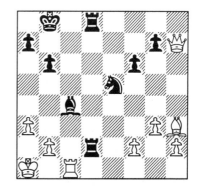

Prior to annotating this game in 1996, I'd believed that it was, if not totally sound, at least presentable. But I made the psychological, if not technical mistake of turning on Fritz. It turns out that White can inflict grievous damage with 28 f4! (not 28 ♕xg7? ♖d1 29 ♖b1 [or 29 ♕h6 ♗b3] 29...♖xb1+ 30 ♔xb1 ♗b3 and Black wins) 28...♖d1 (if 28...♗g8 29 ♕xg7 ♖c2 30 ♔b1; or 28...♗b3 29 fxe5 ♖c2 30 ♖b1) 29 ♕b1!! forcing simplification to a win-

ning ending: 29...♖xc1 30 ♕xc1 ♗b3 31 fxe5 ♖d1 32 ♕xd1 ♗xd1 33 exf6 gxf6 etc.

Instead White panicked with:

28	b3? 2:28	♗xb3	2:16
29	♕xg7 2:28	♘c4	2:17
30	♖xc4 2:28	♗xc4	2:17
31	♗g4 2:28	♖e8	2:17
	0-1		

Game 28
J.Speelman–A.Martin
British Championship (round 6), Torquay 1982
English Opening

After an insipid opening, my position in the early middle-game was, if not bad, far from inspiring. Against a fundamentally very sensible player like Andrew Martin, this would have been extremely difficult to win by normal means; if easy to draw.

Then my attention became drawn to a queen sacrifice, which, if not totally sound, certainly had a lot going for it. By renouncing the lady for two minor pieces, I was able to free my game and set up serious positional pressure both along each of the long diagonals from my two previously dormant bishops; and along the d-file. Allied with the tactical possibility of combining the dark-squared bishop and my knight to attack the enemy king, the temptation proved irresistible.

I've combined some new notes with my original ones in the October 1982 *BCM*; and have enclosed the latter in inverted commas for the sake of clarity.

1	♘f3	♘f6
2	c4	g6
3	g3	♗g7
4	♗g2	d6
5	0-0	0-0
6	b3!?	

Somewhat insipid. In avoiding main lines, White gives Black the opportunity to play 6...♘e4 7 d4 c5. Subsequently, I discovered that this is a direct transposition to a famous game Keres-Szabo, Hastings 1954/55, which continued 8 ♗b2 ♘c6 9 ♘bd2 and now:

a) Here Szabo captured 9...♘xd2? 10 ♕xd2 ♗g4 11 d5. Keres was later left with the white-squared bishop against the knight, out of play on a5; and won well with a splendid kingside attack.

b) 9...♗f5! was recommended by Keres as an improvement and has been played several times since. At the time I felt that 10 ♘h4 was 'alright for White'. In fact after 10...♘xd2 11 ♕xd2:

b1) 11...cxd4 12 ♘xf5 gxf5 13 ♗xc6 bxc6 14 ♗xd4 is about equal (Keres).

b2) 11...♘xd4!? is also very playable.

b3) 11...♗d7 looks odd, but in a game Romanishin-Fedorov, Nikolaev Zonal 1995, Black followed up with 12 d5 ♕a5! when an exchange of queens would take most of the poison out of the position. They agreed a draw after 13 ♕c1 ♘d4 14 ♖e1 b5 15 e3 ♘f5 16 ♘xf5 ♗xf5 17 ♗xg7 ♔xg7 18 cxb5 ♗d7 (after 18...♕xb5 White gets in e4-e5) 19 a4 a6 20 ♗f1 ♖fb8 21 ♕b2+ f6 22 ♖ec1 ♔f8 23 h4 axb5 24 axb5 ♕b4 25 ♖xa8 ♖xa8 26 ♖a1 ♖b8 27 ♖a4 ♕e1 28 ♖a1 ♕b4 29 ♖a4.

6   ...   e5
7   ♗b2

7 d4?! is dubious in view of 7...exd4 8 ♘xd4 c5!

7   ...   c5!

Erecting a central wall to neutralise the newly fianchettoed bishop.

8   ♘c3   ♘c6
9   d3

If 9 e3 ♗f5 is a nuisance since after 10 d3 (10 h3? ♗d3) 10...♕d7 White can't get in h3.

9   ...   h6
10 e3   ♗f5
11 h3   ♕d7
12 ♔h2   ♖ab8

Very playable, though at the time I was more concerned about 12...♗e6, intending ...d5.

12...g5!? was played in a game Grigorian-Tukmakov USSR Championship 1977 (although the position was reached by a totally different move order). They continued 13 ♘g1 g4 14 ♘e4 ♘h7 15 f4 gxh3 16 ♘xh3 ♗g4 with a mess which eventually ended in a draw.

13 ♕d2 0:56

13 ♘d5! was better, freeing the position since Black can't take – if 13...♘xd5?? 14 cxd5 ♘e7 15 e4 traps the bishop.

13 ...   g5! 0:36

Giving the bishop a retreat so that now 14 ♘d5 can be met by 14...♘xd5! which is very acceptable for Black.

If instead 13...a6 14 ♘d5! is that much better than a move previously since 13 ♕d2 looks more useful than 13...a6 if the centre opens up.

14 ♖ad1 1:08 **a6** 0:40

Black has done rather well out of the opening and could even claim a slight space advantage, which White very much wants to challenge with d4.

'I couldn't see where I was going until the idea of the queen sacrifice hit me, initially just as a fantasy, then, on inspection, as a real possibility.'

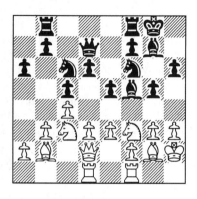

15 d4!? 1:21

'It would be rash to say that this is sound but it is playable since White gets two minor pieces, powerful play on the dark squares and, above all, an extremely compact position in which Black will find no targets. A queen is a serious matter; but the dark squares are too, as White turns the position on its head.'

15 ...   cxd4 0:47

'Black might consider 15...e4 or 15...g4; or precede either move by 15...cxd4. But it would take extraordinary self-control to refrain from taking the lady.'

16 exd4   exd4
17 ♘xd4! 1:27

Although it took another six minutes to play this, I could just as well have done so at once. 17 ♘e2 is legal. After something like 17...♘e4 18 ♕c1 d3 19 ♘ed4 White may well regain the pawn; but Black will have

plenty of time at least to equalise in the meantime.

17 ...   ♘xd4
18 ♕xd4   ♘g4+
19 hxg4 1:27   **♗xd4** 0:47
20 ♖xd4 1:28   **♗g6** 0:52

20...♗xg4! looks better to me now. True, after 21 ♘e4 (21 ♘d5!?) 21...f5 22 ♘xd6 (not 22 ♖xd6? fxe4!) 'the enemy king is exposed while ♖xg4 is in the air'. But the important thing for Black is to reconcile himself to the idea that he must undertake something, indeed brave a certain amount of danger, to consolidate his material advantage. If he just sits there than White will be able to create extremely serious threats.

21 c5! 1:32

'White has a gorgeous position, but it would be nice to get something more than just piece play. Now I'm threatening 22 ♖xd6, followed by ♘d5 aiming at f6; or 22 cxd6 with a passed pawn.'

21 ...   ♖be8 1:06
22 ♘d5 1:44

If 22 ♖xd6 ♕xg4 23 ♘d5 ♖e6! 'White is OK, but I felt the tension had been reduced too early. Obviously, Black will have to return some material. But if he ever gains control or even just a few targets for his queen then the position may turn rapidly in his favour.'

22 ...   f6?! 1:06

Played immediately. But 'I think the move 22...♖e6 is

probably better. Black's problem after ...f6 is that should White ever win this pawn then there will be no shelter for the king on the dark squares – it would be nice to keep this move in reserve as an answer to a discovered check. The move certainly pleased me.'

23 ♘e3

'A beautiful square for the horse. As long as the exchange sacrifice (perhaps a misnomer) ...♖xe3 isn't too strong then White's position remains superbly co-ordinated.'

23...♖xe3 24 fxe3 d5 worried me at the time. However, after 25 ♗xd5+ ♔g7 26 ♗c4 ♕e7 27 ♖d6 White is first and decisively so since if 27...♕xe3 28 ♖d7+! wins.

23...♖e6 24 ♖fd1 ♖xe3 is another idea for Black.

23 ... ♕b5
24 cxd6 ♕e2

'24...♕d7 may be better but White already has a fine position. After the text, Black offered me a draw. But I didn't find it too hard to refuse – for one thing after 15 d4!? I felt obliged to play to a finish.'

25 ♗c3 ♕xa2
26 d7 ♖d8
27 ♖d6 ♔h7

'He wants to threaten ...♕xb3. 27...♔g7 may be better but by now I believed in White's position.'

28 ♘d5 ♕a3
29 b4! 2:04 ♕a4 1:49

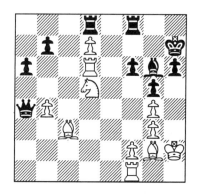

30 ♖a1!

Not 30 ♖e1? ♖xd7 31 ♖xd7+ ♕xd7, when:

a) 32 ♖e7+ is playable but seems a waste of such a good position.

b) 32 ♘xf6+ is an attempt to improve on this, but White is too loose for this to work, e.g. 32...♖xf6 33 ♗xf6 ♕xg4 (33...♔g8 first is also possible since now White could try 34 ♗d5; though Black can simply move his bishop, 34...♗f5) 34 ♖e7+ ♔g8 35 ♖g7+ ♔f8 36 ♖xg6? ♕h5+ wins.

30 ... ♕b5 2:19

After half an hour's thought. Black wanted to bail out with 30...♖xd7, but 31 ♖xf6! wins outright: 31...♕xa1 32 ♖xf8 garnering a whole piece.

30...♕b5 was the only alternative, since he must keep on the d-pawn: if 30...♕c2 31 ♘xf6+ ♖xf6 32 ♗xf6 wins.

31 ♖d1

'31 ♖a5 is also strong, but this keeps more control.'

31	...	♕e2
32	♘xf6+	♚h8
33	♖e1 2:20	♕c4 2:29
34	♗a1!?	

'I was starting to get short of time, myself; and the various forcing lines seemed rather confused,' e.g. 34 ♘d5+ ♚h7 35 ♖e7+ ♖f7 and:

a) 36 ♖e8 ♖xf2 37 ♘f6+ ♚g7 38 ♘e4+ ♕xc3!

b) 36 ♗e4! I dismissed this at the time with a question mark due to 36...♗xe4!, but in fact after 37 ♖xf7+ ♚g8 38 ♖e7 White is actually winning by force: 38...♗xd5 (or if 38...♕f1 39 ♖e8+ ♚f7 40 ♖f6+ ♚g7 41 ♖ff8+ ♚h7 42 ♖f7+ ♚g6 43 ♖g7 is mate) 39 ♖e8+ ♚f7 (39...♚h7 40 ♖xd8 ♕xc3 41 ♖f8) 40 ♖xd8 ♕xc3 41 ♖f8+.

34	...	♕a2
35	♚g1	♕c4

Of course, he had no time to think. 35...♚g7, threatening ...♕xa1!, would have been better; though White can simply reply 36 ♗d4.

I now found a way to improve the position by getting my king to g2 so as to use the h-file. Not only is this a good plan, but it is especially hard to meet in time trouble when a player, fired up by his adrenaline, is usually ready only to meet forcing lines.

36	♗f3	♕b3
37	♚g2	♕c4

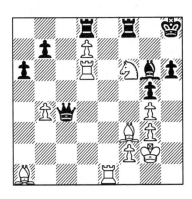

38	♘e4+	♚h7
39	♘xg5+!	hxg5
40	♖h1+	♚g8
41	♖xg6+	♚f7
42	♖g7+	1-0

Game 29
J.Speelman–V.Knox
British Championship (round 10), Torquay 1982
King's Indian Defence

Four rounds after the game with Andrew Martin, I got a chance to 'sacrifice my queen' for the third time in the tournament; though this time there was no speculation involved whatso-

ever – the price for Her Highness was total destruction of the enemy position.

1	c4	c6
2	e4	e5
3	♘f3	d6

4	d4	♘d7
5	♘c3	g6
6	♗e2 0:10	♗g7 0:13
7	d5!? 0:16	

Now that Black has spent a tempo on ...♗f8-g7, it seems reasonable to close the centre since later he is likely to 'lose a move' with ...♗g7-h6. White threatens dxc6 followed by ♕xd6. My opponent decided after just five minutes to close the centre.

7	...	c5!? 0:18
8	♗e3	♘gf6
9	♘d2	h5
10	a3	a6
11	b4	b6
12	h3 0:57	♗h6 0:38
13	♗xh6	♖xh6
14	♘f1	♔f8
15	♘e3 1:10	

White wants to get in h4 but first redeploys the knight. In fact 15 h4 at once looks a good idea. Perhaps I was concerned that in that case Black might try to create trouble somehow, but I don't see it now. Neither 15...b5 16 cxb5 axb5 17 ♗xb5; nor first 15...cxb4 16 axb4 a5 seems to work.

15	...	♔g7 0:42

This was played after only two minutes' thought. The thrust 15...h4!? looks better, with the idea of fighting for the dark squares.

16	h4! 1:16	

Now White gets some control of the dark squares on the kingside.

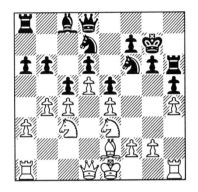

16	...	♘f8

I don't particularly like this. Of course, it is nice to open the bishop's diagonal; but now White gets the chance to exchange on c5 without having to reckon with ...♘xc5.

17	g3	♕e8
18	bxc5 1:27	bxc5 1:01

18...dxc5 would be extremely unstable.

19	♖b1 1:28	

Despite the exchange of Black's bad bishop, this position is very difficult for him since the d6-pawn is so weak. White is well placed to attack on the queenside by bringing out the queen, which may be helped by ♗d1–a4. And in the bishop's absence, f4 may even sometimes be a good move. Meanwhile, Black will find it very hard to create counterplay on the kingside, particularly after his next move.

19	...	♘8h7? 1:05

An ugly self-block. 19...♖h8 looks normal.

20 ♔f1 1:47 **♘g8?!** 1:18

Preparing ...f5. But by taking the pressure off e4, this now permits:

21 ♕a4 1:52 **♕d8** 1:39

21...♕xa4 22 ♘xa4 would be extremely unpleasant for Black, but 21...♗d7 22 ♕a5 f5 would at least have caused some confusion.

22 ♕c6 1:53

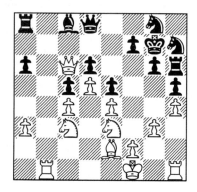

22 ... **g5?** 1:46

Not a bad move positionally since it frees the rook and provides lateral defence of the d6-pawn. But with the f5-square gaping the queen 'sacrifice' screams out to be played.

22...♘e7 would have prevented the queen sacrifice, but after something like 23 ♕b6 ♗d7! 24 ♕xd8 ♖xd8 25 ♖b6 ♗c8 26 f4 f6 27 ♔f2, or perhaps ♔g2 to avoid any trouble later on the f-file, the space advantage and control of the b-file combined with Black's disarray on the kingside add up to a huge advantage.

In this line Black would do better to start slugging with 26...f5!?, but 27 fxe5 dxe5 28 ♘a4 fxe4 29 ♘xc5 ♘f5 30 ♘xf5+ gxf5 31 ♖xh6 ♔xh6 32 ♔f2 ♘f6 33 ♖b1 still looks very good for White.

23 ♕xa8! 2:00 **♗h3+**
24 ♖xh3 **♕xa8**
25 ♘f5+ **♔g6**

To defend the h5-pawn. If 25...♔f8 26 ♘xh6 g4 27 ♘xg4 ♕c8 and White can choose between 28 ♔g2 hxg4 29 ♖hh1 and 28 ♘a4 hxg4 29 ♘b6 ♕c7 30 ♗xg4, both winning easily.

26 ♖b6

Obviously, White is in no hurry to surrender the superb stallion on f5 for Black's pathetic rook.

26 ... **♘hf6**
27 ♔g2 2:08 **gxh4** 2:01

Other moves are equally hopeless. If 27...♘e8 28 ♘xh6 ♘xh6 29 hxg5; or 27...♘xe4 28 ♘xe4 ♔xf5 29 ♗d3; or 27...g4 28 ♖h1 ♘xe4 29 ♘xe4 ♔xf5 30 ♗d3 ♔g6 31 ♘xd6+ etc.

28 ♘xh6 **♘xh6**
29 ♖xh4 2:13 **♘hg4** 2:05
30 ♗xg4 **hxg4**
31 ♖xd6 **♕b8**
32 ♖xg4+ **♔h5**
33 ♖xf6 **♔xg4**
34 ♖f5 2:19 **1-0** 2:13

6 Prelate Power

This chapter features three endings in which formally 'bad' bishops dominated opposing knights.

The first two examples include a pair of rooks while the final one ends as a pure minor piece ending.

Game 30
J.Speelman–G.Sax
Thessaloniki Olympiad 1988
English Opening

This game isn't particularly distinguished up to about move 30; but I was very pleased with the way in which my rook and bishop were able totally to dominate my opponent's rook and knight in the endgame.

1	♘f3	♘f6
2	c4	c5
3	♘c3	♘c6
4	d4	cxd4
5	♘xd4	♕b6!?

This was played almost immediately. Around this time, I had been having good results with 5...e6 6 a3. The point of this is to avoid the complications after 6 g3 ♕b6 7 ♘b3 ♘e5 when White is forced to

engage his opponent with 8 e4 ♗b4 9 ♕e2.

In this move order, the attempt to disrupt White with (5...e6 6 a3) 6...♕b6? is very dubious since White can reply 7 ♘db5! And if 7...d5 8 ♗e3 (not 8 cxd5 ♘xd5 9 ♘xd5 exd5 10 ♕xd5 ♗e6 with a vicious attack) and now:

a) 8...♕d8 9 cxd5 ♘xd5 (9...exd5 gives White the extra option of 10 ♗f4! which looks very strong, e.g. 10...d4 11 ♘c7+ ♔e7 12 ♘xa8 dxc3 13 ♕xd8+ ♔xd8 14 bxc3) 10 ♘xd5 exd5 11 ♕xd5! and Black has almost nothing for the pawn.

b) Black can try to cause disruption with 8...d4 but after 9 ♘xd4 (not 9 ♘a4? ♕a5+ 10 b4 ♘xb4 11 ♗d2 ♘e4 12 axb4 ♗xb4; but 9 ♗xd4 ♘xd4 10 ♕xd4 ♗c5 11 ♕f4 0-0 12 b4 also looks very strong) 9...♘g4 10 ♘a4 ♘xe3 11 ♘xb6 ♘xd1 12 ♘xa8 ♘xb2 (or 12...♘xf2 13 ♔xf2 ♘xd4 14 e3 ♘f5 15 ♘c7+ ♔d8 16 ♘b5) 13 ♘c7+ ♔d8 14 ♘cb5 Black has insufficient compensation for the exchange. So Sax forced me to commit the knight a move earlier.

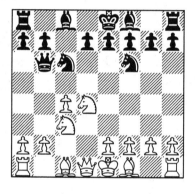

6 ♘b3

After 11 minutes' thought. The clock times were now 0.15-0.03.

In fact 6 ♘db5 is also far from ridiculous. It seems to lead to unclear lines after 6...a6 7 ♘a4:

a) 7...♕d8 8 ♘bc3 ♖b8 (8...b5 9 cxb5 axb5 10 ♘xb5 doesn't give much) 9 e4.

b) 7...♕a5+ 8 ♗d2 ♕d8 (not 8...♘b4? 9 ♘d4 and if 9...♘e4?

10 a3 wins material) 9 ♘bc3 ♖b8 10 e4.

6 ... e6
7 a3!? 0:15

Not 7 ♗e3 when 7...♕b4 is unpleasant. I played 7 a3 immediately so obviously it had been decided upon during the previous think. He now took 21 minutes before trying it on with:

7 ... ♘e5? 0:24

As in the 6 g3 line. Here, however, White not only controls c4 but also has no weakness on the c6-h1 diagonal. Black's alternatives were:

a) 7...d5 is possible, but 8 ♗e3 ♕d8 is a very pleasant version of a Tarrasch for White.

b) 7...♘a5 is also conceivable.

c) 7...d6 is perhaps the most sensible when 8 e4 ♗e7 9 ♗e3 ♕d8 10 ♗e2 leads to a fairly normal-looking 'Maroczy bind' Taimanov Sicilian. We could compare the position after 1 e4 c5 2 ♘f3 e6 3 d4 cxd4 4 ♘xd4 ♘c6 5 ♘b5 d6 6 c4 ♘f6 7 ♘1c3 a6 8 ♘a3 ♗e7 9 ♗e2. Here Black has lost time with his queen, but ♘d4-b3 is certainly not a manoeuvre which White would have undertaken voluntarily.

This line has been played from time to time with very reasonable results for Black – perhaps because a Taimanov Sicilian is not normally what White is going for when he opens 1 c4 or 1 ♘f3.

8 ♗e3!

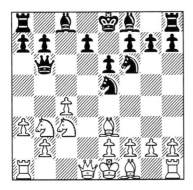

This seems more or less to refute Black's idea. After just five minutes he decided on the very modest

8 ... ♕d8

Rather abject, but although Black has lost two tempi with his queen and played ...♘c6-e5, White's extra moves – a3 and ♗e3 – lack bite; and ♘d4-b3 isn't very helpful either. So White's advantage is still within bounds.

Instead 8...♕c6 9 ♘d4 ♕c7 is sensible (unsurprisingly, 9...♕xc4 is bad after 10 ♖c1 ♘d5 11 ♘cb5 ♕a2 12 ♖c2 a6 13 b3 ♕xc2 14 ♕xc2 axb5 15 ♘xb5). But White has lots of good moves: 10 ♖c1, 10 ♘db5 ♕b8 11 c5 and 10 ♗f4 all spring to mind

9 ♗f4! 0:32

He now took a further 18 minutes on:

9 ... d6 0:47

If 9...♘xc4 10 e4 is very nasty; and both 9...♘g6 10 ♗d6

and 9...♘c6 10 ♘b5 (also possibly 10 c5) 10...e5 11 ♗g5 are pretty unpalatable.

10 c5! 0:48

Using the lead in development to attack Black's centre immediately.

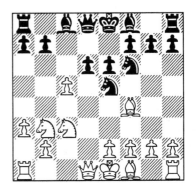

10 ... a6 0:55

If 10...♘h5 White can immediately force events with 11 ♗xe5 dxe5 12 ♕xd8+ ♔xd8 13 ♖d1+! (13 0-0-0+ leaves the f2-pawn undefended) 13...♗d7 14 g4 ♘f6 15 ♗g2 ♔c7 16 g5 ♘e8 which is pretty good after 17 ♗xb7 ♖b8 18 c6 (not indulging in 18 ♖xd7+ ♔xd7 19 c6+ ♔c7) 18...♗xc6 19 ♗xc6 ♔xc6 20 ♘a5+ ♔c7. Now 21 ♖c1 is simple and strong; while 21 b4, although it invites 21...♖xb4 also looks very good after 22 axb4 ♗xb4 23 ♖c1 ♗xa5 24 0-0.

11 e3 0:57

This looks rather lax. I imagine that 11 g3 may be better and 11 ♖c1 is also possible.

11 ... ♕c7 1:09

Against the more trenchant 11...b5!?, White can reply normally with 12 cxd6 ♕xd6 13 ♘a5 ♕c7 or 12 ♗e2 ♗b7 13 0-0 ♖c8 14 ♖c1; but he can also go for broke with 12 ♘d4!? and if 12...♗b7 13 ♘dxb5!? (13 ♘cxb5 axb5 14 ♗xb5+ ♔e7 15 c6 ♗a6 16 0-0) 13...axb5 14 ♗xb5+ ♘c6 15 cxd6 when the three pawns for the piece give reasonable play, particularly since Black cannot develop with the most natural move 15...g6? in view of 16 ♕f3! ♖c8 (16...♔d7 avoids losing back material) 17 ♗e5 ♗g7 18 d7+!

12 cxd6 1:02   **♕xd6** 1:20

12...♗xd6 13 ♕d4! (13 ♖c1 ♕b8 14 ♘d2!) is most unpleasant. It is important that Black doesn't have time to drive the bishop away from f4 since 13...♘h5? (13...0-0 14 ♖d1 ♘e8 15 ♘e4 ♘c6 16 ♗xd6 ♘xd4 17 ♗xc7 ♘xb3 18 ♗b6 is clearly better for White) 14 ♘e4 wins immediately – Sax.

13 ♗e2   **♗e7**
14 0-0   **0-0** 1:41
15 ♖c1 1:19

Sax now took seven of his remaining nineteen minutes before acquiescing in:

15 ...   **♕xd1**

15...♕b8 was conceivable with the point that if 16 ♕d4 ♘c6 stays alive.

16 ♖fxd1   **♘c6**

White's lead in development gives him a potentially very serious advantage. Of course

Black has few weaknesses, apart from the b6-square, but it will be extremely hard to develop without allowing some sort of blow.

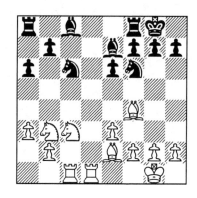

17 ♗d6?!

After just three minutes I decided on this reasonable but somewhat too minimalist approach. I should have gone for more with 17 ♘a4! (17 ♗f3 e5 is much less good) and if 17...e5 (17...♘d5 18 ♗g3 leaves Black in terrible trouble) 18 ♗g5 when:

a) The move that Black wants to play is 18...♗e6?, but it encourages 19 ♘bc5! – Sax.

b) 18...♘d5 19 ♗xe7 ♘dxe7 (or 19...♘cxe7 20 ♗f3 ♗e6 21 ♘bc5 and White will win at least a pawn) 20 ♘b6 ♖b8 21 ♘c5 ♖e8, and here White can cash in at once with 22 ♘xc8 ♘xc8 (22...♖exc8? 23 ♘d7 ♖a8 24 ♘b6; 22...♖bxc8 23 ♘xb7) and now even more ambitious than the simple 23 ♘xa6 bxa6 24 ♖xc6 ♖xb2 25 ♗xa6 is 23

♜d7 keeping up the pressure.

17	...	♗xd6
18	♜xd6	♜d8!
19	♜xd8+	♞xd8 1.50
20	♞a4 1.30	

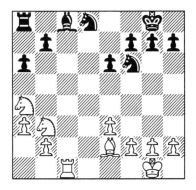

20	...	♗d7

After three more precious minutes. 20...♞d5!? was more combative. Here:

a) 21 ♗f3 ♗d7 22 ♞bc5 (maybe even 22 ♞ac5 ♗c6 23 ♞a5 ♜c8 24 ♞d3) 22...♜c8 23 ♗xd5 ♗xa4 24 ♜c3! ♗c6 25 ♗xc6 ♜xc6 26 ♜d3 ♜c8 27 g4 (perhaps 27 g3) and now:

a1) 27...a5 28 ♜d7 b5 is extremely risky. After, for example, 29 ♞b7 Black has got to try 29...♞c6 since 29...♞xb7 30 ♜xb7 simply wins a pawn. Then 30 ♞d6 ♞e5 31 ♞xc8 ♞xd7 32 ♞a7 b4 33 axb4 axb4 33 ♞c6 b3 looks better for White, but the b2-pawn is also a little weak. So perhaps White could try 30 f4 first.

a2) 27...♚f8 is more controlled. 28 b4 ♚e8 29 ♚g2 (29 ♜d6 ♚e7 30 ♜b6 ♜c7 31 ♚g2

a5) 29...a5 keeps White's advantage within bounds.

b) So I guess that White really ought to go for more with 21 e4 which one would like to avoid – it weakens the dark squares and very slightly exposes the pawn – but is necessary to maintain the initiative.

21	♞b6 1:31	♜b8 1:53
22	♞xd7!?	

After only four minutes, I continued with the minimalist approach – 22 ♞c5 would have maintained the pressure in a more complex way. Seeing this now, in July 1997, reminds me forcibly of Fischer's famous exchange of knight for bishop against Petrosian. I can't believe that this wasn't at least part of my motivation at the time.

22	...	♞xd7
23	♜c7	♞b6
24	♞c5	♞d5

This took him three minutes. If 24...♜c8 25 ♜xc8 ♞xc8 26 ♗f3 ♞d6 27 b4! fixes the queenside with a serious advantage.

25	♜d7 1:43	a5 1:57

To forestall b4, but this does weaken b5. If instead 25...♞f6 26 ♜d6 with a clear plus.

26	♗b5	b6

And this gives White control of c6.

27	♞e4 1:50	♞f6 1:57

By eliminating my knight, Sax hopes to stabilise the position sufficiently to hold the draw. The thing is that knights are particularly well suited for probing against weaknesses, so he is happy even to create another one – the doubled f-pawns – to get rid of them. Perhaps an even more important consideration for him was that knights are very hard to control when you're short of time.

28 ⚘xf6+ 1:50 **gxf6** 1:58
29 ⏛d6

29 f4 was possible at once.

29 ... **⚔g7**
30 f4!

To discourage ...e5. Up to here, this game hasn't been anything special, but the reason I have included it is my handling of the ending which has now arisen: White strives to get a complete grip without allowing the knight to get out and become active.

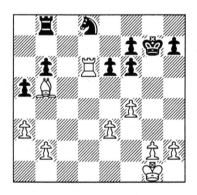

30 ... **⚔f8**
31 ⚔f2 **⚔e7**
32 ⏛d7+ **⚔f8**
33 ⚔f3

By now I'd almost caught up

on the clock: 1:56-1:57.

33 ... **⚘b7**
34 b4!

Of course, White must keep the knight locked in.

34 ... **axb4**
35 axb4 **⚘d8**
36 g4 **⏛c8**
37 ⏛d6?!

A perfectly good move. But, not wanting to commit myself in time trouble, I passed up the chance of 37 ⚔a6!, cementing the bind which I had managed to impose five moves later.

37 ... **⏛b8**
38 h4 **h6**
39 ⚔e2 **⚔e7**
40 ⏛d7+ **⚔f8**

I didn't record clock times past move 35 – so I guess we must both have been pretty short.

41 ⚔f3 **⏛c8?!**

The first move after the time control allows me to establish full control.

42 ⚔a6! 2:06 **⏛a8** 2:07
43 b5! 2:06

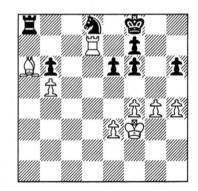

This very unusual plan is predicated on the control which it allows White to exert over the black pieces. By immuring the bishop on a6, White blocks the a-file and also controls c8, so making it impossible for the black rook to become active while the white one remains on the seventh rank; unless the knight can manage to move. But the knight is in trouble, hampered by the rigidity engendered by the doubled f-pawns. It has only two possible normal escape squares – e6 and f7; and Black is likely to have to make a very serious concession to free one of these.

There is one further possibility, though, which White must watch for. When the black rook is on a8 and the white one on d7 the move 1...♘c6 will occasionally be possible. Usually, White would win against this at once with 2 bxc6 ♖xa6 3 c7, but if White has weakened his king's pawn cover then 3...♖a3+ (or 3... ♖a4+ if the king is on the fourth rank) followed by 4...♖c3 will place it behind the newly passed c-pawn. However, even this won't help if the black king is on the eighth rank for then White will still have 5 ♖d8+. Black must now react quickly in the next couple of moves, before White can get a bind on the kingside. If White can get in h5 and f5 then there will be a cast-iron winning plan. Taking care

to avoid ...♘c6 as in the paragraph above – the rook can just sit on c7 for example, White will get his king to d4 and play e4.

If Black plays ...e5 then a stroll to d7 will end the game. But otherwise White can play e5 and, using repeated zugzwangs, he will gradually be able to penetrate with the king to f6. The rest will be a massacre – cf analysis diagram A1.

43 ... ♔e8 2:10

Fairly natural but the wrong way. The king needs, now or later, to go to g7 to try and create trouble on the kingside – and to get off the back rank in the hope of ...♘c6.

The three other possibilities were 43...♔g7, 43...f5 and 43...h5. We're still a bit far from the end to prove a definite win here, but they do all look very promising for White:

a) If 43...♔g7:

a1) 44 f5? is the wrong way round: 44...h5! and if 45 e4 hxg4+ 46 ♔xg4 exf5+ 47 exf5 ♘c6! works perfectly here 48 bxc6 ♖xa6 49 c7 ♖a4+ 50 ♔f3 ♖c4 51 ♔e3 b5 52 ♔d3 ♖c1 with a draw.

a2) 44 h5 f5 45 e4 is correct: 45...fxg4+ (45...♘c6 doesn't work here: 46 exf5 exf5 47 bxc6 ♖xa6 48 c7 ♖a3+ 49 ♔e2 ♖c3 50 g5! b5 51 g6 ♔f6 52 gxf7 ♔g7 53 f8♕+ ♔xf8 54 ♖d8+; or if 45...fxe4+ 46 ♔xe4 ♘c6 47 bxc6 ♖xa6 48 c7 ♖a4+

49 ♔e5 ♖c4 50 ♔d6 and wins)
46 ♔xg4 ♔f6 (Black can also
force matters himself with
46...e5 47 f5!) 47 ♖c7 ♔g7 48
f5 (in view of the note to
46...♔f6, 48 e5 isn't important)
48...♔f6 49 ♔f4 e5+ 50 ♔g4.

Despite the irritation caused
by having to guard against
...♔g5 – so the white king can't
just go for a walk – this structure seems to be winning, viz.
50...♖b8 51 ♖a7 ♔g7 52 ♖d7
♔f6 (or 52...♔f8 53 ♖d6 ♔g7
54 f6+ ♔f8 55 ♔f5) 53 ♖d6+
and if 53...♔e7 54 ♖xh6 f6 55
♖h8! or 53...♔g7 54 f6+ ♔f8
55 ♔f5 ♘e6 56 ♔xe5 must presumably be winning in the long
run.

b) If 43...h5 44 g5 fxg5 45
hxg5 ♔g7 46 ♔g3 (46 e4 first
invites 46...♘c6, but in fact 47
bxc6 ♖xa6 48 c7 ♖a3+ 49 ♔e2
♖c3 50 f5 exf5 51 exf5 is winning here since the king can't
hide from the threat of g6)
46...♔g6 47 e4 and:

b1) 47...♘c6 48 ♔h4 ♘b4 49
f5+ exf5 50 exf5+ ♔xf5 51
♖xf7+ must be winning, e.g.
51...♔e5 52 g6 ♘d5 53 ♗b7
♖a4+ 54 ♔g5 ♖g4+ 55 ♔xh5
♖g1 56 ♗xd5 ♔xd5 etc.

b2) If 47...f6 48 gxf6 ♔xf6
49 e5+ ♔g6 50 ♖e7 ♔f5 51
♔f3 (threatening ♖g7-g5 mate!)
51...♔g6 52 ♖e8 ♔f7 53 ♖h8
♔g7 White doesn't have anything better than 54 ♖xh5 ♘f7,
but this leaves him a pawn up
with a good structure and both

black pawns pretty weak.

c) 43...f5 was also possible of
course. It is conceivable that
Sax prefaced it with 43...♔e8
44 ♖c7 so as to avoid the simple win of a pawn with 44 gxf5
exf5 45 ♖d5, but I would have
been extremely loath to lift the
bind so cheaply. Instead 44 e4
would have led to lines somewhat similar to the thicket of
variations analysed later. And
while there must be differences
– quite possibly important ones
– I think it is time for a little
tree surgery at this point.

44 ♖c7

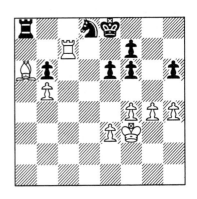

44 ... f5!

A reasonable try. I had
thought that the 'only sensible
alternative' 44...h5 lost simply
after 45 g5! (not 45 e4 hxg4+
46 ♔xg4 f5+! 47 exf5 exf5+ 48
♔xf5 ♘e6 with some chances)
which cramps Black further and
incidentally leaves the h-pawn
vulnerable on h5.

Although this is true, it does
require a slight refocusing by

White. 45...f5 (45...fxg5? is hopeless since 46 hxg5 ♔f8 47 e4 ♔g7 48 f5 kills the knight stone dead) 46 e4 and now:

a) 46...fxe4+? 47 ♔xe4 ♔f8 48 ♔e5 ♔g7 is easy since White can now simplify with 49 ♖c8 ♖xc8 50 ♗xc8 ♔g6, when the simplest win is 51 f5+! exf5 52 ♗xf5+ ♔g7 53 ♔d6 f6 54 g6 ♘b7+ 55 ♔c6 ♘c5 56 ♔xb6 etc.;

b) 46...♔f8! should also lose but is better psychologically. Now of course White would like to win 'cleanly' by maintaining the bind. But if he does pig-headedly play e5 then this will prevent the king from entering the black position, e.g.

b1) 47 ♔e3 ♔g7 48 ♔d4 ♔g6 49 e5 ♔g7 50 ♔c4 ♔f8 51 ♔b4 ♖b8 52 ♗c8 ♖a8 and Black is bound to break out whilst White is trying to get the bishop into play: 53 ♗d7 ♖a1 54 ♗c6 ♖c1! seizes control – not 54...♖f1? 55 ♖d7 ♖xf4+ 56 ♔c3 ♘xc6 57 bxc6 ♔e8 58 ♖xf7 ♖f1 59 ♔b2 winning.

b2) So the correct line is 47 exf5!, temporarily lifting the bind, which would be obvious to a machine but requires a slight change of mind-set from a person. After 47...exf5 White can now win rather simply by forcing off the rooks in order to win the f5-pawn. In the resultant position the h5-pawn, fixed on a light square, is also very vulnerable and the white king

can advance through the centre, viz. 48 ♖c8! ♖xc8 49 ♗xc8 f6 (49...♔g7 50 ♗xf5 ♘b7 51 ♔e3 ♘d6 52 ♗d3; and 49...♘e6 50 ♗xe6 fxe6 51 ♔e3 are absolutely hopeless) 50 ♗xf5 ♔g7 51 ♗d7 etc.

In the introduction to the above variations, I described 44...h5 as the only sensible alternative, but in fact 44...♔f8 is far from stupid. Now White wants to get in f5 and h5. However:

a) If 45 h5 f5 46 e4 fxg4+ 47 ♔xg4 f6 is a very good version for Black.

b) And 45 f5 h5! 46 e4 hxg4+ 47 ♔xg4 ♔g7 48 ♔h5 ♔h7 White's bad kingside structure is a serious matter which means that even though he can force the rook to the eighth rank with zugzwang I don't see a win.

c) So he should start with 45 e4! ♔g7 (if now 45...h5 46 g5! ♔g7 47 f5; or if 45...f5 then simply 46 exf5 exf5 47 gxf5 is very strong, e.g. 47...f6 48 ♔g4 ♘f7 49 ♗c8 ♖a4 50 ♔h5 ♖xf4 51 ♔g6 ♘e5+ 52 ♔xf6 ♘g4+ 53 ♔g6 ♘e5+ 54 ♔h5) 46 f5 and if 46...h5 47 g5 wins, otherwise White gets what he wants – cf analysis diagram A1.

45 e4

Threatening simply to take twice, after which the extra doubled pawn's control of e5 would make life very easy

45 ...   fxg4+

a) 45...f6 would at least have

given the knight a square; though of course White must be winning.

b) 45...fxe4+ 46 ♔xe4 f6 must also be losing. White's problem is to get the king in without allowing serious counterplay. There are two possibilities here. 47 f5 was my first reaction, but perhaps 47 g5 is even better. Black can then set up a temporary blockade by moving the knight to f7, but he has too many weaknesses and White has too much space, e.g.

b1) 47...fxg5 48 fxg5 hxg5 49 hxg5 ♘f7 50 g6 is utterly deadly since the pawn gets to g7.

b2) 47...♘f7 48 gxf6 ♔f8 49 ♖c6 and wins.

b3) 47...hxg5 48 fxg5 ♘f7 49 gxf6 ♔f8 and here, instead of the simple 50 ♖c6, White can even sacrifice a piece with 50 ♖c8+ ♖xc8 51 ♗xc8 ♘d6+ 52 ♔e5 ♘xc8 (52...♘xb5 53 ♗xe6) 53 h5 ♔f7 54 h6 ♔g6 55 ♔xe6 ♔xh6 56 ♔d7 ♘a7 57 f7 ♔g7 58 ♔e8.

46 ♔xg4   ♔f8
47 f5! 2.15   ♔g7?! 2.38

47...exf5+ was a little better, but 48 exf5 ♔g8 49 ♔f4, intending ♔e5-f6 and so forcing 49...f6, must be hopeless in the long run, although it is slightly messy, e.g. 50 ♔g4 ♘f7 51 ♔h5 and now:

a) 51...♔g7? 52 ♗c8 is simple. 52...♔f8 53 ♔g6 ♘d6 54 ♗a6 leaves White even more in

control.

b) 51...♖d8 52 ♔g6 (also 52 ♗c8 ♘e5 53 ♗e6+ ♔f8 54 ♖b7 ♖d4 55 ♖xb6 ♘f3 56 ♔g6 etc.) ♘e5+ 53 ♔xf6 ♘g4+ 54 ♔e6.

c) 51...♘e5!, centralising the knight, is much the most natural. i.e. 52 ♔xh6 ♖d8 and:

c1) Now something like 53 ♗c8 ♖d4 54 ♗e6+ ♔f8 55 h5 ♖b4 56 ♖b7! ♖xb5 57 ♖b8+ ♔e7 58 ♔g7 ♖b1 (58...♘g4 59 h6 wins trivially) 59 ♖b7+ ♔d6 60 ♔xf6 ♘g4+ 61 ♔g5 is presumably good enough, but Black can make some trouble with 61...♘e3 or perhaps 61...♘f2.

c2) But White can win technically with 53 ♖c8! ♖xc8 54 ♗xc8 ♘f3 55 ♗e6+ and the h-pawn is too strong: 55...♔f8 (or 55...♔h8 56 ♔g6 ♘xh4+ 57 ♔xf6) 56 h5 ♘h4 57 ♔h7 ♘g2 58 h6 ♘h4 (or 58...♘f4 59 ♗c4) 59 ♗c8 ♔f7 60 ♗d7 ♔e7 (60...♔f8 61 ♗e6) 61 ♔g8 and wins.

48 ♔f4

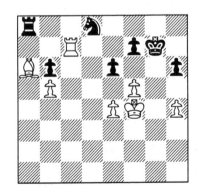

White is definitely winning now, since Black can prevent an eventual ♗f6 only by allowing the equally fatal e5 and f6+.

48 ...   **♔f6**

If 48...exf5 49 exf5 ♔f6 50 ♖d7 and repeated zugzwangs force a decisive entry: 50...♖b8 51 ♖a7 (zugzwang) 51...♔g7 52 ♔e5 ♔g8 53 ♔f6 ♔f8 54 ♖d7 ♖a8 55 ♖c7 ♖b8 56 ♖a7.

It is all over: zugzwang again. If 56...h5 White can simply reset with 57 ♖d7 ♖a8 58 ♖c7 ♖b8 59 ♖a7 and now:

Analysis diagram A1

a) 59...♔g8 60 ♔e7 ♔g7 (60...f6 61 ♔xf6 ♔f8 62 ♔g6 ♔g8 63 ♖e7 ♔f8 64 f6 ♖a8 65 ♖h7 ♔g8 66 f7+) 61 ♖d7.

b) 59...♔e8 60 ♔g7 f6 61 ♔g8.

49 e5+   **♔g7**
50 f6+   **♔g6**
51 ♔g4 2:20   **♖b8** 2:52
52 ♖a7

52 h5+ ♔h7 53 ♖e7 ♖a8 54 ♖e8 was equally effective. I guess I may have been worried about stalemate at the time but I don't see how Black can play for it in practice.

52 ...   **h5+**
53 ♔f4   **♔h6**
54 ♖e7   **♔g6**
55 ♖e8   **♔h6**
56 ♖f8!

Zugzwang.

56 ...   **♔g6**
57 ♖h8

And again.

57 ...   **♘c6**

If 57...♖a8 58 ♗b7.

58 bxc6   **♖xh8**
59 c7   **b5**
60 c8♕   **♖xc8**
61 ♗xc8   **b4**

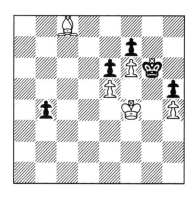

62 ♗xe6!   **1-0**

Although this caused immediate resignation, had I seen the more artistic line discovered by Jonathan Mestel, I would have considered playing it: 62 ♗a6!? b3 63 ♗d3+ ♔h6 64 ♗b1 b2 (Black hopes for stalemate, but White can walk down a ladder to capture the pawn) 65 ♔e4! ♔g6 66 ♔e3+ ♔h6 67 ♔d3! ♔g6 68 ♔d2+ ♔h6 69 ♔c2 etc.

Game 31
J.Speelman–M.Petursson
Novi Sad Olympiad 1990
Sicilian Defence, 3 ♗b5+ variation

The Icelander Margeir Petersson is a fine defensive player, not only prepared but even happy to contest the grimmest positions; partly, I presume, on the grounds that his opponents, even though it is they who might appear to be exerting the pressure, often eventually crack in frustration at his stubborn, immovable solidity. He is also, when he holds the reins, an excellent squeezer; though both of these modes at the chessboard are in sharp contrast to his extremely pleasant disposition away from it.

In this hard-fought battle, a pretty innocuous opening led, with a good deal of co-operation, to a position in which I was exerting some pressure. I then allowed it to dissipate to reach a most interesting ending just five moves before the time control.

In general, positions with just a few pieces on the board may not look 'sharp' in the conventional sense that there are dragoons of tactical fusillades waiting in the wings. But just beneath the apparently innocuous surface, a vicious if short tactical battle raged as I fought to dominate his pieces and he to

free them; while the strategic subtext also involved a fierce struggle for control of the light squares.

Sadly from an aesthetic (if not a practical) point of view, the battle only really lasted the five moves up to the time control. But the domination which I achieved, while less dramatic than that in the previous game, was equally effective on this occasion.

1	e4	c5
2	♘f3	d6
3	♗b5+	♗d7
4	♗xd7+	♘xd7
5	0-0	♘gf6
6	♖e1 0:10	e6 0:05
7	d3!? 0:16	

By playing 6 ♖e1, White threatened, if that is not too strong a word, c3 followed by d4; and so induced ...e6 rather than the slightly more aggressive 7...g6, after which 8 c3 and 9 d4 is quite good. Now, however, the main line with 7 c3 ♗e7 8 d4 cxd4 9 cxd4 d5 10 e5 ♘e4 is known to be fine for Black. So instead I switched to a slower development, intending first to develop ♘b1-d2-f1-g3 before finally getting in the d4 advance.

But this is very insipid and

Black must be fine as long as he reacts well.

7 ... ♗e7 0:09
8 ♘bd2 0:22 **0-0** 0:12

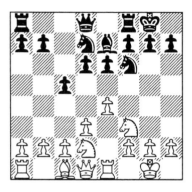

Half a decade later, Loek van Wely played 8...b5 at once against me in a Dutch League match. Loek plays for the extremely strong de Variant team from Breda and I had been persuaded, for the one and only time in my decade in the Dutch League, to play for my club Volmac's second team.

Unfortunately, this manoeuvre was punished since I now attempted to exploit the early thrust with 9 a4!?, but after the simple 9...a6 10 h3 0-0 11 ♘f1 he provoked me with 11...♘b6 12 a5!? ♘bd7 13 ♘g3 ♘b8! 14 e5 ♘fd7 15 exd6 ♗xd6 16 ♘e4 ♗e7 17 d4 ♘c6 18 ♗e3 c4. The a-pawn is horribly weak. I now thrashed around with 19 ♗g5 ♗xg5 20 ♘exg5 ♘f6 21 ♘e4 ♘xe4 22 ♖xe4 ♘xa5 23 ♘e5 ♕d5 24 ♖h4 ♘c6 25 ♕h5 h6 26 ♘xc6 ♕xc6 27 ♖a3 f5! 28 ♖g3

♖f6, but this is clearly winning and he converted in 17 more moves.

9 h3 0:28
If 9 ♘f1 ♘g4!? is possible, en route to e5. Black wants to reposition one of his knights on c6 to fight for the d4-square. While he can always do so with ...♘d7-b8-c6, I felt that he would slightly annoy me if it went via e5, threatening to exchange. In fact I could just move the knight away from f3: 10 ♘d2, when 10...♘ge5 11 f4 ♘c6 12 ♘f3 is a reasonable way to play the position.

9 ... **b5** 0:24
10 ♘f1 0:32 **c4?!** 0:29
10...♘e5 was fine for Black.
11 ♘g3 0:36
If 11 d4 at once, Black can reply 11...d5 12 e5 ♘e4 after which I would have probably acquiesced in exchanging it. So in accordance with the plan started by 7 d3, I first moved the knight, now threatening d4 after which Black, unable to go in to e4, would be a little congested.

11 ... **cxd3** 0:33
12 cxd3 0:36 **♘e5** 0:36
After gaining some time advantage in the opening, Petursson had now caught me up. We then stayed roughly balanced until move 20, but thereafter I remained very slightly ahead. And the clock was to be very significant in the critical stages of the ending.

I now chose a fairly minimalist move, simply establishing my centre. But 13 ♘h2 was also possible, keeping an extra pair of minor pieces on the board – in principle the player with a space advantage should avoid exchanges, hoping to profit from the congestion which the opponent may suffer from.

13 d4 0:39   **♘xf3+** 0:36
14 ♕xf3 0:40   **d5** 0:38
15 e5 0:41   **♘d7?!** 0:44

After this, the knight turns out to be on rather a restricted circuit; more important, I get the immediate chance to create some trouble by attacking g7. So 15...♘e8 was better.

16 ♘h5 0:53   **♔h8** 0:46

If 16...g6 17 ♘f4 with an edge.

17 ♕g4 0:58   **♖g8** 0:49
18 ♗d2! 1:06

The reason for going here rather than the more obvious e3 is so as not to interrupt the rook's defence of the e5-pawn:

a) 18 ♖e3? is much too crude. After 18...♖c8 19 ♖f3 ♖c4 Black is already hitting the e5-pawn.

b) If 18 ♗e3 I was concerned about 18...♖c8 19 ♖ac1 ♖c4, when 20 b3?? is met by 20...♘xe5. But 20 ♕f3 is sensible, hitting f7: 20...♖f8 (20...f6 21 ♘f4 is unpleasant) 21 b3 ♖xc1 22 ♖xc1 is quite a good version for White.

18 ...   **♘b6** 1:08

The 19 minutes spent on this fairly unremarkable move must have reflected, above all, his discomfort.

If 18...♖c8 19 ♖ac1 ♖c4 White can play 20 b3 immediately.

19 b3 1:09   **♖c8** 1:09
20 ♖ac1 1:11   **♗a3** 1:10

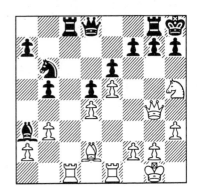

21 ♗g5! 1:12   **♖xc1** 1:21

Normally, Black wouldn't exchange like this since it appears to concede the c-file. But in his 11 minutes' thought, Petursson has decided that White will be obliged to recapture with the bishop.

22 ♗xc1!? 1:19

Of course, I would have liked to play 22 ♖xc1, but I wasn't sure about the main line: 22...f6! (the pathetic 22...♗e7 23 ♗xe7 simply cedes White a large safe advantage) 23 exf6 gxf6 24 ♗xf6+ (not 24 ♘xf6? ♗xc1 25 ♕h4 ♕c7 26 ♘xg8 ♔xg8 winning for Black) 24...♕xf6 25 ♕xg8+ ♔xg8 26 ♘xf6+ ♔f7 27 ♖c7+ ♔xf6 and probably now 28 ♖xh7. While I felt that White must be doing pretty well here, I didn't at all like the fact that the bishop will soon be capturing on d4.

I tried to find other tactical ways to make this work, but they didn't seem adequate. For instance, (22 ♖xc1 f6) 23 ♘f4 sets up the crude trap 23...♗xc1?? 24 ♘g6+ hxg6 25 ♕h4 mate, but Black can simply take the piece with 23...fxg5 24 ♘xe6 ♕e8 25 ♖c7 ♗e7! when White's compensation for the piece is surely insufficient.

22 ... ♗e7 1:24

22...♗b4? hits a rook again, but in this case White can ignore the 'threat' with 23 ♗g5! when if 23...f6? 24 exf6 gxf6 25 ♘xf6 ♖xg5 26 ♕xg5 ♗xe1 27 ♕e5! results in a quick win – 27...♗xf2+ 28 ♔xf2 ♕f8 29 ♔g1 doesn't help at all.

23 ♗e3 1:19 **♘d7** 1:33
24 ♖c1 1:26 **a5** 1:33

Preparing to exchange one of his weak queenside pawns. I used the time this entails to improve my kingside.

25 g3 1:31 **a4** 1:35
26 h4 1:33 **axb3** 1:36
27 axb3 1:36 **♕b6** 1:38
28 ♘f4 1:38

Threatening 29 ♘xd5.

28 ... ♖d8 1:40
29 ♘h3! 1:39

Threatening 30 ♗g5 to force off the bishops, after which g7 would be that much weaker and alternatively the c5-square

would beckon for the knight.

29 ... ♖a8 1:43

Of course if now 30 ♗g5 the bishop can simply retreat to f8, But strangely, it is quite a good idea to force the exchange of the white knight for the black bishop.

30 ♘g5 1:43

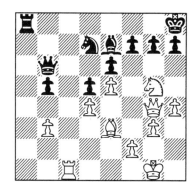

30 ... ♗xg5 1:46

Margeir was concerned to limit my attacking chances which would flare up after 30...♔g8 31 h5.

Now if 31...♗xg5 32 ♗xg5! Black is in serious trouble since he doesn't have time to stop h6: 32...♔f8 33 h6 g6 leaves the black king in a real draught and White's next move might be 34 ♕d1, preparing to infiltrate.

So Black is morally obliged to try 31...h6, when White would keep a good game with the simple 32 ♘h3, but the critical line is 32 ♘xf7! ♔xf7 33 ♕g6+ ♔f8 (not 33...♔g8 34 ♗xh6 ♗f8 35 ♗xg7!)

After considerable analysis I

believe that this is quite good for White; but Black does have a single reasonable way to play the position – see line b32 below.

a) Here in my original notes in *Informator 50* I suggested the immediate 34 ♗xh6 gxh6 and then 35 ♖c3, but this is gilding the lily since it gives the bishop a good square on g5:

a1) 35...♗g5? loses the a8 rook to 36 ♖f3+ ♔e7 37 ♖f7+ ♔d8 38 ♕g8+ ♔c7 39 ♕xa8.

a2) Instead Black must check first 35...♖a1+ 36 ♔g2 ♗g5 37 ♖c8+ (if 37 ♖f3+ ♔e7 38 ♕g8 ♘xe5 39 dxe5 ♔d7 40 ♖f7+ ♗e7) 37...♗d8 38 ♕xh6+ ♔e7 39 ♕g7+ ♔e8 40 ♕g6+ ♔e7 41 ♕g5+ ♔e8 and White has a draw but no more.

b) 34 ♖c3 first keeps control of g5 for one more move. The only, if obvious, disadvantage is that Black can attack the rook. But it seems that in response White can always just take on h6, e.g. 34...♗b4 35 ♗xh6 and:

b1) 35...♗xc3 36 ♕xg7+ ♔e8 37 ♕g8+ ♘f8 38 ♕xf8+ ♔d7 39 ♕xa8 ♗xd4 and White should win.

b2) 35...♖a1+ 36 ♔g2 ♗xc3 37 ♕xg7+ ♔e8 38 ♕g8+ ♘f8 39 ♗xf8 ♔d7 40 ♗c5.

Unsurprisingly, White's bishop and queen combined with the enormous passed h-pawn will easily defeat Black's almost naked king, particularly since White can often get a

passed e-pawn as well and Black has only minimal counterplay.

The variations, which I've tried to cut down to a less than totally unreasonable quantity, are considerably more enjoyable for White than Black:

b21) 40...♕d8 41 ♕f7+ and:

b211) 41...♔c8 42 h6 ♖a2 43 h7 ♗e1 44 ♕g8! ♖xf2+ 45 ♔h3 wins.

b212) 41...♔c6 42 ♕xe6+ ♔b7 43 ♕f7+ ♔c6 44 e6 ♖a8 45 h6 (threatening h7, h8♕ and ♕d7 mate) 45...♗a5 (or 45...♕e8 46 h7 ♖d8 47 ♕a7 ♕xe6 48 ♕b6+ ♔d7 49 ♕b7+ ♔e8 50 h8♕+) 46 h7 ♗c7 47 h8♕ ♕xh8 48 ♕d7+ ♔b7 49 ♕xb5+ ♔c8 50 e7.

b22) 40...♕c6 41 ♕f7+ ♔c8 42 h6 ♕d7 43 ♕g8+ ♔b7 44 h7 and wins.

b23) 40...♕b7 41 h6 ♖a8 and now the simplest is 42 h7 ♕c8 43 ♕f7+ ♔c6 44 h8♕! ♕xh8 45 ♕xe6+ ♔c7 46 ♕d6+ ♔c8 47 ♕c6+ ♔b8 48 ♗d6+ ♔a7 49 ♕xc3 etc.

b24) 40...♕a6 is the most

challenging, aiming to play ...b4 to generate some play of his own. But after 41 ♕f7+:

b241) 41...♔c6 42 ♕xe6+ ♔b7 43 ♕f7+ (there is no need for 43 ♕d7+ ♔a8 44 e6 b4 45 ♔h2 ♖h1+ when Black get lots of checks – though in fact White can escape) 43...♔a8 (if 43...♔c6 44 e6 ♕c8 45 h6 ♖a8 46 h7 ♕c7 47 e7 ♕d7 48 ♕f6+ ♔c7 49 ♕b6+ ♔c8 50 h8♕+; while 43...♔b8? allows forced mate: 44 ♗d6+ ♔a8 45 ♕e8+ ♔b7 46 ♕b8+ ♔c6 47 ♕c7 mate) 44 e6 b4 45 ♔h2 ♖e1 46 e7 ♕c8 47 e8♕ ♕xe8 48 ♕a7 mate.

b242) 41...♔c8 42 h6 b4 43 ♔h2 ♕f1 is perhaps the most entertaining line, but White can force mate starting 44 ♕xe6+ ♔b8 45 ♕d6+ ♔c8 46 ♕c6+ and now if 46...♔d8 47 ♗b6+ ♔e7 48 ♕f6+ ♔e8 (48...♔d7 49 ♕d6+ ♔e8 50 ♕e6+ ♔f8 51 ♗c5 mate) 49 ♕e6+ ♔f8 50 ♗c5 mate; or 46...♔b8 47 ♗d6+ ♔a7 48 ♕d7+ ♔a6 49 ♕c8+ ♔b6 50 ♗c5+ ♔b5 51 ♕b7+ ♔a5 52 ♕b6 mate.

b3) 35...gxh6! (best) 36 ♖f3+ ♔e7 37 ♖f7+ ♔e8 38 ♖f4+! ♔e7 39 ♕f7+ ♔d8 40 ♕g8+ and now:

b31) If 40...♗f8 41 ♖xf8+ ♘xf8 42 ♕xf8+ ♔c7 43 ♕xa8 ♕xd4 44 ♕a5+! wins since after 44...♔c8 45 ♕a6+! ♔c7 46 ♕xe6 ♕e4 47 ♕f7+ White can simply push the e-pawn.

b32) I had thought that if

Black retained the two pieces, the white queen and rook would be too strong. But Black can fight on with 40...♔c7! 41 ♕xa8 ♗c3! attacking the d4-pawn. I can't then see better than 42 ♕h8 (if 42 ♕a3? ♗xd4 43 ♕d6+ ♔c8! Black is better) 42...♗xd4 43 ♕xh6 when play would perhaps continue with 43...♗xe5 44 ♖f7. In any case, although the h-pawn is very strong, Black is well centralised and White has a real fight on his hands.

31 ♕xg5 1:43 **♔g8!** 1:50

Not 31...♖e8? when 32 ♕e7! wins at least the f-pawn.

32 ♕e7 1:47 **♕b7** 1:50

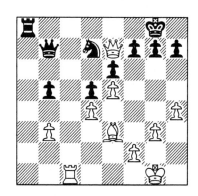

33 ♗d2?! 1:47

This quick move more or less forces the endgame which follows. But I now think that it would have been a much better idea first to interpose 33 h5! h6 and then continue 34 ♗d2 ♖c8 35 ♖a1 ♘c5 36 ♕xb7 ♘xb7 37 ♗b4 as in the game. Here White is much better placed on the kingside since it is vital to stop the black king walking out along the light squares into the centre; and h5, which can if necessary be supported by g4, greatly assists that.

In this line, Black must prevent h6. For if 33...♖c8 34 h6 ♖xc1+ 35 ♗xc1 ♕c8 36 ♗d2 (better than 36 ♕g5 g6 37 ♗a3 f6! 38 exf6 ♔f7) 36...g6? (36...♘f8 37 hxg7 ♘g6 38 ♕b4 is awful but relatively best) 37 ♗b4 ♕f8 38 ♕xd7 ♕xb4 39 g4! ♕f8 (if 39...♕e1+ 40 ♔g2 ♕e4+ 41 ♔g3 ♕d3+ 42 f3 stops the checks or if 39...♕a3 simply 40 ♔g2) 40 g5 the bind on the kingside unsurprisingly leads to a forced win: 40...b4 (or 40...♕b8 41 ♕e7 b4 42 ♕f6 ♕f8 43 ♔f1 and mates) 41 ♔g2 ♔h8 42 ♕d6 ♔g8 43 ♔g3 (zugzwang) 43...♕xd6 44 exd6 ♔f8 45 ♔f4 ♔e8 46 ♔e5 ♔d7 47 ♔f6 ♔xd6 48 f4 ♔d7 (or 48...♔c6 49 ♔g7) 49 ♔xf7 ♔d6 50 ♔e8 etc.

33 ... ♖c8 1:51
34 ♖a1 1:50
If 34 ♖xc8+ ♕xc8 35 ♗b4 ♘b8 gets the knight out with a perfectly acceptable position.
34 ... ♘c5! 1:51
The only way to break out.
35 ♕xb7 1:50 **♘xb7** 1:51
As mentioned in the introduction, this deceptively quiet-looking position is in fact very tense. Although the pawn structure, with White's two central pawns fixed on dark

squares, might look formally as if it favoured the knight, temporarily, at least, a more important feature is the steed's offside position which makes it hard for it to get to a decent square.

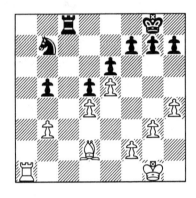

If he can activate the knight without undue cost, then Black may get an excellent game. But otherwise the knight will be a liability, subject to attack by the white rook; and there will be a knock-on effect of making the b5-pawn weak.

I suspect, however, that when entering this ending I had probably rather overestimated White's chances, for there is a very important tactical point. The obvious plan, after putting the bishop on b4, is to penetrate with 1 ♖a7, but this often runs into the tactical retort 1...♘d8 2 ♗c5 ♘c6 3 ♖ (moves) ♘xe5!

I can't remember now when I realised this problem, but I don't believe that it was as early as it should have been – i.e. before playing 33 ♗d2.

36 ♗b4 1:50 **f6!?** 1:54

In time trouble, Petursson decides on an immediate attack on the white pawn chain and also prepares to get his king out; but the e6-pawn is weakened.

Instead 36...♘d8? 37 ♗c5 ♘b7 38 b4 is very bad for Black, since the attempt to get play with ♘xc5 39 bxc5 ♖b8 fails to 40 ♖a6 b4 41 ♖b6!

But 36...h5 was a sensible alternative, when 37 ♖a6 is the obvious reply (if instead 37 ♖a7!? ♘d8 38 ♗c5 ♘c6 39 ♖b7 ♘xe5!? [39...b4 is also possible here] 40 ♖xb5 ♘d3 41 b4 ♖a8 42 ♖a5 ♖b8 43 ♖a4 is a pretty bad version for White, but White could start with 37 ♔g2). Now the attempt to go active immediately leads to disaster: 37...♖c1+? 38 ♔g2 ♖b1 39 ♖a7! ♖xb3 40 ♗e7! trapping the knight. So Black must retreat with 37...♘d8! 38 ♗c5.

White is now threatening to consolidate with 39 b4, after which the b5-pawn would be in terrible trouble. Black has only one challenging reply: 38...b4!

using tactics to undermine the bishop. White now has a big choice of plans:

a) Black's main idea is that if 39 ♗xb4 ♘c6 40 ♗c5 ♘xe5! regains the pawn. Although, in fact, this may still be good for White since the b-pawn is very dangerous, e.g. 41 b4 (also maybe 41 ♔f1 first: 41...♘d3 42 b4 ♖b8 43 ♖a4) 41...♘c4

Now after 42 b5 ♖b8 43 b6 the passed pawn is far advanced, but the rest of White's position isn't very wonderful. To support the pawn – which should ultimately win a piece – White needs six moves: ♔g1-f1-e2-d3-c3-b4-b5; which will give Black time either to get his king across, or to try create counterplay on the kingside.

Perhaps instead White should first bring his king into play with 42 ♔f1 – or play 41 ♔f1 a move earlier.

b) 39 ♖b6 ♘c6 40 f4 stops ...♘xe5 but further weakens the light squares. Black can get his king out via g6 and even in a pretty co-operative line like 40...♔h7 41 ♔f2 ♔g6 42 ♔e3 (42 ♖b7 f6) 42...♖c7 43 ♗d6 ♖c8 44 ♔d3 ♔f5 45 ♖b7 ♔g6 46 ♗xb4 ♘xb4+ 47 ♖xb4 ♖c1, which is the best rook ending that White can possibly get, Black's counterplay looks likely to be enough to escape with a draw.

c) 39 ♖b6 ♘c6 40 ♖b5 is another way of stopping ...♘xe5.

But after 40...♖a8 Black will soon be threatening to get active and a possible, if somewhat contrived, repetition goes 41 ♖b6 ♖c8 (threatening ...♘xe5 again) 42 ♖b5 ♖a8 etc.

My impression of these is that if White has to play f4 and allow the black king to get active then even if he wins the b4-pawn it won't be clear. So perhaps it is best to exchange the e5-pawn for the b-pawn as in line a.

d) But when I showed the game to Daniel King, he pointed out that if White is going to have to play f4 then he should do so immediately: 39 f4. The advantage of this is that b4 is now really en prise since the e5-pawn has an additional protector. Black can choose either to sacrifice the b-pawn to get his king out or to defend it and neither plan is very clear:

d1) 39...♘c6 40 ♔f2 ♔h7 41 ♔f3 ♔g6 42 g4.

Analysis diagram D1

By doing without ♖b6, White

has gained an important tempo which he has used to get in g4, confining the enemy king. As a result the black monarch is quite short of squares and there are even lines in which White generates mating threats.

d11) Thus if 42...♖c7 43 ♖a8 is very dangerous with the idea of 44 ♖h8, when if Black captures 44...hxg4+ 45 ♔xg4 White is already threatening mate in one! For instance:

d111) 43...♘e7 44 ♖h8 hxg4+ 45 ♔xg4 f6 46 h5+ ♔f7 47 ♖b8 is over since the b-pawn is falling and Black can hardly move – if the rook goes off the second rank ♖b7 will win the knight; while if the knight vacates e7 then ♖f8 is mate!

d112) 43...f6 44 gxh5+ is no better: 44...♔f5 (or 44...♔xh5 45 ♖h8+ ♔g6 46 ♔g4 as in the variation d111) 45 h6! ♔g6 (if 45...gxh6 46 ♖f8!) when most crushing of all is 46 f5+! ♔h7 47 exf6 gxf6 48 fxe6.

d12) 42...hxg4+ 43 ♔xg4. Now if 43...f5+ (43...♔h6 44 f5 exf5+ 45 ♔xf5 ♔h5 46 e6 fxe6+ 47 ♔xe6 wins easily) the white king simply retreats: the c6-pawn is then dreadfully weak and, without the possibility of ...f6xe5 to undermine the bishop, it is tremendously strong on c5.

So Black must try 43...f6, when it looks simplest to take straight away with 44 exf6 so that if 44...gxf6 45 f5+ exf5+ 46

♔f4. Black could instead re-capture with the king 44...♔xf6 in which case White would have preferred to have interpolated h5+. But White can play 45 ♖b6! with a big advantage since if 45...♘e7 46 ♗xe7+! – if the knight gets to f5 Black has counterplay – 46...♔xe7 47 f5 the rook ending is very good for White

d13) Black's most combative try is 42...f6.

This invokes ideas for White of 43 f5+ exf5 44 e6. But here Black will get another pawn with check – 44...fxg4+ 45 ♔f4 g3 46 ♔xg3 ♔f5 is sensible, when if 47 ♗d6 ♖c8 48 e7 ♘xe7 (and maybe 48...♘xd4) 49 ♗xe7 ♖c3+ gives Black lots for the piece. (This looks inadequate but it suggests that possibly White could have tried 41 g4 first earlier in this variation and if 41...♔g6 then 42 ♔g3.)

Instead White might sacrifice some pawns to misplace the black king with 43 exf6 gxf6 44 f5+ exf5 45 gxh5+ ♔xh5 46 ♔f4 which looks pretty unpleasant since after 46...♔xh4 47 ♔xf5 ♔g3 48 ♔e6! f5 49 ♔xd5 White is in control: if 49...f4 50 ♖xc6 ♖xc6 51 ♔xc6 f3 52 d5 stops the pawn.

While if Black retreats with 46...♔g6 White can even play 47 h5+ if he wishes.

d2) However, all these lines in which Black goes passive are predicated on the idea that he must defend his b-pawn. Instead 39...♔h7 leads to a completely different complex of variations.

Now White could and probably should simply continue with 40 ♔f2, when if 40...♔g6 41 ♔f3 ♔f5 42 ♖a7! is annoying; so instead Black could play 41...♘c6 42 g4 transposing to variation d1 above.

At first I thought 40 ♗xb4 instead of 40 ♔f2 would be strong, since 40...♖c1+ 41 ♔g2 ♖b1 42 ♗e7 ♘b7 43 b4; and 40...♖b8 41 ♗a5 ♘b7 42 ♖b6 ♖a8 43 ♗b4 are both very bad.

But Black should simply advance his king, 40...♔g6! White can't block him since if he moves the king to f3 then ...♖b8 will gain the advantage – b3 will be en prise with check.

So the question is whether White has time to establish a bind on the queenside. The most natural line is 41 ♗c5 ♔f5 42 b4 ♔e4 and now perhaps 43 b5 to cut out the threat of ...♘c6xd4.

Analysis diagram D2

This extremely critical position is so far from the game that I am going to give a few lines then leave it to any interested researcher to see if they can be improved upon.

d21) 43...♖b8 44 b6 ♘c6? 45 ♖a3! keeps the black king out of White's position.

d22) But 43...♖b8 44 b6 ♘b7 is tricky since if 45 ♗d6 ♘xd6 46 exd6 ♖b7!! (46...♔xd4 47 d7 ♔c5 48 b7 and queens a pawn) stops both the pawns – whenever White puts his rook on the seventh rank to force the advance of one of them, the black rook will be able to end up behind it, i.e. if 47 ♖a8 ♔xd4 48 ♖c8 ♔e3 49 ♖c7 ♖xb6 50 d7 ♖d6 is good for Black. (At first I'd failed to notice this excellent square in the middle of Black's pawn mass.)

d23) 43...♖b8 44 b6 ♔d3 (or 43...♔d3 at once) is conceivable to avoid the king being cut off by ♖a3!

d24) 43...♘b7!? 44 ♖a4! (44 ♖c6 ♖a8 45 ♖c7 ♖a1+ 46 ♔f2 ♘xc5 47 dxc5 ♖a2+ can only be good for Black) 44...♔f3 45 ♖a3+ ♔e4 46 ♗b6! (not 46 ♖c3 ♘xc5 47 dxc5 ♔d4!). Now the black rook gets in but his knight is awful: 46...♖c1+ 47 ♔f2! (if 47 ♔g2 ♖b1 48 ♖a7 ♖b2+ 49 ♔h3? ♔f3 50 ♖xb7 ♖b1 51 ♔h2 ♖b2+ 52 ♔h3 ♖b1 drawing) 47...♖b1 48 ♖a7 ♖b2+ 49 ♔e1 ♖xb5! 50 ♖xb7 ♔f3 (if 50...♔e3 51 ♔d1 ♔d3 52 ♔c1

escapes), reaching the following position:

Although Black has no pawns for the piece the hyperactive king and pin give him drawing chances. But now White has a useful tactical trick: 51 ♔d2 and if 51...♔xg3 52 f5! ♔h3 (52...exf5 53 e6!) 53 fxe6 fxe6 54 ♔e3.

51...g6 is better and perhaps 52 ♖b8!? ♔xg3 53 f5! when if Black ignores the pawn then 54 f6!? followed by ♖b7xf7, going into a rook ending, will be very dangerous; while 54...gxf5 (54...exf5 55 e6! again) 55 ♖b8+ unpins. Still, either of these lines would have afforded serious resistance.

37 f4 1:51

Very ambitiously maintaining the bind. The more modest 37 exf6 gxf6 38 ♖a6 was quite possible, when a likely line would be 38...♔f7 39 ♖b6 ♘d8 40 ♖xb5 ♘c6 41 ♗c5 (if 41 ♖c5 ♔e8 42 ♗c3 ♔d7 threatens 43...♖b8; though 44 ♖b5 looks reasonable) when Black can get some counterplay by advancing with 42...e5.

37 ...   fxe5 1:55

Margeir wanted to clarify which way I would recapture, though since I didn't really want to capture on f6, this is a slight concession. If Black now plays ...h5, the g5-square will be available for the bishop.

38 fxe5 1:54

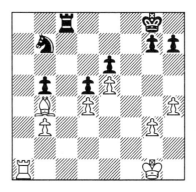

38 ...   ♔f7? 1:56

But it is only after this that White is able to consolidate his control of the position. The correct move was 38...h5!, both fighting for the light squares and creating an alternative route for the black king to advance without allowing the knight to be pinned. White has two plausible continuations:

a) The natural 39 ♖a6 is presumably what put Petursson off, but after 39...♔f7 (again not 39...♖c1+? 40 ♔g2 ♖b1? 41 ♖a7 ♖xb3 42 ♗e7) 40 ♖b6 (40 ♖a7 ♖c7 is an important tempo down on the game) Black should be able to create serious

counterplay while White is winning the b-pawn, by advancing his king towards e4 and even f3.

White can react either by bringing out his own king to f3, in which case ...♖c1 will create counterplay; or by blocking the c-file with ♗c5, when the black rook can't use that line but his king will reach e4, e.g. 40 ♖b6 ♘d8 41 ♖xb5 ♔g6 and:

a1) 42 ♔f2 ♔f5 43 ♔f3 ♖c1 and I can't see how White can get control. If 44 ♖b8 ♘c6 45 ♖f8+ ♔g6 46 ♗c5 ♘xe5+; or 44 ♗d2 ♖f1+ 45 ♔e2 ♖g1, when if 46 ♖b8 ♘c6 47 ♖f8+ ♔g4 (not 47...♔e4?? 48 ♖f4 mate!) 48 ♔f2, simply 48...♖xg3 49 ♖f4+ ♔h3 with the advantage; or 44 ♗c5 ♖c3+.

a2) 42 ♗c5 ♔f5 43 ♖b6 ♔e4 and now:

a21) 44 ♔g2 ♘c6 45 b4 (maybe 45 ♔h3 or 45 g4!?) 45...♘xd4 46 ♗xd4 ♔xd4 47 ♖xe6 ♖b8 and the d-pawn supported by the king ought to give Black enough counterplay.

a22) 44 b4 ♔f3 and:

a221) 45 ♔h2 ♖a8 46 b5 ♖a2+ 47 ♔h3 ♖a1 (not 47...♘f7? 48 ♖a6) is an immediate draw.

a222) 45 b5 is an extremely risky winning attempt. White can now block the a-file with ♖a6, but if Black does ever activate either piece it could become dire.

b) The alternative is to try to bring the king up quickly with 39 ♔g2 (also perhaps 39 ♔f2) but after 39...♔h7! (39...♔f7? 40 ♖a7 ♖c7 41 g4! ♔g6 42 ♔g3 would transpose back into the game) nothing looks very promising, e.g.

b1) 40 ♖a7 ♘d8 41 ♗f8? ♘c6 42 ♖xg7+ ♔h8 43 ♖f7 ♔g8 and Black wins.

b2) If 40 ♔h3 ♔g6 41 ♖a7 ♘d8 42 ♗f8 ♘f7 defends and even 42...♘c6 43 ♖xg7+ ♔f5 44 ♗c5 ♔e4 45 g4 ♘xd4 isn't absurd.

b3) 40 ♔f3 ♔g6 41 g4 (if 41 ♖a7 ♘d8 42 ♗f8 ♘f7! is still fine – but not now 42...♘c6? 43 ♖xg7+ ♔f5 44 ♖g5 mate).

Now premature activity with 41...♖c2? fails to 42 ♖a7 ♘d8 (if 42...♖b2 as usual 43 ♗e7) 43 ♗f8 hxg4+ 44 ♔xg4 ♖g2+ 45 ♔f3.

So Black should play 41...♘d8 42 ♗c5 (after 42 ♖a6 ♘c6 43 ♗c5 ♘xe5+ 44 dxe5 ♖xc5 45 ♖xe6+ ♔f7 Black must hold) 42...♘f7! (42...♘b7 43 b4 ♘xc5 44 bxc5 ♖f8+ 45 ♔g3 hxg4 46 ♔xg4 ♖f2 47 ♖a6

is certainly good for White).

White now has no time for 43 g5 in view of the threat of 43...♘xe5+. Instead he could try:

b31) 43 ♔f4 ♘h6 and

b32) 43 b4 ♘h6 44 gxh5+ ♔xh5 are similar. If White attacks the e6-pawn, Black will defend it with ...♖e8. White can win the b-pawn, but meanwhile the h4-pawn will go after which the g-pawn will be extremely nasty.

b33) 43 ♖a6 hxg4+! (43...♖e8? 44 g5! puts yet another pawn on a dark square but sets up a serious bind, since if 44...♔f5 45 ♖a7 ♘h8? 46 ♖xg7 the knight can't get out in view of 46...♘g6? 47 ♖f7 mate!) 44 ♔xg4 ♘h6+ 45 ♔f4 ♖e8 46 ♖b6 ♔h5 47 ♖xb5 ♔xh4 48 ♖b7 g5+ is similar to lines b31 and b32.

b4) Finally, there is 40 ♗e7, hoping either to dominate the knight or to force a favourable rook endgame. Now:

b41) Now the precipitate 40...♘d8? is unpleasant after 41

&xd8 &xd8 42 &a6 since Black must go passive with 42...&e8.

It is clearly better for Black first to activate the king, after which he should be able to hold the rook ending, e.g.

b42) 40...&g6 41 &a7 &d8 42 &xd8 &xd8.

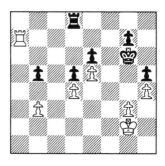

White can of course repeat (e.g. by 43 &f3 &c8 44 &f4 &f8+ 45 &e3 &c8 46 &f4 in line b422) and it seems that he should do so since if:

b421) The race after 43 &e7 &f5 44 &xg7 &e4 45 g4 &xd4 looks very nice for Black.

b422) 43 &f3 &c8 44 &e7 (44 &f4 &f8+! 45 &e3 &c8 doesn't help White since 46 &d3? encourages b4! and 46 &f4 is a repetition) 44...&f5 45 &xg7 &c3+ 46 &g2 &xb3 47 &g5+ &e4 48 &xh5 &xd4 is also good for Black since if:

b4221) 49 &g5 &c3 50 h5 &c8 the b-pawn is already very dangerous.

b4222) 49 &h8 &xe5 and the king is already close. If 50 h5 &f6 51 &g8 &f7 52 &g4 &c3 prevents White from touching

down, after which Black's own passed pawns will be very dangerous.

39 &a7! 1:55

Only now, when the pinned knight can't retreat to d8, is this correct.

39 ... &c7 1:56

40 g4! 1:56

It is important to stop the king becoming active.

40 ... &g6 1:58

41 &g2 1:59 **h5** 2:00

Black can't activate the rook, since 41...&c2+ 42 &g3 &b2 43 h5+! (43 &e7 would also win, as usual) 43...&h6 (or 43...&g5 44 &e7+) 44 &xb7 &xb3+ 45 &h4 &xb4 46 g5 is mate!

42 &g3 2:01

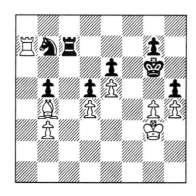

After the immense analytical exertions of the last few moves, this position already hardly requires variations. The point is that once White's king gets safely into the game and his counterpart is restricted, Black has no real opportunities for counterplay. So he either has to shed a pawn for little more than nothing; or sit there.

But If Black sits then the combined pressure of White's three pieces and the strain of holding the e6- and b5-pawns will soon reduce him to zugzwang.

42 ... ♖f7?! 2:12

If 42...hxg4 43 ♔xg4 then:

a) 43...♔f7 44 ♔g5 g6 45 ♔h6! ♖d7 46 ♗d6 wins at once.

b) 43...♖d7? 44 h5+ and:

b1) 44...♔f7? walks into a mating net: 45 ♔g5 ♖c7 46 ♖a8.

b2) 44...♔h6 45 ♖a6 ♘d8 46 ♖d6! ♖xd6 47 exd6 wins the knight for the d-pawn.

b3) 44...♔h7! is toughest, but after 45 ♖a6 ♖c7 (45...♘d8 46 ♖d6) 46 ♖xe6 ♖c1 47 ♖b6 ♖d1 (or 47...♘d8 48 e6) White can win absolutely cleanly with 48 ♖xb7 ♖xd4+ 49 ♔g5 ♖xb4 50 h6 ♖xb3 51 ♖xg7+ ♔h8 52 e6 ♖e3 53 ♔f6; and 48 ♗c3 is also quite good enough.

c) 43...♔h7 is best:

c1) Now there are some splendidly thematic variations after 44 ♗a5 ♖f7? 45 ♗b6 and, for example:

c11) 45...b4 46 ♖a8 ♔g6 47 ♖c8 ♖d7 48 ♖h8 ♔f7 (48...♖e7 49 h5+ ♔f7 50 ♔g5) 49 ♔g5 g6 50 ♖c8 ♖e7 51 ♖c7 ♖xc7 52 ♗xc7 ♔e7 53 ♔xg6 ♔d7 54 h5 ♔xc7 55 h6.

c12) 45...g6 46 b4 ♔g7 47 ♖a8 ♖f8 48 ♖xf8 ♔xf8 49 ♔g5 ♔g7 50 ♗c7 ♔h7 51 ♔f6.

But in this line Black can fight with 44...♘xa5! 45 ♖xc7 ♘xb3. If instead 44 ♔g5 ♖f7! and 44 h5 g6 are both annoying.

The clearest seems to be 44 ♖a6 ♖c1 (44...♘d8 45 ♗a5! ♖c6 46 ♖a7 is another way to trap the beast) 45 ♗e7! ♖d1 (45...♖c7 46 ♖xe6 is hopeless) 46 ♖a7 ♖xd4+ 47 ♔g5 ♖e4 48 ♖xb7 ♖xe5+ 49 ♔g4! (49 ♔f4 ♖f5+ 50 ♔e3 ♖f7! is unnecessary). Now White wins the b-pawn as well since if 49...d4 50 ♗f6!

There are also alternatives to 42...hxg4 but they are pretty trivial as long as White doesn't get excited and simply takes on h5 when he can:

i) I seem to remember at the time being slightly worried about 42...♔h7, but of course White can just capture 43 gxh5 and Black's counterplay will never amount to anything much.

ii) 42...♔h6 is simply bad after 43 ♖a6!

iii) If 42...♖d7 43 ♖a6 ♔f7 (or 43...♘d8 44 ♗a5 ♔f7 45 gxh5) 44 gxh5.

43 ♖a6 2:08 **♖f1** 2:17
44 ♖xe6+ **♔f7** 2:19
1-0

Here Black resigned without waiting for 45 ♖e7+.

If instead 44...♔h7 45 g5! ♖g1+ (or 45...♖d1 46 g6+ ♔h6 47 ♗e7) 46 ♔f2 ♖g4 47 g6+ ♖xg6 48 ♖xg6 ♔xg6 49 e6 ♔f6 50 e7 ♔f7 completes the absolute domination of the knight.

Game 32
J.Speelman-J.Ehlvest
Linares 1991
Nimzo-Indian Defence, Rubinstein variation

After the rather oppressive density of the previous two games, I am sticking very much to the point in the final game of this chapter. In this game I achieved little from the opening, but various mistakes by both players in an initially more or less equal ending, led to a fascinating duel as my king and formally bad bishop tried to catch my opponent's stray knight.

(I'm afraid that you are spared the usual bombardment of clock times because the envelope containing this tournament appears to have gone AWOL.)

1	d4	♘f6
2	c4	e6
3	♘c3	♗b4
4	e3	0-0
5	♗d3	d5
6	♘f3	b6
7	a3!?	

Trying to exploit Black's move order. If instead 7 0-0 ♗b7 we would have transposed to a standard variation often reached by 4...b6 5 ♗d3 ♗b7 6 ♘f3 0-0 7 0-0 d5. In that case, 8 a3 can be met by 8... ♗d6, but of course here that is impossible because if 7...♗d6? 8 e4.

| 7 | ... | ♗xc3+ |
| 8 | bxc3 | ♗a6 |

| 9 | cxd5 | ♗xd3 |
| 10 | ♕xd3 | ♕xd5! |

A novelty – and a good one. If instead 10...exd5 White can iron out his pawn structure (after castling) with c4, when the bishop and central control confer some advantage.

| 11 | 0-0 | c5 |
| 12 | ♖e1 | |

Preparing e4.

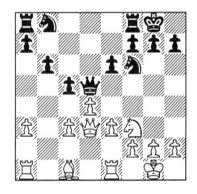

12	...	♕e4!
13	♕e2	♖c8
14	♗b2	

If 14 ♘g5 Black can equalise with 14...♕g4!, offering an unwelcome exchange of queens, and if 15 ♘f3 Black can at the very least repeat with 15...♕e4.

14	...	♘bd7
15	♖ac1	h6
16	♘d2	♕b7
17	e4	

Finally succeeding in playing e4. But Black has used the time this has taken to organise to develop very harmoniously and is now able to force all the rooks off, reaching a roughly equal position.

17	...	cxd4!?
18	cxd4	♖xc1
19	♖xc1	♖c8
20	♖xc8+	♕xc8
21	♕d3	♕c6

In *Informator* I commented that 21...b5! would have been better, with the following possibilities:

a) The idea is to meet the natural 22 f3 with 22...♘b6!? when:

a1) If 23 ♕xb5!? ♕c2 isn't entirely clear but is certainly frightening.

a2) If 23 ♕c3 ♕d7! when ...♘a4 is coming with tempo.

a3) 23 d5? loses a pawn to 23...exd5 24 ♗xf6 gxf6 25 exd5 ♕c5+.

If line a1 really is good for Black – and since it is nothing to do with the ending I'll leave that question open – then White should try to find an alternative to 22 f3.

b) 22 h3 prevents 22...♘b6 in view of 23 d5 exd5 24 ♗xf6 gxf6 25 exd5 with a clear plus for White, but Black can simply revert to 22...♕c6!? when White would have preferred to have played f3 rather than h3.

c) So perhaps 22 ♔f1!?

| 22 | f3 | ♘e8 |

22...b5 was possible at once.

23	♕c4	♕xc4
24	♘xc4	f5
25	♔f2	

This ending is about equal, since White's central control and potentially powerful bishop is offset by Black's presently dormant queenside pawn majority.

25 ... fxe4?

This is wrong because it gives the white king the f3-square.

25...b5 26 ♘a5 ♘d6 was about equal; while 25...♘ef6!? 26 ♔e3 fxe4 27 fxe4 ♘g4+ 28 ♔f4 ♘xh2 29 ♘e3 h5! is also possible.

26	fxe4	b5
27	♘a5	♘d6
28	♔f3!	

If 28 ♔e3?!, 28...♘b6 hits c4 with tempo.

28 ... a6?!

He should probably have played 28...♘b6 at once. 29 ♗c3 and:

a) 29...♘dc4 30 ♘c6 a6 gives

White the choice between 31 &b4!? and the more adventurous but perhaps better 31 ♘d8! ♘xa3 32 ♘xe6.

b) 29...♘bc4 30 ♘c6! a6 (after 30...♘xa3 31 ♘xa7 the b5-pawn is weak) and 31 ♘d8!? looks necessary here since if 31 &b4 ♘b7!, preparing a5.

29 &c3   ♘b6
30 &b4   ♘bc4?

He should have played 30...♘dc4, though 31 ♘c6 keeps the edge.

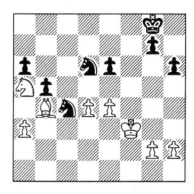

31 e5!!

31 ♘c6? failed to 31...♘b7!, but this anti-positional looking move happens to be very strong.

31 ...   ♘f5

Other possibilities were:

a) 31...♘e8 32 ♘xc4 bxc4 33 &a5! followed by ♔e4 and d5.

b) If 31...♘xa5? 32 exd6 I stopped here in my original analysis with 'and wins'. This may well be true, but when I carried the line further, it turned out that Black does have some serious defensive resources:

b1) 32...♘c6 33 d7 (not 33 ♔e4? ♘b8) 33...♔f7 34 ♔e4 to be followed by 35 d5 is pretty simple.

b2) But 32...♘b7 33 d7 ♔f7 34 ♔e4 ♔f6! is better,. e.g. 35 g4 (preparing h4 and g5+; if 35 d5 a5 36 &xa5 ♘c5+!) 35...g5 (not 35...a5 36 &xa5 ♔e7 37 d8♕+ ♘xd8 38 &xd8+ ♔xd8 39 ♔e5 with an easily won pawn ending) 36 h3 ♘d8 37 d5 e5! (37...♘b7 38 d6 [38 ♔d4 e5+ 39 ♔e3] 38...a5 39 &c3+ looks fairly simple) 38 &a5 ♔e7 39 ♔xe5 ♘f7+! (the pawn ending is lost after 39...♔xd7 40 &xd8 ♔xd8 41 ♔d6 a5 42 ♔c5 b4 43 axb4 a4 44 ♔c4 ♔d7 45 ♔c3 ♔d6 46 ♔b2 ♔xd5 47 ♔a3) 40 ♔f5 ♔xd7 41 ♔g6 ♘e5+! 42 ♔xh6 ♘f3 43 &b4 a5 44 &xa5 ♔d6 and if 45 &d8 ♘g1 46 ♔xg5 ♘xh3+ Black has chances of exchanging off the g4-pawn for the knight to reach the drawn position with 'bishop and the wrong rook's pawn'.

c) If 31...♘f7 32 ♘xc4 bxc4:

c1) In my original annotations I gave 33 &e7?, but this is unclear after 33...♘h8! 34 ♔e4 ♘g6 35 &b4 ♔f7 36 g3 when:

c11) If 36...♘e7?? 37 &xe7 ♔xe7 38 ♔e3 ♔d7 39 ♔d2 ♔c6 40 ♔c3 ♔d5 41 g4! Black runs out of tempi first, e.g. 41...g6 42 h4 g5 43 h5 a5 44 a4 ♔e4 45 ♔xc4 ♔f4 46 ♔c5 ♔xg4 47 d5 and wins.

c12) But 36...a5!! is much

stronger: 37 ♗xa5 (or 37 ♗c5 ♔e8 38 d5 exd5+ 39 ♔xd5 c3 40 ♗e3 c2 when the c-pawn will take ages to round up) 37...♘e7 38 a4 (if 38 d5 exd5+ 39 ♔e3 ♔e6 40 ♗c3 ♘c6 41 a4, Black has at least 41...h5 42 a5 d4+) 38...♘d5 and the blockade makes the win extremely problematical.

c2) 33 ♗d2! is much stronger than 33 ♗e7. The knight is after all four moves away from d5 so White can easily get in ♔e4 followed by d5.

32	♘xc4	bxc4
33	♔e4	

The black knight has nowhere to go, so White is able to advance the d-pawn next move.

33	...	h5
34	d5	♔f7
35	d6	♔e8
36	♗d2	

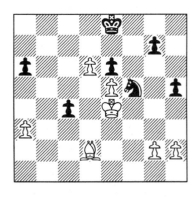

36	...	♔d7

Perhaps Black had to expend two tempi on weakening the kingside pawns with 36...♘h4! 37 g3 (it would be madness to

embark on an adventure like 37 ♔d4 ♘xg2 38 ♔xc4 ♘h4 39 ♔c5 ♔d7 40 ♔b6 ♘f3 41 ♗c3 ♘xh2, when Black is winning!) 37...♘f5.

37 g3?

Here Ehlvest, very much a bishops man, pointed out that the right plan is 37 ♗g5! ♔c6 38 h3 (threatening g4 in a position in which the knight can't escape via h4) 38...h4 (or 38...♘g3+ 39 ♔d4 c3 40 ♔d3 and the pawn will soon be devoured) 39 ♗d2, intending ♗d2-e1–f2, and only then ♔f3-e2-d2-c3xc4 and wins.

37	...	♔c6
38	♗f4	♔d7
39	h3	♔c6
40	a4	♔d7
41	g4	hxg4
42	hxg4	♘h4
43	♗g3	♘g6
44	♔d4	♔c6
45	♔xc4	

White has won the c-pawn, but at the cost of badly weakening his kingside.

45	...	♘h8
46	♔d4	

Instead 46 ♔b4 ♘f7 47 ♔a5 ♔b7 48 d7 ♘d8, threatening mate, forces White to retreat.

46	...	♘f7
47	♗h4!?	♘h6?

47...g5! 48 ♗f2 ♘h6 49 ♗e3 ♘f7! is sufficient to draw. With two weaknesses – on e5 and g4 – White will have to sacrifice one pawn to get things moving. I had thought that this would be simple, but White can try 50 ♗d2 ♔d7 51 ♗c3 (51 ♔c5 ♘xe5 52 ♔b6 ♘xg4 53 ♔xa6 ♘e5 is equal) 51...♔c6 52 ♔c4 ♘h6 53 ♔b4 ♘xg4 54 ♔a5 ♘e3 55 ♔xa6.

Now he hopes to get the a-pawn moving quickly, but 55...♘c4!, tying the bishop to c3, is fine (not 55...g4 56 ♗e1! and if 56...♘f5 57 ♔a7 g3 58 ♔b8 g2 59 ♗f2 White is winning). The most critical line seems to be 56 d7! ♔xd7 57 ♔b7 g4 58 a5 g3 59 a6 g2 60 ♗d4 ♘a5+! 61 ♔b6 ♘c4+! 62 ♔c5 (62 ♔b7 ♘a5+ repeats; while 62 ♔b5 ♘xe5 63 a7 ♘c6 draws) 62...♘d2! 63 a7 ♘b3+ 64 ♔c4 ♘xd4 65 a8♕ g1♕ 66 ♕a7+ with a draw.

48	♗g5	♘xg4?
49	♗e3	♘h2
50	♔e4	♘g4

If 50...♘f1 51 ♔f3! (but not 51 ♗f4? g5!) 51...♘h2+ 52 ♔g3 ♘f1+ 53 ♔f2 ♘h2 54 ♗f4 ♘g4+ 55 ♔f3 ♘f6 56 exf6 gxf6 57 ♔e4 wins (Ehlvest). The line

continues 57...e5 58 ♗xe5 fxe5 59 ♔xe5 ♔d7 60 ♔d5 a5 61 ♔c5 ♔d8 62 ♔b6 ♔d7 63 ♔xa5 ♔xd6 64 ♔b6.

51 a5

Placing Black in zugzwang.

51 ... ♔d7?

A step in the wrong direction since White can now force his king to c5 – though whether he is then winning is far from clear. 51...g6 was correct, or for that matter 51...g5. The point is that the position with the pieces on these exact squares is decisive zugzwang even without the black g-pawn – i.e. White to play still can't win – see the analysis below.

52 ♗f4

Threatening to win at once with 53 ♔f3.

52 ... ♘f2+

52...g5 53 ♗xg5 ♔c6 54 ♗e3! is decisive zugzwang since Black is to move.

53	♔e3	♘d1+
54	♔d4	

54 ... ♔c6?!

This seems obvious, since if 54...♘f2 55 ♗g3 ♘g4 56 ♔c5 the penetration is obviously very worrying. But in fact after 56...♘e3 matters are far from clear, though White may just be winning, e.g. 57 ♗f4 and now:

a) The obvious 57...♘d5? traps the knight in mid board. After 58 ♗d2 g6 White is able to triangulate 59 ♔c4 ♔c6 60 ♔d4 ♔b5!? and now:

a1) 61 d7?! ♘e7 62 d8♘! should also be enough, but certainly not 62 ♗g5? ♘c6+ 63 ♔e4 ♔xa5 64 d8♕+ ♘xd8 65. ♗xd8+ ♔b5 66 ♔f4 ♔c6 67 ♔g5 ♔d5 68 ♗c7 a5 69 ♔xg6 a4 70 ♔f6?? (70 ♗a5 still draws) 70...a3 71 ♗a5 ♔c4 and the pawn queens!

a2) It is much better to continue the triangulation: 61 ♔d3! ♔c6 62 ♔c4 ♔d7 63 ♔c5 g5 64 ♗xg5 ♘c3 65 ♔b6 and wins.

b) 57...♘c2! is tougher: 58 ♔b6 ♘b4 59 ♔b7 (not 59 ♗d2? ♘c6! 60 ♔xa6 ♘xe5 61 ♔b7 ♘c6 with a draw) g5 60 ♗g3 g4 61 ♔b6 (zugzwang) 61...♔d8 62 ♗e1 ♘d3 63 ♔xa6:

b1) If 63...♘xe1 64 ♔b5! (but not 64 ♔b7?? ♘d3 or 64 ♔b6?? g3 when Black queens with check) wins since the knight can't stop the pawn and if 64...g3 65 a6 g2 66 a7 g1♕ 67 a8♕+ ♔d7 68 ♕b7+ and mate in two.

b2) 63...♘xc5 64 ♔b7 ♘c4! (if 64...♔d7 65 a6 ♘c6 66 ♗g3 wins) 65 ♔c6 ♘xd6! 66 a6! (but not 66 ♔xd6 ♔c8 with a draw) 66...♘c8 67 ♗h4+ ♔e8 68 ♔c7 ♘a7 69 ♗f2 ♘b5+ 70 ♔c6 ♔d8 71 ♔xb5 ♔c8 72 ♗g3 and the king can't cross the diagonal.

55 ♗e3!

After this White has a simple demonstrable win.

55 ...   g5!
56 ♗xg5?

But this lets Black off the hook, after which I believe he should still have drawn. 56 ♗g1! was correct. I rejected this because of 56...g4 57 ♔d3 g3 58 ♔c2?? ♘f2! and Black wins! But a move earlier White has an easy win with 58 ♗d4! (threatening 59 ♔d2) 58...g2 59 ♔c2!

56 ...   ♘b2?

56...♘f2 would still have drawn!

57 ♗e3!   ♘a4
58 ♔c4   ♘b2+
59 ♔c3   ♘d1+
60 ♔d4   1-0

Black has no defence to 61 ♗g1 followed by devouring the trapped beast. So Ehlvest resigned.

This is the critical position.

Black to play loses quickly after

    1 ...   **♔d7**

If 1...♘h2 2 ♗f4 ♘g4 3 ♔f3 traps it at once.

    2 ♗f4   **♘f2+**

    3 ♔e3   **♘d1+**

    4 ♔d4

Threatening ♗e3.

    4 ...   **♘f2**

Or 4...♘b2 5 ♗e3 ♔c6 6 ♗g1 ♘a4 7 ♔c4 ♘b2+ 8 ♔c3 ♘d1+ 9 ♔c2 as in the game.

    5 ♗g3   **♘g4**

    6 ♔c5

But as far as I can see, White can't 'lose a move'.

    1 ♗f4   **♘f2+**

    2 ♔d4   **♘g4!**

    3 ♔d3   **♘f2+**

    4 ♔e3   **♘d1+**

    5 ♔d4

Not 5 ♔d3? ♘b2+ 6 ♔d4 ♘a4 7 d7?? ♔xd7 8 ♗e3 (if 8 ♗d2 ♔c6 9 ♗b4 ♔b5 10 ♗a3 ♔xa5 11 ♔c4 ♔b6 and the knight escapes) 8...♔c6 9 ♔c4 ♘b2+ 10 ♔c3 ♘d1+ and wins!

    5 ...   **♘f2!**

5...♘b2? 6 ♗e3 loses in the usual way.

    6 ♗e3

    6 ...   **♘h1!!**

But not 6...♘d1? 7 ♗g1 or 6...♘g4 7 ♔e4! and it is Black's turn to move.

    7 ♗f4

Not 7 d7? ♔xd7 8 ♔c5 ♔c7!

    7 ...   **♘f2**

    8 ♗g5

8 ♗d2 ♘g4 comes to the same thing. White's problem is that the only square for the bishop which really controls the knight is e3. If the knight is on f2 then ...♘h1 defends.

    8 ...   **♘g4!**

8...♔d7 also seems to hold since if 9 ♔c5? Black replies 9...♘e4+ 10 ♔b6 ♘xg5 11 ♔xa6 ♔c6 12 d7 ♘f7!

    9 ♗e3

While with the knight on g4 Black can play:

    9 ...   **♘h2!**

Threatening to emerge via f3-h4-f5. If the white king could go to e3 then he could transfer the move, but after:

    10 ♔e4   **♘g4**

It is still White to play.

7   Blood on the Board

After the rather oppressive rectitude of the previous chapter, I wanted to finish with a much more relaxed spread of battles royal.

Originally, I had envisaged quite a large selection of games, but when I came to this section the pages were already groaning under the analytical load; so I decided to settle for half a dozen examples of serious hackery ranging over a period of more than twenty years.

Game 33
J.Speelman–A.Miles
British Championship, Morecambe 1975
English Defence

One of the biggest psychological problems in playing chess, is to strike the proper balance between the moves which one wants to play; and those which one believes one ought to play.

Certainly, one should aim to remain as objective as possible, at all times. But in the heat of battle this is, of course, extremely difficult.

This is one area in which the difference between strong players and weaker ones is particularly marked. If you talk to a grandmaster after the game, then he may not give the impression of objectivity – there are some notorious optimists around – but the moves which he plays will probably belie his words.

Although this game was played more than twenty years ago, I have rather a clear memory of the feelings – though of course not the exact calculations – which led me to lash out on move seven.

My decision was the result of a heady cocktail of respect for my opponent combined with an under-estimation of my position! When I started to think at move seven, I felt that it should be rather good for me; but then I began to have doubts. If Black can get in ...f5 successfully, then he may get a good game.

At some point the extreme idea of h4 occurred to me. And presumably the more I looked at it the more I wanted to play it. Eventually, I decided to give in to my cruder instincts.

1	**c4**	**b6**	0:10
2	**♘c3** 0:07	**♗b7**	
3	**e4** 0:10	**e6**	
4	**d4**	**♗b4**	
5	**♕c2**		

For the main alternatives 5 f3 and 5 ♗d3 see my game (eighteen years later) with Zsuzsa Polgar (Game 35).

At the time, the position after 4 ♕c2 was almost totally unexplored. Nowadays, the main line is 5...♕h4. (I suspect that Tony actually suggested this move in the postmortem!?) In any case, Korchnoi introduced this idea in his Candidates match with Polugayevsky a couple of years later, albeit in a slightly different position: 1 d4 e6 2 c4 b6 3 e4 ♗b7 4 ♕c2 ♕h4!? 5 ♘d2 ♗b4 6 ♗d3 f5 7 ♘f3 ♗xd2+ (7...♕g4 is better) 8 ♔f1? (8 ♗xd2 ♕g4 9 ♘e5 ♕xg2 10 0-0-0 fxe4 11 ♗e2 gives White very serious chances for the pawns) 8...♕h5 9 ♗xd2 ♘f6 10 exf5 ♗xf3 11 gxf3 ♘c6, reaching the following position.

Korchnoi eventually won that game, starting with 12 ♗e3 0-0 (Polugayevsky-Korchnoi, Evian sixth matchgame 1977).

Interestingly, I reached exactly the same position in a game in 1993, but with both sides having lost two tempi: 1 c4 b6 2 d4 ♗b7 3 ♕c2 e6 4 e4 ♕h4 5 ♘d2 ♗b4 6 ♗d3 ♕g4 7 ♔f1 f5 8 ♘gf3 ♗xd2 9 ♘e5 ♕h4 10 ♘f3 ♕h5 11 ♗xd2 ♘f6 12 exf5 ♗xf3 13 gxf3 ♘c6 (M.Quinn-Speelman, Dublin Zonal 1993).

Although I was aware of the Polugayevsky-Korchnoi game, I certainly didn't know that they had reached this exact position. I chose instead, to castle long and won in 31 moves: 14 ♗c3 0-0-0 15 ♖e1 ♖he8 16 ♖e2 ♕h3+ 17 ♔e1 ♕xf3 18 ♖g1 ♕f4 19 ♖xg7 exf5 20 ♕d2 ♖xe2+ 21 ♔xe2 ♖e8+ 22 ♔f1 ♕xh2 23 ♗xf5 ♘e7 24 ♗d3 ♘g6 25 f3 ♕h1+ 26 ♔f2 ♖f8 27 ♕g5 ♘h4 28 ♔e2 ♕xf3+ 29 ♔d2 ♘e4+ 30 ♗xe4 ♕xe4 31 ♕g4 ♖f2+ 0-1.

Despite the result, it turned

out after the game that my opponent had been well prepared for the English Defence. This was a first round game and he had played a quick game with Tony Miles that very morning for publicity purposes in which Tony had also chosen the English Defence!

Not being prescient, in 1975 Miles chose a slightly less ambitious plan.

5 ...   ♗xc3+!?

To make sure that White's queenside pawns end up doubled. 5...♘e7 is also playable at once.

6 bxc3   ♘e7

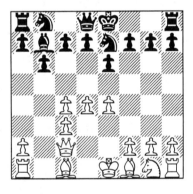

This is where the fun starts. I liked my centre and bishops but got nervous about ...f5, so:

7 h4!?

7 ♗d3 f5!? 8 f3 and 7 ♘f3 are normal. But 7 h4 does have some point in that it makes 7...f5 and 7...d5 rather dubious, viz.

a) 7...f5 8 exf5 ♘xf5?! (if 8...exf5 9 f3 intending ♗d3 and

♘e2 leaves White with some advantage) 9 ♗g5 ♕c8 10 ♖h3! threatening g4. That it where I left it in my original notes in *The Chess Player* in 1975 (volume 10, Game 52). (The notes to this game are based on those but heavily revised.) Black might consider 10...h6, but 11 g4!? is a strong answer.

b) If 7...d5 – which I doubt if Tony considered at all – 8 cxd5 exd5 9 e5 c5 10 ♘f3 leaves White with a pleasant advantage.

7 ...   0-0
8 ♖h3!?

Once loosed from the fetters of playing 'properly', I carried on playing the moves I wanted to!

8 ...   d6

8...f5 was playable here, though after 9 exf5 Black ought again to acquiesce in 9...exf5 rather than 9...♘xf5 10 ♗g5.

9 ♗d3   e5
10 f4!? 1:10

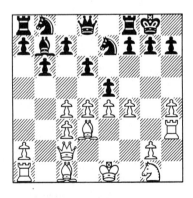

Although this is consequent,

it is extremely provocative. Presumably 7 h4 and 8 ♖h3 had caused a serious rush of adrenaline!

Nowadays, I record clock times after almost every move, but in those days I only did so occasionally. By this stage I had already used one hour and 10 minutes of the two and a half hours which we used to dispose of in those days, while after his next move Tony was up to one hour and four minutes.

10 ...   f5 1:04

Black's alternatives were:

a) 10...♗c8? simply encourages 11 f5.

b) 10...♘bc6? 11 d5 ♘a5 12 f5. In 1975, I gave this as 'clearly better for White'. I guess that White's attack is very dangerous but today I wouldn't be quite so certain that after 12...f6 Black hasn't got time to generate annoying counterplay on the queenside. One defensive idea is to play ...♔h8 and ...♘g8.

c) 10...exf4 11 ♗xf4 and:

c1) Black can gain some time with 11...♘g6 but this is not a good idea since 12 ♗g5 f6 13 ♗e3 is very nice for White:

c11) If 13...♗c8 14 ♖h2 f5?! 15 exf5 ♘xh4 (15...♖e8 16 ♕f2 ♘xh4 17 ♔d2 wins) then the dynamic 16 f6!? is strong and 16 g4 looks even better – if 16...♖e8 17 ♕f2 and wins.

c12) 13...f5? 14 exf5 ♘xh4 15 ♗e4 and again White is

winning.

c2) 11...♗c8 12 ♖h2 f5 13 ♘e2. I stopped here in my original analysis, but Black has 13...fxe4 14 ♗xe4 ♗f5! which gives him a very reasonable game positionally as long as he doesn't lose at once. And indeed after 15 ♗g5 ♗xe4 16 ♕xe4 ♘bc6 Black does seem to stay afloat.

11 exf5 1:23   **exd4**

11...e4 12 ♗xe4 ♗xe4 13 ♕xe4 ♘bc6 was an unclear alternative. After 14 g4?! h5! (14...♖e8 15 ♖e5) 15 ♖e3 hxg4 16 d5 ♘xf5 17 dxc6 ♕xh4+! (not 17...♘xe3 18 ♗xe3 ♕xh4+ 19 ♔d2 ♖ae8 20 ♕d5+) 18 ♔d1 ♕f2 19 ♕d5+ ♔h7 20 ♖e1 Black has a lot of play for the piece.

12 cxd4 1:28

I think that this natural recapture is probably a mistake. If White can maintain his kingside structure then he should be doing very well. So instead he could try 12 h5 when:

a) 12...h6 13 cxd4 (the very crude 13 g4 is also possible) 13...♘bc6 14 ♕c3 d5 15 g4 and White has a wonderful position precisely because the counterblow ...h5 is impossible.

b) If 12...c5 or 12...♘c6 then 13 h6 looks very strong. The h-file will probably open and Black will always have to worry about White's dark-squared bishop which will create havoc if the long diagonal opens.

12 ...   ♘bc6
13 ♕c3 1:38   **d5!**

If 13...♘xf5 14 d5! is very good for White:

a) 14...♕e7+ 15 ♔d1 ♘a5 (15...♘cd4 16 g4!) 16 ♗b2.

b) 14...♕e8+ 15 ♔d2.

c) 14...♘cd4 15 g4 ♕e8+ 16 ♔d1 ♕g6 17 ♖g3! wins.

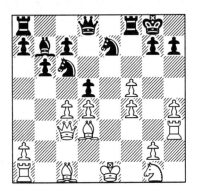

Now, however, things are quite different. The long diagonal will be blocked at least for several moves and Black can hope to mobilise quickly to embarrass White's king.

14 ♘f3

If 14 g4 h5! breaks up White's kingside phalanx. Perhaps White can try 15 f6, but after 15...♖xf6 16 g5 ♖e6+ 17 ♔f1 dxc4 18 ♗xc4 ♘d5 White's light squares, in general, and his king, in particular, look dangerously vulnerable.

14 ...   ♘xf5
15 g4 1:46   **♕e8+**
16 ♔d1

Of course I could also have played 16 ♔f2!? which would

equally have been quite unclear. Indeed, I suspect that this may have been stronger: it is nice for the king to have some pawns to protect him and the variations over the next few moves look fairly good for Black. But there is such a lot of excitement later, that I'll leave my assessment at that.

16 ...   ♘d6 1:52

If 16...♘h6 17 ♖g3 then in my original notes I suggested that White is threatening '♘g5 unclear', but in fact f5 would be more to the point. In any case White seems to be on top:

a) If 17...♖d8 18 c5! keeps White's king safe.

b) 17...dxc4 18 ♗xc4+ ♔h8 19 f5! (but not 19 d5? ♘a5 20 ♗b2 ♖g8 which looks horrible for White). The crude threat of ♗xh6 is now irritating, so Black can retreat either ...♘g8 or ...♘f7. It is all extremely messy but I don't think that White is doing badly.

17 cxd5   ♘e7
18 ♕c2 2:05

This purports to threaten ♗xh7+, but I suspect that Black should ignore this with 18...♘xd5 (both 18...h6 and 18...h5 are conceivable) 19 ♗xh7+ ♔h8 20 ♘e5 (not 20 ♗g6 ♘e3+! 21 ♗xe3 ♕xe3 and White is coming apart at the seams) 20...♘b4 21 ♕b1 when White has won a pawn but he is rather loose. Rather a blasé assessment, perhaps, but there are pages of complicated variations to come.

It seems to me that this is a turning point. After Black's next move, which voluntarily moves His Majesty onto the long diagonal, there are lots of unclear lines, but White is trying to win them. Previously, things were simply unclear; and some lines looked extremely dangerous for White.

18 ...   ♔h8?!
19 ♘e5   ♘f7

If Miles had wanted to play ...♘xd5 then he would probably have done so a move earlier. But 19...♘xd5 was still very playable and seems to lead to a draw after 20 h5 ♘xf4 21 ♗xf4 ♖xf4 22 ♘g6+ (not 22.♕b3 ♘f7!) 22...hxg6 23 hxg6+ ♔g8 when:

a) 24 ♕b3+ ♔f8 25 ♖h8+ ♔e7 26 ♖xe8+ ♖xe8 gives Black tremendous compensation for the queen.

b) 24 ♕h2 is much safer since 24...♕a4+ 25 ♔d2 ♘e4+!? (or 25...♕b4+ 26 ♔c2 ♕a4+ 27 ♔d2 is immediate perpetual) 26 ♔e3 ♖f3+ 27 ♖xf3 ♘f6 (27...♘g5 28 ♖e5 looks good for White) 28 ♖xf6 ♖e8+ 29 ♔d2 ♕b4+ is still perpetual.

20 h5

Getting on with the real business of bringing the c1-bishop to life. After 20 ♗xh7 ♖d8 (not 20...♘xe5 21 dxe5 g6? [21...♖d8] 22 h5!) Black takes

aim at the white king.

20 ...   ♘xe5
21 dxe5   ♕d7

If 21...h6 22 g5! hxg5 (or 22...♕d7 23 e6 ♕xd5 24 gxh6 ♘f5 25 hxg7+ ♘xg7 26 h6) 23 h6 g6 24 e6! and White crashes through.

22 e6   ♕xd5
23 h6

23 ...   ♖f6 2:14

If 23...♖fd8 24 ♕c3 ♕d4 25 ♕xd4 ♖xd4 26 ♗b2 wins simply.

But 23...♕xe6 is another matter:

a) Originally, I thought that 24 ♕c3?! was the move here, but Black has a defence:

a1) Not 24...♕f6? 25 hxg7+ ♔xg7 26 ♖xh7+ ♔g8 27 ♕xf6 ♖xf6 28 ♖xe7 with a won position for White.

a2) 24...♕xg4+? is a mistake, e.g. 25 ♔c2 ♖f6 (25...♔g8 26 ♖g3!; 25...♖f7 26 hxg7+ ♖xg7 27 ♗xh7!; 25...♘f5 26 hxg7+ ♕xg7 27 ♗b2) 26 hxg7+ ♔g8 27 ♕xf6 ♕xh3 28 ♕xe7 and wins.

a3) 24...♖f6 25 hxg7+ and Black can fight on with 25...♔g8 (25...♔xg7 loses to 26 g5 ♕xh3 [26...♘d5 27 gxf6+ ♔f8 28 ♕a3+ c5 29 f5] 27 gxf6+ ♔h6 28 fxe7). After this I haven't been able to find a convincing knockout blow:

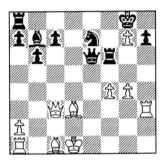

a31) 26 ♗xh7+ ♔f7 and:

a311) 27 g8♕+ ♖xg8? (see a312) 28 ♗xg8+ ♔xg8 29 f5 ♕d7+ (29...♕d6+ 30 ♕d2) 30 ♔e1 ♘d5 31 ♕e5.

a312) 27 g8♕+ ♘xg8! 28 ♗f5 ♖d8+ 29 ♗d2 ♕d6 and:

a3121) Unfortunately if 30 ♕xc7+ ♕xc7 31 ♖h7+ ♔f8 32 ♖xc7 ♖fd6!; or 30 ♖h7+ ♔f8 31 ♖xc7 ♕xf4!.

a3122) 30 ♖d3 ♕e7 31 ♕c4+ ♔f8; or 30 ♔c2 ♘e7 (and not 30...♖xf5 31 ♖h7+!).

a313) 27 f5!?

a32) 26 f5 is also possible without ♗xh7+, though both 26...♕d6 27 ♗b2 ♘d5 (27...♖f7 28 f6) 28 ♕d2 ♖d8 and 26...♕f7 are very messy.

b) But today I believe that White should play the cruder 24 hxg7+! ♔xg7 and now:

b1) Not 25 ♖xh7+ ♔g8 when:

b11) 26 ♖e7 ♕xe7 (26...♕xg4+ 27 ♕e2 ♗f3 28 ♗h7+ ♔h8 29 ♗b2+) 27 ♗c4+ ♖f7!

b12) 26 ♕c3 ♖f6 (not 26...♕xg4+ 27 ♔c2 and wins).

b2) But 25 ♗b2+!

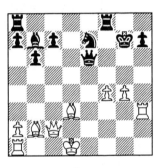

By playing 24 hxg7+ first, White has forced Black to open up the long diagonal.

Now if 25...♔g8 26 ♕c3! ♔f7 (26...♕xg4+ 27 ♔c2 ♕g2+ 28 ♔b3) 27 ♔c2 (27 ♖xh7+ ♔e8) 27...♗e4 (27...♘d5 28 ♖xh7+ ♔e8 29 ♖e1) 28 ♖e1 ♗xd3+ 29 ♖xd3 wins, so Black must try 25...♔f7 when 26 ♔d2! seems to win, viz.

b21) 26...♔e8 27 ♖e1 ♕xg4 28 ♖xe7+ ♔xe7 29 ♕xc7+.

b22) 26...♖ad8 27 ♖e1 ♗e4 28 f5 ♕d5 (28...♘xf5 29 gxf5 ♕xf5 30 ♕xc7+ ♖d7 31 ♖xh7+) 29 ♖xh7+ ♔e8 30 ♖xe7+ ♔xe7 31 ♖xe4+ ♕xe4 32 ♕xc7+ ♖d7 33 ♕xd7+ ♔xd7 34 ♗xe4 wins.

b23) 26...♖fd8 attempts to

improve on the previous variation. White should probably play 27 ♖xh7+ at once and then:

b231) 27...♔g8 28 ♖e1 ♗e4 29 ♖xe7 ♕xe7 30 ♕c4+ ♗d5 31 ♕xd5+ ♖xd5 32 ♖xe7 ♖ad8 33 ♖e3 wins.

b232) 27...♔f8 28 ♕c3 ♖xd3+ 29 ♕xd3 ♗e4 (or 29...♕xg4 30 ♖h8+ ♘g8 31 ♖e1 ♕xf4+ 32 ♔c2) 30 ♖h8+ ♔f7 31 ♕d4 ♖xh8 32 ♕g7+ ♔e8 33 ♕xh8+ and wins.

b233) 27...♔e8 28 ♖e1 ♗e4 29 f5! ♕d5 (29...♗xd3 30 ♖xe6 ♗xf5+ 31 ♔c1 ♗xe6 32 ♗f6) 30 ♗f6 ♕xd3+ 31 ♕xd3 ♖xd3+ 32 ♔c1 ♖d6 33 ♖xe4 and wins.

24 ♗b2 2:15

24 ... ♖xf4?
After this White wins quite simply since the rook turns out to be loose to a later ♕xc7+.

If 24...♕xe6 25 hxg7+ ♔xg7 (25...♔g8 26 ♗c4) 26 f5, intending g5.

But 24...♖xe6! would still have put up massive resistance: 25 f5 (25 ♕c3 ♖g6! 26 ♔c1?? ♖c6!) 25...♖c6 26 ♕e2 and:
a) 26...♕d7.

In principle, I try to avoid using a computer during analysis, but here I weakened and used Fritz 2. (Now we're up to Fritz 3 and 4; it was quite a while ago – *JS 1997.*) Here is what we came up with:

a1) The attempt to be clever with 27 ♕e5? leads to disaster after 27... ♘d5 28 hxg7+ ♔g8 and now:

a11) 29 ♔d2 ♖e8 and:

a111) Of course White would like to play 30 ♖xh7, but after 30...♖xe5 31 ♖h8+ (31 ♗xe5 ♘f6 32 ♖h8+ comes to the same thing) 31...♔xg7 32 ♗xe5+ ♘f6 33 ♖ah1 ♖c2+! 24 ♔xc2 ♗xh1 refutes this fantasy.

a112) 30 ♕d4 ♖d6 31 ♖xh7 ♘f6! defends (but not 31...♔xh7 32 g8♕+ ♔xg8 33 ♕h8+ ♔f7 34 ♕g7 mate) when if 32 ♕xf6? ♖xd3+.

a12) 29 g5 ♖e8 30 g6 ♘f6!

a2) But the crude 27 hxg7+ ♔g8 28 f6 ♘g6 (28...♖d6 29

fxe7 ♗a6 30 ♕e4 ♖xd3+ 31 ♔e1 wins – Fritz 2) 29 ♖xh7 threatens f7+, amongst others, e.g. 29...♔xh7 (29...♖xf6 – Fritz 2 – 30 ♗xf6 ♔xh7 31 ♕h2+ ♔g8 32 ♕h8+ ♔f7 33 g8♕+ ♖xg8 34 ♕h7+ ♔e6 35 ♕xg8+) 30 f7 ♕xd3+ 31 ♕xd3 ♖d6 32 ♗d4 and White wins.

b) 26...♕f7 27 hxg7+ ♔g8.

Here I initially I hallucinated that:

b1) 28 ♖xh7? wins immediately, missing that after 28...♔xh7 29 ♕h2+ Black has 29...♖h6! (Fritz 2); while if 29 f6+ ♘g6.

b2) Given this then a human being immediately thinks of 28 ♖c1! to stop the lateral defence, when if 28...♖d8 29 ♖xc6 and 30 ♖xh7! wins. And lines like 28...♖d6 29 ♖xc7 ♖ad8 (29...♗a6 30 ♖xh7!) 30 ♖xe7 ♖xd3+ 31 ♖xd3 ♖xd3+ 32 ♔e1! are equally hopeless.

b3) Whereas the immediate Silicon reaction was 28 f6 ♘g6 29 g5 ♗c8 (29...♖d8 30 ♕h5 ♖xd3+ 31 ♖xd3) 30 ♗xg6 (this is the move that a person takes a

long time to find – you see that it is legal but would much prefer to find some other continuation which doesn't expose the white king) 30...♕xg6 31 ♖xh7! (Fritz 2) and in fact this does seem to win, though the main lines must be well beyond the computer's horizon except at a slow time limit:

b31) 31...♔xh7 32 ♕h2+ ♗h3! 33 ♕xh3+ ♔g8 34 ♕b3+ ♔h7 (34...♕f7 35 g6) 35 g8♕+ ♕xg8 36 ♕d3+ ♕g6 37 ♕d7+ ♔g8 38 ♕xc6 ♖d8+ 39 ♔c1! ♕xg5+ 40 ♔c2.

b32) 31...♖d6+ 32 ♔e1 ♔xh7 33 ♕h2+ ♗h3 34 ♕xh3+ ♔g8 35 ♕h8+ ♔f7 36 ♕xa8 ♖e6+ 37 ♔f2 ♕f5+ (37...♕c2+ 38 ♔g1) 38 ♕f3.

b33) 31...♗g4 32 ♖h8+ ♔f7 33 ♕xg4 ♕d3+ 34 ♔e1 ♖e6+ 35 ♔f2.

25 ♔c1!

Not, however, 25 ♕c3? when Black plays not 25...♖f1+? 26 ♔c2 ♖f2+ (26...♕g2+ 27 ♔b3) 27 ♔b1, but 25...♖xg4!

25 ... ♘g6

Forced since if 25...♕xe6 26 hxg7+ ♔g8 27 ♗xh7+ ♔f7 28 g8♕+ ♘xg8 (or 28...♖xg8 29 ♗xg8+ ♘xg8 30 ♕xc7+) 29 ♗xg8+ ♖xg8 30 ♕xc7+ and, as mooted in the note to 24...♖xf4?, the rook will die.

26 ♕c3! 2:21

Now this wins by force.

26	**...**	**♕c6** 2:28
27	**♕xc6**	**♗xc6**
28	**hxg7+**	**♔g8**

29	♗xg6	♖f1+
30	♔c2	♖f2+
31	♔b3	♖xb2+
32	♔xb2	hxg6
33	♖f1!	

(see following diagram)

The cleanest win.

33	...	♔xg7
34	♖f7+	♔g8
35	♖hh7	♖e8
36	♖fg7+	♔f8

37	e7+	1-0

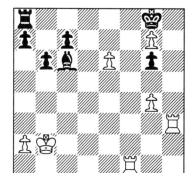

Game 34
V.Korchnoi–J.Speelman
Brussels (SWIFT) World Cup 1988
Pirc Defence

The April 1988 Brussels tournament was the first of the six in the GMA's (Grandmasters Association) first, and as it turned out only, World Cup cycle. The others took place in Belfort (France) and Reykjavik in July and October 1988; and Barcelona, Rotterdam and Skelleftea (Sweden) in April, June and August 1989.

Each of the 25 participants had to play in four of these tremendously strong tournaments, and by the luck of the draw I happened to be in the first four. I started splendidly in Brussels with two wins and three draws. But the enjoyably chaotic victory below in round six was, I fear, the apogee not only of this

tournament but of my whole World Cup campaign.

Following these three wins, I lost twice – to Karpov and Sax – without adding a further victory, to fall back to earth on plus one: a mundane performance which I failed even to emulate in any of the other three tournaments. Still, this game – which Viktor, unwisely approached by a journalist immediately afterwards, characterised as 'silly' – was a very nice way to reach my peak.

The notes are a slightly expanded version of those in *New in Chess*, No.5 1988.

1	d4 0:03	d6 0:01
2	e4 0:03	g6 0:01
3	♗e3 0:13	♗g7 0:03

4 ♘c3 0:13

If instead 4 f3, 4...c5 is very possible

4 ... a6 0:06

This rather cheeky move is more or less the 'main line' at the moment (i.e. in 1988). Black leaves the knight on g8 to stop a quick ♗h6 and starts to expand on the queenside. He plays ...a6 rather than ...c6 since he hopes to get in c5 later, preferably in one move.

5 a4 0:15

Of course White doesn't have to play this. If he prefers, something like 5 ♕d2 is perfectly sensible. However, Nigel Short beat me in just sixteen moves starting with this move at last year's British Championship (i.e. Swansea 1987) – so there must have been an obvious temptation to repeat it!

5 ... ♘f6 0:10
6 h3 0:15 **0-0** 0:14
7 ♘f3 0:18

So we've transposed to an offshoot of the Classical Pirc. In his booklet *Developments in the Pirc and Modern Systems 1984-87* Nigel Davies christened this the 'Spassky system' which isn't unreasonable since Spassky has often played this line.

Against Nigel, I now played 7...b6 (actually the move order was 6...b6 7 ♘f3 0-0) 8 ♗c4 ♘c6 9 e5 ♘e8 10 ♗f4 ♘a5 11 ♗a2 c5 12 dxc5 bxc5 13 0-0 ♖b8 14 exd6 ♘xd6? 15 ♘d5

e6?? 16 ♗xd6! 1-0.

I knew vaguely of a game Ligterink-Timman where Black had played ...c6 instead of ...a6 and here played 7...d5!? At the board, round about the time of 5...♘f6, it suddenly clicked that it is quite conceivable to play d5 here anyway. So:

7 ... d5!? 0:21
8 e5 0:20

8 exd5 ♘xd5 9 ♘xd5 ♕xd5 10 ♗e2 would give White a small edge, but Korchnoi has never been one to shirk a challenge!

8 ... ♘e4 0:23

Of course Black must engage – the two minutes expended were merely because I was late back to the board.

9 ♘xe4 0:20

9 ♗d3 is also quite possible but would be unlikely to constitute a refutation – if in fact 7...d5 really is bad then 9 ♘xe4 will be the way to prove it.

9 ... dxe4 0:23
10 ♘g5 0:22

After 10 ♘d2 c5!? then the b6-square is very inviting for White – the disadvantage of having played 4...a6 rather than 4...c6. However, Black might try 10...f5 instead.

10 ... c5 0:27
11 dxc5 0:22 **♕c7** 0:29
12 ♕d5!? 1:17

After 55 minutes! In Ligterink-Timman, Dutch Championship 1987, White played 12 ♗c4 ♘c6 13 ♘xe4 ♕xe5 14

♘c3 ♗e6 15 ♗xe6 ♕xe6 16 0-0 ♖ad8 17 ♕c1 ♗xc3 18 bxc3 ♖d7 when, despite the extra pawn, White is clearly worse and Jan won in 109 moves (remember, though that in this game the pawn was on a7 rather than on a6, which is probably slightly in Black's favour – there is no weakness on b6).

JS 1997: But he played ...a6 four moves later anyway! 19 ♖e1 ♖fd8 20 ♕b2 ♕f5 21 ♕b3 h5 22 a5 a6 23 ♕a4 g5 24 ♖ab1 ♕g6 25 ♗d4 ♖c8 26 ♖e3 f6 27 ♖e6 ♕f5 28 ♖be1 ♔f7 29 ♕c4 ♕d5 30 ♕d3 ♖h8 31 ♕e2 ♕f5 32 ♕c4 ♔g6 33 ♖1e3 g4 34 ♕e2 ♔f7 35 h4 ♖hd8 36 ♕c4 ♔g6 37 ♕e2 ♖xd4 38 cxd4 ♘xd4 39 ♕c4 ♘xe6 40 ♕xe6 ♖d1+ 41 ♔h2 ♕f4+ 42 ♖g3 ♕xf2 43 ♖xg4+ hxg4 44 ♕xg4+ ♔f7 45 ♕xd1 ♕xh4+ and Black won the ending 64 moves later.

Instead after 12 ♗c4 ♘c6 White can certainly try 13 e6!? (he can also play 12 e6 at once). After 13...f5 the position is extremely sharp, e.g.

a) 14 ♕d6!?? is almost good for White but not unnaturally loses to 14...exd6 15 cxd6 (15 e7+ d5!) 15...♕xd6 16 e7+ ♗e6! etc.

In general White has dangerous attacking possibilities, but the position could also rebound upon his head. I suspect that Black isn't lost and hence must be 'fairly OK'.

b) *JS 1997:* The line was tested later in the year in the game Hodgson-McNab, British Championship, Blackpool 1988, but far from conclusively: 14 0-0 f4 (14...♗xb2!?) 15 ♗c1 ♕e5 16 h4 h6 17 ♘h3 ♘d4 18 c3 ♘xe6 19 ♘xf4 ♖xf4 20 ♗xf4 ♕xf4 21 ♕d8+ ♔h7 22 ♕xe7 ♕f8 23 ♕xf8 ♗xf8 24 ♖fe1 ♘xc5 25 b4 ♘d7 26 ♖xe4 ♘f6 27 ♖d4 ♗f5 28 ♖e1 ♖c8 29 ♖e3 ♔g7 30 ♗e2 h5 31 ♖c4 ♘d5 32 ♖xc8 ♗xc8 33 ♖e8 ♗f5 34 ♖b8 ♘xc3 (34...b5 35 axb5 ♘xc3 36 bxa6 wins for White) 35 ♖xb7+ ♔f6 36 ♗c4 ♔e5 37 a5 ♘d5 38 b5 axb5 39 ♖xb5 ♗e6 40 ♗xd5 ♗xd5 41 a6 1-0.

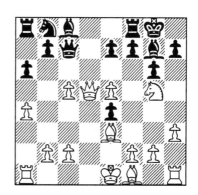

| **12** | **...** | **h6** 0:41 |
| **13** | **♘xe4** 1:17 | **♖d8** 0:53 |

Quite an ambitious move, aiming to force the white queen offside or else provoke an immediate piece sacrifice. 13...♗e6 was a sensible alternative and if 14 ♕d2 ♕xe5 (*JS 1997:* also 14...♖d8 15 ♗d3

♗f5 – Fritz) 15 ♘c3 (15 ♗d3? f5 and 16...f4):

a) 15...♘d7 – which I didn't consider during the game – 16 ♗e2 and now simply 16...♔h7 is quite okay for Black.

b) *JS 1997:* The weaker 15...♘c6 led eventually to defeat in a game Polak-Dudas, Czech Championship, Pardubice 1991: 16 ♗d3 ♘d4 17 0-0 ♕h5 18 ♘e2 ♘xe2+ 19 ♕xe2 ♕h4 20 c3 ♗d5 21 f4 e5 22 f5 e4 23 ♗c2 ♗e5 24 ♕g4 ♕xg4 25 hxg4 ♔g7 26 ♖ad1 ♖fd8 27 ♗d4 ♖e8 28 fxg6 fxg6 29 ♖fe1 ♔h7 30 c4 ♗c6 31 b4 e3 32 ♗xe3 ♗c3 33 ♗d2 ♗d4+ 34 ♔h1 ♖ad8 35 ♖xe8 ♖xe8 36 ♖e1 ♖f8 37 ♗e4 ♖f2 38 ♗xc6 bxc6 39 ♗e3 ♗xe3 40 ♖xe3 ♖a2 41 ♖e7+ ♔g8 42 b5 ♔f8 43 ♖c7 ♖xa4 44 b6 1-0.

14 ♕a2 1:18

In the bulletin, Korchnoi suggested 14 ♕b3 as an improvement. I don't quite understand this since after 14...♕xe5 15 ♘c3 (else b2 hangs) 15...♘c6 White can't play 16 ♗c4 in view of 16...♘d4 and Black has excellent play for just one pawn.

During the game, being perhaps rather over-optimistic about my position, I was more concerned about 14 ♘d6!? exd6 (14...♗e6? 15 ♕xb7) 15 exd6 when White has three good pawns for the piece:

a) Perhaps Black should simply develop with 15...♕d7 16

c3 ♘c6 with an unclear position.

b) At the time I was more interested in simplifying with 15...♗xb2 and now:

b1) 16 dxc7 ♖xd5 17 cxb8♕ (17 ♗c4? ♘c6 18 ♗xd5 ♗xa1) 17...♗c3+ 18 ♔e2 ♖xb8 is excellent for Black.

b2) But 16 ♕b3! ♕a5+ 17 ♗d2 ♕xc5 (17...♕xd2+ 18 ♔xd2 ♗xa1 19 ♗c4 looks very good for White) 18 ♕xb2 is an unclear mess where White looks to be doing quite well.

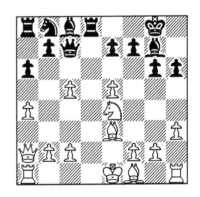

14 ...   ♗f5? 1:06

A blunder which ought to lose! I wanted, of course, to play 14...♘c6 first:

a) 15 f4 ♘xe5 is fine for Black. (*JS 1997:* for if 16 fxe5 16...♕xe5 17 ♗d3 ♗e6! 18 ♕b1 f5 with the advantage)

b) However, I feared 15 ♗c4 when:

b1) 15...♘xe5 16 ♗b3 looked uncomfortable to me, but in fact Black can play 16...♗f5 when:

b11) The natural 17 ♘c3 may

not be very good. Black can play 17...e6 and if 18 f4 simply 18...♘c6 or 18 g4!? ♕c6 or 18 0-0 ♗xh3!? is at least a draw.

b12) However 17 ♘g3! contains more poison. If 17...♕a5+ 18 ♔f1 White has lost the right to castle but he is a pawn up and it is very hard to find a weakness in his position to latch onto.

b2) 15...♗f5 is more natural. However, after 16 ♗xf7+ Black faces something of a dilemma:

b21) 16...♔h7 is more desirable in terms of keeping a safe king, but after 17 f3! (not 17 ♘ moves ♘b4) White seems to be doing well, e.g. 17...♕xe5 18 0-0 e6!? 19 ♖ae1 and if 19...♖f8 (or 19...♖d7) 20 ♘d6.

b22) Instead 16...♔f8! seems correct and after 17 f3 ♕xe5 now:

b221) 18 ♗c4 looks plausible, daring Black to take on e4 which opens the f-file. But after 18...♗xe4 19 fxe4 ♕g3+! Black is doing well.

JS 1997: In fact, winning fairly easily, e.g. 20 ♗f2 ♕xg2 21 ♖f1 (or 21 ♖g1 ♕xe4+ 22 ♔f1 ♖d2) 21...♕xe4+ 22 ♗e3+ (22 ♗e2 ♕b4+ mates) 22...♗f6 23 ♔f2 ♔g7 and the white king is hopelessly exposed.

b222) Of course White must play 18 0-0 when 18...e6 trapping the bishop looks good for Black, but White now has tricks like 19 ♕b3!? ♔xf7 20 ♕xb7+ ♘e7 and either 21 ♖ae1 or 21

♘d6+ ♔f8 and then 22 ♖ae1 causes some confusion.

JS 1997: It is wrong to check first since if 21 ♘d6+? ♔f8 22 ♖ae1 the cold blooded 22...♗xc2! extricates the slightly menaced bishop (not 22...♕xb2? 23 ♕xb2 ♗xb2 24 g4 and if 24...♗xc2 – 24...♗g7 and 24...g5 are better – 25 ♖f2! with the advantage). As far as I (and Fritz) can see White has no good continuation, so that Black emerges with a substantial advantage.

21 ♖ae1 at once is therefore much better:

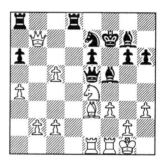

b2221) Of course Black can easily draw here with 21...♖db8 22 ♕d7 ♖d8, when White is ill-advised to avoid repetition with 23 ♘d6+ ♔f8 24 ♕c7 in view of 24...♗xc2 (even with the queen defending the c5-pawn) when the discovery 25 ♗xh6 ♕d4+ 26 ♗e3 ♕xa4 is good for Black.

b2222) 21...♖ab8 22 ♕xa6 is dubious because of 22...♕xb2 (if instead 22...♖xb2 23 ♘d6+ ♔f8 24 ♘c4!) 23 g4! when

White regains the piece, for if 23...♗xe4? (23...♖a8 24 ♕c4 doesn't change much) 24 fxe4+ ♗f6 (24...♔e8 25 ♕xe6) 25 ♖xf6+! ♔xf6 26 ♖f1+ ♔g7 27 ♕xe6 ♘g8 28 ♖f7+ ♔h8 29 ♕xg6 soon wins.

b2223) But 21...♗xe4 22 fxe4+ ♔e8 is very possible, though White has at least a temporary initiative.

b2224) Perhaps the safest winning attempt is to head for the ending with the sequence 21...♕xb2 22 ♘d6+ ♖xd6! (not 22...♔f8 23 ♕xb2! ♗xd2 24 g4! as above) 23 ♕xb2 ♗xb2 24 cxd6 ♘d5.

In any case, I ought to have played 14...♘c6 and if necessary chosen one of the sensible lines from the diagram.

Returning to the game:

15 ♘g3 1:19 **♗xc2?** 1:08

Of course 15...♗e6 was forced in view of the haymaker in the next note.

16 ♗c4? 1:19

Played almost instantly. Unfortunately, 16 ♕c4! (found by John Nunn on the evening after the game) causes a major accident. Black has nothing less unpalatable than 16...♗f5 17 ♘xf5 gxf5 when White is winning.

16 ... **♕a5+** 1:14
17 ♔e2 1:19 **♘c6!** 1:15
18 ♗xf7+ 1:22

Consequent but extremely risky. However, if, for example, 18 ♖hc1 ♗d3+ 19 ♗xd3 ♖xd3!

(but not 19...♘b4? 20 ♗d2!) and Black has abundant compensation for his single pawn deficit.

18 ... **♔h7** 1:22
19 f4 1:22 **♘b4** 1:27
20 ♕e6 1:26 **♘d5!** 1:28

Black's problem is very simple: how best to get at the enemy king. The answer is equally simple. The dark squares are the key to His White Majesty's comfort and so the defending bishop must be removed. The threat of 21...♘xe3 is now most unpleasant.

21 ♗d2 1:42

I had expected 21 ♕xd5 ♖xd5 22 ♗xd5 ♕b4, when materially White is doing quite well but in view of the looseness of his position he is in trouble.

21 ... **♗d3+** 1:33
22 ♔e1 1:42

Of course not 22 ♔xd3 ♘xf4+.

22 ... **♕xc5** 1:34
23 f5 1:48

With serious time trouble approaching, Korchnoi tries to force Black to take perpetual check. Luckily for me, however, there is a way to win with a forcing sequence.

23 ... **♘e3** 1:39
24 ♕xg6+ **♔h8** 1:39
25 ♘h5 1:49

(see following diagram)

25 ... **♘xf5!** 1:48

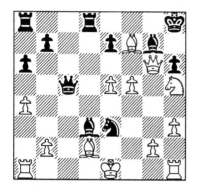

Since this wins by force, there is no real need to look for alternatives. And once I saw 32...♕xh2+ in the game continuation, the choice was clear. But I think I first examined (*JS 1997:* the notes in *New in Chess* don't make this clear) 25...♘c2+ 26 ♔d1 ♗e2+ 27 ♔xe2 and then:

a) 27...♖xd2+ to see whether Black can win with checks. However, after 28 ♔xd2:

a1) 28...♕e3+ 29 ♔xc2 ♖c8+ 30 ♔b1 ♕e4+ 31 ♔a2 ♕xa4+ is only perpetual.

a2) Instead Black could try

28...♖d8+ 29 ♔e2 ♕xe5+ (29...♕e3+ 30 ♔f1 ♗xe5 31 f6! is extremely messy, but at worst White can play 30 ♔f1 (30 ♔f2) 30...♘xa1 31 ♕xg7+ ♕xg7 32 ♘xg7 ♖d1+ 33 ♔e2 ♖xh1 34 ♘h5 which looks good for Black, though the knight on a1 is very bad for the moment.

b) *JS 1997:* 27...♕xe5+ is possible, but 28 ♔f1 (28 ♗e3 ♖d2+!) 28...♖xd2 29 f6! (29 ♕xg7+ ♕xg7 30 ♘xg7 ♔xg7) 29...♕e2+ (29...♘e3+ 30 ♔g1 ♖xg2+ 31 ♕xg2 ♘xg2 32 fxg7+ ♔h7 33 ♔xg2 is equal) 30 ♔g1 ♕e3+ 31 ♔h2 ♗xf6 is also extremely messy.

26	♘xg7 1:46	♕xe5+ 1:48
27	♔f2 1:49	♕d4+ 1:49
28	♔e1 1:49	♕h4+! 1:51
29	g3 1:50	♕e4+ 1:51

Switching to the light squares for the final assault.

30	♔f2 1:50	♕e2+ 1:51
31	♔g1 1:50	♗e4 1:51
	0-1	

Viktor resigned in view of 32 ♖h2 ♕xh2+! 33 ♔xh2 ♖xd2+ 34 ♔g1 ♖g2+ etc.

Game 35
Zsu.Polgar–J.Speelman
Hilversum-Volmac, Dutch League 1993
English Defence

This game was played in the final match of the Dutch League between Volmac Rotterdam and Hilversum. The competition had been a two-horse race between these two clubs. But we had outdistanced Hilversum and required only three points from the ten-board match to win on tie-break.

I had lost my first game against Zsuzsa Polgar in Brussels 1985 but had equalised the score two years previously in that year's Volmac-Hilversum match. Now, in view of the team position, she felt obliged to go for me:

1 d4 0:00   **e6!?** 0:01

Before the game, I had spent quite some time trying to decide how to avoid her rather solid repertoire. But it was only as I arrived at the board that I thought of this particular way of wriggling out of her theoretical vice.

2 c4 0:00   **♗b4+** 0:01
3 ♘c3 0:04

Here Zsuzsa had expected me to transpose back into a Nimzo with 3...♘f6, but I decided fairly quickly on:

3 ...   **b6** 0:04
4 e4 0:05   **♗b7** 0:06

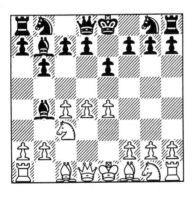

So we've reached a proper 'English Defence'. Here White normally chooses between 5 ♕c2, for which see Speelman-

Miles (Game 33), 5 ♗d3 and 5 f3. As usual, I'll give a précis of theory without getting too involved:

a) If 5 ♗d3 f5!? 6 ♕h5+ g6 7 ♕e2 ♘f6 8 f3 ♘c6! (8...fxe4 9 fxe4 ♗xc3+? 9 bxc3 ♘xe4 10 ♘f3 gives White excellent compensation) and now:

a1) 9 e5? ♘xd4 10 ♕f2 ♘h5 11 ♕xd4? ♗c5 is a well-known trap. Instead White can fight with 11 g4!? when he may win a piece, though his position is a mess.

a2) 9 ♗e3 fxe4 10 fxe4 e5 11 d5 ♘d4 12 ♕d1 ♘xe4 13 ♗xe4 ♕h4+ 14 ♔f1 ♗xc3 15 bxc3 ♕xe4 16 ♗xd4 exd4 17 ♕xd4 0-0+ 18 ♘f3 ♖ae8 and Black won easily in Burger-Ehlvest, Saint Martin Open 1993. But White was outrated by almost 300 rating points.

b) If 5 f3 Black must choose between 5...♕h4+ and 5...f5:

b1) 5...♕h4+ 6 g3 ♗xc3+ (to avoid 6...♕h5 7 ♗d2 when if 7...f5 8 exf5 ♕xf5 9 ♘b5! is a nuisance, as in Ree-Miles, Amsterdam 1978) 7 bxc3 ♕h5 8 ♘h3 f5! and Black gets play on the light squares and a good pawn structure in return for White's lead in development and two bishops.

b2) 5...f5 6 exf5 ♘h6 is a lot more fun. White can wimp out with 7 ♗xh6 ♕h4+, but otherwise Black gains a very serious lead in development for his pawn(s) after, for example, 7 fxe6 ♘f5 8 ♘ge2 0-0. A recent drastic example, also involving Hans Ree (White against Morozevich), was a rapidplay playoff game from Tilburg 1994: 9 ♕b3? (White should presumably play 9 ♗f4) 9...c5 10 exd7? ♘xd7 11 d5 ♘e5 12 ♘f4 ♕h4+ 13 ♔d1 ♘d4 14 ♕a4 ♖xf4 15 g3 ♕h5 16 ♗xf4 ♕xf3+ 17 ♔d2 ♕xh1 18 ♖d1 ♕xh2+ 19 ♔c1 ♘g6 0-1.

My memory of the theory was extremely hazy, but, rather surprisingly, Zsuzsa knew considerably less; and she chose a third possibility.

5 d5!? 0:14

This is rather accommodating, but White's centre is sufficiently solid for her to retain a reasonable position.

5 ... ♕e7 0:15
6 ♗e2?! 0:35

Twenty minutes is a long time to think this early and clearly she was already a bit concerned:

a) In the postmortem, we looked at 6 ♘ge2 which may well be better. The main point is that Black should not try to play analogously to the game. For if 6...♘f6 (6...exd5 is quite playable to force 7 exd5 – of course not 7 cxd5 ♕xe4 – and then 7...♘f6) 7 f3 exd5 8 cxd5 c6 9 dxc6 ♘xc6?! (9...dxc6 is equal) 10 a3 ♗xc3+ (10...♗d6 is unclear) 11 ♘xc3 d5?! then White can safely take the pawn with 12 ♘xd5! (the

cowardly 12 ♗g5? dxe4 13 ♘xe4 ♖d8 is good for Black) 12...♘xd5 13 ♕xd5 ♖d8 (if 13...0-0 14 ♗g5) 14 ♕g5! and despite his lead in development Black is an serious trouble, e.g. 14...f6 15 ♕h5+! g6 16 ♕h6 ♘d4 17 ♔f2 with a huge advantage.

b) 6 ♗e3!? ♘f6 (there is no need for the over-ambitious 6...f5!?) and now:

b1) 7 e5 ♘e4 8 ♕g4? (8 ♕d4) 8...f5 is awful for White.

b2) 7 ♗d3 exd5 8 exd5 c6. Here White could bail out with 9 ♘ge2 cxd5 10 0-0 dxc4 11 ♗xc4, when he may well win back the pawn while Black is completing his development; but Black is certainly fine. Instead if 9 dxc6 ♘xc6 (9...dxc6 is equal) when 10 ♘f3 runs into 10...♘g4 or if 10 ♘ge2 ♘e5.

6 ... ♘f6 0:22

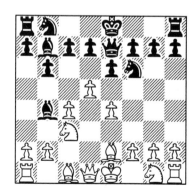

7 f3?! 0:37

This is very slow and extremely weakening. White

should only play moves like f3 if she can keep control, and here there is an obvious way for Black to detonate the position immediately.

I was more concerned about 7 ♗g5!? when 7...h6 is plausible: 8 ♗h4!? (this is an attempt to play for the advantage; if 8 ♗xf6 ♕xf6 9 ♖c1 Black is comfortable) and now:

a) 8...♗xc3+ 9 bxc3 ♕a3 10 ♕d4 (10 f3 ♕xc3+ 11 ♔f1 and White has compensation for the pawn) 10...♘xe4 11 ♕xg7 and:

a1) 11...♕xc3+? 12 ♕xc3 ♘xc3 13 ♗f6 ♘xe2 14 ♗xh8 ♘xg1 (14...♘f4) 15 ♖xg1 d6 leaves White with excellent winning chances.

a2) 11...♖f8 is unclear.

b) 8...exd5 is a more sober approach, and after 9 exd5 0-0 10 ♘f3 ♖e8 perhaps White should immediately surrender the right to castle with 11 ♔f1 when she has been inconvenienced but does still retain her centre.

c) 8...g5 9 ♗g3 ♘xe4 is extremely risky, but it doesn't actually lose at once and has the virtue of winning an important pawn and forcing White's hand. After 10 ♕d4 ♘f6 White can play:

c1) 11 ♗e5 is too eager: 11...c5! is the only move but a good one.

c2) If 11 h4 Black must avoid 11...♖g8? 12 hxg5 hxg5 13 ♖h6! when the knight has no-

where to go! Instead 11...c5 leads to a complete mess after, for example, 12 ♕d3 exd5 13 hxg5 dxc4 14 ♕xc4 ♘e4 15 ♖xh6 ♖f8 (15...♖g8 16 g6!?) 16 ♗h4.

c3) White might conceivably stay calm with 11 0-0-0, though 11...d6 regains some control.

There is also another move instead of 7 ♗g5 – 7 ♕d4. After the game I looked this variation up in *The English Defence* by Keene, Plaskett and Tisdall. I was amazed to find that this very position had been reached in Tartakower-Réti, Gothenburg 1920. After (7 ♕d4) exd5 8 exd5 ♕e4 Black was already very comfortable.

7 ... **exd5** 0:26
8 cxd5 0:38 **c6** 0:27
9 dxc6 0:39 **♘xc6** 0:29
10 ♘h3 0:41

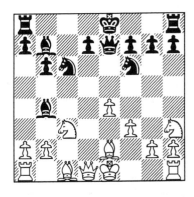

10 ... **d5!** 0:31

A pretty easy decision. Obviously, I couldn't see anywhere near the end of the complications, but it was fairly clear that

Black would be doing okay. And when you have a lead in development but a structural disadvantage it is almost always right to institute tactics if you can.

11 exd5 0:44 **0-0-0** 0:32
12 ♗g5 0:51

More or less forced. If 12 0-0 White gets gunned down along the central files: 12...♗xc3 13 bxc3 (I guess that 13 dxc6 ♖xd1 14 cxb7+ ♔xb7 15 ♗xd1 ♗d4+ 16 ♔h1 is best here, but Black has a big advantage) 13...♖xd5 14 ♕c2 (or 14 ♕e1 ♖e5 15 ♘f4 g5) ♕c5+ 15 ♘f2 ♘d4 and wins.

12 ...   ♖he8! 0:46

This was much more difficult. I saw much of the game continuation but not the haymaker at the end. So instead of 12...♖he8, I also considered 12...♕c5.

13 ♗xf6 1:09

The only move. If 13 ♘f4 ♕e5 14 ♗xf6 gxf6! transposes back into the game, whilst 14...♕xf6!? is also good.

13 ...   gxf6! 0:51

13...♕xf6 14 0-0 ♗xc3 15 bxc3 ♕xc3 looked good for Black, since if 16 ♘f2 ♕e5! (it is vital to stay on the a1-rook) 17 dxc6!? (if 17 ♗c4 ♘a5 Black is clearly better) 17...♖xd1 18 cxb7+ ♔xb7 19 ♖axd1 (of course, if 19 ♗xd1 ♕xa1 wins) 19...♕xe2 20 ♖d7+ ♔a6 21 ♖xf7 ♖e7 (also 21...♕xa2!?) and Black should

win.

But I certainly couldn't be sure that there wasn't some horrific accident lurking in this line whereby I would be pole-axed on the c-file. And since 13...gxf6 also looked very nice, it wasn't too difficult to acquiesce in the maiming of my pawn structure.

In the postmortem, Zsuzsa said that she had been pleased by 13...gxf6 since it made her position much nicer unless Black could do something at once. And indeed this was a very reasonable point of view. In fact, I believe that it was only while she was contemplating her next move that it suddenly struck me that the defence which she now employs is fatally flawed.

14 ♘f4 1:14

Obviously 14 ♔f1 loses horribly: 14...♗xc3 15 bxc3 ♖xd5 16 ♕xd5 ♕xe2+ 17 ♔g1 ♕e3+!? (the repetition doesn't hurt Black but in fact it is best to leave the queen on e2) 18 ♔f1 (not 18 ♘f2 ♕e1+! 19 ♖xe1 ♖xe1 mate) ♕e2+! 19 ♔g1 ♘e5! 20 ♕d6 ♘xf3+ 21 gxf3 ♕xf3 etc.

14 ...   ♕e5 0:52
15 ♕d2 1:24

If 15 ♕c1:

a) 15...♘d4 is wrong since 16 0-0 ♗xc3 (16...♔b8 17 ♗d3 ♗c5 18 ♔h1 ♗d6 19 g3 ♕e3!? with compensation), which seems to win at once, runs into

17 ♗d3!!

b) But the momentarily calmer 15...♖xd5! is very strong, e.g. 16 0-0 ♗c5 (better than 16...♗c5+ 17 ♔h1 ♗e3 18 ♘fxd5) 17 ♘d3 ♕d4+ 18 ♔h1 and Black can choose between 18...♗xc3 19 ♘xc5 ♗xb2 20 ♘b3 ♕e5 and 18...♖xc3 19 bxc3 ♗xc3, both of which should win.

15 ...   ♗xc3! 0:54

15...♘d4 16 0-0-0! is quite nice for Black, but White keeps going. Still if I hadn't had my 18th move in reserve then I might have been vaguely tempted.

16 bxc3 1:24   **♘b4** 0:54

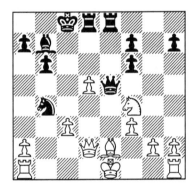

17 ♔f2? 1:29

This loses at once. White can fight harder but she is already in terrible trouble, viz:

a) 17 0-0-0 ♘xd5 18 ♘xd5 ♖xd5 19 ♗d3 ♖ed8 20 f4 (20 ♖he1 ♖xd3 21 ♖xe5 ♖xd2; or 20 ♕e2 ♖xd3 21 ♕xd3 ♖xd3 22 ♖xd3) 20...♕d6 21 ♔c2 (21 ♗f5+ ♔c7 22 ♕c2 ♕xf4+ 23

♔b2 ♖xd1 24 ♖xd1 ♖xd1 25 ♕xd1 ♕xf5) and now the most artistic win is 21...♖xd3 (also 21...♕a3) 22 ♕xd3 ♕xd3+ 23 ♖xd3 ♗e4 24 ♖hd1 b5! after which there is no defence to Black's plan of bringing his king to c4.

b) 17 ♖d1 ♘xd5 18 ♘d3 and now:

b1) Black can now force an ending a pawn up with 18...♕xe2+!? 19 ♕xe2 ♖xe2+ 20 ♔xe2 ♘xc3+ 21 ♔e3 ♘xd1+ 22 ♖xd1. I suppose, though, that the shattered king-side pawns give White some hope of salvation.

I feel that there ought to be a way to conclude the game here by force.

b2) 18...♕g5 doesn't achieve this. White has to defend with only moves, but they aren't difficult: 19 ♕xg5 fxg5 20 ♖c1.

Here 20...♗a6 21 c4 ♘e3 22 ♔f2 runs into possible trouble on the c-file, and although 20...♘e3 looks cleaner, after 21 ♔f2 ♘xg2 22 ♖hg1! ♘f4 23 ♘xf4 gxf4 24 ♖c2 White is still fighting.

b3) If there is a 'forced win', then 18...♕c7 is the way to go about it, though the lines are extremely complex: 19 c4! (not 19 ♔f2 ♘xc3 20 ♖c1 ♖xe2+ 21 ♕xe2 ♘xe2 22 ♖xc7+ ♔xc7 23 ♔xe2 ♗a6 and wins) 19...♘e3 20 ♖c1 and here Black can probably win by 20...♖xd3!? (the materialistic 20...♘xc4 isn't bad of course) 21 ♕xd3 ♘xg2+ 22 ♔f2 (22 ♔f1 looks awful, e.g. 22...♘f4 23 ♕f5+ ♔b8 24 ♖c2 ♘xe2 25 ♖xe2 ♕xc4 26 ♕c2 ♗a6) 22...♘f4 (22...♕c5+? doesn't work very well, though Black can win the queen for two rooks after 23 ♔xg2 ♖g8+ 24 ♔f1 ♕g5 25 ♔f2! [the only move] 25...♕g2+ 26 ♔e3 ♖e8+ 27 ♔d2 ♖d8) 23 ♕f5+ ♔b8.

If Black can get control of the c5-f2 diagonal without allowing the white queen to get too active, then he should win:·

b31) Originally, I'd thought that 24 ♖he1 would be unclear, but I'd missed 24...♖e5! (precisely to seize the diagonal) 25 ♕xf6 (if 25 ♕xf4 ♖xe2+ 26 ♔g3 ♖g2+!) 25...♕c5+ 26 ♔f1 when 26...♗c8! wins immediately (also 26...♘h3 27 ♔g2 and then 27...♗c8!)

b32) If 24 ♗d3? or b33) 24 ♗d1?, 24...♗c8 wins in either case.

b34) 24 ♖c2 looks best, but after 24...♗c8 25 ♕xf6 ♕c5+ 26 ♔e1 ♘d3+ 27 ♔d1 ♘f2+ 28

♔c1 ♘xh1 Black should win.

White might try to improve with 26 ♔f1 to 'misplace the black bishop', but 26...♗h3+ 27 ♔e1 ♘d3+ 28 ♔d1 ♘f2+ 29 ♔c1 ♘xh1 should win anyway.

c) In a game, White might try to avoid the ending in variation b1 above by playing 17 ♖c1. However, after 17...♘xd5 (not 17...♕xf4?? 18 cxb4+) 18 ♘d3 ♕e7 19 ♔f2 (if 19 c4 ♘f4! or 19 g3 ♘f4 20 gxf4 ♗xf3 21 0-0 ♗xe2 wins) 19...♘f4! 20 ♖he1 and now:

c1) If 20...♘xd3+? 21 ♗xd3 ♕c5+ 22 ♔f1 ♖xe1+ 23 ♖xe1 ♕d5 24 ♖d1 White is fighting hard.

c2) 20...♕c5+! is the right move and seems to force victory after:

c21) 21 ♘xc5 ♖xd2 22 ♘e4 ♗xe4 23 fxe4 (23 ♔e3 ♖xe2+) ♖xe4 (23...♖xe2+ 24 ♖xe2 ♘d3+ 25 ♔e3 ♘xc1 26 ♖c2) 24 ♔f3 ♖dxe2 25 ♖xe2 ♖xe2! (not 25...♘xe2?! 26 ♖c2! f5 27 ♖xe2 ♖xe2 28 ♔xe2 ♔d7 with an unclear pawn ending) 26 ♔xf4 ♖xg2 and wins.

c22) 21 ♔f1 ♖xe2 22 ♕xf4 (22 ♖xe2 ♘xd3) ♖xe1+ 23 ♘xe1 ♗a6+ 24 c4 ♖d4 wins.

17 ... ♘xd5 0:54
18 ♘d3 1:31 **♘xc3!** 0:56

This is what she'd missed. Black is now winning after:

a) 19 ♖he1 ♕d4+ (the simple 19...♕xe2+ also forces a won pawn ending) 20 ♔f1 ♖xe2 21 ♖xe2 ♘xe2 22 ♔xe2 ♗a6.

b) 19 ♗f1 ♕d4+ 20 ♔g3 ♖e3 21 ♔h3 ♔b8.

c) The desperate 19 ♕xc3+ ♕xc3 20 ♖hc1 fails to 20...♖xe2+ 21 ♔xe2 ♖xd3.

After about a quarter of an hour's thought White resigned.

0-1

As I explained in the introduction, we were playing this game under rather unequal conditions since Zsuzsa had to win at all costs; and therefore avoided quieter lines in the opening. Nevertheless, it is my quickest ever win against a grandmaster.

Game 36
J.Speelman-Z.Azmaiparashvili
Spanish Team Championship, Menorca 1994
Irregular Opening

Although this game is rather slight and I played pretty abysmally just out of the opening, I've included it in this book for the very pretty finish in which my rook, bishop and knight rout a queen, rook and bishop, even though the enemy queen can initially give several checks.

1 d4 0:00 **d6** 0:00
2 e4 0:04 **♘f6** 0:00
3 f3 0:06

This system is somewhat inconvenient for Black if he wants to avoid a Sämisch

King's Indian. Indeed White also retains the option of developing his knights to b1-a3 and g1-e2-c3 against an orthodox King's Indian set-up with ...e5.

The most usual reply here is 3...e5, though White has some edge after 4 dxe5 dxe5 5 ♕xd8+ ♔xd8 6 ♗c4. Seven weeks later in the Olympiad, I tried 3...d5!? against Paul van der Sterren – see the following game. 'Azmai' found a different way to stir up some confusion.

3 ... e6!? 0:10

4 ♗e3 0:16 **♗e7** 0:10
5 c4 0:23

5 ♘h3 would be good if Black were to allow it to go to f2 unscathed. But 5...e5! equalises at once.

5 ... **0-0** 0:11

If 5...d5 6 cxd5 exd5 7 e5 ♘fd7 8 ♘c3 ♘b6 9 ♗d3 White is better.

6 ♘c3 0:24 **c5** 0:19
7 d5 0:31

7 dxc5 dxc5 8 ♕xd8 ♖xd8 9 e5 ♘fd7 10 f4 is only slightly better for White if at all.

7 ... **a6** 0:19
8 a4 0:32 **b6** 0:20
9 ♗d3 0:38 **♗b7?!** 0:26

Provocation! The bishop is biting on granite here. 9...♖a7 was normal or maybe 9...♘bd7 when White can choose between 10 b3 with a slight advantage and the more ambitious 10 f4!?

10 ♘h3 0:40

10 ♘ge2 was a very playable alternative, and by defending f4 would have nullified the game continuation.

10 ... **e5** 0:26

Since the white centre is very well defended, it makes some sense to block and then try to percolate round the edges. But of course White has a pleasant advantage.

11 g3 0:46

If 11 ♘f2 Black can play to control the dark squares with 11...♘h5 and if 12 g3 ♗g5!; or 12 ♕d2 ♘f4 causes trouble.

11 ... **♘h5** 0:28
12 f4 0:49 **exf4** 0:28
13 gxf4 0:50 **g6** 0:28
14 ♖g1!? 0:57

This looks very appealing; but the knight on g7 will be an excellent defender.

14 ... **♘g7** 0:30

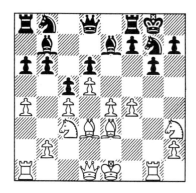

15 ♘g5? 1:06

Despite nineteen minutes' thought, I missed 16...f6! Instead 15 ♕f3 was more sensible.

15 ... **♗xg5!** 0:30
16 ♖xg5 1:07 **f6!** 0:30

Of course not 16...f5? 17 exf5 ♘xf5 18 ♗xf5 ♖xf5 19 ♖xf5 gxf5 20 ♕h5 when the black king is in serious danger. But after the rook has retreated, Black can detonate the centre.

17 ♖g1 1:14 **f5** 0:31
18 ♕f3 **fxe4!?** 0:37

Black can play 18...♘d7 first, but White can still retreat with 19 ♗c2.

19 ♘xe4 1:17 **♘d7** 0:37
20 ♗c2 1:24 **♕h4+?!** 0:40

Despite his rather dubious

opening play, 'Azmai' has seized the initiative following my weak 15th move. But now he tries to cash in too early.

20...♘f6 or 20...♘f5 were sensible, and Black can also consider embarking upon an adventure with 20...♘e5 21 ♕e2 ♕h4+ 22 ♔d1! (not 22 ♔d2? ♖xf4!) 22...♘xc4!? (22...♖xf4? doesn't work when it gets recaptured without check 23 ♗xf4 ♕xf4 24 ♖f1, to be followed by 25 ♘xd6, but the restrained 22...♘f7 is fine) 23 ♕xc4 when:

a) 23...♕h5+? 24 ♕e2 ♕xd5+ 25 ♔c1 is very unconvincing.

b) But 23...♘f5 24 ♗d2! (not 24 ♗f2? ♕xf2; while if 24 ♕d3 ♕xh2 Black is taking a lot of pawns and White is still very loose) is very unclear after 24...♕xh2 25 ♖e1 (25 ♕f1? ♗xd5 26 ♖h1 ♘g3) 25...♘d4 or 24...♘d4 at once.

21 ♗f2 1:29 **♕e7** 0:42
22 0-0-0 1:31 **♘e5** 0:43
23 ♕e2 1:39 **♖xf4** 0:43

Consequent, but after my reply, he ought to have sacrificed the exchange.

24 ♗g3 1:31 **♘h5??** 0:47

This disastrous misjudgement follows from Black's previous moves in which he appears to have got White on the run. If the rook moves back along the file, for example 24...♖f7, White will play 25 ♘xd6! And 24...♖g4 is bad after 25 ♖gf1!

But after 24...♖af8! Black would have had reasonable compensation for the exchange.

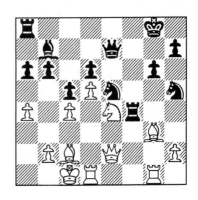

25 ♕xh5! 1:36

This simple queen sacrifice turns the game around. White develops a ferocious initiative which turns out to be sufficient for immediate victory.

25 ... **gxh5** 0:49

If 25...♖xe4 26 ♗xe4 gxh5 27 ♗xe5+ ♔f8 28 ♖df1+ ♔e8 29 ♖g8+ ♔d7 30 ♗f5+ ♔c7 31 ♖g7 wins.

26 ♗xf4+ 1:37 **♘g6** 0:49

Or 26...♘g4 27 h3 with a winning material advantage.

27 ♗g5! 1:38 **♕e5** 0:52
28 ♘f6+ 1:40 **♔h8** 0:52
29 ♗xg6! 1:42

29 ♘xh7 ♔xh7 30 ♗xg6+ is also sufficient. But once I'd worked out this infinitely more aesthetic route, I couldn't possibly pass it up.

29 ... **hxg6** 0:52
30 ♖de1 1:42 **♕xh2** 1:00

He might as well. If 30...♕d4 31 ♖e7! ♕xc4+ (31...♕xg1+ is

the game but with White's h-pawn still alive) 32 ♔b1 ♕d3+ 33 ♔a1 escapes the checks immediately.

31 ♖e7! 1:42 **♕xg1+** 1:00
32 ♔c2 1:42 **♕f2+** 1:01
33 ♔b3 1:47 **♕f3+** 1:01
34 ♔a2 1:42

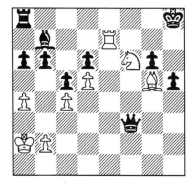

Black has run out of checks and must now return the queen, after which White simply emerges a piece up thanks to the dual threats along the seventh rank.

34 ... **♕xf6** 1:01
35 ♗xf6+ 1:43 **♔g8** 1:01
36 ♖xb7 1:43 **b5** 1:01
37 ♖g7+ 1:43 **♔f8** 1:01
38 ♖h7 1:43 **bxa4** 1:01
39 ♗c3! 1:45

Of course, 39 ♖h8+ ♔f7 40 ♖xa8 ♔xf6 is also an easy win. But this is even cleaner.

39 ... **♖e8**
40 ♖h8+ **♔f7**
41 ♖xe8 **♔xe8**
42 ♗f6! **1-0**

Game 37
P.van der Sterren–J.Speelman
Moscow Olympiad 1994
Irregular Opening

This game was first annotated in the *British Chess Magazine*, March 1995.

1 d4

I played Paul Van der Sterren many times when we were juniors. Although I won the first game, a Closed Sicilian I believe, as White, thereafter Paul became somewhat of a *bête noire*, beating me five times or so without reply. There was then a long gap until a couple of years ago when we started

meeting each other in the Dutch League. We've had two games so far, in both of which I have been Black. Both involved ...e6 systems and after successful time-scrambles I have managed to score 1½.

This time, however, after consultation with my captain (i.e. the *BCM*'s Editor, Murray Chandler), I decided at a critical stage of the Olympiad to aim for chaos from the very start of the game and so opted to play a

...d6 system.

1 ...   d6
2 e4

This was somewhat of a surprise since Paul normally replies 2 ♘f3, but I did guess his next move before he played it.

2 ...   ♘f6
3 f3

This aims, if allowed, to transpose into a Sämisch King's Indian. I've faced it four times, as far as I can remember, and previously had always played into the ending with 3...e5 4 dxe5 dxe5 5 ♕xd8+ ♔xd8 6 ♗c4 ♔e8 etc. I lost against Kramnik, drew with some pain against Korchnoi and had it twice in the Lloyds Bank Masters 1993, scoring 1½/2.

But 3...e5 hardly creates chaos and so I decided to vary.

3 ...   d5!?
4 e5   ♘g8!?

This was a spur of the moment decision. 4...♘fd7 is normal.

5 c4   e6
6 ♘c3

White could instead fix the pawn structure with 6 cxd5!? exd5 7 ♘c3.

6 ...   dxc4!

Although Black has all his pieces on their original squares, the weakening f3 does give him some immediate chances. If now 7 ♗xc4 c5 is slightly annoying. This hits the centre and the d-pawn is temporarily pinned – if 8 dxc5?? ♕h4+ – so

that Black can hope to get play with ...cxd4 and ...♘c6. So Van der Sterren decided to stop ...c5 with:

7 ♗e3   ♘d7!

This defends the c-pawn since if 8 ♗xc4? ♘xe5 and is much better than 7...♘c6 8 f4! when the c4-pawn can be defended only by the ugly 8...♘a5. Now 8 f4 ♘b6 is annoying for White, so he decided to pin the knight. This is not bad but it does commit the queen to a somewhat exposed square.

8 ♕a4   ♘e7
9 ♗xc4   ♘f5
10 ♗f2   c6

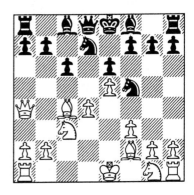

Here Van der Sterren had a long think. Unfortunately, I've lost my score sheet and so I don't have the clock times, but I guess he took half an hour if not more.

I was expecting 11 ♕d1 and during the wait I had more or less decided on 11...c5!? (11...♘b6 12 ♗b3 ♘d5 is one alternative) 12 dxc5 ♗xc5 13

♗xc5 ♘xc5 14 ♕xd8+ ♔xd8
when I was rather optimistic
since the black knights might be
very irritating, but in fact the
simple 15 ♔f2! keeps control
and after, for example, 15...♔e7
White is slightly better.

Instead my opponent decided
upon a pawn sacrifice which
looks frightening for Black but
is probably only equal against
sensible defence.

11 ♗d3!?   ♘b6

11...♘xe5? 12 ♗xf5 loses;
and 11...♘c5? 12 dxc5 ♕xd3
leaves White with a massive
grip, e.g. 13 ♖d1 ♕a6 14 ♕xa6
bxa6 15 ♘e4 en route to d6.

12 ♕a5   ♘xd4!

Not 12...♕g5? 13 g4 ♘e3?
14 h4 (14 ♘e4 ♕f4) 14...♕f4
15 ♘ce2! and wins.

It took me some time to pluck
up the courage to take the pawn,
but at least this does make sense
of Black's previous moves. Although White has a lead in development and the knight is
very exposed on d4, the queen
on a5 is very badly posted.

13 ♖d1

He played this very quickly. I
was slightly expecting 13 0-0-0,
though this would give Black a
check on g5 *in extremis*.

13 ...   c5
14 ♘ge2   ♘c6!?

If 14...♘xe2?! 15 ♗xe2 (15
♔xe2!?) 15...♘d7 16 ♕a4 gives
White a huge initiative.

But 14...♗d7!? was a reasonable alternative, e.g. 15 ♘xd4

cxd4 and now:

a) If 16 ♗xd4 ♕h4+ 17 ♗f2
♕b4 18 ♕xb4 ♗xb4 19 0-0
♗xc3 20 bxc3 ♗c6 Black
should be fine.

b) During the game, both of
us thought that 16 ♘b5 would
be good for White. But in fact
after 16...♘d5 17 ♕xd8+ ♖xd8
it isn't so clear, e.g. 18 ♗xd4
(18 ♘xd4 ♗b4+) 18...a6 19
♘d6+ (19 ♘c3 ♗b4) 19...♗xd6
20 exd6 f6.

15 ♗b5   ♕c7

16 ♗xc6+??

A terrible mistake after which
Black is already better. Van der
Sterren played this move to free
b5 for his knight but he should
have maintained the pin for another move with 16 ♘e4 when:

a) 16...♗d7 is sensible and
should lead to approximate
equality after 17 ♗xc6 ♗xc6 18
♘d6+ ♗xd6 19 exd6 (or 19
♖xd6 0-0 with equal chances)
19...♕d7 20 ♕xc5.

b) 16...♕xe5?! is almost sui-
cidally provocative, but if it

were possible then Black would love to play it. During the postmortem Paul found the good reply 17 ♘d4!? when:

b1) 17...♗d7 18 ♗xc6 ♗xc6 19 ♗g3 ♕h5? (19...♕xd4 20 ♖xd4 cxd4) 20 ♘b5! is crushing.

b2) If 17...♕c7? Black gets his just desserts after 18 ♗g3 e5 19 ♗xc6+ bxc6 20 ♗xe5!

16 ... ♕xc6
17 ♘b5 ♘d5!

Black could equalise with 17...♗d7 18 ♘d6+ ♗xd6 19 ♖xd6 ♘c4 20 ♖xc6 ♘xa5 21 ♖xc5 ♘c6, but after a little checking I satisfied myself that the text move is simply good. Unless he takes immediate action, White will be a pawn down with a bad game and so the following transaction is almost forced.

18 ♖xd5 b6!

This intermezzo is the justification of 17...♘d5!

19 ♕a4 exd5
20 ♘c7+

The attempt to attack with 20 ♘d6+ ♔d7 simply doesn't work, e.g. 21 ♕f4 ♗xd6 22 ♕xf7+ ♗e7 23 ♘f4 ♖f8 and wins.

20 ... ♔d7
21 ♕xc6+ ♔xc6
22 ♘xa8 ♗e7

This is the end of the complications instituted by 17...♘d5. The knight on a8 is trapped and after White loses the beast, taking the b6-pawn with it, material will be equal; but Black will have a big advantage.

23 ♘f4

Threatening 24 ♘c7! and so preventing 23...♗a6, though Black is happy to lose the two bishops in return for a free run on the light squares.

23 ... ♗e6!

Better than the impulsive 23...g5?! which would leave a weak pawn on g5 and weaken the f6-square.

24 ♘xb6 axb6

I was lucky that in regaining his pawn Van der Sterren had to cede me a further asset: play down the a-file.

This ending is extremely unpleasant for White due to the black central phalanx and the weakness of the e5-pawn. Although it is natural to remove one of Black's bishop pair, White's next move does lose control of the d5-square which can now be occupied by the king; after which the black game practically plays itself.

25 ♘xe6!? fxe6
26 ♔d2 ♖a8!

Forcing either horrible passivity with 27 ♖a1 or the move played, which seriously weakens White's queenside structure. White would like to set up a blockade with b3 and a4, but now the pawn may get fixed on a3 as indeed later occurs. It will be easier for Black to set up a passed pawn than with the white queenside untouched; and the b3-square is an inviting long-term target for the black king.

27 a3 d4
28 ♖e1 ♔d5
29 ♖e4

This ugly move is the only way to protect the e5-pawn and prevent immediate expansion with ...c4.

29 ... ♖f8

30 ♔c2!

If 30 a4 Black can switch back with 30...♖a8! 31 b3 b5! I hadn't worked out all the details at the time, but it would be surprising if this weren't winning for Black and indeed after 32 axb5 Black has:

a) 32...♗g5+? 33 ♔d3! (33 ♔e1 ♖a1+ 34 ♔e2 ♖a2+ 35 ♔f1 ♖b2 36 ♖g4 ♗d2 37 ♖xg7 ♖xb3 38 ♖d7+ ♔c4 wins for Black) 33...♖a3 (33...♖a2 34 ♖e2) allows the piece sacrifice 34 ♗xd4! cxd4 35 ♖xd4+ when White is fighting hard.

b) 32...♖a2+. This was my intention but I had not seen that after 33 ♔e1 ♖b2 34 ♖f4 Black has 34...♗d8! (34...♖xb3 35 ♖f7 ♗g5 36 f4 is much worse). By including the bishop in the attack before regaining material, Black is able to co-ordinate all three pieces and win easily, i.e. 35 ♖f7 ♗a5+ 36 ♔f1 ♖xb3 and Black can now answer 37 ♖d7+ with 37...♔c4, intending ...d3 and ...♖a1+. He will win material or even mate in just a few more moves.

30 ... b5!

But not 30...♖f5? when Black can win the e-pawn, but at the cost of allowing a blockade: 31 a4 ♖xe5 32 ♖xe5+ ♔xe5 33 ♔d3 ♔d5 34 b3 and there is no way to make progress.

31 h3?!

In time trouble this makes life slightly easier for Black since the g3-square is now undefended – see the next note. But 31 b4 ♔c4, for example, is winning as well.

31 ... ♖f5
32 b4!?

If 32 ♗g3 ♖g5 forces the exchange of rooks due to the weakening 31 h3. After 33 ♖g4 ♖xg4 34 hxg4 c4 the ending is easily won for Black. Unless White plays f4 the e5-pawn will soon fall, but if he does play f4 then ...♔e4 will initiate a fatal invasion.

| 32 | ... | ♖xe5 |
| 33 | ♖xe5+ | |

If 33 bxc5 ♖xe4 34 fxe4+ ♔xe4 35 c6 ♗d6 the c6-pawn is easily surrounded and Black wins trivially.

33	...	♔xe5
34	bxc5	♗xc5
35	♔d3	♔d5
36	f4	g6

It is always nice in a bishop ending to be able to move a pawn onto a square of the right colour (opposite to one's own bishop's).

No doubt, there are several ways to win now. Presumably, it would be sufficient to exchange the d4-pawn for the a3-pawn, after which Black must win in the end. But I preferred if possible to exchange the d4-pawn for a kingside one, leaving the weakling on a3 as a target for later. A little thought convinced me that although we might reach an ending of bishop and the wrong rook's pawn against king, this could only arise with the white king way over on the wrong side of the board.

| 37 | ♗g1 | |

If 37 g3 Black could play 37...g5 anyway.

37	...	♗d6
38	g3	g5
39	♗xd4	

Or 39 fxg5 e5 and wins easily.

39	...	gxf4
40	gxf4	♗xf4
41	♗b2	♗d6
42	♗c1	

I had expected 42 ♔e3 e5 43 ♗c1 ♗c5+ 44 ♔f3, but Black can win with 44...e4+ 45 ♔f4 e3 when the pawn ending after 46 ♗xe3 ♗xe3+ 47 ♔xe3 ♔c4 is hopeless, as equally is 46 ♔f3 ♔c4 47 ♔e2 ♔c3 etc.

42	...	♗c5
43	♔c3	e5
44	♔b3	e4
45	a4	bxa4+
46	♔xa4	

White has succeeded in eliminating his weakness, but after Black's next move the white king is permanently cut off from the action.

| 46 | ... | ♔c4 |

47 ♗h6   e3
    0-1

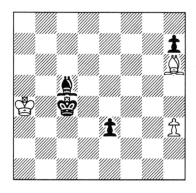

Van der Sterren resigned. White must give up his bishop for the e-pawn. Black will be left with bishop and wrong rook's pawn, but it will be easy to remove the white h-pawn without allowing White's king into the h1 corner.

It is important that the white h-pawn is only on h3. If it could reach h5 then the ending would be problematical at best, since the black king would have to take a long detour to capture it before rushing towards the h1 corner to head off its counterpart. But of course if, immediately after 48 ♗xe3 ♗xe3 or later, White tries h4 then Black can always fix it with ˙49...h5 before taking it with the bishop.

Game 38
J.Hjartarson–J.Speelman
Copenhagen (Politiken Cup) 1996
French Defence, Burn variation

I have included this final example on account of the quite splendid mess which occurred round about move 26: it is seldom that one sacrifices a piece for quite such a slow attack, particularly when the main point is to try to sacrifice a further exchange.

I first annotated this game in *New in Chess*, No.6 1996, and have just added the clock times, without any other significant emendations.

1 d4 0:07   **e6** 0:01
2 e4 0:10   **d5** 0:01
3 ♘c3 0:10   **♘f6** 0:03
4 ♗g5 0:10   **dxe4** 0:03
5 ♘xe4 0:10   **♘bd7** 0:04
6 ♘f3 0:12   **♗e7** 0:06
7 ♘xf6+ 0:06   **♗xf6** 0:06
8 h4!? 0:14   **h6** 0:14
9 ♗e3 0:18

Here the bishop doesn't prevent ...e5. He should have chosen between 9 ♗xf6 and 9 ♗f4.

9 ...   **♕e7** 0:22
10 c3 0:20

If 10 ♕d2:

a) 10...e5 is normal.

b) 10...b6!? is also possible now that the queen is on d2 – White would like to have organised ♗c4 and ♕e2 but didn't have time. During the game I vaguely looked at 11 0-0-0 ♗b7 12 ♗e2 0-0-0, preparing to play ...c5 soon, and if 13 g4 e5 14 g5 exd4 (14...hxg5 is also very good of course) 15 gxf6? dxe3 16 fxe7 exd2+ 17 ♖xd2 ♖de8 is tremendous for Black.

10 ... e5 0:26
11 d5 0:31

Too ambitious since it loses time and the d5-pawn is weakened.

11 ... ♘b6 0:31
12 ♕b3 0:38 **0-0** 0:36
13 ♘d2 0:40 **♖d8** 0:47
14 c4 0:44

14 ♘e4? ♘xd5 15 ♗c5 ♕e6 doesn't work at all.

14 ... e4 0:47
15 ♕c2 0:55 **c6** 0:56

To bust up the white centre as quickly as possible.

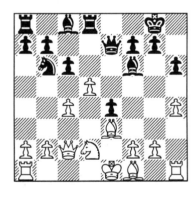

16 dxc6 1:05

If 16 ♕xe4 ♕xe4 17 ♘xe4 ♗xb2 18 ♖b1 ♗e5 is extremely nice for Black.

While if 16 ♘xe4:

a) 16...♗xb2 17 ♘g5 (17 ♕xb2 ♕xe4) 17...hxg5 18 ♕xb2 with a mess.

b) 16...cxd5 17 ♘xf6+ ♕xf6 18 0-0-0 and here Black has at least:

b1) 18...♗f5 19 ♕c3:

b11) 19...♕xc3+ 20 bxc3 ♘xc4 21 ♗xc4 dxc4 22 ♖xd8+ ♖xd8, winning a pawn since if 23 ♗xa7? ♖a8.

b12) But in this line 19...♕e6! may be even better.

b2) Not 18...d4 19 ♕d2!

b3) But 18...♗g4 is playable and if 19 ♖d4 ♗f5 20 ♕c3 ♘xc4 21 ♗xc4 dxc4 or 19 f3 d4 20 ♖xd4 ♖xd4 21 ♗xd4 ♕xd4 22 fxg4 ♖d8.

16 ... bxc6 0:58
17 ♗e2 1:07 **♗f5** 1:01

Threatening to take the h-pawn and so morally forcing White to sacrifice a pawn.

18 g4! 1:25

If 18 g3 the best is 18...♕b4 (also possible is 18...♗d4 at once or 18...♖ac8!?, intending ...♘d5 next) 19 ♖b1 ♗d4! still preventing castling since d2 hangs.

18 ... ♗g6 1:01
19 g5 1:27 **hxg5** 1:02

19...♗d4 was also conceivable and after 20 h5 ♗xe3 21 fxe3 21...♗h7 (or 21...♗f5) 22 gxh6 ♕g5 23 0-0-0, maybe even 23...♕xe3.

20 hxg5 1:27 **♗xg5** 1:02
21 0-0-0 1:28 **♗xe3** 1:04

In the postmortem Johann suggested 21...♗f6 to stop the

rooks doubling on the h-file. But I have to admit that I didn't even consider it since I hate to give my opponent breathing space in such a position.

22 fxe3 1:28 **♕g5** 1:14

I had been intending the alternative 22...♕c5!? while waiting for 20 g4, when we have:

a) 23 ♕c3 is bad here because after 23...♘a4 24 ♕b3 ♘xb2! White has to recapture with the queen 25 ♕xb2 ♕xe3 and here I calculated the line 26 ♖h2 ♖ab8 27 ♖dh1 f6! (not 27...♔f8?? 28 ♖h8+ ♔e7 29 ♕e5+) 28 ♖h8+ ♔f7 and wins.

b) But then I changed my mind in view of 23 ♖h3! ♗f5 24 ♖g3 ♕e5 25 ♖dg1 g6 when White has very reasonable play for the pawn.

23 ♕c3! 1:31

Here 23 ♖h3 ♗f5 24 ♖h5 ♕xe3 is winning.

23 ... **♘a4** 1:20
24 ♕a3 1:31 **♘xb2!?** 1:27

Continuing to deny White any breathing space, but it seems that he has at least a draw. However, 24...♕g2 25 ♖de1 leaves the knight misplaced, while 24...♘c5!? looked very unclear.

25 ♔xb2 1:36 **♖ab8+** 1:31
26 ♔c1 1:38

And not 26 ♔c2?? when 26...♖d3! wins immediately.

26 ... **♕f6?** 1:35

A blunder. 26...♕e5 was correct. Black's threat is still 27...♖d3 28 ♗xd3 exd3 when if 29 ♘b1 or 29 ♘f1 ♖(x)b1+! wins. White can defend with:

a) 27 ♘b1 ♖d3 28 ♗xd3 exd3 29 ♘c3 ♕xe3+ 30 ♖d2 ♕d4 when White can, and probably should, force a draw at once with 31 ♖dh2! ♕f4+! – during the game I only saw 31...d2+?? 32 ♔d1! winning – 32 ♖d2 ♕d4 33 ♖dh2.

b) 27 c5? gives the knight the c4-square, but after 27...♖d3 28 ♗xd3 exd3 29 ♘c4 ♖b1+! 30 ♔d2 ♖xd1+! 31 ♔xd1 ♕e4! causes a total catastrophe (certainly not 31...♕a1+?? 32 ♕c1 ♕xa2 33 ♕b2 ♕xc4 34 ♕b8 mate) 32 ♖h2 (if 32 ♖f1 ♕g4+!; or 32 ♖g1 ♕f3+) 32...♕g4+! 33 ♔d2 ♕g1 trapping the rook!

c) But the best move is 27 ♖h4!!

(see following diagram)

As we shall see, this beautiful move prevents 27...♖d3. It also prepares to double on the h-file if White gets a move.

c1) Unfortunately if Black now plays 27...Rd3? 28 Bxd3 (not 28 Rdh1?? Qa1+ 29 Kc2 Rb2+ 30 Qxb2 Rxd2+) 28...exd3 29 Rd4! c5 30 Qa5!! not only protects the rook but also threatens Rd8+, so 30...Qe7 (or 30...Re8 31 Rd8 Qa1+ 32 Nb1 d2+ 33 Kxd2 and wins) 31 Rf4! (not 31 Rd5? Qf6 32 Nb1 Rxb1+ 33 Kxb1 d2+) 31...Qe5 and now 32 Rd4 would repeat, but White can improve with 32 Nb3!, successfully untangling. And now both 32...d2+ 33 Kxd2 (33 Qxd2? Qa1+!) 33...Re8 34 Qxc5 and 32...Qxe3+ 33 Qd2 Qe5 34 Re1 are hopeless.

c2) Of course not 27...Rxd2? 28 Kxd2 Rb2+ 29 Kc1 Rxe2 30 Rd8+.

c3) 27...Rd7 is an idea. One point of this is to take the rook off the back rank so that if:

c31) 28 Nb1?? Qa1 (now that Rxd8+ has been prevented) and Black wins: 29 Rxd7 Qxb1+ 30 Kd2 Rb2+ 31 Kc3 Qc1+ 32 Kd4 Rd2+.

It also prepares to double on the b-file. But now White has the splendid positional riposte:

c32) 28 c5! This vacates c4 for the knight and incidentally opens the fourth rank for the rook in case of the thematic exchange sacrifice on d3.

Now 28...Rdb7 fails to 29 Nc4!, while if 28...Rd5 29 Nc4 is still good: 29...Qa1+ (not 29...Rxc5 30 Rdh1) 30 Kc2 Rxd1 31 Bxd1 and here a further point of c5 is revealed: if 31...Qb1+ 32 Kd2 Rd8+ White can block with 33 Nd6!

c4) In view of this 27...c5! seems best. Now Black does threaten ...Rd3. But after 28 Nb1! (not 28 Rdh1?? Qa1+ 29 Kc2 Rb2+ 30 Qxb2 Rxd2+) he can't carry out his threat: 28...Rd3? 29 Rdh1! and wins.

So 28...Rxd1+ 29 Bxd1 is forced. Although Black has only two pawns for the piece, he does have reasonable chances since White is temporarily rather badly co-ordinated and the e3-pawn is weak. The best continuation here is probably 29...Bf5 to prepare to improve the king's position (29...Qg3 30 Rh1 Qg2 31 Re1 Qg3 32 Re2 only misplaces the queen). Play could continue 30 Rf4 Be6 when Black will defend the e-pawn with ...f5 if necessary.

27 Rhf1? 1:41

But 27 Nb1! gives White the advantage: 27...Rd3 28 Bxd3 exd3 29 Nc3, and of course here I was intending 29...d2+

(29...♕f2 30 ♖d2 ♕xe3 31 ♕d6! is hopeless), but after 30 ♔xd2 (30 ♖xd2?? ♕xc3+!) 30...♕f2+ 31 ♘e2 ♖d8+ 32 ♔c1 White wins, e.g. 32...♖b8 33 ♕xa7! ♖b1+ 34 ♔d2 ♖b2+ 35 ♔c3 ♖c2+ 36 ♔b4.

27 ... ♕e5 1:35

28 ♘b1 1:42

With the rook on the f-file, 28 ♖f4? is simply bad since after c5! (of course not 28...♖d3? 29 ♗xd3 exd3 30 ♖d4! as in the analysis above) 29 ♘b1 ♖d3! winning. Now White is forced to take it and after 30 ♗xd3 exd3 his position collapses.

28 ... ♖d3! 1:38
29 ♗xd3 1:44 **exd3** 1:38
30 ♘c3 1:45

Not 30 ♖f2? ♖xb1+!; or 30 ♖d2? ♕a1 31 ♕b3 (31 ♖b2 d2+) 31...♖xb3 32 axb3. But 30 e4!? ♗xe4 31 ♘c3 (31 ♖de1? d2+!) 31...♗g6 comes to the same thing.

30 ... ♕xe3+! 1:41

If 30...d2+? 31 ♔xd2! ♕h2+ 32 ♘e2 ♗h5 33 ♖fe1 ♗xe2 34

♖xe2 ♖d8+ 35 ♔c2 wins.

31 ♖d2 1:47

Here Johann offered a draw, but I thought I had at least enough for the rook.

31 ... ♕d4 1:44
32 ♕a5?! 1:48

If 32 ♖h1?! ♗e4 33 ♖e1 f5 cements the bishop. But perhaps 32 c5 was better.

32 ... c5 1:44
33 ♖e1 1:52 **♗f5** 1:50

Threatening ...g5, after which I could just put the bishop back on g6 and advance the g-pawn.

34 ♖f1 1:54

I had vaguely noticed the very computer-like 34 ♖e7, but it is slow and badly weakens the back rank. Indeed after 34...g5 35 ♖xa7 ♖b4 36 ♕a3, which I had seen, there is 36...♕e5! (Fritz) 37 ♖a8+ ♔g7 38 ♖d8 ♕e1+ 39 ♖d1 ♕e3+ 40 ♖d2 ♖xc4 41 ♕b3 ♕e1+ and wins.

34 ... ♖b4 1:51
35 ♕a3 1:54 **♗e4** 1:53
36 ♖b2!? 1:55

I had completely missed that this was legal. Not, by the way, 36 ♔d1 ♖xc4 37 ♕xa7 ♗f3+!

36 ... d2+ 1:55
37 ♔d1 1:55

Of course not 37 ♖xd2?? ♕xc3+! 38 ♕xc3 ♖b1 mate.

37 ... ♕d3 1:58
38 ♖f2 1:58

Here my time record ceases until the control on move 40.

38 ... ♗f3+

I wanted to play 38...♖xc4 but was, quite correctly as it

turns out, worried about 39 ♕xa7! (if 39 ♖bxd2 ♖xc3 40 ♖xd3 ♖xd3+ 41 ♕xd3 ♗xd3 the weak a-pawn gives White some chances, but Black must be doing pretty well) and now:

a) If 39...♗f3+ 40 ♖xf3 ♕xf3+ I had seen 41 ♘e2! but not 41...♕f2, found by Fritz of course. However, after 42 ♕b8+! (not 42 ♕a8+? ♔h7 43 ♕h1+ ♖h4 44 ♕g1 ♕xg1+ 45 ♘xg1 ♖h1 and Black wins) 42...♔h7 43 ♕g3! White defends with a big advantage.

b) If 39...♖xc3? I was concerned about 40 ♕b8+? ♔h7 41 ♕h2+ which I thought might win. But as we found in the postmortem there is 41...♕h3! (Petursson) with a big plus.

But of course White has a huge hit in the middle of this: 40 ♕xf7+! and mate in a couple more moves.

39 ♖xf3   ♕xf3+
40 ♔xd2   ♕f4+?

40...♖xc4! was clearly better, capturing while White still has some co-ordination problems.

41	♔d1 2:04	♕f1+ 2:09
42	♔d2 2:05	♕xc4 2:12
43	♘e2 2:07	♕d5+ 2:12
44	♔e1 2:07	♕h1+ 2:29
45	♔d2 2:09	♕d5+ 2:33
46	♔e1 2:09	

Here after a fairly long think I offered a draw which he, of course, accepted immediately. It may look a little wimpy to make a draw here, but the knight is a very good defender:

a) If 46...a5 47 ♕c3!, preparing 48 a3, prevents Black repairing his pawn structure.

b) 46...♖h4 looks good, e.g. 47 ♕g3 ♖h1+:

b1) And here the natural 48 ♔f2 ♕f5+ is rather unpleasant:

b11) 49 ♘f4? g5 50 ♖b8+ ♔g7! (50...♔h7 51 ♕d3!) 51 ♕c3+ f6 52 ♖b7+ ♔h6 53 ♔g2 ♕e4+ 54 ♕f3 ♖g1+.

b12) So 49 ♕f4 is forced, but 49...♖h2+ 50 ♔e3 is quite dangerous for White since the king really has to walk with the knight misplaced – and Black certainly keeps a perpetual in hand, e.g. 50...♕e6+ 51 ♔f3 ♕h3+ when 52 ♔e4 is forced – not 52 ♕g3 ♕f1+.

b2) But I was slightly concerned about 48 ♘g1!, e.g. 48...♕d4 (not 48...♖xg1+? 49 ♕xg1 ♕e5+ 50 ♖e2) 49 ♕b8+ ♔h7 50 ♖h2+! ♖xh2 51 ♕xh2+ ♔g6 and here Black should perhaps take the last white pawn: 52 ♘e2 ♕a1+ 53 ♔f2 ♕xa2 54 ♕g3+ with a draw.